A MAN'S WORLD

A MAN'S WORLD

A Gallery of Fighters,
Creators, Actors, and
Desperadoes

Steve Oney

THE UNIVERSITY OF GEORGIA PRESS
Athens

To the memory of my father,

Robert Oscar Oney

Publication of this work was made possible, in part, by a
generous gift from the University of Georgia Press Friends Fund.

"The Method and the Madness of Hubie Brown," "Robert Penn Warren Finds His Place to Come To," and "Getting Naked with Harry" are used by permission of *The Atlanta Journal-Constitution.* "The Casualty of War," "The Big Mocker," "Fallen Angel," and "The Talented Mr. Raywood" are used by permission of *Los Angeles* magazine.

Paperback edition published in 2019
by the University of Georgia Press
Athens, Georgia 30602
www.ugapress.org
© 2017 by Steve Oney
All rights reserved

Most University of Georgia Press titles are
available from popular e-book vendors.

Printed digitally

Library of Congress Cataloging-in-Publication Data

Names: Oney, Steve, 1954– author.
Title: A man's world : a gallery of fighters, creators, actors,
and desperadoes / Steve Oney.
Description: Athens : The University of Georgia Press, [2019]
Identifiers: LCCN 2018047767| ISBN 9780820354989 (pbk. : alk. paper) |
ISBN 9780820355047 (ebook)
Subjects: LCSH: Men—Biography. | Celebrities—Biography. |
Men—Anecdotes. | Celebrities—Anecdotes.
Classification: LCC CT120 .054 2019 | DDC 920.71—dc23
LC record available at https://lccn.loc.gov/2018047767

This book was originally published in 2017 by Mercer University Press.

CONTENTS

ACTORS 179

DESPERADOES 237

A MAN'S WORLD

INTRODUCTION

No one taught me how to be a man.

Not my father. While imbuing me with a strong work ethic, a moral compass, and the sense that I was loved, he did not weigh in once I came of age on what comes next. Defending myself, solving problems, handling myself socially, taking risks—the basic business of life in a man's world—he had little to say about these.

Not my coaches at Atlanta's Peachtree High School. Ed Tatum, the baseball coach—a lean and leathery throwback who strutted across our immaculately landscaped diamond wielding his tar-blackened Fungo bat like it was a swagger stick—referred to those of us who suited up for him by a one-size-fits-all term of endearment: "Sorry hounds." He responded to a student who tossed a rock onto the field by making him crawl on all fours to where the offending object lay, fetch it in his mouth, crawl back, and drop it like a dog dropping a bone. Jim Thomason, the football coach, was a more cautionary tale. He'd blown out both knees during his playing days, and by his mere presence—he goose-stepped along the sidelines—he suggested that this was not too high a price to pay for victory. His favorite exhortation: "Suck it up and go." The two embodied opposite ends of the masculine spectrum. One was about inflicting punishment, the other about enduring pain. I had no doubt that in the years ahead there would be a need to do both, but by the same token I felt that unless I was destined for a career as a boxer—or a star in sadomasochistic films—the lessons were of limited utility.

The sole adult male who during my high school days came close to pointing the way was the most improbable. Avowedly pantheistic (Greek gods only), seemingly pansexual, and quirkily attired (he wore his tie in the casual Onassis knot popularized by shipping magnate Ari), Gayle Goodin shepherded me through English composition as a senior.* An over-the-top literary enthusiast, he turned lectures into performances. He was also a taskmaster who required not just weekly themes but outlines in advance. Goodin whetted my interest in writing. Early in the final quarter, I contracted a ferocious case of mononucleosis. My throat swelled shut. In ten days I dropped from my normal weight of 195 to 169 pounds and ended up in the hospital. I was sick a long time. When I was well enough, I phoned Goodin to say I wanted to complete his course. He replied that if I was willing to make up the back assignments while keeping pace with the current ones, he'd give me a shot. I earned an A. This was the greatest accomplishment of my youth. Goodin's ability to present literature as a delight yet insist on discipline and excellence awakened me. After graduation, I broke into tears when he declared: "You will become."

The University of Georgia in the early 1970s was finally catching up to colleges in the rest of the country. Anti-Vietnam-war protestors surrounded the president's home, and marijuana smoke wafted through the dormitories. For all that, it remained a big, old Southern party school. Fraternities were not only the locus of the fun but provided the portals to manhood. Political connections, business opportunities, and friendships—all were forged at the antebellum houses along Milledge Avenue and Lumpkin Street. (Girls were in effect locked inside sororities, but the frat boys held those keys, too.) I envied the brothers' nonchalance. Whether cavorting on their front porches on lazy afternoons in Izod shirts, khakis, and Bass Weejun loafers or shaking a tail feather on football Saturdays to black soul bands pumping out Major Lance and James Brown covers from stages on their lawns, they seemed, from where I stood on the sidewalk, graceful and self-assured. They already *were*. But, as Goodin had said, I had to *become*. So rather than attend pledge week I wandered into the Memorial Hall office of *The Georgia Impression*, the student magazine.

At 18, I was on fire for the New Journalism practiced by Gay Talese, Hunter S. Thompson, Nora Ephron, and, most of all, Tom Wolfe. In the dash of my 1968 Camaro I kept a copy of Wolfe's essay "Why They Aren't

---

* Gayle Goodin was on the faculty of DeKalb College, where thanks to an innovative program in my county school system I took university-level classes while a senior at Peachtree.

Writing the Great American Novel Anymore." The piece began as a screed against the sclerotic literary establishment, but it soon opened up into an ode to the adventurous life of magazine writing. The career offered all the benefits of journalism—consorting with outlandish characters, carousing in dives—with few of the downsides, namely daily deadlines. Maybe more appealing, Wolfe maintained that those at the top of the game were the new modern masters. I spent most of my undergraduate years trying to acquire the requisite skills. I incorporated fictional techniques—dialogue, extended scenes—into the nonfiction stories I wrote for the *Impression*. I'd found a métier, and that was hugely significant. When people tell you that you're not defined by what you do, they're wrong. You *are* what you do—action *is* character.

That the writing of magazine articles would constitute my initiation into a man's world was not something I expected or consciously pursued. When at 22, I landed a job at *The Atlanta Journal & Constitution Magazine*, the largest circulation publication between Washington, D.C., and Miami, I simply wanted to write interesting stories. Luckily for me, I arrived barely a month after Georgia native Jimmy Carter had been sworn in as president. The South suddenly mattered, and the editors of what had been a stodgy outfit were in an expansive mood.

During my five years at the *Journal & Constitution* magazine, I wrote pieces about crime, politics, and business. But mostly I turned out profiles of fascinating men. Some were powerful (U.S. Senator Herman Talmadge), others troubled (Bruce Janoff, an Emory University professor who disappeared after leaving a note that read "If anyone cares to understand, I know what Bartleby must have felt like"). I specialized, however, in writers. I've included in this collection my lengthy portraits of the great Pulitzer-Prize-winner Robert Penn Warren and the Southern gothic novelist Harry Crews. But it was the experience of doing another, shorter author profile that was the most personally illuminating.

A few minutes after I met Tennessee Williams at his bungalow in Key West, he pulled me close and in a theatrical whisper said, "I know you're a nice man and won't hurt me." I had done enough research to realize how emotionally fragile my celebrated subject was. My reassurances calmed the playwright, and soon he was leading me on the sorts of adventures he delighted in staging for visitors. There was a drunken lunch at a Duval Street restaurant where Williams flirted with the waiters. There was an intense encounter with a wealthy Texas divorcee seeking Williams's advice about her love life. There was dancing late into the night with the divorcee and her fetching daughter to Sinatra tunes wafting from a juke box at a waterside bar that overlooked—in a Williams-esque touch—a cross ablaze with Christmas lights. Somewhere along the way the playwright and I sat down long enough to talk about his new drama, *Tiger Tail*, which in a few weeks would premiere in Atlanta and was the reason I had come. After a frenetic two days, I drove to Miami and caught a flight home.

A month later my article was in print—and *Tiger Tail* had debuted to disastrous reviews. The reception was so mortifying that I didn't think Williams would show his face in Atlanta, but one evening shortly after the premiere there he sat in a cozy booth at a fancy restaurant. At his side was a beautiful boy who did not seem of voting age. After introducing us, Williams waved a hand at his companion and in a tone both self-deprecatory and outrageous said to me, "Send him a copy of your story so he'll know who I am." I was flattered, but the next day, as I dropped the piece in the mail, I realized that I also felt something else. I wanted to find within myself the brilliance, style, bravery in the face of long odds, and willingness to flout public opinion that the playwright possessed. "Tennessee," I wished I'd said the night before, "I wrote the story so I'd know who *I* am."

Understanding oneself by writing about others isn't what they teach at the Columbia School of Journalism, and it probably shouldn't be. In-depth magazine profiles are works of reporting, not self-therapy. But just as actors must bring themselves to the characters they portray to make those characters come alive onscreen, writers must bring themselves to the people they write about to make those people come alive on the page. If, by so doing, the writer learns something about himself, the payoff is twofold: a work animated by a life and a life animated and deepened by the work.

In 1982, I moved to Los Angeles, where I became a staff writer at *New West*, soon to be rechristened *California*. There and in the years that followed at other publications—*Esquire*, *GQ*, *Playboy*, *Premiere*, *The New York Times Magazine*, and *Los Angeles*—I repeated the drill I'd begun in Atlanta. I took on a variety of assignments (an exploration of the Hollywood left, an oral history of the Charles Manson case). Mostly, however, I profiled fascinating men. The more of these pieces I produced, the more decided my opinions became about what counts in a man's world. Ultimately, this is what I concluded: First, men must be adept at fighting. Second, they must create. Third, the presentation of a public persona—call it acting—is all-important. Finally, men must be willing to explore their inner darkness.

By fighting, I'm not talking about fisticuffs, although Herschel Walker, the University of Georgia Heisman Trophy winner and subject of a profile I did for *Playboy*, plunged into mixed martial arts as he neared 50 because he wanted to exchange blows with guys half his age. No, by fighting, I'm talking about a part of the male psyche that seems to demand some form of combat. For Chris Leon, a Marine with a screwed-up boyhood whose story broke my heart, the war in Iraq offered a way to reclaim his life even as it took him to his death. For Jake Jacoby, an aging police reporter I wrote about in the aftermath of L.A.'s frightening "Night Stalker" murders, covering the cops gave him a chance to come to grips with the legacy of his disreputable father. A man's world revolves around conflict with others and himself. What combination of nature and nurture makes this so, I can't say. All I know is there's no way to duck it.

As for creating, Robert Penn Warren told me something that became a credo: "It may be said that our lives are our supreme fiction." He meant that each of us traffics in self-invention. This is not, of course, just the province of men, but it is a through line in the lives of those who interest me. That's what drew me to the late NBC president Brandon Tartikoff (not incidentally a student of Warren at Yale), who perfected primetime TV programming as it's practiced today. It's also what drew me to the architect John Portman, builder of modern Atlanta, whom I wrote about because I'd long been obsessed with his work and whose wild hairdo embodies his design philosophy.

Part of the act of self-invention involves putting on a public face. That's what actors do, sometimes in very different ways. When I profiled Nick Nolte for *Premiere*, I was astonished by the painstaking lengths he goes to fashion that face. Harrison Ford, whom I profiled for the same magazine, is the opposite. What you see is what you get, and if he doesn't want you to see it, you won't.

Most problematic: A man's life may not require him to court danger, but it demands that he be open to it if it comes. Harry Crews called this "getting naked." His theory, as he articulated it to me, was that "you can only find out about a thing when you're vulnerable to the experiences of the world." Crews believed that the payoff is personal renewal. Not that this process always ends well, for the distance between walking on the wild side and self-destructive behavior or even criminality can be razor thin. Gregg Allman, lead singer of the Allman Brothers Band and subject of my first piece for *Esquire*, came close to killing himself with heroin. Craig Raywood, a high-end conman I spent nine months researching, betrayed his gifts as an interior designer, defrauded his friends, and went to jail. He crossed the line. To write about him, I had to cross the same line. By this, I mean that I had to make the empathetic leap—crucial to all creative endeavors but especially to writing profiles—between my life and his. Not only did I have to size up Raywood, but I had to imagine being Raywood. It was wrenching.

The majority of the men portrayed in *A Man's World* could be judged successes, but a few are not. Moreover, my categories are somewhat arbitrary. Harry Crews could as easily be considered a fighter or creator as a desperado. Herschel Walker, a genuinely self-invented man, is as much a creator as a fighter. Nick Nolte could as easily be seen as a desperado as an actor. The simplest thing to say is this: Each of these men was dealing with something I felt I needed to deal with, too.

Which brings me back to my father. My earliest memory of him dates to before I was old enough to talk. He got it in his head that if I could only say Kluszewski, the challenging last name of the feared Cincinnati Reds slugger Ted—a player so massive he cut the sleeves off his jerseys because they constricted his upper body—I could pronounce just about any word. Each syllable—CLEW-ZOO-SKI—is the equivalent of a sharply hit grounder, and as Dad, a lifelong baseball fan, dandled me on his knee, he had me repeat them again and again: CLEW-ZOO-SKI, CLEW-ZOO-SKI. Not until I could intone each fragment singly then combine them into the whole did he stop. Although it would be my mother who taught me how to read, my father's bequest was more elemental. That mouthful of ethnic poetry bespoke an America of belching factories and muddy rivers, immigrant laborers and sunburned farmers, lonesome distances and pulsating nightclubs. To give a country boy, which my father was, credit, it even conjured the brutal poetry inherent in the figure of Stanley Kowalski from Tennessee Williams's *A Streetcar Named Desire*. CLEW-ZOO-SKI. I grew up besotted by language.

That was a great gift, and during my early years there were others. By the time I was 6, I could hit a baseball, and by the time I was 10 I could occasionally hit one out of the park. But that's where it ended. While my father was good at raising a boy, he was not so good at raising a man. Fighting, creating, acting, exploring dark places—he surely had knowledge of all, but he was incapable of articulating it to me. On the rare occasions he did venture an opinion his comments seemed so beside the point and possi-

6

bly even harmful that I was grateful for his more typical silence. Not that I blame him. In the end, I'm not sure it was his job to do more than position me to be the father to myself. As for Coaches Tatum and Thomason, there may not be wisdom in inflicting punishment, but the older I get the more I think it is necessary to know how to endure pain. Gayle Goodin is in a different category. I can only say thank you.

On my desk, I keep a hand-made ballpeen hammer. According to family lore, my great grandfather Hiram hewed the handle from a sturdy piece of persimmon wood before heading west to participate in the Pikes Peak gold rush. When I turned 40, my father gave it to me. If the clanging consonants in Kluszewski are raw ingredients, this is a tool. That's all most fathers can impart. In a man's world, the rest is on you.

—Steve Oney

FIGHTERS

By fighting, I'm not talking about fisticuffs. No, by fighting, I'm talking about a part of the male psyche that seems to demand some form of combat. A man's world revolves around conflict with others and himself. What combination of nature and nurture makes this so, I can't say. All I know is there's no way to duck it.

Herschel Walker Doesn't Tap Out

Playboy, December 2011

On a hot summer afternoon, Herschel Walker, wearing a *Best Damn Sports Show* T-shirt and Clinch board shorts, strides into the 2,500-square-foot main room of the American Kickboxing Academy in San Jose, California. At six-foot-one and 219 pounds, he is, in a word even his friends use to describe him, a freak—a magnificent physical anomaly. Walker's trapezius muscles flare above his shoulders like the wings of an avenging angel—one who happens to have a 21-inch neck, a 48-inch chest, and just 2.4 percent body fat. His 33-inch waist, the result of the 3,500 sit-ups he has done each day since he was a teenager, is essentially nonexistent, a mere transition to his 25-inch thighs. Open-faced and handsome with an easy smile, strong nose, and tiny ears set far back, Walker appears to be ageless. That, however, is not so. In a few months he will turn 50.

Between 12 and two every Monday through Friday, the red tatami-mat-textured floor of the kickboxing academy is the scene of a mixed martial arts workout that Walker, who knows something about the subject (1,000 push-ups have also long been part of his daily regimen), calls "without a doubt the hardest training I've ever done." MMA demands excellence in half a dozen disciplines—among them boxing, wrestling, jujitsu, judo, and Muay Thai boxing. The sport likewise requires absolute cardiovascular fitness, and sessions conclude with set after set of sprints and bear crawls. First and foremost, however, it is about fighting, and fighting is what this temple to MMA stresses above all else.

As Walker squares off against a light heavyweight named Kyle Kingsbury, he is surrounded by the best of the best. In one corner Cain Velasquez, MMA's premier heavyweight, grapples with up-and-comer Mark Ellis, a 2009 NCAA Division I wrestling champion. In another corner Josh Thomson, a standout MMA lightweight, rolls with the highly ranked Josh Koscheck. Elsewhere Daniel Cormier, an erstwhile Olympic wrestler, and Luke Rockhold, a vaunted contender, practice holds and parry blows. In this arena the most dangerous fighters in the world regularly butt heads.

Walker, the former tailback who led the University of Georgia to the NCAA football championship in 1980, won the Heisman Trophy, and went on to a storied 15-year pro career (mostly with the Dallas Cowboys), first walked into the American Kickboxing Academy just two years ago. "He came to the gym very accomplished in other areas," says Bob Cook, who has trained Walker from the start and stands at the edge of the room, watching him work. "But he had a beginner's attitude. He got here early, stayed late and mopped the floors afterward. Never has there been a time he has taken the easy route. If we run sprints, box five rounds, and wrestle 30 minutes, he never opts out. Some people come in and say, 'Don't punch me in the face.' Herschel came in with a fighter's attitude. He's been punched plenty in the face."

"I'd rate Herschel today at a midrange pro level, and that's a high compliment," adds AKA founder and proprietor Javier Mendez, who kneels alongside Cook. "He's the strongest man I've ever worked with, and his striking and grappling were always good. But his wrestling and jujitsu are now at another level. He's worked hard to learn them."

Walker has also worked hard to dispel doubts expressed by some in the MMA hierarchy. The sport, though not officially organized until 1993 (until then it was little evolved from the unregulated "tough guy" matches of an earlier era) and not sanctioned by a state athletic board until 2000, has quickly developed a fierce, well-informed following and a proud lore. Dana White, president of Ultimate Fighting Championship, MMA's top promotion company, scoffed, "He's too old for football but thinks he's young enough to fight? Fighting is a young man's sport. You need speed, agility and explosiveness—all that goes with age." For Walker, such cracks, in a friend's words, "were like lighter fluid."

In his professional MMA debut in 2010, Walker defeated the relatively untested Greg Nagy in three rounds by a technical knockout. In January 2011, against the far tougher Scott Carson, who boasted a 4–1 record and is a protégé of UFC stalwart Chuck Liddell, Walker scored a more impressive victory. After absorbing a vicious kick to the face in the contest's opening seconds, he took Carson to the ground with a ferocious left and then pummeled him with a flurry of knees to the ribs and punches to the head that caused the referee to call the contest before the first round had concluded.

Skeptics still abound, pointing out that Walker's fighting style is basic and safe. "He's not the alpha male yet," says one. "He's about controlling the opponent and staying out of trouble." Still, those who have followed his progress believe he is becoming an undeniable force. "It's crazy to see how good he's gotten," says Velasquez, who bested the formidable Brock Lesnar in 2010 to win the UFC's heavyweight belt. Although 20 years younger than Walker, Velasquez has functioned as the older man's mentor, teaching him how to plot strategy and avoid the brutal knee and arm bars that can prompt even the greatest to submit, or tap out. "He's picked up the game fast. He just has to keep building."

Now, in the stultifying steam bath that is July in central California, Walker is preparing for a third fight. His opponent has yet to be named, but the unanimous opinion is that the match will present a huge step up in difficulty. "They'll pick somebody tough," says Mendez. "They'll elevate the level of competition. He's going to face someone much more experienced than the last guy. It's going to take Herschel being here every day for three months to get ready, but once he makes up his mind, that's what he'll do. He doesn't mess around." Even so, Walker acknowledges how unlikely it all is. "What am I doing in there running around with those 20-year-olds?" he asks as he emerges into the AKA lobby, sweat pouring from his face, brow furrowed. For a serious man, the soft-spoken ex-NFL star is not without a sense of absurdity. "Am I really 50? It's weird."

To those who have known Herschel Walker through the years, it is not surprising that he has decided to plunge into a sport in which there are no pads, pain can be inflicted in a dizzying number of ways, and the playing field is an unforgiving fenced enclosure known as "the cage." Vince Dooley, Walker's coach at the University of Georgia, recalls that on Sundays during the college football season, a day when most players were too sore from Saturday's game to crawl out of bed, Walker would attend tae kwon do classes. "I've never seen anything like it," says Dooley. Michael Irvin, Walker's Dallas Cowboys teammate and now an analyst for the NFL Network, says, "When Herschel was the baddest motor scooter on earth, he'd say, 'I want to fight Mike Tyson.' I'd say, 'Herschel, do you know what that guy does to people? Let's just beat the Redskins next week.' But he believed he could beat Tyson. MMA is par for the course for him." Troy Aikman, the Cowboys quarterback during Walker's final seasons in Dallas and now a broadcaster for Fox, also believes his former teammate's latest incarnation is apt. "When Herschel decided to get into it," he says, "an acquaintance of mine involved in MMA told me he didn't give him a chance. I replied, 'I've seen enough of this guy over the years that I wouldn't bet against him on anything.' He's highly driven. He doesn't take on anything halfheartedly. He runs a heck of a lot hotter than people realize. He's a killer."

Walker's rationale for entering the world of MMA is not what many may imagine. "People think I'm doing this for the money," he says, "but I say, 'Guys, I don't need the money. The businesses I've built since I got out of football provide a bigger payday than any fight can bring me.'" (Walker donated the purse from the Carson bout to his Dallas church, Oak Cliff Bible Fellowship.) Nor, he adds, is he mentally unbalanced. In 2008 Walker made news by revealing that he suffered from dissociative identity disorder—what would once have been called multiple personality disorder. In *Breaking Free*, his book about his battle to come to terms with the condition, he writes that in its throes he had experienced fits of murderous rage. But after years of therapy, he says the problem is now under control. "The story people want to hear is that I'm out of whack. But that's not me. I have not become an MMA fighter because I have an anger issue." The truth, he adds, is both simpler and more complex.

Few successful American athletes have enjoyed as varied a career as Walker has. Even as he was leading Georgia to a national football title, he was competing on the collegiate track circuit, running a 9.1-second 100-yard dash and briefly holding the world's record in the 60-yard event. Before the start of a senior year that would almost surely have seen him break nearly every NCAA rushing mark, he became the first college underclassman to bolt not just to the pros but to the fledgling USFL. The New Jersey Generals (soon to be purchased by Donald Trump) signed him to a multimillion-dollar contract. When the upstart league folded after three seasons, Walker joined the NFL's Cowboys. In Dallas he not only played football but, to prove he could, danced with the Fort Worth Ballet. In the 1992 Olympics he competed on the United States' two-man bobsled team, finishing seventh.

As Walker sees it, MMA is simply a new challenge. "One night I was watching *The Ultimate Fighter* on Spike TV," he says, "and someone said, 'We're the best athletes in the world.' I thought, That's a bold statement. I thought, I'm not trying to be arrogant, but I've always thought of myself as being one of the best athletes in the world. I've always wanted people to say, 'Herschel Walker wasn't just a great running back but a great athlete.' So I said, 'I'll give it a shot.'"

Thus began Walker's pilgrimages to San Jose, where he spent four months living in a hotel room before his first fight and six months prior to his second. This was indeed a new challenge, and for Walker challenges are not to be taken lightly. "I don't see in between," he says. "I see only the white and the black. You win or you lose. There's no such thing as just playing well. You do the job or you don't do the job. I don't want to be just a fighter. I want to be a great fighter."

As Herschel Walker and Julie Blanchard, his fiancée, jog through his Dallas neighborhood, Texas-size manifestations of ostentatious wealth loom everywhere. Vaquero is a gated enclave of spanking new châteaus and palazzi, sculpted lawns and country-club amenities (a meandering golf course, jewel-like tennis courts, even stocked ponds with fishing poles at the ready). It has been home to celebrities (the Jonas brothers), major leaguers (the Texas Rangers' Josh Hamilton), and CEOs too numerous to name. "You can order room service at your house," says Walker, who a mile into the run speaks with the effortlessness of someone who could do this for hours. Indeed, it is only 7:30 on a summer morning, but he has been up since 5:30, already knocking out 2,000 sit-ups and 500 push-ups and then answering emails. As far as Walker is concerned, two and a half miles of roadwork before his business day starts is a form of cooling down.

In contrast to some of the larger estates on his street, Walker's 7,300-square-foot, $2.5 million Mediterranean villa is relatively modest, but it is far beyond the budget of most of the fighters who train at the American Kickboxing Academy. "I'm a different kind of MMA guy," he says matter-of-factly. "My life is different." Walker's stone driveway abuts a koi pond and fountain. Spanish arches grace the façade of his house. Inside there's a wine cellar and a screening room. Upstairs a gym is under construction.

Walker has lived here for only several months. During the previous 10 years he was ensconced in a sleek downtown Dallas penthouse. But with Christian, his 12-year-old son by his marriage to ex-wife Cindy, approaching the age when a big yard seemed mandatory, it was time to move. "Christian is my little man," he says.

Breakfast finds Walker and Blanchard, a dark-haired woman who is a vice president at CBS Outdoor Advertising, seated in Vaquero's well-appointed clubhouse. Walker's diet is more idiosyncratically Spartan than his idiosyncratically Spartan fitness routine. He eats only one meal a day, dinner, and is particular even then, limiting himself to lentil soup, salad, bread, and an occasional chicken cutlet. He cheerfully admits to washing down Kit Kat bars with Coca-Cola. "Nutritionists say that's bad for you," Walker concedes but then demands, "If that's so, why am I doing okay with it?" (Walker's physique is so flawless that he appeared nude in *ESPN The Magazine's* 2010 "Body" issue.) Still, he loves the ritual of dining. Even over an empty plate he relishes the give and play of conversation between friends amid the clinking of glasses and silverware. After the waiter brings Blanchard her eggs and bacon and Walker a solitary glass of iced tea, he takes her hand and says a simple prayer: "Dear heavenly father, please bless this food that nourishes our lips, and bless our family."

For all his ferocity in the MMA cage, Walker is inherently sweet-natured and deeply religious. He does not drink alcohol, and he does not curse. His idea of fun is to romp around his back porch with Christian and Cheerio, a golden retriever puppy that has the run of the place, or to plop down in front of any of his several televisions, all of which are generally tuned to DVRed episodes of *Judge Judy*. A criminal justice major in college, he agrees with her no-nonsense verdicts and finds her acerbic worldview amusing.

Not that Walker allows himself much time for relaxation. Most days he is flying to New York, Las Vegas, Detroit or Fort Lauderdale. If he is in Dallas, he is tied up in endless rounds of conference calls. Although he made his first fortune in football, he has made a second one in the food business, and running it is an all-consuming affair. Walker launched Renaissance Man Food Services 12 years ago as "a little family concern" with just one offering—home-style chicken tenders prepared from his mother's recipe. In the following decade he appeared at hundreds of culinary trade shows across the country. "I always say to ex-athletes, 'Guys, your name will get the door open, but unless you've got some substance you can't get a seat.'"

Today Walker's company consists of two divisions, including a recently purchased hospitality unit, and employs 300 people. Corporate offices are in Georgia. From three plants in Arkansas he distributes chicken sliders, chicken wings, chicken breast fajita strips, and a host of other food items to clients that include the MGM Grand, Caesars Palace, the Hard Rock Café, and McDonald's. Last year his sales topped $80 million. "Somebody told me we're the largest minority-owned chicken company in the United States," he says, adding after a deadpan pause, "I don't know if that means anything, as we may be the only minority-owned chicken company in the United States."

.Walker has achieved the dream of every famous jock, trading on his notoriety to create an enterprise that has paid for expensive toys (his 63-vehicle custom-car collection features a $250,000 Shelby KR) and should enable him to take care of himself and his family into perpetuity. He estimates his fortune at $25 million. If he wanted to he could coast from here on out. Yet Walker does not know how to coast.

"I think what people don't realize is that we all have to get up and fight it every day," he says during an afternoon lull in his schedule. "Life isn't easy. Life is not easy. People think things ought to be given to you, but nothing is given to you. You gotta go out and earn it. Sometimes you gotta take it. Every day I get up and fight. Every day I've got to fight."

Jerry Mungadze was in his office in the Dallas suburb of Bedford one evening several years ago when he picked up the phone and heard Herschel Walker say, "I'm in trouble." A psychologist who specializes in posttraumatic stress disorder, Mungadze met the football legend in the building's lobby. "Herschel was very distraught," he says. "He was crying. He was in pain. He was hurting emotionally."

Walker sought out Mungadze, whom he'd known casually since the 1980s, because a few days earlier he had armed himself with a handgun and driven to a meeting with the intention of killing a man whose sole offense had been to keep him waiting for the delivery of a custom automobile. According to Walker, an insistent voice inside his head said, "You don't disrespect me. I've spent too much time with people disrespecting me." He believes he would have committed murder had he not seen a "Smile, Jesus Loves You" bumper sticker on the rear of his intended victim's hauling van. The familiar maxim broke the spell. Still, he had come shockingly close to shooting someone—and not for the first time. On several occasions he had pointed a gun at his wife's head, and more than once he had played Russian roulette. "I was on my way to prison," he says, "or being dead."

Mungadze met with Walker for weeks and arrived at a controversial diagnosis. Many psychologists believe that dissociative identity disorder, or DID, as it is better known, is not so much a bona fide condition as hysteria born of depression. This view holds that for every Sybil, the real-life character suffering from a genuine split personality on whom the Sally Field film of the same name is based, there are thousands who contend with something less dramatic. But Mungadze was convinced that Walker had DID. "His was not one of the depressive syndromes. He was not clinically depressed."

People close to Walker were incredulous. "I know him better than anybody," his father told a reporter from *The Atlanta Journal-Constitution*, "because I raised him. This is my first knowing about that." In an attempt to

17

make light of the revelation, Vince Dooley, Walker's college coach, said, "I like the personality he had when he ran the football."

Initially Walker was also uncertain. Seeking a second opinion, he entered a California psychiatric hospital for three weeks as an outpatient. "For the first couple of days," he recalls, "you say to yourself, 'I'm not like these people here. I'm not like these people.' Then, all of a sudden, it hit me. I was just like those people. The diagnosis was right—is right. That's what it was. That's what it is."

As Walker came to understand, the source of his disorder could be traced to childhood. Although he grew up in a large, supportive churchgoing family in the rural Georgia town of Wrightsville, he had been a frightened boy (he was terrified, for instance, of entering his darkened home alone) who was dealt two of youth's cruelest cards. "I was chubby, what my parents called big-boned to keep from having to call me fat," he says, "and I had a terrible speech impediment. I'd have to slap myself repeatedly on the arm just to get a word out." By way of illustration, Walker takes a breath and with consonants catching on the back of his teeth mumbles, "*c-c-c*-could not *s-s-s*-say *w-w-w*-what was on *m-m*-mind."

An overweight stutterer gripped by a resulting lack of self-esteem, Walker was, in his words, "a doofus" who in elementary school was so unpopular that the only way he could get fellow students to talk with him at recess was by bribing them with his lunch money. Schoolmates called him Herschel the Girlshul. "By eighth grade I'd been beaten up 15 times," he says. "On the last day of eighth grade I got beat up again. I went home and watched *Gilligan's Island* and said, 'That won't happen to Herschel again.' I was tired of it. I said, 'Let's do something about it.'"

In 1975, which he calls his "year of independence," the 13-year-old Walker began forcing himself to stay up alone in the house at night and started reading books aloud in front of a mirror. "I read *Cowboy Sam* over and over to give me confidence," he says. Walker also inaugurated his exercise program. Not only did he begin doing the thousands of sit-ups and push-ups that still sustain him, he started running barefoot along a lonely country railroad right-of-way and over a course his father plowed for him with a tractor in a field near their home. With the help of the high school football coach, he also invented a piece of brutal but effective training equipment. From an old harness, an oversize tire, and a number of 10-pound shots, he built a weighted sled. After school, while his classmates wiled away their afternoons, he hitched himself to the sled and pulled it around the school track at top speed. "In eighth grade," he says, "if anyone had asked if I'd be a good athlete, it would have been a big fat no with a laugh. By ninth grade I'd gone from being a joke to one of the fastest kids in Georgia."

Walker's athletic feats at Johnson County High School are the stuff of legend. In his senior year he won state championships in the 100-yard dash and shot put and was the most highly recruited football player in America. But the triumphs, he says, came at an enormous cost. To survive the isolation that was his lot and the rigors of his singular pursuit, Walker developed an array of personalities that soon dominated his inner life. Some, like "the sentry," were intended to ward off the taunts of schoolmates. Others, like "the enforcer," were charged with punishing, at least in his fantasies, those who had done him wrong. "The hero" summoned him to ever greater gridiron achievements, while "the warrior" prepared him for combat with opponents. According to Walker, these alters, as therapists who treat dissociative disorders call them, were not just aspects of self but distinct characters with joys, needs, grievances, and aspirations. Day in and day out he heard their clamoring voices.

For a long time it all somehow worked. As Walker writes in *Breaking Free*, his alters usually functioned in concert, transforming him into a veritable athletic superman. At the University of Georgia, he overwhelmed huge linemen and sprinted past swift safeties. In his Heisman Trophy-winning year Walker averaged 159.3 yards rushing per game. "I think as a pure running back he's the best there's ever been," says Dooley. "He had world-class speed, strength, toughness, and discipline. He broke so many long runs for us. Even today he's among the top 10 rushers in collegiate history. Most of the other guys in that group played four seasons. He played only three."

Walker's professional career also produced remarkable highlights. He is the only player in NFL history to have scored touchdowns in a single season on a run from scrimmage of 90 yards or more, a pass reception of 90 yards or more, and a kickoff return of 90 yards or more. Because Walker spent his first years in the USFL, however, some of his greatest achievements—among them 2,411 yards rushing in 1985—go unacknowledged by the football establishment. Moreover, while he had spectacular seasons for both Dallas and the Philadelphia Eagles, he was not everyone's idea of a classic NFL back. The pro game values finesse. Walker featured power. "Herschel was a bruising runner," says Nate Newton, a retired Cowboys offensive lineman. "He wasn't elusive. He didn't have the shakes of an Emmitt Smith." Then there was "the trade," a still hotly debated deal that sent Walker from Dallas to the Minnesota Vikings in return for five players and six draft picks—an unheard-of ransom. The trade was supposed to turn Minnesota into an instant competitor, but due to internal squabbles, the Vikings underused Walker and went nowhere. The Cowboys, meanwhile, parlayed their influx of talent into the foundation of three Super Bowl championship teams. "The trade hurt Herschel," says Michael Irvin. "But I say to him, 'Look at what people think of you. Look at what they were willing to give up.'" Walker is satisfied to let his career numbers tell the final story. If record keepers took into account his combined USFL and NFL yardage—13,787—he would be the fifth-leading rusher in pro history, ahead of Jim Brown, O.J. Simpson, Eric Dickerson, and Ricky Williams.

In 1998, after returning to the Cowboys for his last two seasons, Walker retired. It was then that his dissociative disorder revealed its dark side. "Herschel really went through a hard time after retirement," says Julie Blanchard. Jerry Mungadze observes, "He began acting in ways inconsistent with who he thought he was, and it was devastating. He had personalities that had minds of their own. They felt differently, acted differently, and used language differently."

For Mungadze, Walker's condition was anything but academic. "Once, he, his wife, and I were in the office," says the therapist, "and he threatened to kill her, myself, and himself. I called 911, and the police came. That incident ended with him hitting the door and breaking his fist." Slowly, however, Walker made progress. "By resolving the traumas his alters resulted from," says Mungadze, "the alters started listening to him and following his directions. I think he has now integrated his personalities and is a healthy guy." The odds of Walker exploding in anger today, declares the psychologist, are "practically zero."

"Only over the past couple of years have I been able to look at myself and say I love who I am," says Walker, who is now such a believer in therapy that he has endorsed two mental-health outreach programs directed at people suffering not merely from dissociative disorders but from a full spectrum of emotional problems. Through Freedom Care, a division of Ascend Health Corporation, an operator of psychiatric hospitals, Walker speaks regularly to American armed forces members returning from combat in Iraq and Afghanistan. "I go to a lot of bases and say, 'There's no shame to admit you have a problem.'" Since 2009 the ex-NFL star has appeared at 31 military installations, helping initiate care for more than 6,000 troops. Walker's other program, Breaking Free, is aimed at patients at Ascend facilities, where he helps lead weekly group therapy sessions. "What I'm trying to do," he says, "is tell people there's hope. There are people who've struggled so long they think there is no hope. But there is." For Walker the programs offer an added benefit. "I get a lot of therapy by getting up and sharing and being brutally honest."

Mungadze believes Walker's entrance into MMA is the greatest evidence of his emotional well-being. Although the therapist says his patient's warrior alter—"the one that supports him in his fighting"—is still active, he contends that Walker's more troubling personalities have been silenced. If he were still hearing voices, Walker could not survive in the cage, where the very real threat presented by the fists, feet, and knees of opponents would make such distractions deadly.

Walker's love of MMA is unequivocal. The companionship of his fellow fighters at the American Kickboxing Academy and the attention he has received (his first two bouts aired live on Showtime and drew huge ratings) are gratifying. Even the money, whether he keeps it or not, is a form of respect. Promoters are dangling a $1 million payday for his third fight. "They're making me an offer I can't refuse," Walker says. Most of all he relishes the competition. Since his teens, that is what has kept him sane. For Walker to thrive in the world, he must keep pushing himself to do things others regard as on the edge.

Those who care about Walker are now urging him to walk away from MMA. "We all feel scared," says Blanchard. "His family does not approve. He's done it. He's proved it." Walker hears them but says he will finish on his own terms. After this last fight, he says, "I can guarantee you there will be no more. It really won't make sense for me to continue to fight after this year."

Punk Carter's Cutting Horse Ranch, 30 miles north of Dallas, is an unadulterated slice of old Texas. From its barn, bunkhouses, and stables to its rustic ranch house, the place exudes Western authenticity. On a storm-threatened summer night, Herschel Walker has driven here to discuss an opportunity. The proprietor, Punk Carter, spends most of his days teaching would-be cowboys how to ride and rope, but like a lot of country boys he is also a superb cook who augments his income with a line of spicy ranch hand ketchups and barbecue sauces. He and Walker are both in the food business. Along with a couple of partners, they are developing a nutritional supplement; they believe that a marketing campaign capitalizing on Walker's sculpted physique and his NFL and MMA pedigrees will get their product on store shelves. This evening potential investors have flown in from California.

As chicken and ribs sizzle on a grill, Walker, dressed in a TapouT T-shirt and faded jeans, strolls back to the barn, where Carter's 14-year-old grandson, Brock, is performing rope tricks. Soon enough the boy has his famous visitor atop a mechanical device Carter devised to help instruct greenhorns. At the push of a button, a steer on wheels roars down a narrow-gauge track and the student tosses his lasso. After several tries, Walker gets the hang of it, and the boy graduates him to a more difficult task—bringing down a live calf. This job demands not only precise roping but also expert footwork. It is no easy thing to upend and control an animal that weighs 250 pounds.

Again and again Walker tries. Again and again the calf breaks free. Eventually, however, Walker gets it right. With one leg wedged against the calf's flank, he flips it over, ties its hooves, and flashes a broad smile. He had come to Carter's place to expand his culinary empire, but something entirely different is now on his mind.

"You know," he says as he returns to the main house for his meeting, "a lot of the original cowboys were black. There's no reason I can't be a cowboy. I just might become a cowboy." His grin suggests that while MMA may soon be behind him, he will still be game for just about anything. "To get greatness," he says, "you've got to almost get crazy."

Herschel Walker continues to train at the American Kickboxing Academy, but as of 2016 he had yet to schedule a third fight. In 2015, however, he briefly contemplated rejoining the NFL, telling reporters, "I want to be the George Foreman of football."

The Casualty of War

Los Angeles, June 2007

That Tuesday afternoon, as Jim Leon steered his red Nissan Maxima into his windswept Lancaster neighborhood, he sighed in relief. No government vehicles were parked in front of his beige clapboard-and-flagstone house. Which meant there was no bad news from Iraq, where his 20-year-old son, Marine Corps corporal Christopher Leon, was serving in Ramadi, one of the country's most violent cities. In the four months since Chris deployed, this had become Jim's ritual. Because his job as a lab technician at Quest Diagnostics in Tarzana required him to be at work by 6:30 A.M., he always arrived home early. If anything was wrong, he would at least find out before his wife, Kathi, who kept normal business hours in the billing office of an Antelope Valley urologist.

Like so many streets in Lancaster, Avenue K-9, where the Leons live, is a link in a vast grid of alphabetized avenues running east to west and numbered thoroughfares laid out north to south. An unincorporated desert community just 30 years ago, Lancaster now has a population of 130,000 and sprawls across the top of Los Angeles County. From its chain restaurants to its proliferating subdivisions, it exudes newness and uniformity. The big residential developers are KB, Beazer, Pulte, and Heritage, and the interchangeable versions of paradise they've created are advertised on fluttering banners proclaiming 7 FLOOR PLANS, YOU'LL LOVE IT HERE, or NO PAYMENTS UNTIL 2008. The Leons own a three-bedroom house in Harris Homes, one of the earlier neighborhoods on the desirable west side. The living room, all green and white with a faceted mirror over the fireplace, is dominated by a fabric-and-rope tree for their five cats. A Sony big-screen TV fronts one wall of the den. Plates adorned by Norman Rockwell paintings are mounted to another. But photographs of Chris are the interior's most distinctive element. A shot of him as a towheaded three-month-old hangs near his parents' bed. Pictures of him on a recent Easter and on his prom night top the mantelpiece. The first thing visible on entering the front door is a formal portrait of him in his Marine Corps dress blues. Blond haired and hazel eyed with a square jaw, he radiates self-assurance.

The Leons adopted Chris at birth, making him not less than flesh and blood to them but something more. At the time, they'd been together 12 years and were living in a tiny condo in Agoura. Tall with a thin gray mustache, Jim, who moved to Los Angeles from the Midwest in the 1960s, is urbane, deliberate, and at 72, his wife's elder by 16 years. Dark haired and exuberant, Kathi grew up in the North Valley, and most of her family still lives in the area. Each went through troubled early marriages, and both are deeply religious, regarding faith as a bulwark against an uncertain world. Indeed, Jim—who was raised Jewish—converted to Catholicism shortly after marrying Kathi. For a long time they saw themselves as liberals, but eventually they drifted to the right. Not that they were doctrinaire about it. They opposed abortion and felt that the Republican Party offered the best hope for a culture that fostered life. Jim, estranged from a son and daughter by his first wife, especially wanted a child, and he and Kathi tried hard to have one, invoking the Lord—they prayed constantly—and science. Despite side effects that made her hands ache so badly she had to bandage them, Kathi took the fertility drug Danazol. Nothing worked. Then in fall 1985, Kathi's obstetrician phoned with wonderful news. A 13-year-old patient named Nikki Ruhl was putting her child up for adoption. Were they interested? On November 5, the day Nikki gave birth, Jim and Kathi were at Thousand Oaks' Los Robles Hospital. After the papers were signed and Nikki was granted a few hours to hold her son, the couple took the infant home. They called him Christopher David, but "Baby," Kathi's pet name for him—which even after he joined the Marines she continued to use—emphasized his status in their family as a fragile and precious gift. "It was such a God thing," she says. "He gave us this blessing. You think you're in control, but God is."

Jim and Kathi moved to Lancaster in 1988 because it was a part of Los Angeles where they could afford a new house with a big yard. It took time for Jim to adjust to the one-hour commute to and from work in Tarzana, but soon enough the two were using the same expression used by others in the Antelope Valley for the more urban Southern California they'd left behind: Down Below. Down Below was crime and congestion. But here was a community of like-minded people seeking something better. In its orderliness, Lancaster offered a place of greater safety.

For Jim and Kathi, Chris's childhood was a happy blur. They ferried him to tee-ball games, bought him *Star Wars* toys and skateboards, and enrolled him in one of the Antelope Valley's most elite elementary schools, Desert Christian. Chris and his best friend since second grade, David Meade, played on various roller hockey teams—the Sabres, the Hawks, and the Rangers—at an indoor rink. The only trouble anyone remembered Chris getting into as a boy occurred at the age of seven or eight when he and David set some sagebrush at the end of Avenue K-9 on fire while fooling with matches. They tried to put out the flames with Super Soakers, but when that failed they did the right thing, telling Kathi, who called the fire department, which extinguished the blaze.

Since Chris departed for Iraq, Jim and Kathi had thought back often on those days. They'd also thought back on more recent, harder times. Like many young marines, Chris had gone through a period in his teens when he'd behaved heedlessly. He had nearly destroyed himself with alcohol and drugs. There was a long stretch during which Jim and Kathi despaired of ever reaching him. But Chris fought his way clear, the battle largely taking place in his room. Painted electric blue, it is plastered with posters of Eminem and 50 Cent. A hockey stick autographed by the Kings looks down from one side, a row of Dodger caps from another. Here Chris sought meaning in his life and forgiveness for his trespasses, at 18 scrawling a plea for divine intervention on the closet wall with a Magic Marker:

> I feel like I serve no purpose
> Strivin ta succeed but always
> Fallin ta my knees,
> Please God please
> Let my thoughts guide me
> Light my path
> Don't hide me
> I'll change the world you provided me.

Jim and Kathi were thankful the Marine Corps had given their son a sense of purpose, but they were terrified because it had placed him in danger. Jim was particularly fearful, as he viewed the world so differently from his son. Where Chris was vigorous and confrontational, he was bookish and reserved. He spent his days in a lab coat performing repetitive tasks with names like "enzyme-linked immunosorbent assay." Neither had much patience for the other's interests. The gap had been the source of much tension during Chris's adolescence, but they had gotten through it.

All of this was in the back of Jim's mind on Tuesday, June 20, 2006, when he saw the Father's Day card from Iraq. Greetings for specific occasions are hard to come by in Ramadi. Chris was forced to select one that read "Happy Birthday Dad" and displayed a lighthouse. Inside, he'd written a note that from its spotty spelling to its assessment of past failings was a synopsis of his life:

> Sorry they didn't have any fathers day cards. I know the light house is really gay. I hope you know how thankful I am for having a great man and father in my life. You've done more than youre share of hard work raising me and I know it wasn't easy. Now I'm all grown up and reflecting youre teachings and dissapline on the world. You've made me into a man and I thank you with all my heart for youre sacrifices and determination. Thanks for never giving up on me even threw all the shame I brought upon myself. Thank you for all you've done for me. I couldn't ask for a better father. Happy fathers day. I love you dad. Love, Chris

Jim's eyes filled with tears. Chris had never told him that he looked up to him or regarded him as a source of strength. Maybe he had been a better father than he imagined. Maybe their life in the Antelope Valley had worked out according to plan. When he finally composed himself, Jim called Kathi to tell her everything was okay and that he'd received an amazing card from their son that he couldn't wait for her to read. Ten minutes later, the doorbell rang.

One day during his sophomore year, Chris was standing on the grounds of Lancaster's Paraclete High handing out sticks of gum to some friends when a classmate approached and demanded a piece. Chris refused, and the boy grabbed him by the hair. Chris retaliated with a vicious punch to the mouth. He mostly ended up hurting himself, though, opening a jagged gash across his knuckles. The cut became infected, and the next morning he awakened with a hand as big as a balloon. He missed half a week of classes, but the worst thing was that he didn't care. In fact, he took pride in the entire episode, regarding it as a defining moment.

Paraclete High is on the northwest side of Lancaster, just below Quartz Hill, the area's wealthiest enclave, home to physicians, lawyers, and aerospace engineers employed by the giant Boeing and Northrop Grumman factories that dominate the Antelope Valley's economy. Although affiliated with the Catholic Church, the school draws students of all religions to its yucca-studded campus. Ninety percent of the graduates attend college, and as a freshman Chris had given every indication that he would be one of them, earning mostly As and Bs. The next year had begun just as promisingly, with Chris playing cornerback on the varsity football Spirits, getting into enough games to feel that he contributed to the team's 2001 California Interscholastic Federation Southern Section Championship.

Then the bottom fell out. In his second sophomore semester, Chris received a C in English, Ds in French, biology, and religion, and an F in algebra. Never again would he walk onto the football field. His new sport was paintball, which had him running through the desert blasting away with a $1,300 Angel gun his parents dutifully helped him buy. He'd taken up drinking and smoking, choosing brands—potent King Cobra 40s and nicotine-rich Camel Wides—that he believed gave him gangster credibility. Many weekend nights he stayed out until dawn without calling home. He also started stealing money from Jim and Kathi, even taking Christmas presents intended for his grandparents, returning them to the store where they were purchased, and pocketing the refund.

Jim and Kathi racked their brains to understand what was going on. How could their baby have so quickly become a demon? What had they missed? There had, of course, been signs. When Chris was at Desert Christian, he'd been diagnosed with attention deficit disorder, and his doctor had prescribed Ritalin, then Dexedrine. During his teens, though, he stopped taking the drugs. They made him feel dull. Without them, he was prone to rogue bursts of energy. There was also something else: By the time Chris turned 15, Jim was 66, far older than other boys' dads. Jim lived for baroque music, believing that in the intricacy of a Bach Mass he could hear the truth in all its nuances. Chris loved rap, especially anything by Dr. Dre, and found authenticity in its discordant rhythms and harsh lyrics—to him the truth was a blunt object. They quarreled over control of the CD player. "I'm gonna put you down, old man," Chris would growl, to which his father would retort, "That's very mature." The relationship degenerated. "I felt inadequate," Jim says. "I didn't know what to do for him." Hoping to pick up the slack, Kathi often assumed the paternal role, going camping with her son while Jim stayed at home. In an extreme gesture of solidarity for a 50-year-old mom, when Chris got his ears and tongue pierced, she got a diamond nose stud.

At the heart of it all was a riddle that Jim and Kathi couldn't solve: It was one thing for Chris to accept intellectually that he'd been given up for adoption, but emotionally it was another story. No matter how hard Jim and Kathi tried, he felt detached and betrayed. He didn't know who he was, which meant that the battle to forge an identity fought by every teen was for him doubly intense.

On top of all this, Chris was plainly using drugs. What Jim and Kathi lacked was evidence. Shortly after Paraclete let out for summer 2002 vacation, they found it—a bag of marijuana in their son's things. The discovery produced a moment of clarity for Kathi. "I thought, 'All right, it's time to put the screws to him,'" she says. "I thought, 'I'm gonna show him.'" She phoned the Los Angeles County Sheriff's Department. On a June Sunday as Chris was sleeping, two deputies appeared at the door. After awakening and cuffing him, they put him in the back of a squad car. Since he was a minor and in possession of less than an ounce, they charged him with a misdemeanor and did not transport him to the Lancaster substation. He would be required to attend several Narcotics Anonymous sessions and pay a $400 fine, but ultimately his record would be wiped clean. Chris was devastated and furious. "Fuck you, Mom," he screamed when he stormed back into the house. "Fuck you. Fuck you. Fuck you." He then stomped off to his room, slamming the door behind him.

During this period, Jim and Kathi sought consolation and guidance at the 5,000-member Desert Vineyard Fellowship. Wearying of Catholicism's rigidity and seeking a form of worship that was at once less dogmatic and more vibrantly rooted in Scripture, they had joined in 1999. The Vineyard movement, which grew out of the countercultural Jesus craze, began on Santa Monica Beach during the early 1970s. Preachers wear jeans, sermons are conversational, and the music is guitar-driven soft rock to which parishioners stand and sway with hands uplifted to the Lord. Desert Vineyard, which is presided over by the Reverend David Parker—known to everyone as Pastor Dave—is the second oldest of the denomination's 1,500 churches. The congregation includes Northrop Grumman engineers and businesspeople. But many who attend are troubled—35 percent have experienced substance-abuse problems. Desert Vineyard offers a variety of prayer-based support programs, and Jim and Kathi enrolled in one composed of other parents of children using drugs. "They let us know we weren't alone and weren't failures," says Kathi. "They'd say, 'We've been there. Don't give up.'"

Still, the Leons were at a loss about what to do. One minute Kathi would announce that they were kicking Chris out, but Jim wouldn't hear of it. The next, Jim would declare that he'd lost patience, and Kathi would say that they had to keep trying. They agreed on one matter, though: They were through paying thousands of dollars for private schooling. Their son's days at Paraclete were over.

Chris's junior year at Lancaster High started off disastrously. Forging notes from Jim and Kathi, he skipped classes and attracted the attention of truant officers. His grades dropped even lower: Fs in Spanish, English, algebra, history, and science. Affecting hip-hop style in Enyce sweaters and cargo pants from Shady Ltd., he spent afternoons racing his mom's navy blue Saturn along secluded streets. His favorite was Bulldog Avenue near Quartz Hill, where a tight four-lane turn provides an ideal spot for drifting. To give the car a high-performance roar, he removed its air filter, ignoring warnings that this was a surefire way to burn out the engine, which he did. At night Chris was often at a party house owned by an older guy who kept crack in the refrigerator and loved to brag about the life. Strange girls and ex-cons were always passing through, and four or five people would still be awake at sunrise. Before long, Chris was smoking and dealing methamphetamine, the Antelope Valley's hardcore drug of choice.

"He was a classic Lancaster kid," says David Meade, who stayed on at Paraclete but remained Chris's closest friend. "He screwed around in high school because there's nothing to do here but drink and smoke. You get sucked into it, and it's a nasty cycle. You get your girlfriend pregnant, and you end up in a crappy job to pay the bills. And crystal meth is always a danger. It's the largest problem in our town. There are lots of meth labs on the east side, where people's houses blow up in the middle of the night. This was the road Chris was on."

Jim and Kathi didn't know everything, but they knew enough. During talks with a Lancaster High guidance counselor, they were given two choices: Chris could either attend Desert Winds, a separate campus for delinquent students, or he could enroll in Independent Study. Just two months into his new school, their son was running out of options.

On the periphery of the Lancaster High campus, far from the school's busy quads, is room 306, home of the Independent Study program. The location is intentional and symbolic. Here, students who have rebelled against order being imposed on them are expected to impose it on themselves. Rather than meet in class for lectures and instruction, they work on their own schedules. Whether they read textbooks at home or study online at a cybercafé is immaterial. They're only required to appear in room 306 to submit papers and take tests.

One morning in November 2002, Chris walked through the drab blue door for the first time. Instead of desks lined up in neat rows, there were casually arranged round tables. At the entrance was an area reminiscent of a library checkout counter. In a cubicle formed from tall black filing cabinets sat Cheryl Holland. A 58-year-old mother of two and a teacher in the Antelope Valley School District since 1974, Holland projects empathy and toughness. Almost every inch of her work area is covered with photographs of kittens, singer Céline Dion, and former NFL quarterback John Elway. She loves nothing more than to talk about making a difference in children's lives. Then she'll square her jaw and declare that if a student ever hit her she'd deck him.

"When Chris's parents decided it was time to put the brakes on his tailspin," Holland says, "it was the luck of the draw that he was assigned to me. I took one look at him and realized he just needed a little time to get his head out of his ass. He thought he could continue to be a slacker. He thought he could just go through the motions. I told him that wasn't going to fly here. I told him I'd be nice if he did his work, but if he didn't I'd get down and dirty."

Chris told David Meade that Holland was a bitch and complained to Jim and Kathi that he hated her. "She was in his face," says Kathi, "and he didn't like it. But she got his attention." To Jim and Kathi's relief, Chris responded to Independent Study's unstructured environment, in part because it allowed him to call his own shots, a privilege he had never before been accorded. "The program required him to become accountable," says Holland. "After a while I no longer had to tell him to do his work," adds Kathi. "He just did it." In his first grading period, he earned two Bs and a C.

Shortly before Chris enrolled in Independent Study, he fell in with several boys who'd recently formed a crew whose name could not have been more purposeful: Insanely Determined to Succeed. Aside from Chris, IDS had four other members: Jon Sherman, Sonny Huerta, Alan Iosue, and Chris's old friend David Meade. "We started it for protection," says Jon. "We were kind of crazy and got into a lot of fights. It got dangerous out here." This was one reason Jon recruited Chris. "He just had this strength about him. I wanted him on my side."

The first months Chris was at Lancaster High, the boys of IDS spent the bulk of their time driving the Antelope Valley's backstreets or hanging out in an isolated cul-de-sac near Alan's house known as "the spot." There they drank, talked, and when the testosterone was running high, squabbled.

"We didn't do shit," says Jon, "and that's where we did it." Their regimented desert city felt stultifying. Too much conformity. Too many naysayers. Too few outlets for creativity. They were always up for anything unsanctioned, even if it took them to the party house. "It was a fucked-up time," says Jon. "There were days we'd have $1,000 in our pockets."

All the members of Insanely Determined to Succeed came from middle-class or privileged backgrounds (David's dad was an astronaut who flew on three shuttle missions), and each possessed intrinsic skills or qualities. Sonny could cook so well, people thought he could be a chef. Jon could paint. Alan loved architecture. David followed politics and read voraciously. Chris was different. He didn't pursue an obvious passion, but he was the most alive, the most resilient, the one the others turned to. "My mom died, and afterward I was pretty messed up and got into some trouble," says Alan. "I spent 19 days at juvenile hall. Chris was the first person I saw when I got out. He came over to see how I was doing and talked to my dad. I was having difficulty in school, and he told me to stick with it." While none of the group's members was headed to Harvard, and all except David were going to have difficulty graduating from high school, they were to a one idealistic—which had always been part of the attraction. "When I first got to know Chris," says Jon, "he was hanging around with guys who were much lower in intelligence. He just needed help. He needed brothers."

By the start of their senior year, the boys of IDS had begun to follow their own code. "We had too much respect for ourselves to go on the way we had been," says Jon. "I feel like we ultimately became a reincarnation of King Arthur's knights. If someone fell down, we picked him up. We sought knowledge. We told one another the truth. We pushed ourselves to lead lives of valor."

As Chris started to feel better about himself, two good things happened. First, he found a girlfriend. Analyse Reaves, a Paraclete student from an academic family (her father administers the UCLA physics lab), had long resisted his approaches. During his sophomore year, she'd outright rejected him. "That Valentine's Day she broke his heart," says David. Yet Chris persisted, and when he asked her to go to Disneyland in March 2003, she said yes. Soon the two were inseparable. Not only did she boost Chris's ego and improve his manners ("He was very rough around the edges," says David), she got him to swear off meth. "Until then he didn't have a reason to stop," Analyse says. "I think I helped him find one."

Chris also landed a job, taking the position of stock boy at PetSmart in Lancaster's Valley Central Mall. Initially, he put in just a few hours after school unloading merchandise and helping customers carry purchases to their cars. Eventually, the manager came to trust him, assigning him the task of opening the place on Sunday mornings.

PetSmart is next door to the city's Armed Forces Career Center. All the major branches of the military have offices there, and on breaks Chris would wander down to see what was going on. He gravitated to the space occupied by the United States Marine Corps. Decorated by posters bearing slogans like PAIN IS TEMPORARY PRIDE IS FOREVER and a wall plaque displaying the corps' eagle, globe, and anchor seal, the office was run by Gunnery Sergeant Larry Watts and Staff Sergeant Leann Elizabeth Dixon. Watts is a stern, black Chicagoan, Dixon a white Floridian known to pick up stray animals and nurse them at home. Chris liked them both, but he was even more taken by the Marine Corps itself. As he saw it, the service could provide him a chance to excel as an individual while becoming part of something bigger. The romance, the call to duty, the machismo—the corps was Insanely Determined to Succeed writ large. Here, at last, was an opportunity for Chris to merge the warring parts of his soul. He was so gung ho that he told his parents he was quitting school and joining immediately. Kathi objected, insisting that he get his diploma. As it turned out, the Marine Corps offers a Delayed Entry Program designed for those in his position. On July 22, 2003, with Sergeant Dixon bearing witness, Chris signed up.

"This was Chris's way of redeeming himself," says Jim. "He wanted to do something difficult. I think he was a little elitist about it." David believes Chris saw the Marines as a calling: "He told me God wanted him to do it, that it was a vocation." Jon puts it more enthusiastically: "It was fucking cool."

Chris immersed himself in the Delayed Entry Program. "He was one of my faithful fellows," says Sergeant Watts. "Each Saturday we'd run, do pull-ups and push-ups, and every week I'd go by Lancaster High to see how he was doing with his studies." Chris stopped eating fast food and began downing protein shakes and vitamin supplements. "He started drinking this green goop," says David. "It was awful." He also applied himself to Independent Study. "During his junior year I had to push him," says Cheryl Holland. "But during his senior year all I had to do was guide him. He became a pleasure to have in my life. It was hard for him—he never did learn to spell—but in fact he was smart, a deep thinker." To graduate on time, Chris needed to make up all the classes he'd failed. During his last semester he took seven courses, receiving Bs in six. The sole blemish was a C in food. He also undertook a senior project titled "Becoming a U.S. Marine." Chris accompanied his six-page essay with a cover letter that opened,

> For the past four years I have gone through more struggles than the average high school student.... I never really thought I was going to graduate high school. That was until I started really getting involved in the Marines. My whole outlook on life has changed.... I look forward to becoming a Marine. I will do everything possible in my position to make this country a better place for everyone.

The project received the Independent Study Program's highest mark—a 4, for "Distinguished." On June 10, 2004, Chris graduated from Lancaster High with his class. Several weeks later Jim and Kathi drove him to the Armed Forces Career Center, where a van was waiting to transport him to Los Angeles. From there, it would be on to the Marine Corps Recruit Depot in San Diego, and then Camp Pendleton.

The war in Iraq had entered its second year, but just a few months before, President George W. Bush—whom Jim and Kathi had supported in 2000 and would vote for again in November—had proclaimed, "Mission accomplished." Says Kathi, "It never crossed our minds that Chris would see combat. Our goal had been to get him through school. The Marines helped us achieve it. Iraq felt very far away."

The Leons' living room door opens onto a metal security screen, and through it Jim could see a Marine Corps staff sergeant, a chief warrant officer, and an air force chaplain. Jim made no move to unlock the screen, convinced that if he kept his visitors at bay, what they had come to tell him could not be true. He said nothing. He stared at the men, his hands at his sides. The standoff lasted only a minute, but it felt longer. Finally, Sergeant Jeff Brown, who'd never before had to perform this duty, asked, "Can we come in?"

"I don't know how you guys do this," Jim said after stepping aside.

"Your son, Christopher Leon, has been killed in action," Brown began. As the casualty assist calls officer (CACO, in Marine argot), Brown was in charge, but there was no prescribed protocol. All he had to go on was his memory of what it had been like for his parents when he was a boy and his brother died. He knew he couldn't protect the Leons from pain, but he could at least assure them that the Marine Corps would take care of the myriad details. As he started to explain, however, he saw that Jim had turned white, becoming at once agitated and withdrawn. Brown thought he must be recalling memories of Chris. That was only partly right.

The image Jim could not get out of his mind was of Chris's dead body. His facial features were unchanged, but the animating force—the spirit that had made him Chris—had been extinguished. Eyes gone vacant, mouth slack, he was pasty, cold, rigid, inert. Oddly, he was not in uniform but in street clothes, yet maybe that was fitting. Before he was a marine, he was the son whose Father's Day card was lying open on the den table. Jim fought hard to dislodge the vision. Once he did, though, he felt the first flush of a familiar toxic glow. In 2002, while commuting to Tarzana, he'd suffered a mild heart attack. In 2003, he underwent triple bypass surgery. He was later diagnosed with congestive heart failure. Now he was experiencing the same sensation. Pressure surged in his chest. Sweat beaded on his forehead.

"Would you like me to call an ambulance?" the chaplain asked.

"You'd better."

While the paramedics were en route, Jim phoned Kathi. She was at her desk near the refrigerator in the back of the urology clinic, entering charges into a computer and sending claims to insurance companies, when she picked up. "We've lost Chris," Jim said, his voice breaking. She screamed, "No" and continued screaming until her boss's wife took the receiver from her hand. One of her coworkers attempted to reassure her, saying there had to be a mistake, but Kathi knew better, and as she walked through the crowded reception area she kept screaming. She screamed all the way home and was still doing so when the emergency technicians arrived: "No. No. No." Finally, one of the men said, "You have to stop," but she wouldn't. The advice was an affront from someone who couldn't possibly comprehend what she was feeling. Her baby, the unexpected miracle in her life, was gone.

The EMTs raced Jim to Antelope Valley Hospital, where he was diagnosed as having suffered another mild heart attack and placed in the intensive care unit. Kathi stayed behind and began notifying friends and family members, among them her sister, LoriAnn, and her mother, who because of a bad connection couldn't hear what her daughter was saying, forcing her to repeat, "Chris was killed. Chris was killed." All the while, Sergeant Brown and the other servicemen stood at the edge of the room at parade rest. They would do whatever they were asked, but they would not infringe.

By eight o'clock the Leons' house had filled with people—most from Desert Vineyard. Among them were Dana and Dawn Stewart, whose son, Marine Corps lance corporal Ian Stewart, had been killed in Iraq two years before. "I never wanted to walk in your shoes," Kathi burst out on seeing Dawn, and they embraced. Associate Pastor Paul Lopiccolo led the group in prayer, kneeling in Kathi's living room and assuring her that her fellow church members would keep vigil. That night, after everyone departed, Kathi took strength from the knowledge that others would be beseeching the Lord in her name. "I was too devastated," she says, "to pray for myself."

Of the boys in Insanely Determined to Succeed, Jon heard first. He had just come home from his job at T-Mobile, where he was working to put himself through Antelope Valley College. He called the others. Sonny was attending the California School of Culinary Arts in Pasadena by day while grilling steaks at a Claim Jumpers by night. Alan was selling electronics components in Las Vegas to pay for classes at the Community College of Southern Nevada. David was studying at Pepperdine University while employed in a Santa Monica law firm's collections office. He was the last to learn. He'd turned off his cell phone Tuesday night and didn't find out until the next morning when he picked up a text message from Jon as he was walking to the corner of Wilshire Boulevard and 3rd Street. Suddenly, the palm trees and the Pacific dissolved in a blur of tears. After crying for 15 minutes, David told one of the partners that his friend had been killed in Iraq. He then headed to Lancaster. Up the Antelope Valley Freeway, out of the green basin, and into the dry mountains that rim Los Angeles County he drove. Eventually, he found himself at Jon's apartment. Both of them wanted to visit the Leons, but neither could muster the courage that night.

Over the next several days, as Jim lay in a hospital bed, Kathi leaned heavily on LoriAnn, who'd come from Westlake Village to stay with her. The house was filled with flowers, but Kathi could barely see them, having ruptured blood vessels in her eyes during her screaming. Nor could she eat any of the casseroles and sandwiches members of Desert Vineyard kept dropping off. She had no appetite. "I was just broken down," she says. "My mind had become mush. I couldn't reason." Her biggest concern was the return of Chris's remains. The bodies of fallen American servicemen are initially flown to the Charles C. Carson Center for Mortuary Affairs in Dover, Delaware. The length of time they are kept there can vary widely. Each morning Kathi called Sergeant Brown to see where things stood, but he couldn't get an answer. The only information he could provide was that

Chris's remains were viewable. Unlike many servicemen killed in Iraq, he had not been torn apart by an improvised explosive device. A sniper had shot him. "I never thought I'd want to see a body, especially my son's," says Kathi, "but I was comforted by the fact that I'd be able to."

At 11 P.M. on June 29, a week and a half after Chris was killed, a Delta flight carrying his remains landed at Ontario International Airport and taxied to the gate. Jim had been released from the hospital, and he and Kathi, her parents, and her sister and brother-in-law were standing on the tarmac alongside a Marine honor guard commanded by Jeff Brown. After the passengers disembarked, Chris's casket appeared in the mouth of the cargo hold. Encased in Styrofoam and shrink wrap, it looked like an appliance carton. The marines needed ten minutes to rip away the packing material. They then draped the coffin with an American flag and carried it to a waiting hearse. "It's such a horrible car to see your baby go in," says Kathi. "But at least we got to touch the casket and kiss the flag. We were in such a state of shock. A woman in a ground-level shipping office saw us standing there and opened a locked door and said that if we needed to use the bathroom to come in. It was a tiny thing, but it showed real kindness. We were so grateful." As the hearse pulled away, Jim saluted. Behind the glass wall of a busy concourse, people standing in line were saluting, too.

The next day Kathi and her family went to Lancaster's Joshua Memorial Park to view the body. Jim, in his mind having already seen Chris dead, didn't go. "I just can't take it," he told Kathi. After the family filed out, David Meade and Jon Sherman entered. "I was so glad to see him," says Jon. "I was so glad he was home."

That evening, family members gathered at the Leons' to make memory boards to display at the funeral. Jim and Kathi had assembled a stack of photographs from different periods in Chris's life. As the group began to cut and paste, something unexpected happened—the sadness lifted. Grief, unbearable as it is, offers moments of euphoria, and they were experiencing one, so much so that around ten o'clock Jim rushed out to a Marie Callender's and bought pies. Everyone stayed up late eating and passing around pictures. There was Chris at two with a baseball cap on sideways and a plastic bat in his hands. Here he was at four in a bathing pool filled with frogs he'd collected. A shot of him at ten riding on his skateboard conjured memories of his frequent falls and how he always jumped back up. They laughed at these images, but one taken of Chris in Iraq elicited a different emotion. He's wearing a desert camouflage uniform, with his helmet pulled down low.

Eyes wary, lips set in a straight line, he looks fierce yet mindful. For years his parents had worried that Chris wouldn't find himself, but here was evidence that he had, and it made them proud. "I wouldn't want to tangle with that guy," Jim thought.

The most daunting part of Marine boot camp is the Crucible. A 54-hour training mission during which sleep-deprived recruits each carrying 75 pounds of gear march, crawl, and run more than 50 miles through mock battlefields, the drill amounts to a final exam. It concludes with a ten-mile climb known as the Reaper. Characterized by rocky terrain and nearly vertical ascents, it is Camp Pendleton's most formidable challenge. Shortly before Chris started, he bent over to adjust his boots and heard a loud crack, then felt pain. He'd broken his left foot. For a second, he contemplated what to do. Yet as he looked back on what he'd already been through during the eight weeks since he'd left Lancaster—the loneliness and the exhaustion—he decided to push forward. Every inch of the Reaper was excruciating, as was every inch of a six-mile run that followed, but Chris finished. Boot camp was essentially behind him. The life he'd aspired to since he walked into the recruiting station next to PetSmart lay ahead.

Chris's injury, although not severe, required him to wear a walking cast, and he did not graduate with his class that fall. Accompanying Jim and Kathi to a December graduation ceremony were Analyse and three members of Insanely Determined to Succeed—David, Jon, and Alan. Chris, they all agreed, seemed older, more polite, and for someone who'd been immersed in a culture that prizes toughness, surprisingly more loving. Afterward, everyone went to lunch at the San Diego Yacht Club, snapping pictures of Chris in his uniform with its eagle, globe, and anchor pin as he stood before the sparkling water. He was now a marine. Two days later he walked into a tattoo parlor and had USMC inked onto his right triceps and his last name inked onto his left.

Chris returned to Camp Pendleton for six weeks of infantry training, then reported to Twentynine Palms, home of the Marine Corps Communications School. He wanted to become a radio operator and spent hours learning how to operate the PRC-117 and PRC-119, each about the size and weight of a VCR. Along with bulletproof steel plates, a flak jacket, ammunition magazines, and an M-16 A4 rifle, these machines would become part of the 120 pounds of equipment he would carry in the field. During downtime, he began working out obsessively. At first he just wanted to be strong enough to do his job, but he found he loved physical training. Within months he was bench-pressing 300 pounds and on his way to a green belt in karate.

Because he was close to the Antelope Valley, Chris could go home on weekends. Jim and Kathi's hope that the Iraq war would be over by the time their son finished training had been a delusion. In boot camp, Chris had told them as much. In one of the weekly letters he sent them, many of which were simply addressed "Mom and Dad, Avenue K-9, Lancaster, Ca.," he'd written, "I'm getting kinda scared…. The DIs keep telling us that most of us will go to Iraq for sure, including all infintry. But its OK if I go. I'll come back walking and talking, that is. I don't want you to tell Analyse this. Okay."

Now deployment was drawing nearer. One night Chris and David Meade were hanging out. "Why are you going?" David asked. "So you don't have to," Chris responded. Around this time, Chris attended the funeral of a marine killed in Iraq. Afterward, he dropped in on David at his mom's house, which offers a view of the entire Antelope Valley. The two boys were standing outside looking down on the lights of the town where they'd grown up when Chris said, "The funeral I was at—only one person spoke. If anything happens to me…."

David refused to let Chris finish. "If you're predisposed to it, it'll happen."

But Chris wouldn't be silenced. "If anything happens to me and only one person gets to speak, I want it to be you."

The night before Chris left for Okinawa for final training, Jim and Kathi threw a going-away party. About halfway through the evening, with no explanation or tenderness, Chris told Analyse that he was breaking up with her. They had been together for two years. She was devastated. "He did it in a very cold, very fucked-up way," says David. "She sat outside in her car for two hours. He knew he was going to die and didn't want any attachments." Chris's other friends felt that his motivation had more to do with the deteriorating nature of the relationship. All agree that his behavior was cruel. "He felt he should just break things off," says Analyse. "I never saw him again."

In Okinawa, Chris was assigned to the highly regarded Air Naval Gunfire Liaison Company. Although not as elite as Force Recon, ANGLICO is among the Marines' most demanding outfits. Working in small groups usually no larger than four and typically commanded by a high-ranking fighter pilot, ANGLICO teams are the communications link between ground combat missions and air support, which can come in the form of everything from helicopter gunships to F-18s. It's ANGLICO'S job to call in bomb and missile strikes, and since the missions require precision, units are frequently within 100 yards of their targets. The radio operator must maintain contact between the foot soldiers and the forces aloft. "At first he wasn't proficient with the radios, not that this was surprising," says Captain Adam Blanton of Fifth ANGLICO. A 29-year-old Boise State English graduate who grew up in Riverside County, he was Chris's team leader. "We have the most complicated equipment out there. But he picked things up quickly."

In November 2005, Chris phoned Kathi. He knew that within a couple months he would be in Iraq, and he wanted to meet his birth mom before leaving. "At first my heart sank," says Kathi. "I thought I was going to lose him. But I realized that was my own insecurity, my own problem. I needed to do what was best for Chris. So I dug up the paperwork from the adoption. There was a phone number for Nikki Ruhl's mother. When I called it, I got a forwarding number—and here's the remarkable part. When I reached Nikki's mom, who'd moved to Nevada, she told me the forwarding number was due to be disconnected that very day. If I hadn't called when I did, who knows if we'd ever have found her?"

Nikki was 33, living in Simi Valley and training to be a veterinary technician. Each November 5, ever since that day 20 years earlier at Los Robles Hospital, she'd quietly celebrated Chris's birthday. When he turned 18, she'd begun hoping he'd call. Now, here was Kathi on the phone saying Chris was leaving for Iraq and wanted to meet her. Nikki couldn't hold back the tears. "I was so happy," she says. "Kathi and I talked for two hours. Then I drove to Lancaster a couple of weeks later and spent the afternoon with Jim and Kathi. We looked at pictures and talked about the good and the bad. They made me feel like family." Jim and Kathi were taken with Nikki, and at the end of the visit, Kathi said Chris would be home for the holidays and she'd make the arrangements.

Everything about Chris's 2005 Christmas leave, indeed everything about the weeks before he deployed for Iraq, seemed touched by the miraculous. The day after he got back to Lancaster, he went on a date with Aimey Vaccaro. The two had known each other in grade school at Desert Christian, but they'd lost touch. Just five feet two inches tall and 105 pounds, with straight brown hair with red highlights, Aimey is tiny and saucy. She favors faded jeans and Dooney & Burke bags and drives a white Toyota with the vanity tag AIMEY V. She was attending Antelope Valley College and working at a local clothing store. Chris, who Aimey remembered as "a little pip-squeak," had metamorphosed into a five-feet-ten-inch, 175-pound marine. He liked to show off his ripped upper body and his tattoos, which now included a rosary on one arm and a dragon on his back that he'd acquired in Okinawa. Yet for all his toughness, Aimey found him dear. By night's end, both were smitten. "I liked him," she says, "but I told myself, 'I'm not going to be a 19-year-old girl tied down to a boyfriend in Iraq.'" Still, in the coming days the two spent hours together around a giant Christmas tree at Jim and Kathi's house, wrapping presents and watching DVDs (Jim Carrey's *The Grinch*, an entire season of Fox's rude *Family Guy*). "He was addictive," Aimey says. "It was impossible not to be with him. I gave in."

Chris attended a candlelight Christmas Eve service with Jim and Kathi at Desert Vineyard, then the next morning rode with them to Westlake Village for dinner at his aunt and uncle's home. He supervised the distribution of presents and taught his four-year-old niece how to ride the new bicycle she'd received.

The following day, Chris drove to Simi Valley to meet Nikki Ruhl. He was so nervous that he phoned Aimey three times before he arrived. Nikki was equally flustered, calling Kathi three times as well. Like Chris, Nikki is blond with hazel eyes. "You're so pretty," he said when she came to the door. The two spent the morning together, with Nikki doing most of the talking. She told Chris she had gotten pregnant the first time she'd ever had sex. The reason she'd put him up for adoption was that she'd been so young and scared. If only she hadn't been 13, she added, asking if he could understand. He said he did. She offered to tell him about the 17-year-old boy who was his father. But he didn't want to hear about him. He was just interested in her. Chris spoke of the difficulties he'd caused Jim and Kathi, but he stressed that it was all in the past. He went on about the Marines. Nikki thought he was earnest and cocky, an impressive combination.

In the early afternoon, the two drove to a T.G.I. Friday's, which made the occasion feel like a first date—in many ways it was. Over lunch they discovered all they had in common. Each had found school difficult. Both loved animals. Neither possessed a good sense of direction. Near the meal's end, Chris told Nikki that meeting her had made his life complete. Then he pulled out a picture of Nikki taken the year she'd given birth to him. Jim and Kathi had given it to him when he entered high school. He told her he'd been carrying it ever since and would carry it with him in Iraq.

Chris spent January at Camp Lejeune in North Carolina, perfecting his radio skills. "He went from being merely proficient to being one of the best I've seen," says Captain Blanton. It was also during this period that Chris and Aimey fell in love. Maybe it was the war, maybe it was just luck, but they were open to each other in ways neither had been to anyone before. Despite his rejection of Analyse, Chris realized he needed someone now more than ever, and he was astonished that Aimey was willing to be that person. On January 8, he e-mailed her:

> I just wanted to say thank you. Thank you for being there for me (for us) for what I'm about to go threw 'what we're about to go threw.' You have a lot of courage and strength for what you're taking on. A lot of women in your position can't handle what you're about to go threw. I admire you so much for you're strength.

In February, Chris flew back home for a last few days' leave before deployment. His grandparents hosted a party, and he took Aimey out for a Valentine's Day dinner at Café del Rey overlooking the Pacific in the Marina. The next day he phoned David Meade and suggested a double date. That night, Chris and Aimey and David and his girlfriend, Anna, met at an Islands restaurant. Everyone had hamburgers except Chris, who true to his new obsession with fitness ordered a chicken and lettuce combination. The four then drove to the Sunset Strip, where David had purchased tickets for a Louis C.K. show at the Laugh Factory. After his set, the emcee announced a surprise guest—Dave Chappelle, whose midseason defection from his Comedy Central series had sparked headlines. To Chris, Chappelle was a giant, the stand-up equivalent of Dr. Dre. He loved a sketch called "Black Bush," in which the comedian, playing the president, takes the country to war in Iraq because he doesn't understand the meaning of yellow cake, confusing the weapons-grade uranium his advisers claimed Saddam Hussein possessed for a piece of Duncan Hines. The absurdity of the notion broke Chris up. Seeing Chappelle in person was just the right send-off.

Two days later at 5:45 A.M., Kathi and Jim climbed into the front seat of the family car and an exhausted Chris and Aimey fell into the back for the mad dash down the Antelope Valley Freeway to make an 8:50 flight from LAX to Charlotte, North Carolina. There Chris would change planes for Camp Lejeune and departure for Iraq. Chris slept for the trip's first hour, but by the time they hit the 405 freeway he was awake and furious. Traffic was barely moving—they were never going to make it. "I can't miss this flight," he hissed at Kathi. Around 8:30, they arrived at the US Air terminal, and Chris leaped out. He was too late. An attendant told him he'd have to wait for the next departure at 1 P.M. At first Chris was angry, but when he returned to the car, he smiled. Instead of having to say goodbye in a rush, he could spend the morning with his parents and Aimey. After breakfast at an International House of Pancakes, where they talked about everything and nothing, they drove to a bookstore, where Chris bought copies of *Playboy*, *Maxim*, and *Vibe*. They then stopped at a Starbucks and lingered over coffee. Finally, it came time to head back to LAX. The line for security snaked outside onto the sidewalk, allowing them a luxurious few more minutes together. As they inched along, Aimey held one of Chris's hands and Kathi the other. They took every opportunity to say, "I love you," or exchange kisses with him, not caring if strangers saw them hugging and crying and holding on until they reached the point beyond which only passengers could continue. "You're the best," Jim shouted after his son, and Kathi called out, "Baby." On hearing her pet name for him, Chris turned and smiled. In time, Jim and Kathi would regard these four extra hours as the most valuable gift they had ever received.

The only thing Chris told Jim and Kathi about Iraq was that he could "feel the evil." Ramadi, where he was stationed, was christened "the most dangerous place in the world" by *Time* shortly after Fifth ANGLICO arrived. The city of 400,000 just west of Baghdad was the center of both the Sunni insurgency and Al Qaeda. Block after block had been reduced to rubble.

Fifth ANGLICO found itself in regular daily combat. Chris's 4-man unit was part of a larger 13-man squad that reported to Major David Berke, an F-18 pilot. Sometimes they went out with 1,000-man army battalions, other times with Iraqi forces, and occasionally with small detachments of Navy SEALs. "We were mortared, hit by IEDs, fired on constantly—everything," says Sergeant Jerred Speller, who was part of Chris's team. "We went on the worst of the worst missions, and the most dangerous aspect was that when we received contact, we ran toward it. We have to see the enemy before we can order planes to drop 500-pound bombs. If we don't, there's too much chance for innocent people to get injured."

One day early on, when Fifth ANGLICO was returning from a rural section of Ramadi, Chris was nearly killed. They'd been out with the Delta 149th Infantry in an area riddled with IEDs and were on their way to their vehicles when someone started shooting at them. Speller and the captain managed to dive into a ditch, but Chris took cover behind a haystack, which provided no cover at all. His comrades yelled at Chris to get out of there. When a lull came, he bolted toward them, firing his M-16 over his shoulder.

This was what Ramadi was like in spring 2006. "We'd be out all day on some brutal, ridiculously painful mission," says Major Berke, "and we'd get back to base and all I could do was crawl off to my quarters. Chris, on the other hand, would go straight to a pull-up bar and do a set of chin-ups—while still wearing his gear. Then he'd get to work on his radios."

Chris sought support in daily phone calls and emails to Aimey. Several weeks after reaching Iraq, he wrote:

> Hello my love!
> One more mission down, I miss you so much Aimey! Im so thankful I have you to appreciate and love. Everyday my love for you gets stronger, my heart and soul needs you. Everyday I think of your touch and how I can't wait to have you in my arms again! I LOVE you so much! You give me strength and confidence in everything I do. Knowing there's someone behind me 100 % is breath taking!... I love you with all my heart, soul, body and mind and don't ever forget that.

Everything about their exchanges was heightened, the urgency amplified by the inability to see or hold each other. All told, they had been in each other's presence for less than a month. "When someone isn't there physically," Aimey says, "you have to ask a lot of questions and you begin to know them on a profound level. I could talk to him for hours. Being in Iraq, he'd learned not to take life for granted." It wasn't always easy for her to convey the certitude that he was seeking, but she tried:

> My love, my strength, my faith—
> I miss you so much. Even though I'm having a hard day I know you have it much worse...You said today—"I sometimes think, 'How can someone be waiting for me? How can she make that commitment and take such a big risk?'" My reason: YOU. We have such a special connection that is accompanied by complete honesty—and trust...I read that once in a great while one person comes across another person who is the perfect companion to accompany us in our travels through life... You're mine. Even though you're far away, miles are just location. I will always act in your absence as I would in your presence. I love you with all my heart Chris.

In May, Chris asked Aimey to marry him. She said yes. They set December 30 as the date. Aimey and her mother found a church in Valencia, contracted a caterer, sent out "Save the Date" notices, and at David's Bridal Shop in Northridge bought a gown.

On June 2, Chris emailed David Meade with the news:

> What's up bro, not much here we've had a lot of time off lately because the army unit we work with is packing up to leave and a new one is settling in. But things are going to pick up soon enough... I'm getting married in December and I would be honored if you would be my best man. So how is everything going back in Cali. Man I cant wait to get home. It was 114 today you can't even walk outside without sweating your ass off. And wearing all you're gear and going on foot patrol. Holy shit! Allright Dave I'm gonna get going take care, Chris

On June 11, American and Iraqi troops launched yet another campaign to pacify Ramadi. The plan was to establish fortified outposts in a number of contested sections of the city and use them to create safety zones in the hope that stable social and economic life would follow. "Our objective," says Berke, "was a house on the high ground in southern Ramadi that looked out over a train track and a large neighborhood."

Unlike its surrounding structures, the house that became known as Command Post Iron—or COP Iron—was in excellent shape. Two stories in height and built of stucco-covered stone, it was the perfect location from which to project order onto chaos. By June 20, the building had been in U.S. possession for six days. Parked in front were several Abrams tanks and a number of Bradley fighting vehicles. Spread out on the grounds, 20 or 30 GIs were building sandbag parapets. On the rooftop, which was surrounded by a thick masonry wall, Chris and the marines of Fifth ANGLICO provided cover for the grunts working below. "It was still a very hot area of Ramadi," says Speller. Yet compared with the spots he and Chris had been during previous weeks, this one felt secure, so much so that Speller curled up with a book.

"The thing about Iraq," says Blanton, who was inside the building at the time, "is that you can go forever without anything happening, and then in an instant your life is hanging by a thread." All day the men of Fifth ANGLICO stood watch. When Berke radioed to order Blanton's team to remain in place a few extra hours, no one expressed the least concern. Then the unit came under fire. "Sniper," screamed Speller. He and Lance Corporal Matthew Odom popped their heads up over the wall to scan for signs of the shooter. Chris raced into the house to alert Blanton, then returned to the roof. The fire was coming from the east, not the north, he told Speller. Thirty seconds later, Chris went down. Speller, who was at his side in an instant, saw blood pouring from a wound behind Chris's right temple. "I tried to put a bandage on his head, but the blood was coming out so fast I couldn't make it hold," he says. "He was still breathing, so I kept working. I finally got one wrapped all the way around, and a couple of army medics helped me get him on a litter and downstairs to one of the Bradleys."

Charlie Med, the hospital at Camp Ramadi—the huge base that houses most American troops in the city—is a ten-minute drive from COP Iron. As the Bradley was on its way, Blanton radioed Berke that Chris had been hit. The major raced to Charlie Med and was there when the Bradley arrived. "When they opened the back of the truck, I looked right at him and I knew in an instant he was dead. He was all gauzed up. There was a big hole in his head. I could see the entrance wound. They took him inside, and two minutes later the surgeon came out and confirmed it."

Around 9 P.M., Speller, Odom, and the other men of Fifth ANGLICO carried Chris's body out of Charlie Med, passing through a cordon of marines standing at attention. They then loaded him onto a CH-46 helicopter for what is known as an Angel Flight. As the chopper lifted off, the group on the ground saluted. Several days later there was a service at Camp Ramadi. Blanton maintained his composure until it was over, then walked off by himself and broke into sobs. Afterward, he posted his thoughts on his website: "The loss of Chris hit everyone in the unit pretty hard. I don't think it hit me hardest, but it has affected me greatly and changed the way I do business. I experience a sense of fear I never had before Chris was killed... I still can't believe he's gone. In time I will find my way home from this awful place."

Chris's homecoming came at Desert Vineyard Fellowship a week after the ceremony at Camp Ramadi. The day before, a fringe group had sent a threat over the Internet, vowing to protest the services. As a consequence, a contingent of sheriff's deputies greeted the Reverend David Parker when he arrived at the church. The lawmen were later reinforced by about a hundred members of the Patriot Guards—a motorcycle-riding contingent of veterans and supporters of American troops. But no demonstration ever materialized.

A thousand mourners packed the vast sanctuary. Sitting in front were Jim and Kathi, Nikki Ruhl, and Aimey Vaccaro and her mother. In the middle of the hall sat Chris's Independent Study teacher, Cheryl Holland;

his old girlfriend, Analyse Reaves; and the clerks and managers from PetSmart. Captain Blanton's mother had driven over from Riverside County, and Lieutenant Colonel Joseph Shrader, ANGLICO's commanding officer, had flown in from Okinawa. The boys of Insanely Determined to Succeed—except for one—were there, too. Against the urgings of David, Jon, and Alan, Sonny had decided to go on a long-scheduled family vacation to Mexico. "It was the hardest decision I ever made," he says. Not everyone understood or quickly forgave.

The services began with the old hymn "On Christ the Solid Rock I Stand." Then Reverend Parker delivered a sermon in which he alluded to Chris's troubled teens ("After losing his way, he graduated from Lancaster High") and applauded his service to his country ("He willingly and proudly defended America"). Fulfilling his friend's request, David gave the eulogy. In it he sought to exalt the fraternal ideals of IDS. "I believe that imagination is stronger than knowledge," he said. "Myth is more potent than history. Dreams are more powerful than facts. Love is stronger than death. The way we remember Chris is the way he becomes immortal."

Aimey Vaccaro followed David. She spoke of her love for Chris, calling herself "the luckiest girl there is," but as she looked out on a room filled by their contemporaries, her tone changed. "Not only did Chris die for his country," she said, "but for his friends. I hope that's really a wake-up call. It's up to you to know what life is all about. It's not about the parties and the things we get so worked up about." The lesson of Chris's death, she was saying, was that one's time on earth is finite. Only dedication and accomplishments, not myths and dreams, would properly commemorate him.

The funeral procession then drove to Joshua Memorial Park, where Jim and Kathi received the flag from Chris's casket and a Marine honor guard delivered a 21-gun salute. Several weeks later Jim and Kathi picked up a bronze box adorned with an eagle, globe, and anchor seal containing Chris's ashes and brought it home. They placed it on a granite-topped buffet in the den, where they would see it every day. Their son, Christopher David Leon, was the 2,509th American service member killed in the Iraq war.

A month or so after Chris's funeral, Kathi Leon, accompanied by her sister, Nikki Ruhl, and Aimey Vaccaro, found herself climbing a flight of stairs in a down-at-the-heels mini-mall in east Lancaster. At the top, beneath a sign reading THIS FACILITY IS UNDER VIDEO SURVEILLANCE AT ALL TIMES, was Sanitarium Tattoos, a cramped room dominated by drawings of skulls and crossbones and a table holding needles and inks. Ever since Chris got his first tattoo after boot camp, Kathi had chided him. "Why would you make yourself look so ugly?" she'd ask. "Why have you done something so revolting?" Yet just as she'd at times tried to reach Chris by following his lead in life, now she would do so in death. Proprietor Rick Labosh inscribed a red heart, Chris's birth and death dates, and the words A GIFT FROM GOD onto her right calf. She later returned and had Labosh etch Chris's face onto her shoulder. Even as she was doing these things, Kathi was slightly appalled, but she had passed into a stage of grief where, as she puts it, "nothing is too weird."

In the weeks before and after Kathi's trip to Sanitarium Tattoos, many of those who were closest to Chris also visited Rick Labosh's shop, turning over legs and arms to his needles. Nikki, who felt like she'd now lost Chris twice, had his dates and the words REST PEACEFULLY MY SWEET ANGEL tattooed in a garland of ivy leaves on her left calf. Three of the boys from Insanely Determined to Succeed—David, Jon, and Alan—had their biceps tattooed with jeweled crosses surrounded by the epitaph REST PEACEFULLY CPL. CHRIS LEON. Aimey went to Buzz Bomb, a tattoo parlor on the Venice Beach boardwalk she and Chris had visited together, and had his dog tag and the words A TRUE HERO NEVER FORGOTTEN inked onto her left shoulder blade. En masse, it seemed, those who'd loved Chris were trying, as David had urged in his eulogy, to immortalize him.

By autumn Kathi had gone back to work at the urology clinic, but Jim never returned to Quest Diagnostics. The treatment for his congestive heart failure had adversely affected his kidneys, and he was weak and disoriented. He felt Chris's absence keenly, yet he couldn't cry. Numbness had set in. On many days he never got up from the sofa. Aimey dropped out of college for the semester—holding down her job was triumph enough during a period when she often had to take Ativan to fend off panic attacks and Ambien to sleep—and David entered therapy with an Encino psychiatrist. He blamed himself for Chris's death, believing that if he and the others in IDS had forced him to study harder and avoid drugs he would have joined them in college rather than gone to war. As for Jon, he downed a six-pack of beer many nights to turn out the lights.

The place where the opposing opinions of how to face Chris's death met was his MySpace page. Chris had started the page—which he topped with the motto "My sacrifice is your comfort"—shortly before leaving for

Iraq. Now that he was gone, his friends refreshed the site with postings that reflected their conflicted feelings. David championed the view that Chris's good deeds would give him eternal life. "Chris protected our freedoms," he wrote. "He protected our right to know the truth about what's happening in this country." Aimey, however, often despaired. In an early fall note addressed directly to Chris, she wrote, "I miss you so much baby. It hurts every day. I keep wishing that this wasn't real and that my phone would ring again. I still sign onto MySpace hoping that my new message is from you— but I know that will never happen again." On September 17, the day Fifth ANGLICO returned from its tour of duty in Iraq, Kathi added her voice. "Baby, I can't believe today is going to come and go and we won't have had you home to celebrate. This is really too hard for words." Several weeks later David also came around to this view. "I never knew it took so long to come to terms with something like this. I thought someone died, you mourned for a while, and you moved on. On the contrary, it takes time to accept that a person you love isn't coming home."

Surprisingly, those close to Chris felt their moods lift on November 5—his 21st birthday. Everyone congregated at Jim and Kathi's for cake and margaritas. Nikki, Aimey and her mother, David, Jon, and Alan, and Chris's grandparents and aunts and uncles sat around talking about him. Jim, who on previous visits by his son's friends hadn't been well enough to say hello, joined the party. They passed around Chris's medals, among them the Purple Heart, the Combat Action Ribbon, and the Navy and Marine Corps Commendation Medal. Late in the afternoon, David and Jon walked into the front yard and in a private ritual that they knew would have delighted their friend poured two King Cobra 40s into Avenue K-9. "That day," says David, "marked the first time I could breathe."

On December 30, which should have been her wedding day, Aimey donned a white button-down shirt and white jeans and went to dinner at an Italian restaurant in Lancaster with her mom, sister, and several of the girls who would have been her bridesmaids all dressed in red—the color she'd picked for the big event. The previous night, as she'd reflected on what it would have been like to oversee the final details—the seating, the music, and the flowers—she'd cried. But as she and her friends enjoyed a long evening, she felt peace. "A few weeks earlier, I was a disaster," she says. "But I'm starting to feel okay. I thought, 'A new year is coming. I can carry over the crippling emotion or I can start in a different way.' I've decided to start in a different way."

The next night, New Year's Eve, David's girlfriend threw a party at her Sherman Oaks apartment. The 20 guests ate sushi and drank vodka while listening to rap and rock. Everyone laughed and gossiped until shortly before midnight, when four of the revelers disappeared into a bedroom, closing the door behind them. It was the first time the members of Insanely Determined to Succeed had all been together since Chris's death. Before anyone could speak, Sonny, who after skipping the funeral had avoided the group, broke down. "I've missed you guys," he said. They agreed that Chris would want them all to go on with their lives. Jon then draped a dog tag bearing their friend's likeness around Sonny's neck, and he and the others, each of whom wore similar tags, were back at the party before 2007 began.

Looking forward wasn't going to be as easy for Jim and Kathi. They decided to forgo a massive Christmas tree, opting instead for a tiny artificial one that Kathi decorated with cards bearing handwritten remembrances of Chris. "A son who loved deeply," said one. "A son who was deeply loved," said another. On Christmas Eve, they and other church members who'd experienced loss during 2006 attended a "Blue Christmas" service at Desert Vineyard. As always, on Christmas morning they drove to LoriAnn's house in Westlake Village, where they were joined not just by Kathi's family but by Nikki and her mother. Kathi, dressed in a bright purple sweater and black slacks, and Jim, in a red-checked shirt and khakis, tried to be festive. They looked on as their niece opened her Disney Tea Party Play Set, and they talked about a holiday care package they'd sent to the men of Fifth ANGLICO, who were in Okinawa preparing to redeploy. But after presents were exchanged, their spirits darkened. When LoriAnn pulled out a photo album from the previous Christmas in which she'd pasted pictures of Chris and written a holiday prayer—"For everyone to be together again next year—safe and healthy (Chris home from Iraq)"—they began to cry, and while Jim noted that his newfound ability to shed tears was a step forward, he didn't sound convincing.

"This is our first Christmas without Chris," he said, "and I don't like the fact that there are now 3,000 families that have gotten the same news we got. I resent it. I wish we would get out of Iraq. What we're doing there doesn't make sense."

"But he was a marine," said Kathi. "He was doing what he wanted to do. He was doing his job."

At that, LoriAnn announced lunch, and Jim and Kathi, carrying a box of Kleenex, walked into the dining room.

New Year's was, if anything, even harder. Where Chris's friends saw a beginning, his parents saw an end. On her son's MySpace page Kathi wrote, "Chris there is no happy to this new year. Only the knowledge that we are further apart than ever. It's hard enough that the day changes but we are already into another year. I can't bear the thought of having time continue and making the distance even greater. How do I get past this?"

In stronger moments, Jim and Kathi can both dimly perceive happier times ahead. Kathi has joined a gym in the hope of getting into good enough shape to run in the annual Marine Corps Marathon honoring war dead. Jim has rallied sufficiently to volunteer several days a week at Desert Vineyard. Yet they remain inconsolable. On days when he's not at the church, Jim finds himself sinking deeper into depression. Although he's taking Prozac, the drug can't keep him from fixating on Chris. He frequently pops a DVD of the funeral into the machine in the den, watching it over and over, the images serving as a narcotic. "Kathi doesn't like me immersing myself in it," he says, "but I find it comforting." Kathi's grief reveals itself differently. "I'm flatlining," she says. "I try not to show any feelings at all." But she's only partially successful. Whenever President Bush, someone she once trusted, appears on TV, she changes the channel. Then there are times she picks up one of their many pictures of Chris, presses her lips against it, and whispers, "Baby."

Chris's bedroom is as it was when he last slept there. The Dodger caps still stare down, and the handwritten plea for guidance is on the closet wall. Even little things—a bottle of Calvin Klein Truth Cologne for Men on the chest of drawers and a can of Bud Light on the television cart—are unchanged. To be surrounded by their son's possessions gives Jim and Kathi a sense of security, yet they now know there really is no such thing. Chris went out from Lancaster with its symmetrical streets and identical subdivisions into anarchy. That anarchy has come back to Avenue K-9, shattering the Leons' lives and filling them with doubt. If their son died in an unjust war, they wonder, can there be a just God? Jim and Kathi remain believers, seeing the Lord's hand in Chris's emergence from his difficult adolescence and keeping faith they'll meet him in a better world. But this one holds few allures. They are grateful for Pastor Dave and the others at Desert Vineyard, who regularly check in on them. They are thankful for family members who do the same. They are indebted to the many neighbors who've hung blue-and-gold banners declaring SUPPORT OUR TROOPS from trees and roofs. Their home, though, is as much a prison as a refuge. "We've lost not just Chris but our future," Jim says one late winter afternoon sitting in the den. "There will be no wedding, no grandchildren, no one to leave any of our possessions to. Ahead for us is nothing. It's just a hole."

The Method and the Madness of Hubie Brown

The Atlanta Journal & Constitution Magazine, December 9, 1979

From a vantage point high in some structural-steel arena in a city like Phila-delphia or New York or, for that matter, Atlanta, Hubie Brown, the coach of the Atlanta Hawks, appears to be a slightly mad martinet, a ranting, ban-tam dictator commanding an army of giants. Clad in a loud plaid jacket, a silken shirt open wide at the collar, double-knit slacks, and shiny black shoes, he storms along the sidelines of the National Basketball Association cursing and screaming and throwing his hands over his head in nearly game-long bouts of apoplectic rage. When a call goes against the Hawks, Hubie erupts from his chair at the head of the bench and races toward the offend-ing referee like a bouncer going after an unruly drunk. "What kind of an asshole call is that?" he shrieks. After a string of bad breaks or blown plays, Hubie tromps to the end of the bench, squats down in a catcher's crouch, lectures whatever Hawk happens to be perched there, springs again to his feet, covers his head with both hands, and walks back to his seat moaning, "Oh, Jesus Christ. Oh, Jesus Christ Almighty."

Hubie's timeouts are legendary, and if he's especially angry, he sum-mons his charges into a circle around him near the center of the court. But even a wall of seven-foot-tall athletes cannot muffle Brown's Jersey-shore croak. "What the hell's wrong with you?" he demands. "We've been down the floor 11 times and got only two good shots." Hunched over a miniature magnetic basketball court on which he moves pill-sized metal discs repre-senting the players, Hubie raves about flaws in the team's offensive execu-tion. Glancing up, he starts in on guard Eddie Johnson. "Christ, I'm telling you, Eddie, that you better get your shit together. The ball is precious, but *you* go one-on-one with three guys on you. Christ. And your defense is abominable." He levels Johnson with a gaze. When the player attempts to interject, Brown cuts him off. "You're out. I gotta get somebody who can play." Johnson again tries to counter the charges, but Brown barks, "Hey, am I talking to you in a foreign language? Didn't you hear what I just said?" His face blotched with fiery red patches, his centurion-style gray hair drenched in sweat, Hubie heaps abuse on several other Hawks before the scorer's horn finally blasts to signal a return to action.

In a profession known for hair-trigger tempers and blue utterances, Brown has managed to achieve notoriety not only because of his blistering attacks on referees and players (it is almost a cliché that professional basketball is life's only niche in which a short white man can call 10 leviathan blacks "sons of bitches" and escape with his hide unscathed), but because he is willing to get in the faces of fans as well. If a crowd rides Hubie, he retaliates by spinning around viciously, picking out one of his loudest detractors, pointing at him, and yelling, "Do you want to coach this team, Jack? If you do, get down here. If you don't, shut up."

Roaring through the season like a mean, late summer tempest, Hubie gives every impression that he is utterly out of control. He appears to be a tyrannical blowhard whose main goal is to coerce players by intimidating them. That, however, is only a part of Hubie Brown. What is significant about the coach is not that he bellows and gesticulates but that his histrionics are merely the smoking tip of a coldly rational iceberg. In spite of his game-time pyrotechnics, he is the most glacially methodical coach in basketball. As a result, the Hawks are not so much a team as a ruthlessly directed juggernaut. At times, they seem to function rather than to play. They are meticulously choreographed. Brown calls each of the Hawks' offensive and defensive sets and will not tolerate any deviation from his directives. Just how integral Brown is to the Hawks is readily apparent: more than any other NBA team, the Hawks reflect their coach—both in their highly synchronized style and in their punishingly aggressive zeal.

Brown's success as the Hawks' coach is enviable. When he accepted the Atlanta job in 1976, the Hawks were possibly the worst team in pro basketball. During the previous season, they had won only 29 games while losing 53. Before coming to Atlanta, Brown had coached the Kentucky Colonels of the now defunct American Basketball Association to a league championship in 1975 and to the playoffs in 1976. Although the Hawks suffered a mediocre season during Brown's first year in Atlanta, he led them to the NBA playoffs in 1978. In 1979, the Hawks posted their first winning record in five years and nearly upset the powerful Washington Bullets in the semifinals of the playoffs. By late November of the 1979–80 season, when Brown signed a five-year contract that will earn him around $150,000 annually, the team was at the top of the Central Division and had won 13 games and lost only seven.

In Brown's three years as the Atlanta coach, he has taken a group of players, none widely acknowledged as stars, and molded them into a menacing machine. That Brown at times treats his people like the cogs and bolts of some inhuman basketball mechanism doesn't worry him. "This is a very cold business," he says. "It's either me or them. When my head is on the block, don't think they're going to step up and talk about what a great friend I've been or what a warm heart I have. There's no love in the pros. It's my job to strain their talent until they cry out for mercy. That's what I'm paid to do. And I never have to worry about looking in the mirror and wondering if I've done my job."

On a Monday morning early in the season, the Hawks are clustered around the baskets of the Morehouse College gym throwing up trick shots and bantering with one another when Hubie Brown slips onto the court and walks purposefully toward the jump-ball circle. Silently studying several sheets of statistics, the coach is oblivious to the action. When he reaches the middle of the floor, he stops, tilts his head back imperiously, and stares from one end of the court to the other. Within 10 seconds the players have tossed their basketballs aside and are rushing obediently toward him.

Turning his hazel eyes on forwards John Drew and Dan Roundfield, Brown purses his lips in disgust and snorts disdainfully, "When I pick up the stats and you've got *two* defensive rebounds and you've got *three* for the whole game, then I know something is wrong. We should have beaten Houston, Boston, and San Antonio, but how can we hope to when you two are incapable of understanding the basics?" The coach's face, in quiet moments marmoreal and composed, heats up like a kiln. With his chin stuck out, his lips pulled back in perfect mimicry of an attacking dog, and his eyes fixed on the players like gimlets, he is cowing. "*Should*," he says harshly, "is a bullshit word. It's a bullshit word."

After searching through the columns of data he wields as if they were holy writ, Brown steps toward Drew, the team's leading scorer, the one Hawk whose name is often in the limelight. "When a man calls you a star," the coach begins, "you are supposed to be able to pass. You are supposed to be able to dribble. You are supposed to be able to rebound. You are supposed to be able to score." Halting, Brown jerks in a long breath then roars: "Not just score. Not just score. Not just score."

For the next five minutes, while constantly referring to statistics, Brown unloads on the team. Aided by his assistant, Michael Fratello, the coach converts so many aspects of Hawks' games into percentages and numbers that at times he seems less like a mentor than a sports actuary. He often computes rather than judges a player's value. Stats reveal just how faithfully the team is complying with "the system," Brown's highly orchestrated playing method. The system is the functional outgrowth of what the coach terms "the philosophy." The philosophy is part of the more nebulous "total picture," and, says Brown, it is the very foundation of success. The coach realizes that he cannot convert all of his players to the philosophy, but if an athlete won't at least adapt to the system, he is, in Brown's mind, "not good people," and he is traded.

A methodical recounting of figures that reveal the Hawks' pitiful rebounding, lapses in defense, and shortage of fast breaks serves as a prelude for Brown to home in on what he and most other coaches believe is the Achilles' heel of every professional team—the selfishness of players. Brown waxes more vociferously on player egotism than on almost any other topic.

"You want to know why Boston beat us?" he asks rhetorically. "It's because they have people who pass. They have guys who are unselfish. But not us. Isn't it amazing that we don't have five guys who can play our defense and make the traps? For Christ's sake, isn't it amazing? By Wednesday, we're gonna have five guys who can play. I don't care who they are."

Clearing his throat, Brown extends both hands into the middle of the huddle. The eleven team members grab them in unison and spread out to begin their warm-up drills. Meanwhile, Brown confers with Fratello, a diminutive, curly-haired Jerseyite. Fratello was a high school student when he met Brown, and he is the coach's most trusted adjutant. Together, they are like combative cocks lording over a barnyard of mammoths. With their heads close, their expressions intent, they outline the day's practice, a non-stop session that will be run with the precision of an engine. To Hawks fans, Fratello is known as "Baby Hubie."

Watching a Hawks practice is akin to observing a watchmaker assemble the parts of a fine chronometer. It is at the same time like seeing a straw boss put a road crew through a grueling morning of hard labor. The Hawks work relentlessly on every part of their complicated offenses and defenses and on their opponents' plays as well. Hovering around the periphery of the court, Brown shouts out seemingly unintelligible terms, colors, and numbers that signal the players to concentrate on their full-court press or their fast break or their barely disguised illegal zone defense. The team uses some of the most intricate choreography in basketball, and for a player, a Hawks practice is more like a dress rehearsal than a training session. Brown sees the basketball court as a 94-by-50-foot grid that, if he spaces his players correctly, can be totally controlled. For Brown, control is the only end, the ultimate reward. As the Hawks rush through their routines, the coach screams directions:

"Get to the spot."

"Find the lane."

"Get the rotation right."

While athletic talent is important to Brown, execution is paramount. "We don't have a team that can overpower the best teams in the league," he often says. "We're fragile. So what we do is try to have a lot of set plays with options that we know will free people for good shots. We simply can't physically beat anybody." The Hawks are the antithesis of a championship team like the 1973 New York Knicks, which featured Willis Reed, Walt Frazier, Bill Bradley, Dean Meminger, and Earl "The Pearl" Monroe—basketball artists who demanded great leeway to play well. Instead, Brown's team harks back to the Boston Celtics of the early 1960s, probably the most disciplined club in the annals of pro basketball—and the most successful. "Our people," says Brown "have to be subservient to my goals. That's it."

As the Hawks run through a fast-break drill, shooting guard Terry Furlow lopes off the court grumbling. Earlier, Brown had given the player a new responsibility that could decrease his scoring.

"They're gonna have to pay me more money to play this way," Furlow mutters as he crosses the sideline.

From the other end of the floor, Brown rushes toward the guard shrieking, "Jesus Christ. Jesus F. Christ. If you don't like it here, just get your ass out. Get out."

A minute later, as Furlow goes through the same drill he pauses momentarily near the half-court line and dribbles the ball listlessly. "Hey, big shot," Brown cries, "will you give up the ball? Do you know how to pass it?"

Within seconds, Furlow drives toward the basket, fakes a shot, and throws a bad pass that bounces out of bounds. "What in the name of Christ is that?" Brown screams. Furlow shakes his head and glares at the floor.

A Hawks practice never ends gradually. It just stops. After running drill upon drill, Brown calls the session off and leads his team down a dimly lit flight of stairs to a grim cinderblock classroom. The players fold themselves into tiny school desks while Brown takes a spot at the blackboard and scrawls one word: "Soft." To Brown, people who are soft are selfish, inept, lazy, and worse. "Everybody in the NBA is soft to begin with," he says. "They come here spoiled. They've been the star in high school and college, and they are soft. It's my job to harden them." For 10 minutes, Brown ricochets around the room like an atomic particle in a reaction chamber. Screaming and screeching about the team's weaknesses, he focuses on the previous game. "They have to understand why they lost the last one so they won't make the same mistakes again," he contends. Brown can be righteous and obscene in the same breath. His constant use of the four-letter obscenity for sexual intercourse is less foul than it is sanctimonious. He drops the expletive in at the end and beginning of almost everything he says in the same way preachers in evangelical churches tag "Jesus" onto every admonition. His exhortation finally climaxes in a crescendo of pious fury about the Hawks' lack of discipline, aggressiveness, and intensity. Shrieking so loudly that his voice cracks, he dashes a piece of chalk into a tray, stomps out of the classroom, and zips down the hall toward the Morehouse bowling alley. There, he corrals his nine-year-old son, and for a second they watch a group of students clustered around the long hardwood tongue of the lane. Briefly, Brown's bellicosity subsides. He smiles at the boy, puts his arm around him, and they walk up the stairs.

Later that afternoon, clad in a white Hawks T-shirt and a red team windbreaker, Hubie Brown traipses through a sky-lit hallway of the Sporting Club—a plush, north-side spa—toward its wood-paneled lounge. The John L. Sullivan Bar, a dimly lit retreat hung with boxing prints suggesting a New York City athletic club, is familiar to the Hawks coach. Brown spends much of his spare time here. Immediately after practice, he rushed to the club's gym to film a commercial aimed at attracting new members. Now, as he pulls up a chair at a corner table and orders two happy-hour Bloody Marys, he boasts, "This is a great place. Best like it in town." The Sporting Club offers one of those private havens that are the privilege of the *nouveau riche*: it reminds them of how far they have come. Like most of the trappings of Brown's life now, the club is comfortable. Brown lives with his son, three daughters, and wife, Claire, in a handsome five-bedroom house in the far reaches of suburban Dunwoody. It is a spacious, tastefully decorated home with book-lined shelves and cases of sports memorabilia—all symbols of Brown's hard-won achievements. At times, the amenities of Brown's club and existence must seem unreal, especially in light of the place where he was reared. Brown enjoys the rewards of his success, but he talks constantly of his past, saying that it is the key to understanding him.

Brown grew up in a small, four-unit apartment building in a rough-and-tumble section of Elizabeth, New Jersey, one of many tough port towns squeezed between New York and Philadelphia. He was an only child, and his father, Charlie Brown—a foreman at the Kearny Shipyards—spent most of his free time teaching Hubie how to play baseball. Charlie, as his son called him, and Hubie passed long Saturday afternoons in an Elizabeth park with a bat and a bucket of taped-up balls. The man pitched to the boy until nightfall, and the next morning, as soon as Hubie returned home from 9:00 Mass, the two caught a train for Penn Station in New York then took the subway either to Yankee Stadium or the Polo Grounds, home of the New York Giants. They always arrived at the park before batting practice began and bought $1.75 tickets for seats along one of the foul lines. Throughout the game Charlie would lecture his son about the sacrifices ball players make to get to the majors. Charlie wanted his boy to play professional baseball, and he drilled him incessantly, sometimes ruthlessly. Whenever Hubie suffered a hitless night during Little League baseball games, his father raged at him. "He was a very demanding man," Brown remembers. "My wife, who's very bright, thinks I now have a great ability to punish myself for losses because of the way my father punished me for the times I played badly as a child. I don't know about that, but it is probably the subconscious reason why I really hate to lose."

The Browns never had much money. They had no telephone or car, and sports provided their lone form of recreation. They lived in a hard, Irish Catholic neighborhood of working-class families. By the time Hubie was in grade school, he had taken a job serving 6:30 Mass every morning at St. Elizabeth's Hospital. Each night, he hung out on the streets where he learned how to fight and cuss and fend off bullies by bullying back. Between the unceasing urgings of his father and the survival instincts picked up in corner tussles, Hubie was already a brutal competitor by age 10.

"The really great thing about my childhood," Brown recalls as he slumps back into his chair after finishing the first of his drinks, "is that I had great coaches who drove me." Starting in 1947, when Brown was the catcher on an undefeated St. Mary's Grammar School baseball team that won the New Jersey state championship, he usually played for victorious teams. But not surprisingly, he was not spoiled by success—his father would not allow it, and neither would circumstances. When Brown was in the eighth grade, the Kearny Shipyards shut down, and his father lost his job. For nine disheartening months, Charlie stood in unemployment lines.

During the time that his father was out of work, Hubie watched the family plummet to near destitution. Charlie had always preached to him that if he worked hard enough, he would succeed, but Brown began to tell himself that it didn't matter how hard someone worked if he lost control of his life. A man who has observed Brown closely for years but asked not to be named says, "Hubie comes from a very brutal world where jobs were tough to get. He remembers that. He identifies with that, because he still lives in a brutal world. Coaches have no security. Deep in his heart, I think it really nags him. I think that's exactly why he's so obsessed with trying to control everything about his basketball team and every minute of a game. He wants to have his hand on every single lever that could possibly affect his life, because he remembers when his father couldn't."

By the time Hubie began his freshman year at St. Elizabeth's High his father had taken a job as the school's janitor. Hubie would star in football, basketball, and baseball before earning a dual basketball and baseball scholarship to Niagara University. At Niagara, Brown played guard for the school's great mid-1950s basketball teams, which featured players like Larry Costello, later an NBA star, and Charlie Hoxie, the premier Harlem Globetrotter of the early 1960s. Hubie's father could not afford to travel to the games but told his son to pick out an old man in the crowd and imagine that he had to please that man as if he were his father. (Hubie still observes the ritual. His father died before seeing his boy coach in the pros, but when Brown first took his Kentucky team to the playoffs, two friends bought an empty seat across from the Colonels' bench and told Brown that it was for Charlie.) While Brown was a talented athlete, his playing days ended after college when he realized he was not skilled enough to play pro baseball or basketball. He would instead coach.

Unlike most NBA coaches, men who were either professional players or highly successful in the college ranks, Brown came through the back door by coaching at high schools. One of his first jobs was at Fair Lawn High in Fair Lawn, New Jersey, where in his initial season his team won just two games and his wife had difficulty finding anyone to sit with her in the grandstands. But in two years, Brown took the school to a state championship. Brown got a real leg up in coaching in 1967 when he landed an assistant's job at William and Mary College. The next year, he took a similar position at Duke University. While Brown was in North Carolina, his college teammate, Larry Costello, was named head coach of the Milwaukee Bucks and offered Brown an assistantship there. It was Brown's big break. After three years in Milwaukee, he moved on to the Kentucky job. Two years later, he came to Atlanta.

His second Bloody Mary a memory, Brown orders a coffee. It has been a grueling day, and he has a long evening ahead of him. He and Fratello are in the final stages of editing a basketball coaching pamphlet. Aside from fronting the Hawks, Brown appears at numerous basketball clinics every year and is one of the country's highest paid tutors of the game. During springs and summers, he regularly flies to northeastern cities where he speaks about the sport. Not only does Brown proselytize about his method to other coaches, but he is often on the corporate self-help circuit, talking to companies like Aetna Insurance and IBM about applying his coaching wisdom to the big game of life.

Sometime during his grinding ascent when his triumphs extended no further than the local newspaper, Brown figured out that to get where his ambition was driving him he needed something other than just moxie. An economics major as an undergraduate student and an education major in graduate school, he had been exposed to various systemized, goal-oriented approaches to "making it." Slowly, he developed his own philosophy and system. His fanaticism about three-year, five-prong programs has come to resemble that of the Soviet government although in truth the coach's formula is not unlike any Dale Carnegie self-help scheme—except it's more aggressive and, like so much that comes out of sports, it employs a big helping of jock lingo.

Setting aside his coffee, Brown grabs his left index finger with his right hand and exclaims, "The whole thing finally can be broken down to five things. It's how I coach the Hawks and it's what I tell businesses. You could coach baseball with this system. Or football. It's very adaptive.

"The first thing is that you've got to be totally organized with your goals—daily, weekly, and monthly. That's why we keep such careful records on everything the Hawks do.

"The second thing is that you've gotta have a total philosophy. By that, I mean that in basketball you've gotta understand the game so well that you have a sound system. A sound system is the hallmark of every good coach. It's why a great coach can take a mediocre team against a talented bunch of morons, and he can 'X and O' them to death."

Counting down quickly, Brown adds, "The third thing you must have is discipline. You can treat a player any way you want to as long as it's fair and it teaches him something. By the time they get to the pros, they don't want love. Hell, they're making an average of $137,000 a year."

"The fourth thing is good people, people who will put the team above all else. The big problem with pro ball today is urban blacks. Now, Southern blacks are all right, but these urban kids who come off the streets think the sport is just run-and-gun and dunk-and-shoot, and they're so damn cocky. They just won't fit in."

"The final thing you've got to have," Hubie declares, "is style. We play like blue-collar workers. We bring our lunch pails with us and we wear you out. We're a 94-foot team, and we press and fast break and we control everything we can."

Pushing himself up from the table, Brown picks up the check, pays it, and walks out of the bar. It is already dark, and he has a 30-minute drive home.

That someone as single minded as Brown has made his share of enemies is inevitable. Shortly before coming to Atlanta, Brown was contacted by the owner of the Milwaukee Bucks and asked if he'd be interested in returning to the team as head coach. At the time, Larry Costello was still in charge of the Bucks, and Brown contends that he emphatically said he would not consider the position as long as Costello held it. Not long after Brown talked with the Bucks' owner, *The Milwaukee Journal* printed a series of articles implying that Brown was jockeying to take Costello's job. "That was just fiction," says Brown. "It was so far from the truth. It ruined a great friendship. It's probably the worst thing that ever happened to me in sports." Costello is still bitter about the episode, claiming that Brown was indeed vying for his job. After Brown took the coaching spot in Atlanta, Costello resigned. He now coaches a professional women's team. "I don't want to get into it again," says Costello. "But I will say that Hubie is a real rotten apple. A horrible person. He'll do what he wants to get what he wants."

The fanatical dominion that Brown exercises over the Hawks leaves little room for contentious employees in Atlanta management. Mike Storen, formerly commissioner of the ABA and briefly general manager of the Hawks, maintains that Brown consciously set out to undermine him in the Atlanta job. "He's a sick man," says Storen. "He wants to control everything, and if you get in his way, he'll get you. He plots. He schemes. It's all very deliberate. He ruined my career in basketball." During Storen's short tenure with the team, he and Brown fought over the future of several players and the general style in which the Hawks would be managed. "I thought it would all work out," says Storen, "but Hubie decided he had to get me out of the way." Brown counters, "Storen pulled so much shit while he had that job that Ted [Turner] had to can him." Shortly before owner Turner deposed the general manager in 1978, Storen asked an Omni technician to bug Brown's office phone. The workman refused. The next day Storen was fired. Subsequently, Storen filed a $300,000 suit against the Hawks.

Although Brown has had a number of such front-office disputes, he has done better with former players. True, Lou Hudson, the only bona fide superstar in Hawks franchise history, protested when Brown traded him to the Los Angeles Lakers in 1978. He had been with the team for 10 years and was still one of the game's best pure shooters. But he remains a Brown supporter. "Sure it hurt to leave Atlanta," says Hudson, "but I don't blame Hubie. He did what he thought was right. He's a great coach. No one knows more about the game. No one is better prepared. In Los Angeles, I played for Jerry West, who is a much nicer man. But I've got to say Hubie's a better coach."

Most of the current Hawks share a similar admiration for Brown's knowledge of the game, but few will talk publicly about what it is like to play for a coach who berates them constantly. They cite Brown's propensity for fining players who speak derogatorily about the team. Says one player, "I have to have all my creative outlets elsewhere. I'm just part of a system here." Another adds, "It's okay if you're a machine, but if you're a human being, he can beat you down."

Tom McMillen, the Rhodes Scholar from the University of Maryland who's now the Hawks' reserve center, says, "Hubie's a very intense man whose entire happiness revolves around winning. It's the whole thing with him. He's seen that the NBA is a war and that you can't win with kid gloves on. He has to be autocratic to triumph. Now there are many players in the league who are so egocentric that they could never play for him. They'd clash with him. But I respect what he's done very much. His system, while rigid, is fair and it works. The way he has it set up, we're all rewarded for our efforts. He plays 10 of us each quarter, and we all get our good shots. The difficult thing is that losing is such anathema to Hubie that he tries very hard to make us miserable too. He just doesn't want us to get used to losing. I don't blame him, but it's hard sometimes."

Nowhere is Brown's urge to dominate better illustrated than in his relationships with reporters. The coach's press conferences are akin to papal appearances. After a game, he enters the press room clutching a beer, gazing silently at the mass of journalists waiting for some tidbit about the team. After staring at them briefly, he issues a perfect report on the contest, a state-of-the-game speech replete with esoteric statistics. It spills from his lips like a computer printout. He has a near photographic memory of games and can pinpoint every key shot or block. Following a 10-minute spiel, he often concludes with the warning, "Now I don't want any stupid questions." He berates reporters who do broach ignorant queries by rejoining mockingly, "If you'd ever seen a pro game before, you wouldn't be asking that."

Among sportswriters, there are very definite pro-Brown and anti-Brown camps. The situation is illustrated graphically by the way Atlanta's two daily newspapers cover the team. Darrell Simmons, of the *Journal* is, in Brown's estimation, "a great writer, a fine journalist, a man who understands the sport." George Cunningham, the *Constitution* reporter covering the Hawks, is, says Brown, "a truly sick man who is out to destroy pro basketball in Atlanta. He is the most dangerous threat to our team." At a booster club meeting at the Atlanta Hilton in September, Brown launched into a lengthy diatribe against Cunningham, accusing the journalist of "trying to ruin us." Cunningham's coverage of the Hawks often highlights the play of John Drew and Terry Furlow, the team's most explosive scorers and the two players Brown rides hardest during practices. Simmons usually writes about "team efforts." Cunningham almost never quotes Brown, while Simmons quotes him extensively. Cunningham counters Brown's criticism by saying, "Hubie's a great coach, but he's such a horrible egomaniac that he can't stand any criticism, and he can't stand anyone else getting any publicity. The reason he hates me is that I'm the only media voice in town who will criticize him at all. The rest might as well be on the Hawks' payroll. They follow the party line."

It is Friday night at the crowded Spectrum, home of the Philadelphia 76ers, one of the most talented teams in basketball. With Julius Erving, "Dr. J," at forward and a massive locomotive of a center named Darryl Dawkins, whose dunks shatter backboards and whose 250-pound body has flattened more than a few wiry defenders, the 76ers are star-studded opponents. The Spectrum crowd is unusually unruly. Thursday marked the world premiere of *The Fish that Saved Pittsburgh*, a bit of bad basketball cinema starring Erving, and the team organist is cranking out the disco theme music from the movie while the arena's patrons are screaming for blood, preferably Hubie Brown's. Three nights earlier, the Hawks had handed the previously undefeated Philadelphia team its first loss of the year. 76ers enthusiasts do not want to see their team's record drop from 8-0, to 8-1, to 8-2—all at the hands of the Hawks. As Brown follows his team onto the court, a chorus of boos wafts down to greet him. "Better cool it tonight, Hubie," one fan shrieks. "You're crazy, Hubie." Brown's detractors are located both behind the bench and beneath the Hawks' basket, and as he surveys the scene, he realizes that for an entire evening he'll be caught in a cross fire. Before the game starts, he crouches down and pulls out a small package containing a portrait of Jesus and two Catholic icons. His father gave them to him long ago. Kneeling, he kisses the icons and tucks them into a pocket.

It is a desultory first half in which defense dominates. Neither the 76ers nor the Hawks can muster any scoring. Hubie stomps up and down the sideline, Fratello following as if attached by strings. During a game, Fratello constantly suggests plays and options that might get the Hawks some baskets. Fratello's running charts on a game are so detailed that he is able to inform Brown immediately which plays are working most productively and which defenses are the most stingy. But tonight, very few of Brown's orchestrations are functioning. The coach becomes so despondent that he simply sits on the bench, his head cradled in his hands, as if to watch is too painful. Occasionally he rises to his feet and screams to center Tree Rollins, "Be big, Tree." During one timeout he accuses Eddie Johnson, Dan Roundfield, and John Drew of being "the three stooges of basketball" and says that if they keep playing stupidly he won't be able to abide seeing them on the court any longer. As he walks into the dressing room at the end of the half with the Hawks trailing 38-33, his face is drawn and tired. He simply shakes his head.

At the start of the second half, something in Brown clicks. He is no longer content to sit back. He is up prowling, shifting his shoulders like a boxer. It is a low-scoring game, the kind a coach can influence more easily than a run-and-gun contest, the gritty kind of game won by playing the vicious defenses and set offenses that Brown loves. Even before a minute has elapsed, Brown is shrieking at Dan Roundfield, "Jesus Christ, you're just wasting my time out there. I'm getting you out of the game." When Brown is coaching aggressively, he is a master of operant conditioning. The most universal negative stimulus for a basketball player is to threaten him with the bench, and as the contest heats up, Brown uses it on almost every player.

To reserve guard Charlie Criss, he cracks: "One more pass like that, Charlie, and you're on the bench for the rest of the night."

Then he's back on Drew: "For Christ's sake, John, if you do that again you're out."

Same with Rollins: "Jesus, Tree. Why don't you dunk it? You're the only center in the pros who can't stick it in the hole. Jam it in there or you're through."

Like an overseer on a galley ship, Brown lashes out at whoever appears to be lagging.

But in the contest's last four minutes, he is more like a chess master in a brutal match of speed chess. Bobbing up and down from his seat, touching his fingers to his temples, he screams: "Deny. Deny." The Hawks are attempting to keep the 76ers from passing the ball inside for easy shots.

As the Hawks bring the ball down on offense, Brown shrieks, "31."

As Atlanta drops back on defense, he screams, "Black."

Darryl Dawkins misses a close shot, and as the Hawks walk the ball back up court they have a slight lead. Brown yells, "Be tough. Be smart."

From beneath the Hawks' basket, 76ers partisans are screaming, "Shove it, Hubie." As the team works its offense, John Drew breaks into the open for a good shot. As he goes up with the ball one of the 76ers hits him with a forearm. Drew crumples to the floor, and Brown rushes to his side. His face flushed, the coach is bending over the player when several fans pour onto the court, shooting their middle fingers into his face. Brown stands his ground, glares then smiles as the police step between him and the mob. "We beat you three last year. It'll be four this year," he barks as two burly officers push the people back into their seats.

When Eddie Johnson hits a jump shot with three seconds left to put the Hawks ahead for good at 85-81, Brown raises his hands over his head, clutching his fists. The game ends. The Hawks have won, and Brown shouts his only utterly affirmative words of the night: "Oh yes. Oh yes." He is absolutely joyful, as if this is his one authentic moment of joy, the sole time he is satisfied. For a second, he is in control.

Even in 1979, Hubie Brown's ugly comment about urban blacks raised eyebrows. However, the consensus was that Brown is not a racist—just a blunt guy from Jersey. He continued coaching in the NBA until 2005 and is now a color commentator for pro broadcasts on ESPN.

Hollywood Fixer

Playboy, December 2010

When Kate Moss, just arrived from London, emerges from the Tom Bradley Terminal at Los Angeles International Airport, the paparazzi swarm. Thirty, maybe 40 in number, they will do almost anything to get a shot of the model. All that stands between their two-foot lenses and her multimillion-dollar face is Aaron Cohen. Eyes hidden behind wraparound Ray-Bans, dark-brown hair swept back, the 34-year-old chief of IMS Security is the image of imperturbability. At six feet and 185 pounds, he is not bodyguard big, but it would be a mistake to cross him. As he presses through the jostling throng, Moss clutches his shoulder with one hand while grasping the wrist he has extended behind him with the other. His expression dares her pursuers to make a wrong move. Typically, however, Cohen relies more on cunning that muscle. Why expose a woman whose waiflike visage has graced 300 magazine covers to physical harm when a few well-chosen Hebrew words will part the waters?

"*Tazeez otam achorah*," Cohen says in a voice loud enough to carry above the din. The paparazzi fall back.

"*Tazeez otam achorah*," he repeats, and they fall back again.

Soon enough, a passageway opens through the crowd, offering a glimpse of the Promised Land: a black 750 BMW that has materialized at the curb. It seems like a miracle, yet there's nothing miraculous about it. Two of the paparazzi besieging Moss are not paparazzi at all. Although outfitted with lights and cameras, they are IMS operatives and, like their boss, ex-commandos from Sayeret Duvdevan, an Israeli military unit that specializes in extracting terrorists from the occupied territories (in fact, IMS stands for Israeli Military Specialists). They know that *Tazeez otam achorah* means "Move them backward," and each time Cohen utters the words, they elbow the Nikon-wielding wolves toward the street. The theory is that the paparazzi, like members of any pack, are not so much creatures of free will as easily manipulated animals. Get one to retreat and the rest will follow.

"*Tazeez otam achorah*," Cohen says a final time, and suddenly he and Moss are in the BMW. At the wheel sits another IMS agent. "Thank you.

Thank God," the model says as they pull away. Not that she is home free, as several of the paparazzi give chase in their vehicles. But Cohen, who works frequently with Moss, has an edge here as well. No sooner does their BMW enter traffic than a trail car driven by an operative falls in behind, keeping the paparazzi at bay on the ride to the Chateau Marmont on the Sunset Strip. All told, the task of delivering the model—in town to appear in an ad campaign—safely to her hotel takes four hours and requires six men. The cost: $7,000. "One of these nights the paparazzi are inadvertently going to get someone killed," Cohen remarks afterward, "but it's not going to be one of my clients. The entire time I was thinking, Is this really what our culture has come to?"

IMS exists because the world is more dangerous than ever, and Aaron Cohen knows it. Now is a time when business disputes often end in death threats, trips abroad inspire fear of abduction, and even B-list celebrities attract stalkers. With just 25 operatives (six full-time, 19 on call), Cohen's Los Angeles-based security firm is certainly not the biggest in the business. Yet in composition (80 percent of his men are former Israeli special forces fighters) and areas of expertise (from close protection to counterterrorist training), IMS offers everything. As Cohen is fond of saying, "Walk softly and carry a small Israeli team."

In the nine years since he founded his company, Cohen has worked for a wide range of clients. Entertainment manager Steve Katz first hired him in 2001 to protect Jackie Chan at the premiere of *Rush Hour 2*. The action-adventure star was being stalked by an obsessed woman, and Cohen served as his bodyguard. Since then Katz has frequently engaged Cohen's firm. "A typical Hollywood security guy is a hulking person there to intimidate people," says Katz. "Make no mistake, Aaron is tough, but his real weapon is his mind. He's an extremely sharp tactician. The wheels are always turning."

Lisa Kline, proprietor of the hip Los Angeles fashion boutique of the same name, employs Cohen whenever such customers as Eva Longoria Parker, Britney Spears, or Kate Beckinsale want to shop in private. "He makes sure no one gets near them," she says. "He helps them to and from their cars. He's a professional, but he's intense. He treats every job like a mission—no funny business." Not that there aren't light moments. When the paparazzi appear, as they inevitably do, IMS operatives posted around the Robertson Boulevard store open umbrellas in a synchronized tactic that blocks all sight lines. No one gets a picture.

Far from Hollywood, the sheriff of Houston County, Alabama, also relies on Cohen. Andy Hughes has flown him in on multiple occasions to train his deputies. "He is an active instructor," says Hughes. "He doesn't tell you how to do things, he shows you—shooting in crowds, rescuing hostages. I'm the coordinator of homeland security for my region of Alabama, and if something happens, we will be the first responders. Aaron has taught us what we need to know. I'm not easily impressed. I'm impressed by Aaron."

Then there's a major social services agency in a large Midwestern city. After the agency, which is housed in a 22-story tower, received a series of bomb threats, the director of security contracted IMS to do an assessment. The results were unsettling. Although the building was supposed to be inaccessible to vehicles, Cohen found an opening in a protective cordon of planters and bollards and drove a car that could have been laden with explosives right to the front door. Later, with a few keystrokes on a computer, he emailed a panic-inducing message. "Because Aaron served in Israel, he sees things in a way we Americans just don't," says the security director, who prefers that he and his agency remain unnamed as it continues to be a target. "Aaron suggested a whole range of steps, and we took them. We rewrote our security manual."

Cohen is a rare hybrid of Hollywood heat and military know-how. One moment he'll talk about singer and occasional client Rihanna ("I wish I'd been there when Chris Brown went at her—it would have ended differently"), the next about protecting the powerful and the rich in, as he likes to put it, "austere environments." By this he means not just the violent countries in which some business executives must work but also the exotic lands in which the wealthy often vacation. Colt M4 Commando carbines, 7-foot repeating towers for transmitting radio signals over vast distances, night-vision goggles, level-three under-armor concealment vests and rented helicopters—to Cohen these are simply tools of the trade.

"You don't find many guys like Aaron in Los Angeles," says Rob Weiss, a long-time friend and executive producer of HBO's *Entourage.* "You find actors and writers, but you don't find commandos." That being the case, when Doug Ellin, *Entourage*'s creator, was beset by a security problem last year, Weiss introduced him to Cohen. "It was a situation where someone had crossed a line and needed to be looked at a little closer," Cohen says with characteristic evasiveness. To be more precise, a wannabe Hollywood player was going around town trying to pass himself off as Ellin, who happened to be building a new home and felt particularly exposed. Cohen checked out the house, assessed its vulnerabilities, and suggested solutions. Grateful for the resulting peace of mind, Ellin wrote Cohen into two episodes that aired near the conclusion of *Entourage*'s 2009 season. The story was that a dangerous stalker breaks into the pad shared by the show's fame-seeking ensemble in pursuit of their movie-star leader, Vincent Chase. Their agent, Ari Gold, urges them to hire Aaron Cohen, played by veteran film tough guy Peter Stormare, perhaps best known for his role in *Fargo*. Cohen and his band of Israeli agents become part of the ensemble's lives, introducing a new level of paranoia into the series. *Entourage* being a comedy, it all comes to an absurdly amusing end when the stalker is revealed to be a group of sorority girls after the underwear of posse member Turtle as part of a pledge-week prank. Cohen had entered the popular culture.

On a warm spring morning, Aaron Cohen, clad in a white T-shirt, Gap jeans, New Balance sneakers, and his always present Ray-Bans, walks into the Kings Road Café, an informal yet chic Los Angeles breakfast spot that serves as his unofficial office. "There's only one way in and one way out, and I get a 180-degree view," he says only half joking as he takes his usual seat at an outdoor corner table. "My back is to the wall by second nature," he adds. "When I sit down I do what is called a precision generalization. I know that's an oxymoron, but what I mean is I look at everyone around me. I don't want to come off like Jack Bauer, but I look at shirts to see how they're worn. I'm trained in lies—an itch or a blink, clothing that doesn't match bags. Everyone has a different tell. I know instantly if someone is wearing a pistol. It's always on. I can't turn it off. So I look around until I can dismiss all threats."

Today nothing untoward catches Cohen's eye as the café fills with the usual crowd of screenwriters pecking at laptops and actresses leashing their dogs to sidewalk chairs. But that does not mean the director of IMS can relax. At this very minute, for instance, Cohen is keeping track of Michael Douglas. Before the year is out, the actor will be battling for his life against cancer. But he is currently on a weeklong backpacking trip with his family in Mexico, where drug executions and kidnappings are the worry. Prior to departing, Douglas had contacted IMS, seeking advice on how to stay safe. Cohen's response was to outfit everyone in the party with miniature state-of-the-art global positioning devices. "I'm so excited about this," he says, pulling one of the $300 gadgets from his pants pocket. It's no larger than a cigarette pack. "We sewed them into all of their backpacks. I'm checking in with

Michael twice a day. I call on his cell and say, 'Are you standing next to so-and-so?' And he says, 'Yes.'"

The devices cannot, of course, guarantee that Douglas will avoid mishap, but if something bad does occur he will have a better chance of survival. "It's extremely advantageous to know someone's last coordinates," says Cohen. "In the event of trouble, I'd dispatch my team there. I'd contact the Mexican authorities, the U.S. consulate, and I'd call in some favors from my Israeli friends. We would find him.

"I have this crazy idea that every mother and daughter and every couple traveling in South America will one day have one of these," he adds, turning the global positioning device over in his hands. "Why didn't Natalee Holloway have one of these in Aruba?"

Simultaneously, Cohen is monitoring an international pop diva right here at home—a five-bedroom estate in Sherman Oaks just off Mulholland Drive. He will not disclose her identity because her problem—unlike those of clients he does discuss by name—is ongoing. "She had a number-one album several years ago, and a stalker was introduced into her life," Cohen says. "Then another stalker appeared. He was a crazy who believed she'd ripped off one of his songs. The claim had no merits, but he was making direct threats on her website. The police were called in and found he had a felony assault arrest. I went to the California firearms registry and found he had a registered firearm. At that point she decided to acquire full-time security."

The protection is comprehensive, technologically advanced, and heavily armed. It begins with two dozen closed-circuit cameras in critical areas of the grounds around the singer's home that feed into high-resolution screens in a control room in her basement. Her property is also crisscrossed by invisible radio-frequency beams that tie into a custom-fabricated electric map in the control room. If a breach occurs, the map lights up, pinpointing the spot. The house is guarded 24 hours a day by a revolving team of IMS agents who carry Glock 19 semiautomatic pistols in tactical holsters concealed in their waistbands. Periodically the operatives walk the perimeter, swiping access cards over digital readers to confirm that all areas have been checked. They also monitor the star's website for disturbing emails and chart street traffic to make certain no one is casing the neighborhood.

From the curb, the Spanish Revival house is the picture of tranquility—a circular drive, lovely greenery, gym equipment in back. The singer has relied on Cohen to keep it this way since 2006. The price: $500,000 a year.

Protecting clients is an obsession for Cohen. "He doesn't have an off switch," says *Entourage*'s Weiss. "I don't know what he does to take it easy," adds Steve Katz, the entertainment manager. "I've been out with him, and he's very personable and funny, but he's preoccupied a lot of the time." Although Cohen dines at fashionable Hollywood restaurants at least once a week (his preferred meal: a steak at Dan Tana's), the outings are as much for research as for pleasure. He likes to keep current on Los Angeles nightspots because the stars he represents frequent them. "I'm not a scenester; I never have been," says Cohen, who'd rather ride his Harley-Davidson in the hills above Malibu or hang out at home playing Led Zeppelin on his Martin acoustic. He has a girlfriend, but he deflects even innocent queries about her. "Security," he often declares, "begins with anonymity," and the rule applies just as much to him as to his charges.

To spend time with Cohen is to enter a hyperaware world where not everything is as it seems. During the course of a conversation he may hold forth on stalkers, which in his business are a persistent threat. "They suffer from erotomania," he says, his tone, as always, earnest, almost scholarly. "They believe that they and the celebrity they see on-screen or in concert have a personal relationship. The cause is linked to low self-esteem. My task is to determine if a potential for violence exists." Or he may discuss the challenges of working abroad. "I recently had a job for an American billionaire in Tanzania," he says. "A few weeks before he was scheduled to take his family there, drug lords gunned down several of his employees. He asked me to secure the property, which turned out to be several hundred thousand acres. It was really a military operation, and I hired five trained killers. That's what was required."

For all this Cohen is anything but gung ho. He goes to extraordinary lengths to diminish the chances of confrontation. "The trick in my job is to manage risk, not exacerbate it," he says. "The goal, always, is to avoid a violent outcome. What I do is the opposite of what you see in a movie. In fact, if I ever had to pull a pistol it would be an admission of failure. It would mean I was so far behind that I had been beaten. My task is to see what a client is up against and then make sure it doesn't happen."

In part, Cohen's philosophy derives from common sense, but there is also something else. "Aaron doesn't wear his compassion on his sleeve," says Katz. "But as you get to know him it shows up. He's an amalgam of a counterterrorist and a warm, caring person. He sees himself as the cavalry coming to the rescue. He works so hard because he empathizes with his clients."

Adds one of those clients, "He's not afraid to show you that he's vulnerable, and that actually encourages your trust in him. Most of these guys think they have to be 100 percent granite—not him."

"I come into people's lives when there is a lot of fear and doubt," says Cohen in a voice that suggests he knows a bit about such emotions himself. "You've got to be able to relate to them. In this business you have to want to help people. If you don't, you ought to be doing something else."

"The first thing you need to understand about Aaron is that he is a little Jewish boy from Beverly Hills," says his client Lisa Klein. The stepson of Abby Mann, the Academy Award-winning screenwriter of *Judgment at Nuremberg*, Cohen grew up not only with money but in the highest reaches of Hollywood royalty. Steven Spielberg, Warren Beatty, and Tom Cruise regularly wandered by the house to discuss scripts. Tony Bennett, Dean Martin, and Frank Sinatra dropped in for coffee. James Caan was one of his Little League coaches.

Although Cohen was raised in a rarefied realm, he did not enter it until the age of 10, when his mother, also a screenwriter, married Mann. From the start, he never felt he belonged. "My mom and stepfather were too into their careers and themselves," he says. "I was an attention-seeking kid, and I wasn't getting any at home. I couldn't connect to them, and I acted out. I got into trouble." During his freshman year at Beverly Hills High School, Cohen absconded with the family BMW and charged some $10,000 on his mother's credit card. "When my mom found out what I'd done," he says, "she sent me to military school, the Robert Land Academy outside Toronto. I got a total ass kicking. It was a completely structured environment—beds made each morning, no violations, no attitude. But I found out I loved the structure. In fact, I found out I excelled at it."

After a couple of years Cohen returned to Beverly Hills High School for his last courses and graduation. Unlike others in the class of 1994, however, he was not headed to an Ivy League college or a summer internship at Creative Artists Agency. At Robert Land he'd become fixated on joining the Israeli army, so he bought a one-way plane ticket to Tel Aviv. "A lot of Jewish teenagers go to Israel," says an old friend, "but not very many go to join the army. Aaron had something to prove. He was disgusted with the shallowness of his life in Beverly Hills. He wanted to find his own identity." Cohen puts it more succinctly: "I was a fucked-up kid looking for a family."

Following 14 months of what he calls "a modern-day version of gladiator school," Cohen had acquired an array of lethal skills—chief among them Krav Maga, an Israeli hand-to-hand combat technique that stresses relentless attack. He had also learned the Israeli art of deception known as *mista'aravim*. Working undercover, he would be able to speak convincing Arabic and wear the distinctive red-or-blue-checked kaffiyeh. The payoff: He was accepted not just into the Israeli army but into Sayeret Duvdevan, roughly equivalent to the United States Army's Delta Force, a rare honor for an American. Duvdevan performs a specific and dangerous task. "Our single focus was to undertake stealth counterterrorism operations in the occupied territories," Cohen would later write in *Brotherhood of Warriors*, a memoir he co-authored with Douglas Century. "Every single mission was an attempt to take down a terrorist leader. We were not after suicide bombers, but rather the planners…the command-and-control of groups like Hamas, Hezbollah, and Islamic Jihad." The Duvdevan specializes in serving so-called "terrorist warrants." Bluntly put, the unit abducts murderers and brings them back to Israeli authorities for interrogation.

Thus it was that two and a half years out of Beverly Hills High, Cohen was sitting across from the third-ranking figure in Hamas, at the Palestine Café in East Jerusalem. Hair dyed blond and a tape recorder in hand, Cohen passed himself off as a sympathetic student journalist straight out of UCLA. Armed with only a Beretta concealed in his boot, he was all charm, knowing that if he made even the slightest false move one of the Hamas leader's three bodyguards would shoot him. After receiving a message in a tiny earpiece that his comrades were in place, Cohen leaped across the table and beat his quarry senseless. It was a classic Duvdaven operation: quick and brutal. The terrorist was whisked out of the café. Only when it was over did Cohen real-ize that much of the blood that covered him was his own. So savage was the attack that he'd ripped open his fists.

Cohen had become, by his own admission, an "emotional automaton, a pure fighting machine" able to turn on "an inner killer—a survival mechanism inherent in all of us but rarely used in normal Western society."

After completing his required one-year tour, Cohen did not reenlist in the Duvdevan. He had killed and had witnessed killing. (A teenage girl died in his arms in the midst of a horrific, terrorist bombing at the Dizengoff Shopping Mall.) He was scared—both of dying and of becoming a monster. He was only 21, but to use a phrase common in the Israeli military, his dick was broken—badly. "I didn't stay in Israel because I was burned out," he says. "My Israel wasn't joyful."

Still, no matter how terrifying the experience, it had imbued Cohen with not just a profound feeling of accomplishment but a sense of belonging. "Israel was my mother," he says. "It gave me the attention I needed, and the skills I could use to cope later in life. I always say I was raised in Beverly Hills, but I grew up in Israel."

Back in Los Angeles, Cohen was initially at a loss. "I wanted to do something with what I'd learned in Israel," he says. "I didn't want it to have just been three years of finding myself. But I didn't know what that something was."

The answer came when Cohen applied for work with Professional Security Consultants, a Southern California firm that provided bodyguards to celebrities. The timing was perfect. His first assignment was to protect Brad Pitt. The then rising star had arrived at his Hollywood Hills home one night to be greeted by a stalker named Athena Rolanda. She had broken into the house, put on his shirt, and was waiting for him in bed. "Brad was completely freaked out," says Cohen. "For the next year and a half I was the team leader for six guys providing security at his property 24 hours a day."

After three years with PSC, Cohen went out on his own. From the start, he hired former members of the Duvdevan. "I feel a duty to give back to Israel," he says. More important, Cohen trusts Duvdevan veterans. "I need to have guys on my team I can lean on," he says. "We do what most people would consider complex operations, but the goal is to treat them as if they are second nature. I can't do that unless I know that my guys have a certain level of skill. The Israeli special forces provide that skill."

Former members of the Duvdevan also share Cohen's philosophy, which puts a premium on understatement. Except in rare instances, his men do not make a show of force. Indeed, at a typical property protected by IMS, there seems to be no security at all. As the maxim-loving Cohen likes to say, "What they don't know, they can't plan against."

Over the past several years, Cohen has been trying to nudge his business toward becoming "a lean, private military company." The focus, he says, will be on training police department SWAT teams and other small forces. Indeed, he recently conducted training sessions at two major nuclear reactors (one in Virginia, the other in upstate Michigan), teaching their security guards how to retake the facilities should a terrorist group ever gain control.

"This interests me," he says, "because you have to move fast. Otherwise the reactor's core might melt. You have no time."

Yet because of Cohen's ties to such notable clients as Kate Moss and Rihanna and the publicity he gained from his association with *Entourage*, it is hard to imagine him leaving the world of celebrity. "The irony," he says, "is that I grew up utterly despising Hollywood, but not only am I continuing to work for it, more and more I'm working in it."

In a vacant Pasadena warehouse, Aaron Cohen, an Uzi in one hand and an ammo clip in the other, kicks open a flimsy door and shouts, "Hot range." On cue, mixed-martial-arts-star-turned-actress Gina Carano, also armed with an Uzi, follows him into a narrow passageway adorned with posters depicting ski-masked terrorists. At the sight of each one, the star of *Haywire*, Steven Soderbergh's forthcoming thriller, fires a flame-spurting burst. "Keep shooting until you feel the guy is dead," Cohen urges. "Keep shooting." She does. Soon, the floor is carpeted with shell casings.

"Great. Cool," says Cohen when Carano emerges from the far end of the course, and the two enthusiastically bump fists. As Carano walks off to reload, Cohen remarks, "When Gina started she didn't even know how to hold an instrument. Now she can flow in a tactical situation, firing her machine gun at a pretty advanced level."

On this sunny, Wednesday afternoon, Cohen is deep into coaching Carano for her role as the lead operative of the fictional, private military force at the center of *Haywire*. In the picture Soderbergh will attempt to bring the gritty aesthetic he perfected in *Traffic* to the slick world of espionage showcased in the Bourne franchise. As technical advisor, it's Cohen's job to make sure that the cast gives true-to-life performances. When he's finished with Carano, he puts costars Channing Tatum and Michael Fassbender through their paces.

"God said, 'We shall make them warriors, so warriors they will become,'" Cohen barks as he instructs the actors in the proper technique for drawing and holstering their Sig Sauer P 228 pistols. "The first thing is to keep from shooting yourself in the ass," he advises. Once they have the hang of it, he shouts, "Smash and rock," and they open fire at targets emblazoned with the images of hooded malefactors.

"My goal is to give them a special-op training course," Cohen says as the men go through their paces. "I want them to look natural as they move with weapons. I also am giving them an immersion course in the very intense, emotional experience of working undercover. A couple of my guys are following them everywhere they go, and they have to email me if they spot the surveillance. I've got them living in a watered-down version of the dread and pressure I experienced in the Israeli military."

That's just for starters. "Aaron has become a key part of my brain trust," says Soderbergh. "He's really part of the core creative group on *Haywire*. There's not a single aspect of the script I haven't run by him. When two of the operatives have a phone conversation, I ask him, 'How formal should they be, how colloquial?' I'm also relying on him to make sure that we use the right technology. I don't want Gina carrying a weapon that real operatives wouldn't use. Basically, Aaron has been value added. That's how I describe people I like having around."

This being the case, it's no surprise that when filming begins several weeks later in Dublin, Ireland, Soderbergh casts Cohen as an operative and gives him a line. "It's one of my favorite bits in the film," says the director, who proceeds to enthusiastically recite the dialogue uttered by Cohen's character, "So, what do we know about the Spaniard, Rodregio?" Soderbergh was fascinated by Cohen's zest for the role. "I watched Aaron calibrate himself to react to the other actors as he got into the work. You could see him thinking, 'This is an interesting world, one I could be very interested in.' He looks great on camera, and he's actually a good actor. Someplace in there he's got the timing of a Catskills comedian. Of course, he can also rip your lungs out."

Aaron Cohen insists that he has no desire to get into the movie business. He relishes reality, not make believe, and within days after the production wraps, he's back from Europe, sitting again at his corner table at King's Road Café, eyes hidden by his wrap-around Ray-Bans. This morning, he is obsessing over a new client, whom he will describe only as "a Midwestern manufacturer of a significant cog that's distributed around the world." A former business associate has threatened the manufacturer. "It was pretty direct," says Cohen. "The guy feels my client ripped off one of his ideas. So he emailed him and said, 'Stop selling this product, or you won't ever sell anything again.' We've outfitted my client and his kids with global positioning devices, and cameras have gone up in his home. I'm running what I call a 'tentacle operation.' Not only am I watching my client, but I've got two of my operatives shadowing the guy who made the threats. He lives in Melbourne, Australia, and they're following him 24 hours a day. The purpose is to determine if he is capable of violence. If he buys a gun, meets with suspicious people, or gets on a plane headed to my client's town—we contact the police."

A month into the job, the client has paid Israeli Military Services $50,000. "He was terribly spooked when he first called us," says Cohen. "But he's better now." In the end, this may be all that IMS, or any other protection agency, can offer—the reassurance that comes from knowing every possible measure has been taken. Of course, Cohen also provides comforting intangibles. As Soderbergh puts it, "Aaron reminds me of a line Anthony Minghella once used to describe Harvey Weinstein: 'He's a bull you'd rather have running alongside you than at you.'"

The Real Jake

GQ, May 1986

On the first floor of Parker Center, headquarters of the Los Angeles Police Department, is the Norman "Jake" Jacoby Press Room. A large, cluttered space whose grimy walls are plastered with black-and-white glossies of crime scenes, the chamber functions as the nerve center for police news in Southern California. It takes its name from an old-time reporter, a man who covered the cops back in the 1930s when murder stories sold newspapers, criminals commanded monikers worthy of comic-strip villains, and police beats all across the country attracted a breed of journalists who fancied themselves as hard-living but secretly bighearted chroniclers of life's mean streets.

Those days, and most of the reporters who made them so colorful, are now long gone, but Jake Jacoby, more than fifty years after digging up his first scoop, is still on the job, tracking down leads for a feisty local wire service called City News. At 70, he's lost the hearing in one ear, his hair is a memory, and he's forsworn Scotch whisky, the drink that sustained him during the many years in which he covered L.A. from a phone booth at a now defunct police bar called the Stake-Out. But he has yet to lose a step where it counts, something that his competitors occasionally learn the hard way.

Early on a smoggy summer afternoon, Jacoby was sitting at his corner pressroom desk when one of his four telephones suddenly began jangling. The voice on the other end of the line belonged to a source with a tip that nearly every other reporter in town was hoping for: The members of a special task force investigating "the Night Stalker," a serial killer who since early spring had slain at least a dozen Angelenos, had just returned from San Francisco, where they'd been looking into the murder of Peter Pan, an elderly Chinese man. Depending on what the detectives had discovered, the Stalker might have expanded his range to include the entire state.

"Watch the phones. I'll be right back," Jacoby told his City News Service colleague Mike Blakemore after hanging up. Then as casually as if he were heading off for a cup of coffee, Jacoby eased out of his seat and disappeared into the labyrinthine corridors of the building. Somewhere upstairs, in this bureau or that, his Deep Throat was waiting.

It was hardly surprising that Jacoby was receiving a break on the story. Well over half the calls that come into the press room on its main line—which is shared by all the news organizations that staff the station house—are for Jacoby's ears only and usually begin with the warning "Jake, make sure no one else picked up." Never is this reality more apparent than during one of those sprees of slayings that, like autumn brush fires, seem endemic to California. Jacoby has been in the middle of every serial-killer case within recent memory, and policemen regard him as an expert. In fact, he coined two of the genre's most haunting handles, phrases that have entered the language as code words for the monstrous and the unknown: "the Skid Row Slasher" and "the Hillside Strangler."

"Peter Pan looks better than ever," Jacoby whispered to Blakemore upon returning from his fact-finding mission—the Night Stalker, in other words, had indeed struck in San Francisco. For Jacoby, this piece of intelligence was galvanizing. Though he had been at work since 6 A.M. and it was now a little after 2 P.M., it was time to really get moving.

From a battered metal file cabinet, Jacoby extracted several thick bundles of paper and stacked them on his desk. These were the computer printouts of every crime piece written by a City News reporter during the course of the summer-long crisis, and Jacoby intended to study them all, searching for reports of murders that might be attributable to the serial killer but that initially hadn't been perceived as part of a larger pattern. At first blush, such a task might seem like a waste of time, but Jacoby felt that the new development warranted the effort—if the Stalker had hit the Bay Area, his instincts told him, he had probably also hit other cities.

As a member of the old school of police writers, Jacoby fancies himself part cop. He follows his hunches. A few months before, he had read about a 5-year-old girl who had been held captive in a house trailer in Anchorage for three and a half years but could remember once "living near a beach." Almost immediately, Jacoby's sixth sense told him that this was a child who had been kidnapped in 1981 in the Venice section of Los Angeles. FBI agents checked out his suspicion, found it correct, and reunited little Elvia Vasquez with her overjoyed parents. At the time, Jacoby remarked, "Most of the work I have to handle is gruesome, but once in a while you get some remuneration. This is one of the things I'm most proud of."

Inspired by several such instances, Jacoby began the job of wading through the dozens of dog-eared dispatches. All around him, the pressroom was in its typical bedlam. Dozens of police radios buzzed and squawked from every side of the place. On a table marked "Visiting Press," a beat-up TV was tuned to a soap opera. Reporters from UPI, the *Los Angeles Times*, and other news agencies wandered in and out, taking calls and talking among themselves about the case. To them, Jacoby seemed simply to be tidying up his files.

After an hour or so of reading old news, Jacoby stumbled upon something—a short item about the murder of a couple in the suburban Los Angeles community of Glendale. In late July, Maxson Kneiding and his wife had been found dead in their home. The deed resembled the Stalker's work, but the special task force did not appear to have probed into it.

Leaning across his desk, Jacoby quietly told Blakemore the name of a lieutenant in the Glendale Police Department and asked him to make a call. Blakemore, who is half Jacoby's age and regards his co-worker as his mentor, immediately did so. And he hit pay dirt. The officer was only too happy to tell him that the Glendale authorities were working closely with the task force on the Kneiding murders.

When informed of this, Jacoby smiled widely. Now he felt that if he could uncover just one more part of the puzzle he'd have a great story. This last detail, however, wouldn't come from anyone in an official capacity. It would come from Jacoby's head. Due solely to his years of experience, the reporter knew—even though no one in the police hierarchy would confirm it—that the investigation had reached the stage where an all-points bulletin would be issued for a suspect who had thus far been described only as a dark-haired Latino with crumbling, yellowed teeth. Armed with this final piece, Jacoby believed it was time to start writing.

For the next forty-five minutes, Blakemore and Jacoby hunched over City News's video-display terminal. They were an odd Mutt-and-Jeff team. Blakemore, dressed in jeans, Top-Siders, and a Hawaiian shirt, is intense and antic, a survivor of the Sixties who likes to unnerve lawmen with what he calls "my psychedelic gaze." He actually composed the article while Jacoby—clad in a rumpled old suit and black suspenders—sat at his side, reading over his shoulder. Occasionally, in a low, gravelly voice that along with his heavy jowls and trim, gray moustache gives him a gruffly reassuring, avuncular mien, Jacoby would correct what Blakemore had written or advise him to alter a passage that could be damaging to the investigation. By the time the two reporters were finished, they had crafted a comprehensive piece. The article, which was credited entirely to unnamed sources, not only contained three exclusives but summarized the entire Stalker case.

It was now 5 P.M., and there was still some unfinished business. First, Jacoby decided he didn't want a byline. "I've already had that kind of glory," he said. "Let the kids coming up get some credit." So Blakemore signed his name to the article. Then the two agreed to hold the piece until after 6 P.M. so that by the time it moved on the wires many of the task-force detectives would have gone home, making it difficult for rival journalists to locate them. City News would have the exclusive. With these decisions out of the way, Jacoby, after eleven hours on the job, decided to call it a day.

Early in the evening, when the City News piece began coursing into the offices of its one hundred subscriber newspapers, television news departments, and radio stations, all hell broke loose. The little wire service had scooped every major news organization in town, and editors and news directors were incensed: Why hadn't their people come up with the story? Nightshift reporters were ordered to get on the phone and see if they could recover from this embarrassment, and soon dozens of calls began pouring into Parker Center. By 10 P.M., the clamoring of the pack had created such a commotion that Los Angeles County Sheriff Sherman Block, leader of the task force, came back downtown. In a room bathed in bright television lights, he held a news conference, confirming everything that appeared in the City News article.

By that hour, Jacoby was home in the tidy La Crescenta Valley town of Montrose, sitting on the living-room sofa with his wife of forty-four years, Audrey. They were content to watch the hubbub on the eleven-o'clock news. Because of the sheriff's statements, the TV types had been given a chance to recover and were able to present the new leads as if they'd reported them from scratch. Jacoby, of course, knew better. It was his enterprise that had forced Block to verify several items he would rather have kept to himself a while longer, and the reporter felt an immense sense of accomplishment. But it wasn't the sort of satisfaction most journalists receive from a job well done. After all, there was absolutely no public awareness of his part in the drama, and the financial compensation for his diligence was negligible, to say the least (after half a century as a police writer, Jacoby earns $376 a week and has no pension plan).

Jacoby takes his payment in an old-fashioned kind of currency. As a police reporter, he believes it is his mission to help stem the tide of criminal outrages. For him, it is reward enough to be, as he often terms it, "just someone who sweeps back the waves."

If there was ever an instance in which Jacoby could feel justified in his role, it was the Night Stalker case. In part because of his dispatches, law-enforcement officials decided to handle the investigation quite openly, eliciting the citizenry's help in apprehending the killer. Eight days after Jacoby's big story, Richard Ramirez, a man matching the description Jacoby had published, was cornered by a group of East Los Angeles residents. The next week, he was charged with the Stalker murders.

It is not every day that Jake Jacoby finds himself embroiled in a crime story that attracts national attention. The bulk of his working hours are consumed by the usual sordid tales that come with the territory. Before dawn on most mornings, he is hunkered down in the police pressroom with a phone clasped to each ear and an eye on two other phones that are ringing off the hooks. All the while he is absorbing the static-broken messages of mayhem blaring from seven scanners monitoring twenty-five police frequencies. Bad news flows into him from every part of Los Angeles.

A desk sergeant at LAX is calling to say that a Colombian couple is using a baby girl as a decoy to rob businessmen at the airport. Jacoby laughs and says to the officer, "The kid was only 20 months old, huh? Boy, they break them in early. Tell me, did she have on a skirt or little panties?"

Then an editor is demanding a story on a woman found dead in a deep arroyo near the harbor. After hanging up, Jacoby pulls a calculator from his valise and does some quick computations to determine whether the previous evening's tides could have affected the position of the body.

Next, a detective upstairs is phoning to report the latest on the investigation into the gang-related murder of a mother and her teenage son. As Jacoby jots down notes, his mouth tightens. Before signing off, he tells his source, "I hope you catch whoever did it." Then he grumbles darkly, "I sometimes wonder if we shouldn't start all over again. Back to Adam and Eve. This world of ours is far from civilized."

A few minutes later an officer on the west side is calling to report the latest on the investigation into the execution-style shootings of two UCLA students.

After concluding each conversation with a brisk "Thanks, pal," Jacoby picks up another line. Whenever the chaos momentarily subsides, he turns to his computer, and his fingers start to hunt and peck over the keyboard. Upon finishing an item, he types out a heading—CLIFF-BOTTOM BODY topped the article on the deceased female—and then begins writing his next piece. His prose, while not sterling, is serviceable and bespeaks a bygone era of American journalism. In the world according to Jacoby, crimes are usually "capers," pretty women are often "comely coeds," domestic shootings are "lovers' quarrels," and assaults are generally "foul play."

Yet Jacoby's stories aren't merely catalogues of cop-shop clichés. Not only are his pieces usually filed far ahead of those written by the competition ("He breaks 90 percent of the police news in Los Angeles," observes an AP correspondent), and not only are they remarkably accurate, but they are also informed by his strong law-and-order sensibility. Unlike many young police writers, reporters whose journalism-school professors trained them to see the ongoing conflict between wrongdoers and the police as a contest between two evenly matched teams—each with its own strategies and stars and each to be regarded objectively—Jacoby sees the fight as one between the forces of good and evil. In his view, lawbreakers of all stripes are to be treated with disdain, while tough-talking cops should sit at the right hand of the Lord.

"One of the reasons I admire policemen," Jacoby remarked one busy day during a lull in the action, "is that as a general rule they're fighters. They're trying to improve things, but not like the do-gooders, whose heads are in the skies with their feet planted firmly in the clouds. The police realize they're up against some very tough problems. They have trouble with the DA, who won't prosecute unless he has a good chance of getting a conviction. They have trouble with politicians, who want to please everybody but didn't even want to approve the money for a better fingerprint system. They were at odds with the legislators on even so simple a matter as getting people to wear seat belts. I mean, cops are up against a tough, non-resilient wall. I feel like it's my duty to work with them to make their lives easier."

Such is the spirit that has led Jacoby to devote himself to a branch of reporting that most newsmen see as only a painful but necessary apprenticeship. In fact, many of America's premier journalists—writers like David Halberstam, Jack Nelson, and Russell Baker—started their careers as police reporters, but after a few years of blood and gore they were ready for the more sanitized glory of political writing or editorial-page punditry. (Baker once related to a writer from *More* magazine that he knew it was time to quit covering the cops for *The Baltimore Sun* when he heard a paddy-wagon driver tell a wounded man, "Hurry up and die. I get off in ten minutes.") From the moment Jacoby walked into the police pressroom, however, he was never really tempted by such supposedly higher callings. In the department, he found his home.

Decades before the Night Stalker would terrorize Los Angeles, Jake Jacoby started working for City News Service. It was 1935. Back then, Los Angeles was a last frontier of azure skies spiked by tall palms and Deco towers. But innocent as the city appeared, there could have been no better place to begin a career as a police reporter. Against this town's pastel backdrops and on its dusty streets, crime flourished. This was, after all, Raymond Chandler territory.

"My first big case involved a guy called James the Barber, who was later renamed Rattlesnake James," Jacoby was recalling one quiet morning as he sat at his desk waiting for something, anything, to happen. "I wrote the first story about this fellow—it concerned what appeared to be the accidental death of his pregnant wife in La Crescenta. He had a big piece of property, and she was found drowned in the fishpond. But the autopsy showed that the water in her lungs had come from somewhere else. The sheriff started checking on the guy and found that he was the recipient on the insurance policies for various family members, a couple of whom had also died in mysterious circumstances. Then they found that he was sleeping with his niece, who was the manicurist at his barbershop. The police bugged his place, and I'll never forget what she said to him right before they caught them in the act: 'Let's do it the old-fashioned way.'"

Jacoby laughed at the memory then added, "She turned state's evidence. Later, while the trial was pending, a guy walked into a bar, got drunk, told the bartender that he was James's co-conspirator, and then confessed everything they'd done. It turned out that the two of them had gone into the desert, gathered up a dozen rattlesnakes, put James's wife's foot in the nest and let them bite her. But she didn't die. Because she was pregnant, she was strong. So then they stuck her head in a bathtub and drowned her. I covered this story all the way through to the trial, where James was convicted. Incidentally, in 1939—or maybe it was '38—he became the last man to hang in California's gallows."

Thus christened, Jacoby's career took off. During the last years of the Depression, Los Angeles teemed with criminals. In those days, Jacoby covered everything: the death of movie figures (he reported on the ongoing lawsuits resulting from the murder of silent-film director William Desmond Taylor, a case notable because the chief suspect was the valet, which gave rise to the phrase "the butler did it"), child-molestation scandals, plane crashes. He rode to crime sites with officers in big, open-air touring cars at breakneck speed, lights flashing, sirens blaring. He flew on body searches in small aircraft. He drank with off-duty lawmen in bars that only they frequented: the U.S. Bar, El Correo, Tony's Goodfellow Grill—all gone now. Many a night Jacoby helped close them. (In later years, Jacoby became such a fixture at the Stake-Out that finally an impressively lettered enamel sign appeared over its lone phone booth. It read, "Jacoby's Private Office.") "I could drink them all under the table," he said, "and I won their confidence that way. It's a shame it doesn't work like that anymore. Now newspapers frown on reporters fraternizing with policemen, but there's no better way to get information. If a cop asked me to hold something for a day or two, I always would because that way they'd tell me things they wouldn't tell anyone else."

When he got the green light from a source, though, Jacoby would rush to a public phone or back to the office and produce a piece. After finishing, he'd dictate or type a short title for his work. From the beginning, he had a knack for coming up with catchy, brief headlines—encapsulations known in the newspaper business as slugs. Because Los Angeles once boasted two Hearst papers, many of Jacoby's coinages began screaming from street racks in 72-point type. There was "Handsome Boy," an Adonis among bank robbers; "the Triple Threat Man," a heist artist who jumped the counter of whatever institution he was knocking over, presented a note stating his demands then threatened to kill everyone on the premises; and "the Marx Brothers," a burglary duo notable for disguises.

This was the *Front Page* era, and with his gift for fast writing and alcohol-fueled stamina, Jacoby quickly became a part of a tradition established by his slightly older contemporaries—legendary police reporters who were almost as famous as the stories they covered. The Big Daddies of the craft were Bob Considine, Jimmy Kilgallen, and Damon Runyon of the Hearst newspapers; Al Lewis of *The Washington Post*; and Pat Doyle of *The New York Daily News*. Of the lot of them, Lewis and Doyle were by far the most hard-core practitioners, men who were born to chase ambulances. One day, Lewis achieved journalism's equivalent of hockey's hat trick when he wrote every single story on the *Post's* front page, including a piece about the apprehension of a rapist who'd turned himself in not to the police but to Al Lewis. Doyle, known universally by his nom de guerre—"the Inspector"—modestly referred to himself as "the world's greatest police reporter" and once reportedly removed the oxygen mask from the mouth of a dying man to get a good quote. His memoirs were entitled *In Hot Blood*.

The temptation would be to discount these old newshawks as boozy stereotypes, but that would be a mistake. They were experts at using a priest or a rabbi to wheedle a heartbreaking remark from a murder victim's next of kin. They knew how to sweet-talk an emergency-room nurse or badger a tough motorcycle cop. They understood that the telephone—not the Freedom of Information Act—was a reporter's greatest tool. Moreover, in some philosophical sense that they rarely articulated, they believed that the police beat kept them in touch with the very gristle and bone of life, and that as members of a select fraternity they were privy to truths unavailable to those who lived in a more polite world.

Jacoby thrived on the multiple intoxicants that came with the beat—glamour, romance, power, and access to places high and low. In fact, during the spring of 1941, he met and courted the woman who would become his wife when she served as his source on one of the biggest stories in Los Angeles.

"I used to go to the coroner's office every morning," Jacoby remembered, "and go through all the deaths. One day, there was only one traffic death, but the location wasn't listed. So I called Queen of Angeles Hospital looking for some information on the wreck. They were never very cooperative, but that morning I happened to reach a very nice switchboard operator who was rebelling against the fact that the nuns had told her not to talk to reporters. She not only told me what I wanted to know, but she also told me that Les Brunneman, the gangster who ran the Southern California mob before Bugsy Siegel, was a patient. Brunneman had been shot in Redondo Beach and was recovering there."

The switchboard operator was a pretty blonde named Audrey Keary. Over the next weeks, as Audrey and Jake began dating, she supplied the reporter with information about Brunneman, including the inside dope on what happened one night when the mobster, after sneaking out of the hospital with an attractive nurse for a drink, was assassinated by two gangland rivals. If any of Jacoby's rivals were curious about why his stories on the hit were filled with information no one else could get, their questions were answered two months later when he and Audrey were married.

Over the years, Jacoby has generally had the good fortune to be in the right place at the right time when big news was breaking. In January, 1947, he put out one of the first bulletins on the infamous "Black Dahlia" case, the still-unsolved murder of Elizabeth Short. A tease with a penchant for ebony lingerie (hence the sobriquet), Short was found surgically sliced into numerous pieces in a vacant Los Angeles lot. The killing inspired John Gregory Dunne's novel *True Confessions*.

Yet journalism's primary allure for Jacoby had little to do with the opportunity the profession afforded for vicarious excitement and momentary fame. What Jacoby liked best about the field was that it is based on facts, the sort of verifiable certainties that he had longed for during a somewhat difficult childhood. Jacoby's family lived in L.A.'s Fairfax district, a community made up mainly of progressive Jews. Jacoby's father, however, was never really part of that world. He was, by turns, an auctioneer, a jeweler, and a gambler who scraped by solely on what his son calls "a gift for gab." Jake wanted something more solid for himself. Although he got into reporting when he came down with pneumonia shortly before beginning junior college ("One of my classmates told me to enroll in a journalism course because the homework was so easy that I'd have no trouble keeping up while recovering"), it was this deeper desire to build a career on a sound foundation that fired his enduring passion for the work—and for the police.

Not surprisingly, Jacoby once actually considered becoming a cop. "It wasn't really for the glory, although I certainly believed in what they were doing," the reporter recalled. "To tell you the truth, they had great benefits. Audrey and I had just got married, and I thought it was important to get some good insurance and a pension plan." Audrey, however, wouldn't hear of such a move. She thought it was too dangerous. After a while, Jacoby's impulse passed.

Although Jacoby would never actually don a uniform, he assisted in numerous police investigations (he once allowed himself to be wired while interviewing a murder suspect), and in late 1947 he briefly left journalism to publish a right-wing newsletter that attacked the group he saw as the chief criminal enemy of the United States: Communists. Jacoby's paper was named *Alert*, and it was unabashedly hostile to anyone with leftist leanings, especially those writers such as Ring Lardner, Jr., who would later be blacklisted as members of the so-called Hollywood Ten. As Jacoby fondly likes to recall, "The publication named names." While *Alert's* circulation never exceeded 2,000, many in that small number of subscribers were leading reactionary figures, among them John Wayne, Ward Bond, and Morrie Ryskind, the Pulitzer Prize-winning playwright (*Of Thee I Sing*) and conservative polemicist. Today, Jacoby's friends shake their heads when confronted with the subject of the reporter's sojourn as a McCarthy-era propagandist. But Jacoby makes no apologies for his actions. "If I caused anyone misery, they deserved it," he said. "Those people are the ones who owe the U.S.A. an apology." His affiliation with *Alert* did nothing to hurt his reputation with the police, and in 1952, when Jacoby returned to the newspaper business as the police reporter for the old *Los Angeles Herald-Express*, he was on warm terms with almost every member of the law-enforcement brass.

For the next sixteen years, until the *Herald* underwent the crippling 1968 strike that would change the face of the Los Angeles newspaper world, Jacoby was in his prime, working for the city's dominant daily. He broke story after story, primarily because no one in the city had better sources. At the top of the police department in those days was the legendarily tough-minded conservative William Parker. To the extent that Parker had friends, Jacoby was one of his best. Notoriously shy with the press, Parker seemed to open up only to Jacoby. While other Los Angeles reporters constantly complained about Parker's inaccessibility, Jacoby and the chief had coffee almost every morning in Parker's office. Through Parker, Jacoby became acquainted with the men who would run the police department in the future: Ed Davis, a lieutenant on Parker's staff and chief from 1969 until 1978; and Daryl Gates, Parker's aide and driver and the city's current top cop.

Inevitably, Jacoby's chumminess with the police has led to the charge that he is more cop than reporter. Says Detective John St. John, the LAPD's top homicide investigator: "I talk to him like I talk to any other detective because I know he's not going to hurt me. You can relate things to Jake you wouldn't tell other reporters. At the same time, when he learns something— and on big cases he's very good at seeing patterns I might miss—he'll come up and lay it on me."

Such praise isn't the sort that goes over very well with most editors. When confronted with the allegation that he hasn't been tough enough on the police, Jacoby calmly replied, "I've broken more scandals within the department than any other reporter in this city." Then he cited story after story of police abuses he'd reported: burglary rings, sex scandals, drug smuggling at the airport, and an incident involving one of his best friends, a male officer picked up for soliciting a female undercover detective posing as a streetwalker. Still, a faint haze has lingered over Jacoby's career. "When the *Herald* went on strike," he said, "I tried to get on at the *Times*, but they thought I was too close to the police and didn't want me." Thus Jacoby rejoined City News.

In recent years, Jacoby has been reprimanded twice by his current employer for incidents stemming from his intimacy with the people he covers.

In the first case, he agreed to hold a scoop concerning officers who were robbing Hispanic motorists suspected of being illegal aliens; the *Times* broke the news. In the second, he failed to write up items from the "gig sheet," a police-department memo that reports disciplinary actions taken against officers. In both instances, he maintained, there were mitigating circumstances. In the former, Jacoby said he was waiting for an internal police investigation to proceed before going with his piece; in the latter, he doubted the newsworthiness of the items.

Whenever the topic of Jacoby's ties to the LAPD comes up, it is usually followed by conjecture about his retirement, for implicit in any conversation about his connections to the cops is the notion that he's an anachronism. It has now been eighteen years since he rejoined City News Service for his second stint. During that time most of the country's other great police reporters have stepped down or died. Jacoby, though, shows few signs that he is ready to head out to pasture. "I don't think that a person who's still able should walk away from life," he said. "If I was physically or mentally unable, I'd think about retiring. But I think there's plenty of evidence that shows I'm still on top of the game." The only recent event that even vaguely suggests that he is not quite in mid-season form is that his nickname for Richard Ramirez—"the Valley Invader"—was supplanted by the more chilling "Stalker" moniker that a *Los Angeles Herald Examiner* editor dredged up from an old TV-show title. In the past, almost all of Jacoby's crime designations have stuck.

But doubts about Jacoby's real ability are rarely raised. At an age when most men are slowing down, not only is he still plugging away, he's setting the pace. "He's so good it's frightening," said Pat Brierton, a City News co-worker. Added Alice Crane, a UPI reporter: "Nobody beats Jake." In short, Jacoby has had the good fortune to find and keep his niche in life. He will never win a Pulitzer Prize. Abe Rosenthal of *The New York Times* will never call and ask him to cover the White House. For that matter, most of the Los Angeles television anchor-people who read Jacoby's stories will never know that he wrote them. But such recognition is really meaningless to Jacoby.

"One of the greatest pleasures I've had is the chance to train hundreds of young reporters," he said. Because City News is a shoestring operation, it attracts scores of journalists just out of college, and most of them spend some time under Jacoby's tutelage. "I've tried to advise them as best I can on the delicate matters involved in handling the cops, the crooks, and the victims," he said. From all accounts, he's done a good job. "Jake taught me the business," said his running mate, Mike Blakemore. "He showed me things I could never have learned anywhere else." (Indeed, Blakemore recently graduated to UPI.)

The ultimate tribute, however, has come from Southern California lawmen. To celebrate his forty-eighth anniversary on the job, the Los Angeles Police Department threw Jacoby a barbecue at the police lodge in Elysian Park. Last summer, to commemorate his golden anniversary, there was a repeat performance. At that bash, Chief Daryl Gates told a throng of some 200 officers that Jacoby is "the sort of reporter I wished there were more like, the sort of man we can trust, a man we can tell our secrets to." Later last summer, Jacoby received his greatest compliment when the pressroom was named for him. During a brief ceremony, a drab black-and-white sign printed in the same official typeface that marks the Asian Task Force office, the Juvenile Division, and every other LAPD department was hung above the door. In that instant, Jacoby formally became an institution.

Late on a pleasant Friday afternoon in autumn, Jacoby and Audrey were seated at a desk in a Century 21 Realty office in Glendale. Atop the desk were two tiny "For Sale" signs, one bearing Jake's name and the other Audrey's, identifying both of them as Century 21 agents. Every day following his shift at Parker Center, Jacoby puts in four or five hours as a broker. This is how he makes ends meet, and as the numerous plaques declaring him "Salesperson of the Month" attest, he's done quite well for himself. He owns rental property, and in spite of the miserly wage he pulls down from City News, he has no worries about his dotage.

As evening was coming on, agents scurried around the office trying to close deals before the weekend. Amid the hustle, Jacoby and Audrey discussed their family (they have three daughters) and the pleasures of living far from downtown Los Angeles, where Jake is forced to deal with stories of human tragedy.

Audrey is a pert, outspoken woman, still quite attractive and obviously the center of her husband's life. She's completely behind Jake's efforts to fight crime through the newspapers. "Once when he was working on a hot story, somebody called and said, 'We're gonna kill him'," she remembered. "I said, 'Don't be ridiculous,' and hung up." Tonight, as the two of them talked back and forth, the name of the late gangster Mickey Cohen came up. He ran the mob after Bugsy Siegel's death.

"Jake, don't you dare say we were friends with Mickey Cohen," Audrey admonished.

"But I was. I was his friend. I was his ghostwriter. Back at the *Herald*, you know very well that I wrote stories that appeared under his byline. He was a decent guy. He came to our picnic one year."

"He was nothing but a common crook," Audrey retorted.

"No, not a bad guy. Although every time I was with him, I noticed that he had a habit of constantly washing his hands."

"That's because there was so much blood on them," she shot back.

Jake laughed. Then Audrey laughed. Then they began finishing up some paperwork, as the office would soon be closing. Shortly, the Jacobys would make their way home to the suburbs, where on Saturday and Sunday they would enjoy the peace and quiet. But come Monday morning at 4:40, Jake would awaken to the sound of a radio alarm, dress quietly, down a glass of orange juice and a bowl of bran, and climb into his 1973 Chrysler Newport. He would drive south on the Glendale Freeway, merge onto the Golden State, and proceed downtown. Fifteen minute after stepping out of his front door, he would park in the lot below Parker Center. By the time he walked into the pressroom, the phones would be screaming, and once again he would begin the ceaseless job of sweeping back the waves.

CREATORS

As for creating, Robert Penn Warren told me something that became a credo: "It may be said that our lives are our supreme fiction." He meant that each of us traffics in self-invention. This is not, of course, just the province of men, but it is a through line in the lives of those who interest me.

Robert Penn Warren Finds His Place to Come To

The Atlanta Journal & Constitution Magazine, September 16, 1979

It was getting into the heart of the Vermont summer, and the air was still and heavy. Resting in a wicker chair on his front porch, Robert Penn Warren, sweat dripping from his sharp, freckled nose like a rivulet running off red rock, gazed into the hazy glimmer of late day. "I think a man just dies," he said after a while. His voice was harsh and sibilant. "No heaven. No hell." Tugging a checkered bandana from a rear pocket of his baggy Levis, he wiped the perspiration from his face. "I'm a naturalist," he added haltingly. "I don't believe in God. But I want to find meaning in life. I refuse to believe it's merely a dreary sequence of events. So I write stories and poetry. My work is my testimony." Warren's tone had dropped into a low, croupy register. Limned briefly by the last beams of the sunset, he resembled a statue carved long ago from a hunk of sandstone. He reached for a drink, smiled, then said, "I can't believe I'm talking like this. I can't tell someone why I write. And I'm sure as hell not going to attempt self-psychoanalysis. But let me tell you a story..."

The rhythm of Robert Penn Warren's life now is settled but not sedate. He rises early, fixes his own breakfast, exercises with a set of barbells kept on the living-room floor then dons trunks and a plastic cap and makes the short walk to a bower-hidden swimming hole behind his summer home. He swims nearly a mile in the chilly water, sculling along at a steady, rigorous pace. The clay-bottomed pool is surrounded by ferns and high trees, and in the morning—as thin, miasmic bars of sunlight filter down, dappling the water in tones of emerald and gold—it is Edenic. Here, his body aching slightly from the exertion and his mind free from worries, Warren slips into a creative trance. This is the hour when the images bloom. The swims are never draining, are in fact less taxing than running, the exercise he used to stimulate himself when he was younger. As Warren strokes back and forth through the glittering pond, a poem usually flowers. The past decade has been remarkably fertile. He has revised *Brother to Dragons*, his epic-length verse drama about Thomas Jefferson's murderous nephews, and he has written two novels. In 1980, he will publish his fourth collection of poetry since 1966—his most recent, *Now and Then*, won the 1979 Pulitzer Prize. It was his third. The second came in 1958 for his book of poems, *Promises*. The first came in 1947 for *All the King's Men*, a work of fiction many critics contend is among the finest of the twentieth century.

His swim over, Warren retreats to an outhouse-sized wooden shack poised on the steep banks of Bald Mountain Brook, a rocky creek that meanders behind his home. The structure gives onto a vista of elders and maples punctuated by an occasional white birch. The windows are covered with chicken wire, and even on a hot day cool breezes drift in from the mountains.

Inside, sheets of copy paper are stacked sloppily atop a tiny, rough-hewn desk. Leather briefcases are underfoot. A gray, Hermes typewriter rests on a rickety stand. When Warren is writing fiction or an essay, he sits in a Formica chair behind the machine and pecks out words in a rackety, pensive staccato. But if the morning swim has been fruitful, he plops onto a tattered green-and-orange striped canvas beach chair and jots down bits of a poem in a cramped, barely legible scribble. Warren is a diligent worker. On most days, he spends at least five hours in the tiny room that he and his wife, novelist Eleanor Clark, call "The Coop." Deep in thought, his thinning red hair plastered across his skull and his face flushed from exertion, he looks like an aged fighting cock. He is seventy-four.

Around two in the afternoon, Warren and his wife eat lunch. Her work shack is on the opposite side of the house, an architectural hybrid of a rustic mountain cabin and the jutting, glass geometries of a 1950s vacation retreat. She is first to call it a day, and after stirring around the kitchen, hurriedly dumping bowls of leftover peas and carrots and chunks of beef or chicken into a simmering pot of impromptu stew, she walks to a back window, cups her hands and shouts, "Red, let's eat." If his writing is going well, she has to call several times before he finally emerges, scowling, to tramp up to meet her. Once he has made his way inside, his demeanor softens. Together, he and his wife set the table, feed the dogs—Sophie, a playful mutt, and Frodo a blind, thirteen-year-old pure-bred cocker spaniel—and pour each other drinks. During lunch, the two usually talk about their children. Rosanna, twenty-six, teaches art history and writes poetry. Gabriel, twenty-three, is a sculptor and boat builder. The Warrens remain young in the way parents still raising a family must. Occasionally they gossip about literature and world affairs, but they rarely talk about each other's work.

In mid-afternoon, Warren wanders downstairs from the dining alcove and takes a brief nap. The first floor of the house consists of three bedrooms fronting a central hallway. Standing in his son's room several years ago, his mind drifting aimlessly, the opening sentence of his most recent novel, *A Place to Come To*, "simply popped" into his head. Such unexpected conjuring is not unusual for Warren. More than once when he has been stuck in the middle of a book, he has dreamed whole passages of the story then written them down the next day. Awakening from his nap, Warren reads a new novel or works of Southern and American history. Sometimes he drives into the woods to visit acquaintances like Mr. Newell, a sparrow-thin maple syrup distiller who owns a large sugar bush hidden behind rock walls. Once a week, Warren hikes several miles up a long, sloping grade to a glacial lake where he often spends an hour staring into the Green Mountains. The Vermont forests—lush and quiet—replenish him. He emerges with many of the ideas and images that later well up in his poetry, poetry that brims with the pulsations of the natural world. A couple of years ago, in early fall, he observed wild geese beating south through a gap near the lake. Watching them, he questioned the paths he had followed, the decisions he had made. At least these birds, he wrote in "Heart of Autumn," respond to the tick of a cosmic clock. But why, he asked himself, had he lived the way he'd lived?

At dusk, Warren, his wife, their children, and any visiting friends rendezvous on a screened porch for cocktails. Warren drinks Campari and orange juice and snacks on radishes grown in the family garden. Occasionally, strains of Louis Armstrong waft into the gloaming from a stereo in the living room. These pre-meal gatherings are almost always rollicking sessions of tale swapping. "You see," Warren says, "when I first started thinking about writing novels back in the 1930s, people I knew would sit around all night at parties just spinning tales. The South was a terribly rich country then. Rich tale country. Ironically, what made it so is that it was otherwise a horribly impoverished nation. Tale-telling was entertainment. What distinguishes every writer from the South is that they've got a goddamned honed tale sense. One of the reasons Eleanor and I don't have a television, have never had one, is that we don't want to lose that."

Throughout dinner, usually a simple but hearty feast of baked chicken or roast beef served with good wine followed by tossed salad, the stories continue. Afterward, the forest buzzing in the peaceful night, Warren retires. Sometimes, around four or five in the morning, he awakens briefly, snatching and recording what he can of his dreams. Then he sleeps again.

Robert Penn Warren is an anomaly among American writers. The archetypal American novelist is plagued by angst, alcoholism, poverty, and public indifference to his work. Worse, too many American writers are notoriously unproductive; after one largely autobiographical book, they have little left to say. Unlike their European counterparts, who develop slowly but sturdily, American writers explode after etching fiery, transient paths in the sky. Warren's slightly older peers—F. Scott Fitzgerald, Thomas Wolfe, Ernest Hemingway—all died tragically. The myth of the American writer is that the work destroys the man, but Warren, the man, has endured. He has produced ten novels—efforts that are at once serious and humorous—fourteen collections of poetry, several critical studies, many textbooks, and a compendium of short stories. In 1930, he contributed an essay to *I'll Take My Stand,* an influential collection about his native South.

During the Depression, Warren co-founded *The Southern Review,* one of the nation's best literary journals. In the early 1960s, he wrote two studies of race relations in America that largely recanted the stubbornly recalcitrant opinions he held as a young man. He is one of the country's few Men of Letters, an appellation that usually implies a priggish separation from the immediacy of life in both a writer's work and daily existence. Yet Warren defies that stereotype, too. He is successful, happy, critically acclaimed, occasionally querulous, but largely humble, optimistic, curious, and, in his words, "consumed by the thought of the poem I can write tomorrow."

One late July afternoon, Warren tramped along a new-cut dirt road high in the Vermont hills. He alternately cussed investors who want to use the road to attract vacation housing developments and then, the anger passing, told stories. He wore an old blue knit shirt, drooping jeans turned up at the cuffs, white socks, and hiking boots. He could have easily passed for a cocklebur raconteur back in his hometown of Guthrie, Kentucky. As his voice rasped into the quiet, time and miles slipped by.

"Let me tell you about Uncle Turner," he exclaimed at one point. "He was the uncle of my old Mississippi friends Bill and Cannon Clark, and he was known for miles around because he couldn't tell the truth. He would exaggerate even the simplest of stories. He was one of the greatest orators of his time and place." Warren's laughter pealed out. "Uncle Turner specialized in funeral and Fourth of July orations. He could talk way down deep. And he could say things like, 'He was one of the greatest men in our county. His

Christian virtue shone as an example for us all.' Which sounded good when the kinfolks were laying a sinful old geezer in the ground. It was a lie, of course, but that's why Uncle Turner was so well loved." Poking a scarred cane before him, a battered straw hat pulled low over his brow, Warren pushed ahead at a brisk pace. "Once Uncle Turner was called upon to dedicate a new dam in Tupelo," he added. "He was standing at the podium and all these pompous officials were standing up there with him and he commenced with something like, 'Ladies and gentlemen, we have come to christen this great body of water.' And you know, he was rolling his arms out in great gestures and then he bellowed, 'This lake will be fifty miles long.' And he just stopped there. He had looked over at his wife, and she'd been shaking her head in frantic desperation. Well, he thought a moment and then thundered, 'And it will be two inches wide.' God, can you imagine it? It's a true story. Really is." His eyes watered as he choked down laughter.

Warren has an infectious, ironic sense of humor, and it permeates his work and his conversations. His almost every tale is intended to suggest that man is ultimately a folly-filled creature. During the climb up to the glacial lake and back, the stories spooled out one after another. Warren declaimed on a "horrible poet" of the 1800s who advised young men not to go west because "the West is full of debt dodgers, drunkards, fornicators, adulterers, incest-mongers and you shouldn't join them;" a talented Tennessee newspaper writer "ruined by too much Catholicism and too much Jung" who should have stuck to liquor "because it sure as hell doesn't ruin you half as fast as the others;" and an old friend, a professional baseball player "who sure God drank himself" out of the majors. "It was a good thing," he said. "Pitching was cutting into his hunting time back home." After stopping to spit, he recalled how novelist William Faulkner wrote Albert Erskine, who edited both writers at Random House, that *All the King's Men* should not have glorified "that two-bit, low-brow, redneck fascist Huey Long." A look of amazement lit Warren's face as he remembered the letter. Then he said, "Damn Faulkner must have been drunk when he wrote that thing. It was so incoherent you wouldn't believe it." Making perfunctory stabs with his cane at leaves and rocks, Warren spun out yarn after yarn. It was as if his mind were a Big Top of memories and he a ringmaster calling the past's players to life. Once one act ended, he ordered the troupers down the rampway of time and summoned new ones.

"I can remember my first day as a student at Vanderbilt," Warren said trudging toward home. "I was scared, immature, and totally incompetent to do just about anything. I was a terribly young boy, even younger than my age, which was just sixteen. I was sitting all alone on the steps of one of the buildings there when this massive hand fell across my shoulder with the force of a tumbling chimney. I turned around, saw a grinning, malicious, oafish face and out of that wet mouth came the words: 'Boy, there's only one thing I want to know. Do you ever have evil thoughts?'" Warren parted his lips, flashed his teeth, and brayed. "The only thing I can be thankful for," he added, "is that he didn't give me any time to answer. He introduced himself, said he was secretary of the YMCA and that he wanted to talk with me about Christ. Said that he'd once partaken of whores, liquor, and cussing— which didn't sound bad to me—but that since he'd been saved he'd stopped." Warren bunched his cheeks up incredulously. "What's worse, this fellow had taken to turning in bootleggers because he said Christ told him to. God! That was one tough bugger for Jesus. I remember walking by the track one afternoon. He was a track man. He was winding up to throw the discus. He let it fly and then shouted out: 'Hey, Red Warren, you're some sort of poet, aren't you? Well, boy, that there was poetry in motion.'"

Robert Penn Warren was one of those boys who come out of the Southern hill country with a shock of curly red hair, a freckled face, and hazel eyes. His friends nicknamed him "Red." Early on, his pioneer forebears had migrated from Virginia into North Carolina; by the time of the War of 1812, they had moved into the undulating hill country of that part of Kentucky about fifty miles north of Nashville, Tennessee. They were modestly prosperous people, and Warren's father, aside from having interests in land and a small store, was a banker in the village of Guthrie, a tiny place bisected by the Tennessee-Kentucky line. As a youngster, Warren saw little of his dad— the elder Warren was constantly at his office—and until he was fourteen, the dominant figure in his life was his maternal grandfather, Gabriel Thomas Penn.

Almost from the time he could walk, Warren spent his afternoons with the old man. Grandpa Penn would sit beneath a tree with the boy on his knees and reel off ceaseless stories about the Civil War. The grape shot flew. Sabers rang. Horses, frothing and blood-streaked, carried their Confederate charges into the din of conflict. Fantasies and fascinations of war whirled through Red's mind like the fragments of glass in a kaleidoscope. Before he could read, he knew the power of a story.

While often absent, Warren's father also played a part. If it is true that the secret ambitions of a parent—longings often stunted by adult responsibilities—reappear as doubly strong yearnings in a child, the phenomenon applies especially here. On more than a few evenings during his boyhood, Warren's dad would convene an old-fashioned family reading circle in the living room. The Warrens read poetry and histories of Greece and Rome aloud. "My father was a frustrated poet," Warren remembered. "I'll never forget the time, when I was twelve, when I was foraging through some bookshelves at home. I found this black book stuck way back among the others. I pulled it out, held it open, and I saw his name." Warren's voice cracked with the memory. "I was completely disoriented by the discovery. It was an anthology called *The Poets of America*, and here were the works of my father included in it. That night, when he came home from the bank, I very unsubtly showed it to him. And he said calmly, coldly, 'Give me that book.' We never talked about it again. I think he was ashamed of the poems. He destroyed the book."

There were other early flirtations with literature, but only in the long perspective of time did Warren realize that forces were moving to shape him as a writer before he was conscious of them. He remembers stumbling across a pile of books in his paternal grandfather's attic one afternoon and being fascinated by an illustrated copy of the works of the Italian poet Dante. "I remember that when I found that illustrated Dante I thought how strange, how wonderful that my grandfather had this book," he recalled. "What is very peculiar, though, is this. Much later, years later, I was poring over crumbling papers at the Harvard library while I was working on a critical study of Herman Melville's poetry for an edition of his poems I was doing." Warren's voice quivered excitedly. "I was sifting through these papers when I found a letter to Melville from a literary society in Clarksville, Tennessee, a small town only a few miles from Guthrie. Well, this letter begged Melville to come to my part of the world, this out-of-the-way country to deliver a lecture. They said no price would be too dear for them. They were reading everything he wrote. The document was signed by people from families that were friends of my grandfather. I wonder if he was involved. He must have been."

For all the literary intimations that hovered around the periphery of Warren's boyhood, he took no active interest in writing, pining instead for the life of an outdoorsman or an adventurer on the high seas. During summer mornings, he searched in the woods for butterflies, arrowheads, rocks, and leaves. His hobby was taxidermy, and his love was baseball. Occasionally, he read from the works of Charles Dickens and James Fenimore Cooper—never, however, with a yen to make up his own stories. After graduating from high school, Warren sought a commission from the Naval Academy; more than anything, he yearned to be an admiral of the Pacific fleet. One summer night shortly before he was to leave for Annapolis, he was lying on his back behind a hedge looking at the stars. Standing on the other side of the bushes, his younger brother was playfully tossing rocks into the air. He didn't know Red was resting on the far side, and when he lobbed a large, sharp stone over the hedge it smashed into his brother's left eye. The damage was severe enough that Warren lost most of his vision in that eye, and he abandoned his hope of attending the Naval Academy. Primarily because he and his father had attended numerous football games at Vanderbilt University in Nashville, Warren decided at the last minute to enroll at the small liberal arts school and major in chemistry.

The pivotal moment for Warren at Vanderbilt came early when he was assigned to a freshman English class taught by poet John Crowe Ransom. By the end of the term, his compositions had caught Ransom's eye, and the instructor invited him to enter an advanced English survey course. Warren had quickly grown bored with his science studies and had been covertly reading Ransom's poetry. "His poems set me afire," Warren remembered. "What I saw in his work was someone making poetry out of my world, the world of the woods and the country." Ransom's tutelage proved to be catalytic, as was that of another poet on the faculty, Donald Davidson. Davidson believed that composing clever facsimiles of the classics taught a student more about literature than writing critical essays. For an entire semester, Warren mimicked the styles of every English writer from Chaucer to Thomas Hardy. Under the two men's influence, he began writing poetry.

During the 1920s, Nashville, an otherwise insular city, was the vortex for one of the most influential groups of poets and thinkers ever to gather in America. Shortly before the start of World War I, several Vanderbilt teachers, including Ransom and Davidson, as well as downtown businessmen interested in poetry, formed a literary group called the Fugitives. Its credo: "The Fugitive flees from nothing faster than the high-caste Brahmins of the old South."

Artistically radical, the Fugitives scorned the ancestor-worshipping literature of post-Reconstruction Dixie. Not long after Warren began writing poems, the society's magazine published a couple of them. At eighteen, he was made its youngest member. "They treated me like an equal," he recalled. "Except, I said a lot of foolish things and they told me so." The group met every week, and each session was conducted in a personally friendly but critically cutthroat manner. Warren's poems had to be excellent to earn an accolade from this bunch. "They could be derisive as hell," he said. "But more than anything, that process of close analysis taught me how to write." The group spawned the so-called Southern Literary Renaissance, a movement that ultimately included writers as disparate as Allen Tate and James Dickey. "I've never heard of any other thing like it in America," Warren declared. "We were absolutely wild for poetry." Warren, especially, was consumed by a passion for literature. He memorized T.S. Eliot's "The Wasteland" and decorated his boarding room walls with paintings depicting scenes from the poem. By the time he graduated, he had begun publishing verse in *The Nation* and *The New Republic*.

After leaving Nashville, Warren attended graduate school at the University of California Berkeley and Yale before leaving for England in 1928 on a Rhodes scholarship. During these years, he lived entirely from fellowship money; the occasional $10 he received for a poem or a review was used to purchase a good bottle of whisky. It was shortly before he left for Britain that Warren began to consider writing fiction. He had scorned novels as "vile, dreadful stuff written by hacks" until he met the established author Ford Madox Ford and the rising young short story writer Katherine Anne Porter. They gradually convinced Warren that the novel was a legitimate literary form. But it was not until Warren arrived at Oxford, where he was lonely and homesick, that he decided to write a story in the hope that the project would help him cling to his pleasant memories of the South. Laboring on his fiction at night, he produced a novella called *Prime Leaf,* a story of tobacco warfare in Kentucky. The piece was a harbinger of Warren's later novels, works almost always tied directly to historical events, and it riveted him to the idea of becoming a novelist. After returning from England, he cancelled a fellowship at Yale ("I didn't have time to write a damn doctoral thesis") and began searching for a teaching position to support him while he wrote.

Shortly before taking his first job at a Memphis college, Warren made his contribution to *I'll Take My Stand,* the volume of essays about the South. The book champions agrarianism as a way of life. Warren's passions had been chiefly aesthetic until his involvement with the project, but during his correspondences and conversations with a group of Nashville friends who edited it, he began to outline many of the philosophical tenets that would sustain him for most of his days. In numerous ways *I'll Take My Stand* is obtusely unenlightened. Yet in spite of the work's unreconstructed point of view, some of the essays espouse a bold and intoxicating romanticism. The Agrarians embraced a Jeffersonian belief in the salubriousness of life on the land; they insisted on the nobility of the individual; they were skeptical of technology. Warren's piece was called "The Briar Patch." Liberal for an era in which most Southern whites believed blacks should be denied any schooling, it now seems racist in its plea for separate but equal education. Warren admitted that his views on race had been "unfortunate," but he bristled when defending the general thrust of the book, especially its views on industrialization.

"I'd been very much struck by something that Henry Adams, the historian, said about the test of modern man being how he would deal with the machine. He said the machine would end up riding the man instead of the other way around. I feared that then, and I still do. I think we were really pretty perceptive to attack rampant technology so early."

On a balmy summer night, his elbows propped on the dinner table, Warren was fulminating on the decadence and decline of the Western world. In between bites of green beans and chicken and glasses of Spanish wine, he excoriated oil company executives, fumbling energy department bureaucrats, and soft-headed jurists. It had been a long, sumptuous meal that Warren's wife had begun preparing early in the afternoon. Three years ago, Eleanor Clark was partially blinded by macular degeneration. At first, the condition seemed hopeless and was emotionally devastating. Clark had written several books and in 1965 had won the National Book Award for her non-fiction account of the men and women who work in the French oyster industry, *The Oysters of Locmariaquer.* Her vision stabilized about six months after she was stricken, allowing her to perceive dim, impressionistic glimpses of the world and return to her writing. Composing sentences by drawing giant Magic Marker letters on blank sheets of newsprint then transcribing these jottings with a large-type typewriter while peering through a lighted magnifying glass, she wrote a book about the fight to regain control of her life.

Eyes Etc.: A Memoir details how Clark meticulously arranges every pot, pan, and scrap of food in her kitchen to foster a reliance on memory, not sight, when she is cooking. Her meals are triumphs of culinary determination, but she solicits no sympathy and in fact discourages pampering. She is a strikingly handsome, green-eyed Connecticut Yankee with high, bold cheekbones and a thick mane of straw blond hair. Her literary and political roots extend deep into the New York of the 1930s—a world populated by Communists and revolutionaries. She was a Trotskyite, although she labored harder on essays for publications like *The Partisan Review* than on implementing social reforms in America. Her marriage to Warren is one of sweet collaboration wed to a propensity for ceaseless oratorical battle. They disagree on politics, people, literature, psychology, and economics. She is the liberal Eastern aristocrat. He is the clodhopper scholar with dung on his boots and poetry in his heart. For twenty-seven years they have had a sturdy, loving marriage. During the months when she was certain she would lose her vision, he read aloud to her almost every night from the works of the blind poet, Homer.

"Pass me the chicken, please," Clark said as Warren concluded his harangue on the vapidity of the political functionaries trying to deal with the energy crisis.

"Yes, darling, here it is." He handed her the platter. The Warrens, daughter Rosanna, and a woman friend sat around a large table in the upper portion of the house. This expansive living area is decorated with an old upright piano, two huge Jack Daniels decanters, a bas-relief map of southern Vermont constructed by son Gabriel, and many pieces of well-worn, comfortable furniture. On one coffee table was an issue of *The Atlantic Monthly* containing a poem by Rosanna. On another was a copy of an academic journal featuring one of her father's poems.

"Thanks, Red," his wife said, taking a chicken breast from the plate.

"You all know they closed the gas station in Jamaica last week," Warren groused. The village of Jamaica, a tiny gathering of proper white New England churches and lodges, is about ten miles down Bald Mountain Brook valley from the Warrens' house.

"We're just going to have to learn to live without cars," Rosanna said. "I'm terribly worried about the mental health of the American people. They're addicted to driving."

"I'm worried about that, too," Clark said.

"Well, I'm worried about their moral health," Warren countered. He smiled. "I've been saying this for a long time, but I think the whole guts have gone out of the American state of mind. Americans now want it done for them. You can trace a lot of this back to that business of the New Deal. Now, I'm a New Dealer. But I don't think you have to make it so easy. One time that old witch lady of the Roosevelt family told me all about it. What is her name?"

"Eleanor Roosevelt," Clark offered, her voice rising slightly.

"No. Damn it. She was a witch, but she didn't have any brains. I mean the bright one. Oh, you know—the one who lives in Washington."

"Who are you talking about, Red?"

"Oh, the famous old witch. Alice Longworth. Yeah. I met her once. The only time I ever saw her, we spent an afternoon together talking about the Roosevelt administration. And she said that the one thing you have to remember about FDR, the one thing that everyone else overlooks, was that he was a cripple in a wheelchair and that he wanted to make all Americans the same way. He wanted everybody to have someone to push them around."

Taking a drink of wine, Warren smiled like a fox. Rosanna and Clark clucked audibly.

"Oh, come on, Red," Clark said. "I can't believe you're saying this."

"Now, just a minute darling," Warren pleaded. "She is a wicked old lady, but she is sharp as hell. As sharp as hell."

"No. No. No. No." Clark's voice exploded each time she said the word.

"Darling, I'm not saying this," Warren begged. "She said it."

"I'm really ashamed of you, Red. To quote this sympathetically is preposterous."

"Well, I'm quoting it humorously, darling. Can't you see?"

"Oh, come on. It's not funny at all."

"It's not only funny, it's half true."

"Stop." Her eyes fixed him.

"I think it's obvious that most Americans are now patients."

"That's ridiculous."

"There's something very profound in the notion, darling."

"I think we'd better stop this right now," Clark said, pounding a glass down firmly on the tabletop. "Stop it before I really get hot."

"Now, what are your politics, darling?" Warren asked, slipping in the dagger. His voice cracked mischievously. "I've forgotten what party you belonged to."

"Oh, Jesus, honey. Will you lay off? You're so obstreperous."

"Well, I'm sure everything I say will be discarded." His tone was at once plaintive and mocking. He smiled. Abruptly, Frodo began barking and howling wildly from beneath the table.

"Yes, Frodo, I agree with you," Clark said, commiserating with the animal and rubbing its head. "Having to listen to him go on like that."

Warren smiled grandly. "That Alice Longworth is a spunky damn dame."

"Red." Her voice buzzed.

Placing a hand on her father's shoulder, Rosanna attempted to placate them both. "You two remind me of those Romanesque carvings in which you've got a little stone soul being torn apart by a devil and an angel." The Warrens laughed, and Rosanna passed the bottle of wine to her father as an appeasement.

"Well, to say the least, the mental health of America is pretty bad," said Clark, her expression calming as she negotiated a return to the original topic of conversation. "There's so much real craziness today. Bizarre murders. You know, in the past, a story like Jack the Ripper became folklore. And Bluebeard became legend. What was his real name?"

"Gilles de Rais," Warren said.

"Thanks. But, ah, these things were so extraordinary when they happened back then. But now it's so commonplace in America that we're inured to it. Son of Sam. The Texas Tower murders. What's really awful is that atrocities happen so often that we accept them as commonplace."

"Yeah," Warren concurred. "You just shrug your shoulders and ask, 'What's the next piece of news?'" Shoving a forkful of salad into his mouth, he chewed pensively then added, "Our civilization is spewing out more and more of its ordure as it goes along. It's a great big machine, and it spews it out, and it's human waste."

In 1939, standing on the northern tip of Capri and looking out to sea toward Europe, Robert Penn Warren was feverish with the knowledge that the world would soon be at war. The Mediterranean island was fertile ground on which to consider a conflict that might destroy civilization. It had already been the site of barbarous decadence. Here, Tiberius, the brooding, vile-tempered Roman emperor, had staged the wild sexual dramas that preceded the decline of his empire. Gazing over the water, thinking of the coming conflagration, Warren felt helpless. Finally, he tossed a stone into the dark brine; it was all he could do. Years later, he wrote a poem about that night. While the range of Warren's poetry is broad both in style and subject, "Tiberius on Capri" is emblematic. His poems almost always deal with history or nature and man's place in them; they almost always incorporate a bloody incident and tie it to a metaphysical rumination. While "Tiberius on Capri" has no story line (many of Warren's longer poems read like fiction; he in fact abandoned short-story-writing because the impulse conflicted with the composition of poetry), it is richly descriptive and binds the grim past of the island and the looming destruction of World War II to a philosophical consideration: What is a man to do in the face of a world in which he is helpless to change things? As Warren has grown as a poet, this confluence of guts and ideas in his work has occurred more and more.

During the past quarter-century, Warren has written a phenomenal amount of poetry, receiving more critical acclaim for his poems than for his novels. Recently he has concentrated most of his efforts on poetry because he feels he might not have enough time left to produce another novel. "My poetry allows me to live so intensely," he said. "It's an immediate transaction with the world around me." Warren's verse pullulates with striking images that can wrench a reader to attention and wonderment, and his best poems stew with sensuality. About dancing with a young woman he wrote:

> Flesh, of a sudden, gone nameless in music, flesh
> Of the dancer, under your hand, flowing to music, girl—
> Flesh sliding, flesh flowing, sweeter than
> Honey, slicker than Essolube, over
> The music-swayed delicate trellis of bone
> That is white in secret flesh darkness.

Yet as evocative as Warren's descriptive touch can be, he is at his weakest when trying to draw conclusions from the rich images. He slips occasionally into didacticism. This tendency toward heavy-handedness springs from his instincts as a novelist. Warren has pared much of the rhetoric from his poetry during the past twenty years, gaining, as a reward, an utter command of a hard, fecund Southern verse style. But there has been a cost. As he has stripped away this tendency in his versification, he has also pruned it from his novels, weakening his fiction. Reviewers have responded harshly to such recent novels as *Flood, Meet Me in the Green Glen*, and Warren's 1977 book, *A Place to Come To*. While the latter novel strongly recalls the dazzling prose that makes *All the King's Men* explode with stylistic pyrotechnics, it is spotty, depending on an intellectual framework, where *All the King's Men* is both cerebral and visceral. Still, as even one of the new novel's harshest critics allowed: "His many admirers will find isolated passages and striking images scattered through the book that are the equal of anybody now writing in English."

A Place to Come To chronicles the life of a displaced Southerner driven from his home by his mother's hatred for the mean, ignorant, hookworm-ridden Yahoos of his native Alabama. The book could be interpreted as autobiographical. Since leaving a teaching position at Louisiana State in the 1930s, Warren has returned to the South only for short visits. But he contends that there is no trace of himself in the novel's narrator, Jed Tewksbury. "He hated the South," Warren said. "I love it. My house in the North is really just a big hotel to me. A place I stay. The South will always be my home." Warren says he was forced from the region by economic necessity. "Shortly after I came back to the South," he recalled, "I began teaching at Vanderbilt. I could have gone to California, but I didn't want to. But after three years in Nashville, they let me go. I couldn't get along with the department head." After leaving Vanderbilt, Warren taught at LSU.

"I loved Baton Rouge," he said. "I had a nice place to live there, and I loved New Orleans. I used to go to a bar there where the bartender would set a bottle in front of me on the table and say, 'Pour 'til you're satisfied.' It was fifteen cents a drink. And they let me keep count of the tab. God that was living. You couldn't find that in the North. But LSU wouldn't give me a $200 raise when I thought I deserved it. So I went to Minnesota to teach."

In the years that followed, Warren often considered returning home. Shortly after he married Eleanor Clark, she suggested that they buy a farm in Tennessee so their children could learn about the South. "I went back," Warren said, "and looked around, but it just wasn't the same anymore. I couldn't find anyone to talk to. Before, I could talk for hours with any dirt farmer sitting on a split rail fence. But the rural South, my South, is vanishing. Because it was such an impoverished place, it was particularly vulnerable to having the TV culture superimposed right on top of it. It's not my South anymore."

It has been more than forty years since Warren lived in the land of cotton, but the region still influences much of his poetry and all of his fiction. The power of Warren's novels, however, has diminished in the decades since he left. It was his sure knowledge of Southern manners, his intimate acquaintance with the subtle nuances of life in Tennessee and Louisiana that fed his best works. *All the King's Men*—the book that would have assured his place in literature had he never written another—is vivified by his knowledge of the region. During Warren's last years in Louisiana, he witnessed the ascension of Huey Long to power. Long's influence at LSU was enormous. The ROTC was his personal army; the football team was his band of gladiators; students with politically powerful parents easily found academic success. While teaching English at Baton Rouge, Warren was caught in the prickly thicket of turmoil spawned by Long. "But the thing you have to remember," Warren said, "is that before Long, Louisiana was a worthless state. No government. No literacy. No hospitalization. No free roads. No schools. No nothing. It was rotten. Huey Long's genius was that he saw this vacuum. Long got me thinking about doing the novel, but I wasn't really interested in him. I was interested in the whole question of power in our age. The Mussolinis and Hitlers. The question of means and ends. I didn't do five minutes of research on Long. I didn't really give a damn about him. I was reading Shakespeare's *Julius Caesar*, William James's works on pragmatism, and Machiavelli. I was interested in how power corrupts absolutely. I saw that at LSU, and that gave the book a setting. But it was about Long in only superficial ways."

The idea to write *All the King's Men* came to Warren one humid afternoon as he sat on the front porch of a cottage rented by his future editor Albert Erskine, at the time a LSU graduate student. Rocking idly on the porch that day, Warren told Erskine he was going to write a play about the recently assassinated Long. He did not yet have a plot for the work, but he envisioned a verse drama with choruses of doctors, policemen, and politicians. The central theme: What good can be made from evil? Warren actually began writing the play in 1938 while sitting beneath an olive tree in the wheat field and vineyard country of Italy's Umbria region. When he finished it, he put it away. He sensed something was horribly wrong with its construction.

Nearly three years later, during his tenure at the University of Minnesota, Warren removed the manuscript from a storage bin and reread it. "I remember distinctly the room where I was then living. I remember the desk. I had an apartment on Lake of the Isles. I almost remember the smells of that day. Strange. Anyway, I read the play again and was utterly dissatisfied with it. It was bad. The characters were all stunted." After pondering the work for several hours, Warren began to be fascinated by an unnamed newspaper reporter who appeared in its last act for staging purposes. Warren thought: Why not make him the narrator of a novel based on the play? Warren named the character Jack Burden and almost by accident created one of the most distinctive narrative voices in American fiction. In Burden, Warren not only had a perfect storyteller—a sardonic, cynical journalist—but a character whose deep emotional problems helped save the novel from becoming a political potboiler. In Burden, Warren embodied many of his theories about history and psychology. "Jack gave me someone I could toy with," Warren recalled. "I could play with some of my notions about America with him—about the meaning of the West, for instance. At one point, Jack runs away from it all in Louisiana—his girl and the Boss, Willie Stark, and the whole mess. He can't stand it anymore. He goes to L.A. Now that's just like an American. We go west to find the new Eden. We've been doing it ever since we came to this country. If you go west, the sheriff back home can't catch up with you. But once you get out there, you find out you're mortal. That's the paradox of America. It's the land of redemption, but it's also a land in which human nature can't be redeemed."

Late one afternoon, as occasional gusts of wind blew out of the mountains bringing slight respite from the heat, Warren sat on his front porch facing a visitor. The room was aglow in the roseate hues of fading day. Ensconced in a comfortable rocking chair, his eagle-beaked, strong-boned, ruddy old face twisted into a frown, he answered the visitor's questions. Except for their voices, there was no sound.

"I'd be interested to know if you're sad now that you're old. Do you have regrets?"

"Ah not really...I have my family and my work. But I don't have many friends left. Most of them are dead." With that, he wavered. "Katherine Anne Porter was a close friend of mine. What a beautiful woman she was—is. There was never anything between us, romantically, but she was very dear to me." His voice cracked. "I went to see her not too long ago in a nursing home. She's dying now. On her deathbed. She's eighty-six years old. Several strokes. It's very painful. If only she could be herself again. Old actresses can turn on the beauty, you know...One minute they have it and...well..."

"I know your life has been a success, but how have you endured the hard times?"

"Life isn't an escalator," he said gruffly. "But nothing horrible has happened. This sounds like a boast, but I'm obsessed, have been and am, with trying to make sense out of things by writing about them, because I regard writing as basically a means of self-knowledge and self-control. It's a way of investigating my own nature. As long as I can write, I'll be all right."

"Now that you're older, are the things you want out of life different?"

111

"Some of the things are obvious, I guess… I'm of a religious temperament, you see, but without religious conviction. I take Christianity as a myth. What it says about the depths of human nature is largely true. But it's not true in the sense of the sacrament being the transubstantiation of the real presence. That's the argument between Catholics and Protestants, but I don't even think it's relevant. What I do think is relevant, and what I want to try to emulate now, is the example of Jesus. But any moral human being wants that. I want to give myself in sacrifice of some sort. To participate in the common body of human life… My poetry lets me do that, but it sounds so trite to say."

"What do you care most about now?"

"The things I prize most about my life are having a happy marriage and having children I take great delight in. They aren't servile. They're goddamn independent. But they love us. And in this life of desperate uncertainties, that's compensation."

"There are other compensations, other rewards, aren't there?"

"Ah, I don't know. I'll just read one sentence from this book." He leaned over and picked up the manuscript of his forthcoming poetry collection, *Life Is a Fable*. After putting on a pair of half-rim glasses, he began: "This is an autobiography which represents a fusion of fiction and fact from varying degrees of perspective." Then he went on. "As a question and answer, fiction may often be more deeply significant than fact. Indeed, it may be said that our lives are our supreme fiction."

The place that Robert Penn Warren has come to in his life is nearly idyllic. There have, of course, been dark times, grim periods when he was haunted by demons. Shortly after he injured his eye as a young man, he feared that he would go blind and drank destructively, rushing off to hidden nooks where he could be alone with his trepidations. His first marriage ended in a painful divorce. During the last years of the entanglement, he could not write at all. For a decade, his life was littered with sheets of aborted verse, works that miscarried for reasons he still doesn't understand. In 1971, he feared that he might be suffering from cancer. He lost weight, energy, and sleep. But a liver biopsy came back clean; later, a doctor would discover that he had been poisoned by a prescription for a minor ailment—athlete's foot. Throughout his life, he has been consumed by feverish contemplations of evil, sin, and the at once bestial and angelic nature of America. Yet his days have breezed ahead pleasantly, determinedly.

In *All the King's Men*, Warren describes the protagonist, Willie Stark, as a man born outside of luck, good or bad. He can spend his life discovering who he really is. Unlike most, he is not prey to fate. Warren, of course, has not lived unaffected by luck. In fact, fortune—in the form of a jagged stone arching over a summer lawn in a small Kentucky town—turned his hand to writing. His hopes of a naval career shattered, he decided to become a poet and spent most of his energy pursuing his ambition. He grew into maturity at a time when it was difficult to ignore how life in the modem world was progressing. He could no longer count on the verities of religion or political ideology or even science to give him his bearings. He sensed that what he could depend on was the constancy of nature, the anchor of memory and history, the safe harbor of family, and the difference he could make by shaping it all into poems and novels. His belief in the power of imagination has sustained him.

One night at dinner, Warren was telling stories, intricate, riotous tales about old Indian fighters, murder trials, Southern ladies, and foreign journalists. He was in his element until the phone rang. Getting up, he answered it. His son, Gabriel—who had spent the last four years building an ocean-going schooner of his own design—was calling from Rhode Island, distraught, as only a 23-year-old can be, over a minor design flaw in the boat. He said he was going to sail it into the Atlantic the next morning and scuttle it at sea. For nearly fifteen minutes, Warren pleaded with him over the phone. Finally, his voice desperate, he shouted, "Son, come home." Returning to the table, he sat quietly before his plate. His eyes were filled with tears.

"He's a hard-headed boy," he finally said.

"He's like his father," his wife said.

Sucking up his breath, shaking his head and clutching the table with both hands, Warren brought the matter to an end. "I can't bear to talk about it." Sighing, he added, "I know he'll come home. I know things will be all right."

Drawing another gulp of air, Warren began telling more stories. Stories about the Civil War, stories about the woods, stories about a woman who deceived her pastor into believe she was saved when, after someone dropped a match down her dress during services, she screamed, "The fire is in me." Stories about time and nature. They were the stories he had lived by.

Portman's Complaint

Esquire, June 1987

For as far as John Portman can see in every direction, he is surrounded by his own buildings. Before him towers the seventy-three-story mirrored silo of the Westin Peachtree Plaza, the world's second tallest hotel. Behind him stands the smaller—but infinitely more influential—Hyatt Regency Atlanta, a structure whose dramatic enclosed atrium was the prototype for what is now one of architecture's most prevalent clichés. On all sides of Portman loom the skyscrapers of Peachtree Center, a honeycomb-like complex that houses the headquarters of Dixie's business elite. To the architect's west are his gigantic furniture and apparel marts. To the east is his monolithic new Marriott. And arching overhead at various dizzying heights are twelve pedestrian sky-bridges. The passageways form a network linking all sixteen of Peachtree Center's Portman-designed buildings, making it possible for businessmen, shoppers, and conventioneers to walk from their cars to their rooms to their meals without ever leaving the environment John Portman created for them.

Yet as Portman strolls through his kingdom what one notices first are not his buildings—the largest collection of major works ever erected in the same city by an American architect—but his hair. The man has a sculpture on his head made out of his own hair, an outrageously conceived, meticulously arranged wave that takes off from one fringe of his balding pate like a tsunami and surfs across his skull, breaking and rising in salty brown swells until it crashes over his opposite ear. Everything else about the sixty-two-year-old architect—his wardrobe, his voice, his mannerisms—is understated. But Portman's do, which dominates a face made up of close-set walnut eyes, a pug nose, and just the faintest trace of jowls, is absolutely wild. It simultaneously manages to hide what otherwise would be a shiny dome while calling attention to itself like some kinetic piece by Alexander Calder. In short, Portman wears his design philosophy right atop his noggin.

Security and frivolity, the fortress and the carnival, a siege mentality married to an irresistible urge to shout "Step right up"—these are the yin and yang of John Portman's approach to architecture, visible, to greater and lesser degrees, in his numerous projects around the country: Embarcadero Center in San Francisco, Renaissance Center in Detroit, Los Angeles's Westin Bonaventure, Chicago's Hyatt Regency O'Hare, and New York's controversial new Marriott Marquis at Times Square. But it is in Atlanta, Portman's hometown, that he has accomplished what other architects only dream of—to build the heart of a city in one's own image.

On a crisp October afternoon, John Portman is wandering across one of his sky-bridges, this one leading from the shopping level of Peachtree Center to the lobby of the recently completed Marriott. The sun-bathed sidewalks far below are deserted, but in this Plexiglas tube pedestrians pass by in a steady flow. Surveying the scene, Portman pronounces, "I'm building a city that will become the modern Venice. The streets down there are canals for cars, while these bridges are clean, safe, climate controlled. People can walk here at any hour."

With that, the architect exits the concourse, strides through a claustrophobic, low foyer—he calls these trademark portals to his buildings "people scoops"—and emerges into an immense chamber whose vaulting walls rise toward a skylight forty-six floors above. "Now, I've been accused of turning my back on the city," Portman confesses in his soft, Southern drawl. "But what I say is that I'm giving the city new spaces away from the turmoil of urban life. I like to think of this lobby as a new town square. Here's a side-walk café. And look over there," he enthuses, pointing to a man curled up in a chair reading a book. "Name me a public place in a city today where you can sit outdoors without anyone bothering you."

Portman delivers this last observation as a challenge, but his tone wavers between imperiousness and vulnerability. The architect's vanity is especially apparent when he's showing off any of the more debatable features of his work, and this lobby illustrates one of his most frequently debunked notions—the idea that downtowns are dangerous, that what they lack are "oases," demilitarized zones created by a circling of the architectural wagons and connected with one another by enclosed walkways. Portman has fashioned similarly cloistered spaces all over Atlanta. Inside the castle gates, however, his buildings are anything but paranoid. In fact, they are just the opposite: riotously freewheeling.

On high in the Marriott lobby, exposed crystal elevators adorned with dozens of little lightbulbs rise and fall; fluttering red streamers dangle like Japanese kites; and volume after multileveled volume of crowded pavilion spaces seem on the verge of exploding from the larger cavity that contains them. Approaching the far edge of the room, Portman stops at a small bandstand surmounted by a grand piano. Adorning each corner of the platform are candelabra festooned with gaudy clusters of lights. "This is my homage to Liberace," he declares without a trace of irony. The bandstand is just the kind of decorative touch that has led Portman's detractors to accuse him of building Disneylands for adults, a charge to which he pleads guilty. "You know, inside all of us is that kid we've repressed," he says. "I like to go down and release that innocence, that enthusiasm."

Portman relies on more than razzle-dazzle. Oddly enough, his designs are also informed by a reverence for nature. Staring down into a pool of water at the core of the Marriott lobby, he says meditatively, "You're never far from the sound of running water in my buildings. And in the lobby of my Hyatt at Embarcadero Center, I installed a sound sculpture featuring tape-recorded birds singing to one another. What I'm doing is exactly what Frank Lloyd Wright did when, say, in his prairie houses, he used stylized wheat shafts in the stained-glass windows. Only I'm doing it with modern technology."

And with modern financing techniques. Portman is the nation's premier builder of mixed-use developments, of self-sustaining villages plopped down in the middle of teeming cities. He designs buildings, and he puts together real estate deals. He chooses materials and hustles bankers. It's as if Donald Trump and Michael Graves were rolled into one. Or as Portman once somewhat more heroically put it: "I'm the Medici to my own Leonardo."

The offices of the family-owned Portman Companies, a group composed of ten subsidiaries, are only a sky-bridge away from the Marriott. In 1986 these enterprises pulled in a combined $400 million. At the heart of the business is John Portman and Associates, the design arm of the empire, where sixty architects labor in a vast open space reminiscent of a newspaper city room. With more than $1 billion worth of projects currently under construction around the world, it is one of the busiest studios anywhere in the United States. In a brightly lit chamber a few flights below the studio stands a scale model of the downtown Atlanta that Portman envisions for the not-too-distant future.

"We control property on fifteen contiguous blocks," the architect says as he hovers over his mock-up metropolis. "We're building a city here. Look there on those blocks to the northwest; we're going to put real urban housing there. And over there, I'm proposing a shopping center. That's a hard one, because I don't own the adjacent lots. I have to woo many competing interests."

As Portman rattles off his plans, he seems like a latter-day Robert Moses, a man for whom influence—not design—is the currency of the realm. No wonder. In Atlanta, Portman has played the role of urban power broker ever since the early '70s, when he served as chairman of one of the most important city planning groups, Central Atlanta Progress.

This is not to say that Portman hasn't been challenged. In a boomtown like Atlanta, fights over turf and policy are inevitable. But Portman has almost always quashed any uprisings. When a group of developers wanted to move the Atlanta airport from its current location in a blue-collar neighborhood south of the city to an affluent northern suburb, Portman led the battle against the plan. The move, he argued, would undermine the economy of a struggling section of town. When MARTA (Metropolitan Atlanta Rapid Transit Authority) executives wanted to lay a subway line through the heart of the city by the traditional cut-and-cover method of construction—a disruptive technique that can close streets for years—Portman again marshaled the loyal opposition. His reasoning this time was more self-serving: business at his own Peachtree Center would have been damaged by the upheaval. Hence the subway tunnel was blasted hundreds of feet below the sidewalks.

To those who disagree with him, Portman's style can be exceedingly abrasive. "John is a screamer," says one Atlanta businessman who's worked intimately with him over the years. "He rants. He turns the ceiling blue. His approach is, 'This is how it's gonna be done because I say so. Period.'"

Portman agrees that he can be a tough customer but claims there's generally a good reason for his tantrums, averring that unlike other developers, he usually takes the long view. Leaning against a wall of his model room, he confides, "Everything I do is designed to make the city a better place. What I care about most is seeing people smile."

Tape-recorded birds, master plans, contented urbanites at work and play—these are the obsessions of a utopian. As John Portman walks through his city, expounding on this and that, he sounds not so much like an architect but a peripatetic '60s savant. In fact, he is positively McLuhanesque: aphoristic, abstruse, all knowing.

What chutzpah! At a time when the primary debate in architecture is between the stalwarts of modernism, who continue to pay homage to the austere forms dictated by the Bauhaus, and the cheerleaders of postmodernism, who mix and match decorative references from bygone eras, Portman is clearly a prophet in the wilderness. And in the eyes of the architectural clerisy, a pretty cockamamie one. Far from winning him respect, his iconoclastic ideas have brought him a reputation as a glitzy philistine.

Oh, a few critics, like Tom Wolfe, have praised Portman. In his 1981 book, *From Bauhaus to Our House*, he stood up for the architect, and he still does. Observes Wolfe: "More than any other architect, he's created what we regard today as downtown glamour. His work is great theater."

Yet on the Richter scale of the architectural establishment, Portman barely registers. Wolfe fears he "will be thrown down the 'memory hole.' He'll be forgotten because the people who write the history are in the intellectual compound, and Portman doesn't know how to play their game." Indeed, in the architectural department of Harvard's Graduate School of Design, Portman's name is only mentioned in passing in the basic survey course.

Portman's friends believe that the architect's failure to garner the approval of his peers grieves him deeply. Irv Weiner, formerly one of Portman's top associates, says, "Architecture is everything to John. The development business is nothing but a vehicle he uses to implement his ideas."

But if Portman is wounded by his dubious status, he certainly doesn't admit it. In fact, he vigorously defends his isolation from the establishment. As far as he's concerned, the modernist movement was bankrupted long ago by its failure to respond to human needs and scale. As for the postmodernists, he regards them as nihilists whose inability to add new ideas to the design vocabulary is reflected by their need to vandalize the styles of other periods. Prideful to the point of disdain, Portman asserts, "I didn't just come up with my ideas overnight. My philosophy protects me from hip shots." What also helps are jobs, which Portman attracts like a magnet. This spring, the first in a chain of Portman Hotels will open near San Francisco's Nob Hill. Meanwhile, a host of enormous Portman projects in the Far East are in various phases of planning or construction. Several developments on mainland China make Portman one of the largest American investors in that country. If this weren't enough, there are his continually unfolding plans for Atlanta—a city that for both better and worse is his abiding work in progress.

Two extraordinary things happened to John Portman on his way to becoming America's most prolific architectural apostate, and both of them involved acts of heresy against the craft he loves.

Portman's first sin was to buck the American Institute of Architects' sanction forbidding members from developing their own projects, and he didn't waste much time committing it. Not long after graduating from Georgia Tech in 1950, Portman informally apprenticed himself to Atlanta's two most powerful real estate developers. "I didn't want to do schoolroom additions," Portman recalls. "I wanted to leave footprints in the sand." Portman's initial foray into developing was modest—a mart for regional furniture wholesalers in what had once been a parking garage. Almost overnight his mart became hugely popular. Portman had anticipated such success and soon made the decision to undertake his first large-scale development project—the one million-square-foot Atlanta Merchandise Mart. When the new structure was finished in 1960, it was the largest building in the Southeast, and Portman was on his way.

"Because of my work in real estate," the architect says, "I was able to see how fast the South was going to grow." In short, Portman foresaw the advent of the Sun Belt and positioned himself as the man who would give shelter to latter-day carpetbaggers when they set up shop below the Mason-Dixon Line.

Around the same time, Portman committed an equally unspeakable transgression by rejecting what was then architecture's holy writ—modernism. Listening to Portman talk about the decision is akin to hearing a defrocked priest discussing his renunciation of the teachings of Rome.

"In 1960, I flew down to Brazil to attend the inaugural ceremonies for the city of Brasilia, the planned city created by the best minds of modernism." Rubbing his eyes as if reliving a painful memory, he adds, "At that time in my life I'd never anticipated anything with the kind of excitement I had for this trip. Well, when I got to Brasilia, I was devastated. It was heartless, lifeless, cold."

Portman left Brasilia with his belief system shaken. "Everything my teachers had told me was crumbling," he says. "Over and over, I thought, 'We don't need new cities, we need old cities restructured in such a way that they respond to human needs.' So I started thinking about how different parcels of land up and down Peachtree Street might work when developed on a master plan. I also started thinking about new forms for buildings. The

Merchandise Mart was just a simple cube. There had to be something different."

For Portman the breakthrough was the Hyatt Regency, his 1967 Atlanta hotel built around an expansive, covered courtyard and punctuated by scores of his patented "Look ma, no hands" details. Before the Hyatt opened, all the experts predicted failure. But once guests began registering, the occupancy rate never fell below 70 percent. Not only that, Atlantans lined up around the block just to take a peek.

It didn't take long for political and business leaders in other cities to notice what Portman was doing down South. His projects had brought to Atlanta what Mayor Andrew Young calls a "vital core." In fact, the mayor now credits Portman's designs, as much as anything else, with Atlanta's "peaceful passage" through the violent era of the '60s. No wonder, then, that shortly after his initial success in Atlanta, the architect was in partnership with David Rockefeller in San Francisco and with Henry Ford II in Detroit. Soon John Lindsay was courting him to revitalize Manhattan's Times Square. For a brief moment, Portman was a sensation. But this was before anyone actually realized just how fully committed he was to his singular vision.

On a rainy fall afternoon, John Portman is sitting on a white sofa in the corner of his Peachtree Center office. "I'm an addict when it comes to collecting art," he says, motioning at the numerous pieces around the room. At the door are two five-foot-tall Jean Cocteau glass sculptures. On the shelves encircling the space are, among others, a Picasso and an Arp. But the featured artist here is John Portman. His unsigned canvasses, executed in vivid reds, blues, and yellows, portray amoeba-like swirls dissolving into one another. It doesn't take a genius to see that their intricately connected shapes are abstractions of the 3-D forms the architect erects out in the real world.

While there's a desk and a conference table in Portman's suite, there's no drawing table—he does most of his designing out in the studio. In the office, he likes to let his mind wander. He speaks in whirling circumlocutions, each idea leading to half a dozen more. But eventually, he always comes back to the notions that have obsessed him since his trip to Brasilia, the fundamental themes of his architecture.

Leaning back on the sofa, Portman begins to lecture. "At the heart of my approach is an unflagging optimism. Because we're moving from an industrial society to a technological one, most people feel a tremendous pessimism. There's confusion, a nostalgia for the past.

"Since World War II," he adds, "we've been living in what I call a period of fragmentation-separation. You know, Einstein said that the world would never be the same after the bomb. How this affected cities was that it caused the inner core to explode. This happens in lots of ways. With freeways, the telephone, TV, man just doesn't need the city. He drives his car out to the suburbs, kicks off his shoes, and shuts himself in."

In Portman's view, more than just the distraction of watching the grass grow keeps suburbanites out of town. The most potent force is fear—fear of the arsenal of random assaults that jolt the sensibilities on most city streets. The middle class is running scared.

"My idea was that I just couldn't see abandoning the cities to the poor," Portman says. "I want to bring the middle class back."

In Portman's mind, one of the keys to an urban renaissance involves getting Americans out of their cars. So he structures his projects in accordance with something he refers to as a "coordinate unit," the distance he believes a person will walk before climbing into "the four-wheeled monster." Hence the sky-bridges, the clustering of white-collar labor and fun zones in his developments.

Portman also has some almost Jungian ideas about certain shapes that he feels people gravitate toward. "Some people claim that I built the Atlanta Marriott as the womb into which I could insert the erection of the Peachtree Plaza," he confesses mischievously. "Now, it's not quite like that, but I do play constantly with the rectilinear and the curvilinear."

But Portman feels that his greatest gift to cities—the subject to which he generally returns in most conversations—is that he's reinjected nature into the urban formula. "I'm preoccupied with nature," he says. "I grew up in an agrarian society. My grandfather had a farm south of Atlanta, and there I fell in love with the stillness of a lake, with flowers. Those are the things I try to put in my buildings."

Where do all these twists and turns lead? To Portman World, a place whose far-flung outposts are, in a real sense, terrariums for humanity segregated from America's mean streets. For a man who professes to love cities, Portman paradoxically hates urban chaos.

As long as John Portman erected his fantasy lands in regional cities such as Atlanta and Detroit, his position as a minor bedazzler of the hinterlands was assured. But in 1985, when Portman finally brought his show to New York City in the form of the Marriott Marquis, the high church of design could no longer afford to write him off as a nuisance building amusement parks for parvenus beyond the Hudson. In the course of a single day, he went from being a nonentity to a public enemy.

On August 31, 1985—the eve of the Marriott's grand opening—Paul Goldberger, architecture critic of *The New York Times*, published a devastating critique of Portman's first contribution to the Manhattan skyline:

"The Marriott Marquis...cost upward of $400 million and it is chockfull of the latest technology. But it is to architecture as the Edsel was to the automobile—awkward, gangling, and out of touch. In the years between the announcement of this project and its completion, almost everything in the world of architecture has changed except Mr. Portman... At a time when architects are coming more and more to understand the importance of modest scale and...even historical elements, the Marriott moves four-square in the opposite direction..."

If the Marriott Marquis had been a Broadway production, it would have shut down the next night. Instead, it stood there like a scorned misfit. Yet, while the architectural nabobs were snickering, the hotel's 1,877 guest rooms were filling up and have remained booked ever since. Meanwhile, the first play to open in the hotel's theater—the British production of *Me and My Girl*—became the hit of the season. Of course, such successes should have surprised no one; Portman's taste has always appealed to that vast majority of expense-account wielding Americans who wouldn't know a Philip Johnson from a Howard Johnson's.

More was behind Goldberger's dismissal of the Marriott than just a dispute over architectural style. From the start, the project was troubled. Shortly after John Lindsay recruited Portman back in the early '70s, the hotel's finances fell through, suspending construction. Then a convention center that was to be built adjacent to the structure was moved downtown. Worst of all, Portman's hotel called for the demolition of two beloved historic buildings—the Helen Hayes and Morosco theaters. Neither structure went gently into the night, as preservationists mounted fierce campaigns to save them.

"You know, fifteen years ago Lindsay brought me to New York to combat the sleaze factor on Broadway," Portman recalls. "To do something positive, we decided we had to build a large structure that could single-handedly be a catalytic element. But that was so long ago, and in those years so many things changed. I ended up feeling like Don Quixote."

Portman sighs then, his voice bristling, adds, "To tell you the truth, if I'd designed the building yesterday, I would have done it the same way. As far as I'm concerned, the Marriott is just what Times Square needed. I've done something no one has ever done in Manhattan—I've given the city space. So what if I've been criticized because the building doesn't feature a collage of postmodern clichés. I firmly believe that once you stop being controversial, you're dead."

The pasting received by Portman's New York Marriott can be attributed in part to the building's controversy-plagued gestation period and in part to the architect's unwillingness to bend to what he regards as the wrong-headed styles of the times. But criticisms pointing up other flaws in the structure—its inaccessibility, its undeniable girth—can't be so easily dismissed. Such charges have trailed Portman around the country—in Detroit, where the shopping sections of the Renaissance Center, which is separated from the heart of the city by a nine-lane highway, have never worked; in Los Angeles, where the stingy entryways to the Westin Bonaventure isolate the building like a space-age medieval keep. But it is in Atlanta, where Portman has controlled the look of the city for a quarter of a century, that his efforts are most vulnerable to the more substantive attacks leveled at him elsewhere.

As much as Portman would like to believe that he is an architect for the masses, many of his Atlanta buildings are forbidding and cold. In fact, his largest structures, such as the Marriott, weren't built for Everyman at all but for those hordes of corporate nomads who migrate in vast tribes to the trade shows that are an integral part of the city's economy. While the architect's work is user friendly to members of these large groups, it has little to say either to individual travelers hoping to appreciate the South's charms or to natives who labor downtown, day in, day out.

"The mentality of Portman's projects," says Richard Rothman, an Atlanta architect who specializes in small-scale buildings and rehabilitating old structures, "is based on providing space for a homogeneous society that is apathetic to those who don't share the wealth. What's worst is that every one of his Atlanta buildings is offensive to the street. The entrances are low and shadowy. And the most terrible thing is all those bridges. Walk around Atlanta, and the town is dead. Everyone is up above in all those glass tubes."

Rothman believes that Portman has been able to get away with building what amount to urban redoubts because he's a victim of the very innovation he pioneered. "Because Portman is his own developer," Rothman contends, "he's not blessed with what I think is a very healthy check-and-balance system. For most architects, part of the job is to review the developer's program. Portman never has the advantage of independent analysis."

Portman has heard such criticisms before, and in recent years he's attempted to modify his work to answer some of the complaints. In his older Atlanta buildings, he's knocked down a few walls to install street-front entrances and shops. In the Peachtree Plaza, he's just completed an inspired redesign of the lobby, transforming it from a dank grotto into a bright space decorated by mauve-and-pink dormers and pediments. In his newer structures, he's designed numerous street-level spaces where he'll one day open boutiques.

But such alterations amount to little more than pushing around the deck chairs. Portman is never going to make major changes because he truly believes that he is right. Time and again, he'll say, "I don't look back. I don't question myself. I'm a producer, and what I do is produce." Portman is to be lauded for having the courage of his convictions, but his assertions, so full of strut and swagger, are also defensive, camouflaging his fear of opening up his buildings to America's streets and everything they represent: danger, yes, but also the vivifying hustle and bustle that makes cities great.

John Portman lives in a large, tranquil house about fifteen miles outside of Atlanta. From this remove, the sturm and drang of building a city seems unimaginable. The dwelling, which he designed in 1964, sits on a wooded slope, and in a placidly abstract way, it resembles a Greek temple. Supported by twenty-four columns—many of them hollow and containing everything from baths to spiral staircases connecting the two main floors—it radiates order and peace. As in almost all of Portman's work, water runs through the house, which on the ground level is really an archipelago of living areas separated from one another by the fingers of a man-made pond.

"So much of what I'm all about is evident here," Portman says, sitting in a butterfly chair in his backyard one warm autumn morning. "This is where I really first brought nature indoors." He smiles and for a second seems content with the world.

The architect spends a great deal of time at his house, which he named Entelechy (Greek for "potential realized"). He and his wife, Jan, have six children. When Portman is not busy being a father, his favorite thing is to hole up in an atelier beside his swimming pool and paint. "One of the things I'm bad at is chitchat," he says.

Not surprisingly, Portman is intensely private, guarding just about every aspect of his personal life. His fortune is considerable, but he refuses to talk about it. (Three years ago, an Atlanta business paper estimated his wealth at $200 million.) His free time is his own, and he's not apt to share it ("John hates cocktail parties," says Irv Weiner, "and I think that's made it rough for him in New York"). Again and again, he parries even innocent inquiries by saying, "Architecture is what I'm about. Let's talk about that."

The architecture that Portman is asked about most often these days is a vacation house he has just completed on Georgia's Sea Island, a secluded haven of old-money WASPs who disdain ostentation and refer to their multimillion-dollar homes as cottages. After Portman purchased three lots and began work on the building he said would contain "everything I've learned as an architect" (he's christened it Entelechy II), it didn't take long for the community's tony denizens to mount a hue and cry. A front-page headline in the *Los Angeles Times* topping a piece about Portman's beach place said it all: HIS DREAM A NIGHTMARE TO NEIGHBORS.

To say the least, Portman's 12,586-square-foot bungalow flies in the face of the typical colonial style found on Sea Island. There are numerous sculpture gardens, a waterfall flowing alongside the entryway stairs, and a mammoth, white concrete latticework roof topped by gazebos and brightly colored abstract pieces. Portman admits that the house is not like the ones next door—"The rooftop is my homage to Dali," he says—but he can't understand the fuss. "I'm an open, straightforward person," he finally says. "I just hate being a phony, which is what I'd be if I went around explaining it all. See, I'm on down the road, thinking about the next thing."

Recently, Portman has turned over some of the day-to-day responsibilities of his operations to his oldest sons. Jack, a Harvard-educated architect, laid the groundwork for the Portman Companies' expansion into China, and Michael has taken over many of the public relations duties that come when working in such distant lands. Meanwhile, Portman has been concentrating on a few projects smaller than those he's normally undertaken in the past. At Atlanta's Emory University, he's just finished a superb new student center and a no-nonsense athletic facility that suggest a new direction. Last year, he and his associates completed the delicate task of redesigning the skating rink and lobbies of New York's Rockefeller Center. But in spite of the fact that he's now into his seventh decade, Portman shows no signs of abandoning downtown Atlanta, which he calls "my ongoing saga."

Wandering the grounds of his estate, he points through some second-growth forest. "See there, you can just make out the skyline," he says with pride. True enough, the needle of the Peachtree Plaza is shimmering there in the morning light.

What Portman has wrought in the sky above Georgia is one thing, but not long ago he put his imprint in the red clay itself. After much debate, Ivy Street—a thoroughfare named for Atlanta's first resident that runs by many of Portman's edifices—was renamed Peachtree Center Avenue. By displacing the town's founding father, Portman has certainly left his footprint in the sand. Now even the maps say John Portman was here. But why he was here and what he was all about—to understand those things, people will have to look beyond the surfaces, away from the streets. For in the end, John Portman is not an architect who faces the world but one who turns flamboyantly from it.

Herb Alpert: Always in Tune

Los Angeles, May 2011

One night in the fall of 1969, in the midst of his unparalleled triumphs as a performer and music executive, Herb Alpert came apart. Onstage in Munich, Germany, with the Tijuana Brass, he was beset by a strange and terrifying sensation. He saw himself sitting in the third row of the audience. For the rest of the evening he watched as someone named Herb Alpert blew the horn. "The question hit me," he recalls, "'Why is that guy seemingly so happy when he's playing the trumpet but so unhappy when he's with a group of people?'"

Alpert's out-of-body experience devastated him, both in its own right and because it indicated a crisis he'd long sensed approaching. "I don't think I had a handle on what I was doing or who I was," he says. "I had money and notoriety, but something was missing." Things only worsened when Alpert returned home to Los Angeles. He picked up the trumpet and could no longer play. Just that quickly he had succumbed to a career-threatening psychosomatic episode. "I started stuttering through the horn," he says.

Alpert needed help. He flew to New York to talk to Carmine Caruso, a trumpet teacher who counseled brass players.

"I said, 'Carmine, what's wrong?'"

"'If I tell you, it won't help.'"

"That intrigued me," Alpert says. "So I ordered drinks and got him a little lushed up. Then I questioned him again.

"'Carmine, what am I doing wrong?'

"'Yursh trying to play the trumpet wiff your mouth open.'

"He was right. I had formed a bad habit. I was playing with my lips apart. I wasn't touching the mouthpiece." Caruso prescribed a series of exercises, but as he predicted, they didn't work.

"My problem," Alpert says, "was inside."

Herb Alpert had lost his sense of self. "He was on a merry-go-round, spinning," says his wife, singer Lani Hall. "He was very successful. He had a record company that kept getting bigger and bigger, but he had to find out who he was. 'Is this defining me?' he asked." Alpert needed to confront everything that was wrong: a faltering first marriage, a career in danger of be-coming more about commerce than music, and the underlying fear that he had lost his identity. It took years of therapy, but he "pulled himself out of it," says Hall. "He worked very hard to do it." She calls Alpert's breakdown "a real blessing." He agrees. "I wouldn't be the man I am if this had not hap-pened."

Forty years later, thanks to that singular breakthrough, Herb Alpert, who fronted one of the emblematic bands of the 1960s, sold 72 million al-bums, and cofounded A&M Records, is pushing himself harder than ever. At 76, when most people are slowing down, he has a new CD, *I Feel You*, coming out on Concord Records. A recent tour of the Northeast concluded with a sold-out performance at Jazz at Lincoln Center in New York.

I Feel You features Alpert on trumpet and Hall on most of the vocals. The CD is plainly the work of the man behind the Tijuana Brass. (It in-cludes a new version of "What Now My Love," one of the Brass's biggest hits.) It is also experimental and far-ranging, establishing Alpert as more than a midcentury artifact. "I feel like it's a blend of pop and jazz, but not fusion," says Alpert. "It's music with its own spin. If I can take a familiar song and put a twist on it, I'll try." The album includes smoky arrangements of such standards as "Cast Your Fate to the Wind" and "Call Me" (a long-ago hit for A&M artist Chris Montez), a reimagining of Van Morrison's "Moondance," and the sorts of Brazilian classics ("Berimbau") for which Hall, formerly the lead singer of Sergio Mendes's Brasil '66, is celebrated.

Alpert is also achieving success as a painter and sculptor. His swirling acrylic-on-canvas abstractions in vivid reds, greens, and violets are, like his music, deeply felt and boldly chromatic. His bronzes are even more pro-found. They are ambitious, emotionally engaging, and powerful. During a four-month exhibit last summer and fall, the Ace Gallery in Beverly Hills displayed 15 of his massive pieces. The two-ton "black totems" were valued at $250,000 each, and most of them sold.

The ultimate outgrowth of all this creative ferment is the Herb Alpert Foundation, which Alpert uses to encourage the imaginative self-expression of others. In an era of diminished budgets for the arts, it has given away more than $100 million, including $30 million to endow the school of music at UCLA, $15 million for the school of music at CalArts, and $4.6 million for P.S. Arts, which funds programs for cash-poor public education across Southern California. The foundation is becoming a major force in Los An-geles philanthropy.

Herb Alpert's house looks down on nearly six rocky acres of Malibu beachfront planted with towering Monterey pines and eucalyptus trees. Its outstanding features—an ornate front door and a Chinese pediment over the foyer—are the work of the baroque designer Tony Duquette. Yet both outside and in, this is a place where the artist in residence has made the most telling statements. Alpert's sculptures command the grounds. With names like *Guardian Spirit*, *Eagle*, and *Ancient Source*, they rise from stone-walled gardens and jutting promontories. Alpert's paintings dominate the interiors. Several hang in the living room. Several more line the halls. Alpert's trumpets—the Chicago Benge, which he played as leader of the Tijuana Brass to record "A Taste of Honey," "Tijuana Taxi," and "Spanish Flea," as well as the German Sonare, which he currently uses for practice and performances—are at the ready in an adjacent recording studio.

By 6:15 each morning, Alpert, clad in a loose-fitting black sweat suit and Nikes, pads into the kitchen. He is lean and fit, his age betrayed only by thinning hair in back and a scruffy gray beard. After flicking on a small oven, he inserts a metal tray that holds a hard sheet of wax. Although his sculptures can reach 18 feet in height, they start as four-to-eight-inch maquettes. As Alpert waits for the wax to become soft enough to shape into one of these miniatures, he downs a glass of NanoGreens, a cloyingly sweet diet supplement fortified with sufficient algae and barley grass powder to stock a health food store. "It's guaranteed to make you feel three months younger," he cracks. Then for 30 minutes he loses himself in his task, laboring less by design than touch. "You have to be free," he says. "I just make shapes that feel good to me. I fool with it until I get a good feeling."

As 7:30 approaches, Alpert wanders into the recording studio to warm up on the Sonare. "There are 240 muscles that need to be in sync to play the horn," he says, and for a half hour he does exercises and runs through arpeggios. Once he's finished, he sits at a Yamaha grand piano and glides over sequences of chords. Later he will return to his trumpet and let loose with renditions of "Desafinado" by João Gilberto and "The Girl from Ipanema" and "Triste" by Antonio Carlos Jobim, the brilliant Brazilian composer whom he knew and admired. "The guy was a genius," Alpert says in his soft tenor voice. "But he was an unpretentious person. Lani and I were going to do an album with him—he would sing in English, Lani in Portuguese—but he passed away."

Alpert is all about art, all the time, and as he goes about his business, he betrays no sense of pressure or anxiety. "For me," he says upon emerging from the studio, "the important thing is not to think or analyze but to accept my own creativity." After navigating a passageway marked by a photo of Stan Getz, the formidable jazz saxophonist whose albums Alpert produced at A&M Records, he enters his painting atelier, an airy space stacked with brushes and smelling of pigment. Alpert has been working on a new piece for a couple of weeks—a few minutes one morning, a few more the next. On this day he is back at it.

An hour later Alpert walks to a service porch, climbs into a golf cart, and rolls away. "Sid, can you unwrap that big piece?" he says to an assistant over a walkie-talkie. He steers along a twisting path that leads to a high-ceilinged, hangar-like structure large enough to accommodate four forklifts and several sculptures in progress. The center of attention is a looming 12-foot-tall monolith. "That started in my kitchen," Alpert says as he pulls to a stop. "For the last month I've either been up on a forklift shaping the clay by hand or standing on the floor using a laser light to guide the guys who help me. I'm intrigued by what makes something good to look at. I'm looking for things that resonate more in the soul than in the eyes." He believes this piece is just about right. In a few days workers will make a mold, which after it sets will be removed and trucked to an Eastside foundry.

As the sun dapples down on this fall afternoon, one week before Alpert must let go of *I Feel You* for mastering and production, he revisits his recording studio. At a large table topped with electronic equipment and two Macs powered by Logic software, he listens to the numbers. He keeps time by slapping his hand on the back of a nearby chair. Glancing at the monitors, whose oscillating waves track surging notes, Alpert shakes his head in wonder. "The thing that's fascinating to me about this technology," he says, "is that it records music in zeros and ones. It's not like the old days." Alpert has been in the music business so long that he can recall the primitive devices that predated tape recorders and captured sound on wire. Now he's digitally sophisticated enough to mix his own albums on a computer. Still, the goal for him is the same as ever—to express genuine emotion. "It's a huge mystery to me," he says, "but this equipment can record feelings."

To spend time with Alpert is to discover that in both music and the visual arts, he prizes unfettered imagination and heartfelt sentiment above all. The artists he most admires are those who trust their guts. Alpert recalls asking Getz, a master of bebop, for instruction in its basic two-five-one chord sequence. "Stan looked at me," he says, "and asked, 'What's that?' I thought, 'That's the sort of freedom I'm looking for.'" Alpert saw the same spirit in another A&M stalwart, the soulful Brazilian Milton Nascimento. "I signed him in 1970," he says. "He was playing intricate things, but he didn't really know what a chord was. Everything he did was intuitive."

Learning to rely on his instincts was central to Alpert's psychological breakthrough; maintaining such faith is sometimes still a battle. Nothing brings out his doubts more than the imminent completion of a project. As "Viola Fora de Moda" from his new CD fills the studio, he begins to tinker. With a few keystrokes he changes the piano track, believing that he is enhancing the entire recording as well as the performance of the vocalist—his wife. No sooner does he finish than she walks in.

Dressed in black from head to toe, pale oval face set off by reddish blond ringlets that accentuate a warm yet assertive smile, Lani Hall is every bit the musician her husband is. "Oh no, you're not remixing something, are you?" she demands, having caught Alpert in the act. "Which one?"

"'Viola.'"

"Why?"

"I was conscious that I didn't put the piano where I wanted it. Here, check this."

As the new version plays, Hall sways to the rhythm, but from her expression it's clear that she dislikes what her husband has done.

"I don't know, hon," she says. "It's now all out of whack for me."

"But..."

"You work on it then, but it just feels all out of whack to me."

With that, Hall disappears, leaving Alpert not so much chastened as bemused. "You know the difference between a female singer and a terrorist?" he finally manages. After a beat, he offers the answer: "You can reason with a terrorist."

But he knows she is right. The two share a creative vision. When he gets off course, she brings him back. "On one level she's almost like a schoolgirl with him," says music mogul Lou Adler, a longtime mutual friend. "She thinks he's the greatest and the most handsome. She's very positive. But she's no flatterer. She can be brutally honest, and she demands that Herb live up to high standards."

When Alpert eventually signs off on *I Feel You*, he has restored "Viola." "I was guilty of doing what I tell people not to do," he says. "It felt good, but I thought I could make it better. I was wrong."

From the start, Herb Alpert was surrounded by music. His mother played the violin, his father the mandolin, his brother the drums, and his sister the piano. Born into a Jewish family in Boyle Heights, Herb grew up in the Fairfax District, where his parents moved when the fortunes of his father, a downtown manufacturer of women's suits and garments, improved. He was eight when he picked up a trumpet from a table stacked with instruments at Melrose Elementary School. "I was very shy," he says. "The horn made a loud noise and spoke for me."

Initially Alpert was just a kid with a toy. "It was a piece of plumbing," he says. His mom and dad, however, were determined to see him master it. Each week Benjamin Klatzkin, a former principal trumpet for the New York Philharmonic, arrived at the Alperts' house at the corner of Fuller and Rosewood. Sitting side by side on chairs in the boy's bedroom, the two worked through exercises in *Arban's Complete Conservatory Method for Trumpet*, a text in print since the 1860s. One afternoon when Alpert was in his mid-teens, he played an étude from the book and looked up to see his teacher crying.

"It's so bootiful," Klatzkin exclaimed.

"I had touched him deeply," Alpert recalls. "It was the first time I thought, 'Gee, maybe I have something.'"

By his junior year at Fairfax High School, Alpert was moving beyond classical music. He was listening to Harry James and Bunny Berigan, particularly Berigan's recording of "I Can't Get Started." Then, he says, "I started listening to progressive jazz, especially everyone's favorite, Charlie Parker." Alpert also had an ear for pop. He fronted a band called the Colonial Trio. After winning the KTLA competition show *High Talent Battle* for several weeks running, his group began picking up wedding and bar mitzvah gigs. Among the Jews of West Los Angeles, Alpert was a minor celebrity.

He enrolled at USC as a music major, but after two years he dropped out. "We had these prerequisite courses like 'Man and Civilization,'" he recalls with a grimace. He was drafted and became solo trumpet with the Sixth Army Band at the Presidio in San Francisco. Alpert grew comfortable playing anywhere, including at funerals. "I once played taps for 14 services in a single day," he says. At the same time the military forced Alpert to face his limitations. "I ran into trumpet players who were much better than me. I realized that if I didn't come up with a style of my own, I was never going to be a professional."

Alpert wed his high school sweetheart, the former Sharon Lubin, whose friend married Lou Adler, then an aspiring lyricist and music manager from East Los Angeles. "You know the expression, 'We went to separate schools together,'" says Adler. "That was me and Herbie. We matched up immediately. When he got out of the service, we said, 'Let's write some songs.'" In 1957, the two went to work at L.A.-based Keen Records for the legendary artists and repertoire man Robert "Bumps" Blackwell. "Our job was to log all the sessions Bumps recorded," says Alpert. "We'd listen to the tapes of the various artists and give them ratings for first verse, second verse, bridge, and third verse. That was how we got our feet wet in the music business."

Keen's main draw was the rhythm and blues singer Sam Cooke. Alpert and Adler struck up a friendship with him, and in 1958, the three wrote one of the singer's top-selling hits, the catchy teen ballad "Wonderful World": "Don't know much about a science book. Don't know much about the French I took."

Cooke articulated what would become Alpert's artistic philosophy. "He was very intuitive," Alpert says. Cooke urged him to value true sentiment over all else. "Sam was trying to start his own label, and one day he auditioned this extremely good-looking guy from the Caribbean," Alpert remembers. "Sam and I stood in the control room listening to him play. Sam asked me what I thought. I said, 'I like him.' Then Sam said, 'OK, turn your back on him and now listen another five minutes.' Which I did, and I realized the guy wasn't sending anything. I didn't get him. That's what Sam wanted me to understand. To him, it never mattered how an artist looked. He didn't care. He always said, 'People are listening to a cold piece of wax. It either makes it or it don't.' What he meant was, 'Trust your feelings. If it doesn't feel good to you, it's not going to feel good to anyone else.'"

In 1959, Alpert and Adler launched Jan and Dean, producing the duo's first album. Alpert brought them a doo-wop tune called "Baby Talk." Their falsetto-infused rendition rose to number ten on the charts, setting the stage for a decade of surf music to follow. Soon afterward, Alpert, Adler, and disc jockey B. Mitchell Reed started a music production company called HerBLou. Although Reed was outgoing, Alpert and Adler seemed unlikely industry operators. "I didn't speak much at all," says Adler, "and Herb spoke less than I did. If we were in a crowded room, I'd hardly get involved in the conversation, and Herb just wouldn't participate." Nonetheless the partners had an innate sense of where pop music was headed.

At 25 Alpert was becoming a *macher*, but he felt unfulfilled. He liked being a producer, but he also wanted to be a performer. The partnership split up. "I kept Jan and Dean," says Adler, "and Herbie took the tape recorder. Those were our only real assets." Reed went back to spinning records. Alpert tried his hand at a singing career. He recorded four singles at RCA under the name Dore Alpert. None made the charts, and Alpert hated the experience: "The recording studio at RCA was very chilly—a cold atmosphere." Worse, when Alpert asked if he could add a trumpet track to one of his songs by using an overdubbing technique he'd been experimenting with, the request was denied. "They said it was against union regulations."

Disenchanted with the music business, Alpert drifted. With striking good looks—jet-black hair, darting brown eyes, and a delicately tapered nose—he tried acting. "But I didn't have what it takes," he says. Music, he realized, was his love. Nights found him at Sardi's listening to Shorty Rogers or taking in Gerry Mulligan wherever he was playing, but when Alpert sat in on trumpet with bands at Hollywood piano bars, nothing clicked. He still hadn't developed his own style. His playing suggested Clifford Brown with a little Louis Armstrong thrown in.

It was during this time that Alpert and young music executive Jerry Moss, then with Scepter Records, started driving to Tijuana to attend bullfights. "I was there for the Hemingway machismo thing," says Moss, "but Herbie experienced it more deeply." The spectacle thrilled Alpert. "There was so much energy and excitement," he says. "The fans drinking wine from bota bags, the brightness of the colors, and the fanfare of trumpets that announced each event—it got under my skin. I was curious to see if I could capture that feeling on a record. I wanted to channel that energy."

Alpert shut himself in a garage studio behind his West Hollywood home. Finally the trumpet was no longer just a piece of plumbing. Indeed, he was not even aware of it as a tangible thing. "It was part of me," he says. Using session musicians and working from a song called "Twinkle Star" by the pianist Sol Lake, Alpert fashioned a number distinguished by two resounding horn tracks, both of which he played, overdubbing them onto tape using the technique RCA had forbidden. "It's amazing what Herbie did," says Moss. "He was an innovator."

Alpert and Moss formed A&M Records, and in the late summer of 1962, it released *The Lonely Bull* by Herb Alpert and the Tijuana Brass. "We had our first hit," says Moss, "and I gave up all my other business and went to work full-time with Herb. By this time we were really good friends." The two completed each other; Moss was relentless, Alpert sensitive. Success seemed inevitable. At first, however, A&M did not get everything right. In the early '60s, the label rejected what became a generation's anthem to libido—the Kingsmen's "Louie Louie." "I thought it was too long and out of tune," says Alpert. A&M also missed a bigger opportunity. It failed to sign the Beatles. Many other labels did, too, Alpert says. "I didn't see what was happening."

The big break for the Tijuana Brass came in 1965 with *Whipped Cream & Other Delights*, the album that featured "A Taste of Honey" and what is arguably the decade's sexiest piece of cover art: a photograph of a dark-haired vixen clad in nothing but shaving cream and scarce little of it. Following *Herb Alpert's Tijuana Brass, Volume 2* and *South of the Border*, both released earlier, *Whipped Cream* made the group a sensation. A&M put together a six-man band that was soon playing in giant arenas and on national television.

In November 1965, the band performed on what was then America's greatest stage, CBS's *The Ed Sullivan Show*. Although awkward and raspy, Sullivan had introduced the country to some of its biggest acts—among them Elvis Presley—and he took the role of national tastemaker seriously. During a rehearsal, he put an arm around Alpert and said, "Herb, I discovered you."

"Ed, it's too late," Alpert replied.

The Brass was already on its way. In 1966, it sold 13.5 million albums, outpacing the group Alpert had missed and Sullivan had ushered into American stardom—the Beatles.

In an era dominated by the Rolling Stones, the Doors, and Jimi Hendrix, the Tijuana Brass was an anomaly. Its music was upbeat, effervescent, and romantic, encouraging intimacy and promising happiness. Herb Alpert provided the soundtrack for that part of the 1960s in which the future felt limitless, subdivisions proliferated, and the cocktail parties never seemed to end.

Many of the Brass's hits became advertising jingles ("Mexican Shuffle" turned into "The Teaberry Shuffle") or themes for television shows (thanks to *The Dating Game*, "Whipped Cream" inspired the fantasies of a generation of bachelors and bachelorettes). Not that Alpert consciously cast himself as the pied piper of the good life. "I made the music that was coming out of me," he says. "I had all these songs in my head that I'd played over the years, and I was mainly drawn by their melodies. Being an instrumentalist, I couldn't do otherwise because I rarely had the advantage of a lyric. Most of the songs the Tijuana Brass did were ones I whistled when I was alone."

Along the way Alpert developed a distinctively bright trumpet sound, although he often discounted the accomplishment. To Miles Davis's remark that he could recognize Alpert's playing after just three notes, Alpert replied, "You hear one note, and you know it's Miles." Alpert also brought Latin-American music into the mainstream, so much so that on meeting him, a surprised Ringo Starr exclaimed, "I thought you were a short, fat Mexican."

The success of the Tijuana Brass positioned A&M Records as a dominant force in the music business. Alpert and Moss could not have been better paired to take advantage of the opportunity. "Jerry brought everything you needed to be successful in business," says Lou Adler. "He was consummate. He could negotiate. He could promote. That allowed Herbie to concentrate on bringing in great artists." Alpert's first coup was Sergio Mendes, the Brazilian pianist and bandleader. "I had no hesitation about signing with an upstart label," says Mendes. "The way Herb approached me felt right." Alpert produced Brasil '66's best-selling debut album. "It was a great experience to be in the studio with him," says Mendes. "We brought the repertoire and arrangements, and he trimmed where we needed trimming and got us to add where we needed to add." While working on the album, Alpert became acquainted with Lani Hall. "We were just friends," he says. "I enjoyed working with someone with such an extraordinary voice."

By 1967, A&M Records was doing so well it purchased the Charlie Chaplin Studios on La Brea Avenue. There, says Adler, the label established itself "as a place for artists to further their art without worrying about the commercial world." The congenial atmosphere was, at Alpert's insistence, the opposite of what he'd experienced at RCA. Soon A&M had signed everyone from the moody pop-psych band Procol Harum to the British blues belter Joe Cocker and a number of English rockers, among them Humble Pie and Spooky Tooth. It was a broad array of talent, but the trend was obvious. "I was looking for edgy acts," says Moss. "I felt that's where the game was going."

Predictably, when a demo by a pair with an innocent sound and a sweet, straight-cut look came over the transom in 1969, A&M rejected it. "Every other label in town had also turned us down," says Richard Carpenter, who'd written the four tracks to showcase the voice of his sister, Karen. "But I thought we had something, and I arranged for the demo to be resubmitted circuitously to Herb."

Alpert's first-floor office, with its fireplace, hooked rugs, and flawless sound system, was a perfect place to immerse oneself in music. "I closed my eyes and played the tape," he recalls. "It wasn't the kind of thing I'd have gone out of my way to listen to, but I could immediately tell that these kids were making the music that was real to them. It was an honest reflection of who they were as musicians. It's the same thing I look for in jazz, and when I find it, it always interests me. On top of that Karen had a remarkable voice. She reminded me of a singer I loved in high school, Patti Page. It felt like she was sitting in my lap and singing just to me."

Drawing on the wisdom Sam Cooke had imparted, Alpert told Jerry Moss that they should sign the Carpenters. So close was the relationship between the partners (they had a handshake agreement) that A&M made the deal. But the group's first album did only modestly well, and many at the label lost faith.

"A lot of people informed Herb, 'This band will never sell. Cut your losses,'" says Richard Carpenter.

Alpert was undeterred. "He said, 'There's something there,'" Carpenter recalls. "He said, 'I'm going to give them another go.'"

Trusting his instincts, Alpert, who two years earlier had enjoyed a rare hit as a vocalist with the Burt Bacharach-Hal David song "This Guy's in Love with You," slipped the Carpenters another Bacharach-David tune. "Herb gave us the lead sheet to '(They Long to Be) Close to You,'" says Carpenter. "It was just lyrics, melody, and chord symbols. I did the arrangement. A&M released 'Close to You' in May 1970."

The record shot to number one, selling more than three million copies in its first run. The Carpenters became the best-selling act in A&M history.

In the fall of 1968, as his breakdown approached, Herb Alpert and his first wife threw a big party at their home on Maple Drive near Sunset, one of the best addresses in Beverly Hills. It was an extravagant affair—backyard tented, wait-staff hovering. Among the guests were Sergio Mendes and Lani Hall. "I watched Lani exploring our house," says Alpert. "We'd had a high-priced designer do it, and it was filled with expensive things out of *Architectural Digest*. I was thinking to myself, 'She must think this is pretty impressive, pretty cool.' A few days later I asked Lani if she'd had a good time.

"She said, 'Well, not really.'

"I said, 'What was the problem?'

"And she replied in pretty strong terms, 'That house doesn't look anything like you. It doesn't feel like you. It's pretentious.'

"When she said that, I thought, 'She has the power to look right through me.'"

In December 1969, deep in the throes of his trumpet block, Alpert disbanded the Tijuana Brass. Not long after, he was divorced. But for Alpert, good came out of bad—he was seeing Hall. "Lani's honesty was irresistible," he says. "She doesn't know the meaning of the word 'lie.' Everything she says is true." For Hall's part, the initial attraction was physical. "His smile had a lot to do with it," she says. "It captured my heart." But the real allure went deeper. "I'd never met anyone that kind. It was pivotal. I thought if I hung around, his true colors would come out. They never did."

The two married in 1974 at Alpert's newly purchased Malibu spread.

Still, Alpert struggled with the trumpet. "It was horrible, horrible," says Hall. "At the time his studio was next to our kitchen. I'd be in there doing the dishes, and I'd listen to him through the wall as he was practicing. He could get out a few notes, but he couldn't play a melody. I'd just break down crying."

Alpert had begun therapy. "Nothing was more important to me than finding my path, finding why I'm here: 'What's my mission in life?' It was not just to be a celebrity or a guy who sold a lot of records. I did that, and it was nice, but it wasn't going to be my salvation. I was looking for my reason for being. I was willing to throw my horn into the ocean if that's what it took to find out. It was a long and winding road. It took years before I felt like I used to feel."

Through it all Alpert signed and produced performers at A&M. Slowly he regained his mastery of the trumpet, but it was 1979 before he had another hit of his own, the funk-influenced "Rise," one of the disco era's most sensual dance numbers. In 1987, he was back in the Top 10 with "Diamonds," which featured his characteristically seductive trumpet work and Janet Jackson on vocals. Meanwhile, thanks to such acts as Supertramp, the Police, Peter Frampton, Bryan Adams, and the Go-Go's, A&M was thriving. America's most innovative label, it had averaged seven gold records and four platinum albums a year for three decades. It was the largest independent record company in the world.

Yet by the late 1980s, Alpert and Moss sensed the business was changing. Not only were new technologies imminent, but the partners could see that in the years ahead it was going to be difficult to run a record company on instinct and a handshake. In 1990, they sold their baby to PolyGram for $500 million.

"Do I miss it?" Alpert asks. "Not for a second. It's a different business now. It's run by lawyers and driven by the bottom line."

The three-story stucco building that houses the Herb Alpert Foundation would be indistinguishable from its neighbors on Santa Monica's 6th Street were it not for the sculptures poking above the walls of its several outdoor patios. Tall and graceful, the pieces signal that this is a place dedicated to art. The interiors, which are hung with a score of Alpert's paintings and include a recording studio, further emphasize the point. In the years since Alpert sold A&M, his life has focused on the intersection between his own creativity and the ability that his financial wherewithal gives him to inspire it in others.

One of his favorite spots is the penthouse. After a meeting with foundation president Rona Sebastian, he settles into a chair and recalls how the sale of A&M Records enabled him to pursue both his artistic and philanthropic instincts. He says his new wealth set him free. His friends concur. "It allowed him to be the man he always wanted to be," says Moss. Adler agrees. "Money hasn't changed him. It has just enabled him to do the things he loves: paint, sculpt, play music, and run his philanthropy."

Alpert's interest in the visual arts had been whetted during the early years of the Tijuana Brass. "Right after I did *The Lonely Bull* and got a little bit of gelt," he says, "I bought a Rufino Tamayo at a gallery." He fell hard for the Mexican master. From then on, wherever the Tijuana Brass toured, Alpert spent his days off in museums. His reaction to Michelangelo's ceiling at the Sistine Chapel was pure jazz: "Holy shit, this guy is on another planet." His response to the sculptures of Henry Moore was an overwhelming desire to run up and hug them.

Soon enough, Alpert had made the leap from enthusiast to practitioner. "I think I had an advantage," he says, "in that I never really studied art. Because I started as a novice, there were infinite possibilities. There weren't any rules." This is not to say that Alpert didn't learn technique, both at the easel and when he took up sculpture. "The Chinese have a saying: 'Before spontaneity comes discipline,'" he says. "In the same way that I learned chords and notes before I could play the trumpet, I learned by trial and error what I could do as an artist."

Alpert's attitude toward philanthropy is much the same—reactive and instinctive. After reading a *New York Times* article last year that said the Harlem School of the Arts was going broke, he picked up the phone. He told Rona Sebastian, "Let's find a way to fix this." Says Sebastian, "Herb is intuitive in his giving. He will respond to a situation he finds intolerable." After she determined that the school could be saved, Alpert wrote a check for $500,000 and challenged other donors to match it. They did, and bankruptcy was averted.

This year the New Roads School in Santa Monica has begun construction on the Herb Alpert Educational Village. Scheduled for completion in 2012, the $10 million-plus project will house middle and high school students and include a 350-seat auditorium. Even more recently Alpert scored a triumph for jazz in Southern California by arranging the move of the Thelonious Monk Institute of Jazz Performance from its longtime home in New Orleans to UCLA's Herb Alpert School of Music. Starting next year students will be able to earn master's degrees on the Westwood campus from a faculty that will boast such guest lecturers as Herbie Hancock and Wayne Shorter.

At the same time Alpert's foundation is widening its range of interests, donating $3.1 million to Modest Needs, a New York-based group that provides temporary assistance to responsible people who've fallen on hard times. The foundation also has given $2.2 million to Adler and his wife, Page, to help start the Painted Turtle, a Southern California outpost of Paul Newman's Hole in the Wall Gang camps for terminally ill children. Every year Alpert personally puts a handful of worthy students through college. They have included an old friend's son and a young man from Africa who is now a prominent politician in Sierra Leone.

As diverse as Alpert's charitable interests have become, they spring from the same place. "Herb was a shy kid who at age eight picked up a trumpet and found his voice," says Sebastian. "He's now trying to help others find theirs."

On a crisp winter evening Herb Alpert and Lani Hall take the stage at Vibrato, the Bel-Air jazz supper club he has operated for eight years. The room, with its cozy wooden interiors, perfect sight lines from every seat, and state-of-the-art acoustics, has drawn performers ranging from Toots Thielemans and Dave Brubeck to Bobby Hutcherson and Chuck Mangione. Which is exactly what Alpert had in mind when he started it. "There are so many great musicians in L.A.," he says. "I run the place so they'll have somewhere to play." This evening Alpert, his wife, and their backup trio will burn through a set that includes several of the Tijuana Brass's greatest hits, a medley of Brazilian pieces, and numbers from *I Feel You.*

In black slacks and blazer over a T-shirt emblazoned with the image of the late Cuban jazz percussionist Mongo Santamaria, Alpert opens with the Spanish favorite "Bésame Mucho," carrying the melody on trumpet. Hall beams as he plays. When she sings Peggy Lee's "Fever," he steps to the edge of the stage and watches with adoration, pumping his fist as she finishes. The couple isn't shy about public displays of affection. They hug and kiss freely.

"We love what we do," Alpert tells the packed house early on. "I love to play the horn. She loves to sing. And we love each other."

Whereupon Alpert serenades Hall with the Lerner and Loewe classic "I've Grown Accustomed to Her Face." Voice glowing and warm, he makes it plain that this is a marriage in which emotion and art go hand in hand. As the song ends, Alpert picks up his Sonare and plays the first few notes of "This Guy's in Love with You."

A couple of days earlier he'd said, "I once read something attributed to Mark Twain in which he advised that you should think of your life in reverse, always asking, 'What will it be like to look back from 60, from 70, and now in my case from 85, or if I'm lucky, 90?' Since I read that, I realized that I'd be more disappointed with the things I didn't do than those I did."

That Championship Season

California, February 1984

Late on a November afternoon, six young executives filed into the NBC boardroom in Burbank to begin reprogramming the network's entertainment schedule following one of the most disastrous fall seasons in the history of television. Seven of the nine new shows NBC had premiered barely six weeks earlier were in cardiac arrest. For the eighth consecutive year, the network was dead last in the prime time Nielsen ratings race.

As five of the programmers took their seats around a large conference table, the sixth—Brandon Tartikoff, the boyish 35-year-old president of NBC Entertainment—approached the large metal chart that dominated the room. The chart was sectioned off vertically into columns representing the nights of the week and horizontally into hour and half-hour segments. It was covered with yellow, green, red, and white magnetic markers that bore the titles of the major networks' 1983 prime time shows.

No one would have blamed Tartikoff if he'd suffered a moment of stage fright. From afar, powerful eyes were upon him. On Wall Street, where stock in the RCA Corporation (NBC's parent company) is traded; on Madison Avenue, where advertisers buy television time; and in the offices of the 215 NBC affiliate stations across the country, every move he made would be mercilessly scrutinized. Even though NBC was about to end its most profitable year in half a decade, its $100 million in reported gross earnings paled beside the $200 million that ABC and CBS were each expected to take to the bank. A columnist for *Advertising Age*, the weekly marketing journal, would soon ask publicly what some of these distant observers were asking privately: "Does Brandon Tartikoff have a special magical immunity that enables him to keep his job despite flunking the Nielsens season after season?"

Although the pressure was immense, Tartikoff was focused on the task at hand. A tall, dark-haired man with sleepy blue eyes and a perpetually calm, slightly bemused presence that belies ambition and inner grit, he knew that in many ways he was simply going to have to start from scratch. Before the fall season had begun, he had budgeted for four hours of programming failure, but now he was facing a scheduling board that revealed six hours of dead shows.

"This ain't working," he said matter-of-factly as he reached up to the Friday night column, plucked off the 8 o'clock marker that read *Mr. Smith*, and tossed it onto a countertop. Then he ran his hand down to the 8:30 slot and detached the marker that read *Jennifer Slept Here*. *Jennifer* might get a chance to sleep on another night, but that would be decided later. Frowning, Tartikoff stripped off the 9 and 10 o'clock entries, and for the moment, at least, that was the end of *Manimal* and *For Love and Honor*.

All over Hollywood, there were people who might gladly have traded in their Mercedes to be eavesdropping on this session, for Tartikoff—who administers NBC's $900 million entertainment budget—was making decisions that would affect scores of writers, directors, production companies, and aides-de-camp. But more than that was happening here. Tartikoff's decrees would dictate what millions of Americans would watch on television every night and thus which actors would become stars, which phrases would enter the national lexicon, and which characters would become folk heroes (he had just pulled the plug on an orangutan with an IQ of 256, a sweet female ghost, a latter-day wolf man, and soldiers at an army base).

While Tartikoff handed down sentences, several of his programming lieutenants jotted notes on legal pads. Others got up and paced the spacious, wood-paneled boardroom. Like their boss, these vice presidents of comedy and series development and dramatic programming were a bit of a curiosity in the buttoned-down world of network television. They were casual, intellectual (one held a Harvard M.B.A., another had majored in English at Brandeis), prone to shoot from the hip, and, to varying degrees, involved in NBC's grand experiment to bring quality to a medium that has often trivialized the nature of human experience.

Getting up from his chair, Warren Littlefield, the bearded vice president of comedy, approached the programming chart and vigorously tapped an index finger against the marker for CBS's new 8 P.M. Monday show, *Scarecrow and Mrs. King*. All season long, the program had been cleaning up against NBC's *Boone*, a gentle one-hour drama about a budding country music star. "This is gonna bite your ass if you don't do something about it, Brandon."

Tartikoff considered his options for a second then went back to work. In a flurry, he discarded the marker for *Boone* and replaced it with cards for two half-hour comedies. Standing back, he examined his handiwork then shook his head. "In order to do the Monday move, you've got to move Wednesday and juggle Friday and Saturday," he said.

"It does have the look of pushing around the deck chairs," said Jeff Sagansky, the vice president of series programming. "And we're not helping Friday."

Picking up the cue, Alan Sternfeld, the vice president of planning, eased out of his seat at the board table and suggested that Tartikoff reschedule one of agent Sandy Gallin's *Live and In Person* variety shows as a stopgap measure on a Friday in December.

But Gallin's variety hours, Ed Sullivan-esque song-and-dance extravaganzas, had bombed when they were broadcast in September. "You want to give a signal that we're really bankrupt," Tartikoff said crisply, "put that in."

"Forget it, Alan," Segansky seconded.

Then someone mentioned that the NBC news department was pushing a documentary on the NATO missiles to fill another Friday night hole.

"Don't miss it, 'Be there,'" Sagansky muttered in a dark reference to the current NBC promotional slogan, which most viewers had refused to obey.

Tartikoff knew only too well how documentaries fare in prime time. "Don't worry about that happening," he assured the group. "I told them, 'Over my dead body.'"

As the session wore on, Tartikoff looked at the edge of the scheduling chart, where the network's new shows clustered like subs on the sidelines. Some of the titles had been jotted down in a kind of shorthand. *M&V P.I.* read one marker. Another simply said *Duck*. Others bore monikers such as *No Man's Land, The Ninja, House of Cards, Hard Knox, Pier 56,* and *Another Jerk.* One merely revealed the name of a producer—Lorne Michaels, creator of *Saturday Night Live.* In many cases, these programs not only hadn't been filmed, they hadn't even been written. And there were other story ideas so speculative that they had yet to be put on markers. They existed only in Tartikoff's mind—a plot mentioned over lunch last week, a concept hatched a month ago in a meeting, something he had dreamed up himself one weekend. This was the kind of haphazard planning that had led the young programmer's harshest critics to refer to him as "Random Tartikoff."

Yet Tartikoff is a believer in inspired accidents. For instance, one day he and Jeff Sagansky had been discussing the problem of casting handsome male leads—many of whom can't act—in starring roles. Suddenly, the two had a brainstorm, something they would privately call *The Man of Six Words.* It begins with the hero getting out of a woman's bed. He says, "Thank you."

Then he chases down some villains. He says, "Freeze!" Finally, the victims thank him for putting away the bad guys, and he says, "You're welcome." End of show. What happens during the rest of the hour? A car does the talking. Thus was born *Knight Rider*, now one of NBC's few bona fide hits. No amount of careful calculation could have concocted it.

In rebellion against adulthood, Tartikoff doesn't wear a watch, but as darkness fell on Burbank this November evening, he knew that time was ticking very, very fast. In five short weeks, he would have to announce a mid-season replacement schedule. Working quickly now, he detached one marker from an early spot on Thursday night and stuck it on Saturday. Then he moved his 9:30 P.M. Thursday sitcom, *Cheers*, to 9 on the same evening, leaving a gap just before the 10 P.M. show, *Hill Street Blues*. He filled it with the *Duck* marker, let it sit there for a second then removed it.

Tartikoff was beginning to play programming chess, a game whose objectives are deceptively simple: to create and schedule shows that will captivate the most television viewers during each week's 22 prime time hours. But there is nothing elementary about the way the game is played. Every move has myriad ramifications. A simple-looking change on Thursday at 9:30 P.M., for instance, will be felt all over the chart—Thursday at 9, Thursday at 10, some other night of the week where a show will be missing. Indeed, programming is considerably more complicated than the game of kings. It is conducted on many levels (the three networks, public television, independent stations, and now the cable companies are playing simultaneously), and it is fought with an arsenal of series, movies, and specials, whose powers— unlike those of a bishop or queen—are subject to the whims of unpredictable forces. Only M.C. Escher could design a game board that would suggest the intricacies of modern network programming. It would be a multidimensional, checkerboard cube made of smoky Plexiglas. And it would shudder and shimmy with vibrations emanating from sources as various as affiliates and sponsors.

Looking around the NBC boardroom, Tartikoff certainly knew that programmers are sometimes forced to traverse a realm where subjectivity and rationality blur and the known world begins to wobble. In fact, he had been in this room on another occasion—as a junior executive—when things just flat-out warped. One fall afternoon in 1978, producer Dan Curtis had arrived in Burbank to pitch an idea for a new show. On the conference table, Curtis set up a circular wooden railroad track atop which he placed a number of handsomely carved train cars and an engine. Like Faberge eggs, the cars came apart, but instead of offering up portraits of the Czar's children, they revealed playgrounds on wheels. Inside one was a lavish dining hall. Another featured a swimming pool. A third contained deluxe sleeping accommodations. This was the prototype for *Supertrain*, an hour-long adventure show. Fred Silverman, NBC's chairman at the time, and the others in the room were knocked out by the presentation. Surely, they thought, the program would be a hit.

Supertrain, of course, was one of the biggest derailments ever, a multimillion-dollar disaster. After a few horrible episodes, it was canceled. Depressed, Silverman surveyed the somber boardroom—a place reminiscent of some Eastern business library—and decreed it jinxed. For much of the next year, NBC conducted conferences at the network's Rockefeller Center offices in New York. Only after nearly $100,000 had been spent converting the Burbank space into a light, airy room done in neutral Scandinavian tones could programmers reconvene there.

Five years later, Tartikoff and his programmers knew that many of the moves they were making in this same room—moves that looked so promising—could have the same sort of hidden faults that had killed *Supertrain*. Still, they worked on, illuminated by a flickering of orange neon from the sign atop Chadney's restaurant across the street. By the time the group disbanded, the large metal chart that had been so orderly when the session began was in disarray. Tomorrow they would rejoin the fray.

Driving home through the suburban tranquility of the San Fernando Valley, Tartikoff's mind was whirring. At 10 P.M., *Bay City Blues* would go on the air. The show had been drawing only a 16 share of the audience, meaning that only 16 percent of the viewers watching at that hour had been turning to it. Tartikoff, an ex-college baseball player, desperately wanted this program about a minor-league baseball team to succeed. Produced by Steven Bochco (creator of *Hill Street Blues*), *Bay City* was deftly written, and Tartikoff took considerable pride in it.

In a sense, *Bay City* was the kind of show that made Tartikoff's job worthwhile in the face of an extreme circumstance. Ten years ago, when he was 24 years old, he was diagnosed with Hodgkin's disease, a malignancy of the lymphatic system. After a harrowing eight months of chemotherapy, Tartikoff warded off the cancer, which is now in remission. But the experience left him with more than just a strong sense of the temporal nature of life. It led him to rethink what he really wanted to accomplish.

"There's a myopia that what you're doing is all meaningful," he says. "It sets in with people in TV. For TV is itself a cancer. People get a taste then they dwell on it all their working hours. I still get caught up, but I'd hate to think that if this job at NBC were the last thing I did in life, and I hope it won't be, that they'd say of me, 'He put on three shows that got 30 shares each.'" Consequently, Tartikoff believes himself to have a very different agenda from that of most people in television. He thinks that the medium can be used to present funny, moving, and original dramatic works. Of course, he has shilled for ratings with the best of them, but he also says he would never schedule such toxic waste as *Love Boat* or *Dynasty*, even if doing so would fill his network's coffers and secure his position.

As Tartikoff negotiated his Ford Mustang around the tricky curves of Coldwater Canyon Boulevard into Beverly Hills, he tried not to let himself become obsessed with these problems. Several years before, he had totaled his car on this road after a vexing meeting in Burbank. Still, it was hard to keep his mind off of *Bay City Blues*. If tonight's episode could draw a 19 share, he thought, the show just might make it.

That night there were two dreams in the life of Brandon Tartikoff. The first, a public dream, had begun days earlier when signals had pulsed outward from towers in New York and Burbank. These blips had carried the dream to a satellite high above the earth. From there, it had traveled back to both coasts, where it was transmitted by microwave and over phone lines to NBC stations in Detroit, Memphis, Boise, Jacksonville, Buffalo, and scores of other towns. Then, from antenna topped by red warning lights, the dream moved again, coursing through the sky to its destination—television sets, millions of glowing tubes in darkened rooms where a pattern of sizzling dots gave the dream its shape. On this particular Thursday night in November, the dots revealed a young man, a pitcher for the Bay City Bluebirds, who was throwing his career away. He was an alcoholic. He and a pretty girl were driving very fast down a two-lane road. They were drinking. They were smiling. They were singing along with the radio. When they rounded the bend in the highway, they didn't see the truck in front of them. There was a screeching of tires, a crash—and terrible silence. The young man was dead. The Bluebirds' owner sobbed. Across America, sharers of the dream cried, too.

The other dream, a private nightmare, usually unfolds later, in the quiet hours of the early morning. Tartikoff will be in bed beside his wife, Lilly,

drifting on the sea of sub-consciousness, when images suddenly heave themselves up like sharks. In this recurring dream, Tartikoff sees himself picking
up a telephone and placing a call to Nancy Mead, an NBC researcher in
New York who often reads him the overnight ratings of network programs.
In the dream, the call goes through, but Mead won't tell him anything. She
keeps procrastinating. Tartikoff poses question after question about how the
previous night's shows performed, but she equivocates. Again. And again.
Finally, by nightmare logic, he reaches out over 3,000 miles and grabs the
woman by the collar, screaming, "Goddammit, tell me. Tell me how we
did."

The next day, Brandon Tartikoff awoke at 7. It was a beautiful early fall
morning, and light fell softly into his room. He traipsed across the hardwood floor and down the hall to the bedroom where his baby daughter, Cal-
la, was sleeping. After cuddling her for a second, he returned to his bed, sat
down on the edge of the mattress, and called New York. This time there was
no screaming, just terrible news: *Bay City Blues* had drawn a 14 share. As the
verdict seeped in, sadness welled up inside of Tartikoff. He had often said
during these weeks: "All I asked was 'Come to the dance and see whether
you like it. Then leave.' But they didn't even come."

    Bay City's dismal performance was more than just a setback for Tartik-
off. The failure also served to symbolize the position in which NBC finds
itself in the mid-1980s. At the 1983 Emmy ceremonies, the network—after
receiving a record 133 nominations—captured 33 awards (ABC won 14,
CBS, 11). With its trophy case full, NBC, by desperation and design, began
in a slightly smug fashion to cast itself in the role of the network that airs
thoughtful and well-written programs. Grant Tinker, who is chairman of
NBC and Tartikoff's boss, is an avowed champion of the sort of literate series he sold to the networks when he was president of MTM Enterprises—
programs such as *The Mary Tyler Moore Show* and *Lou Grant*. It just so happens that such shows appeal to affluent urban viewers between the ages of 18
and 49—the people whom advertisers most want to reach. In an era of frag-
menting audiences, NBC—by broadcasting shows like *Hill Street Blues,
Cheers,* and *St. Elsewhere*—seems to be offering a path for sponsors who seek
"upscale" targets for their sophisticated video hucksterism. A decade ago,
ABC, then the third-place network, began a meteoric rise in the ratings by
selling its attractive demographics. To some extent, NBC is now trying to
follow the same trail. Although its gross ratings have lagged far behind those

of its competitors, the network has managed to come in a close second to ABC in the battle for viewers in the 18-to-49 group.

But good demographics or not, NBC is struggling. Paul Klein, formerly an NBC vice president and now president of the *Playboy* channel, says of his former employer, "If you have a low circulation in TV, you call it quality programming. NBC doesn't operate as a going concern. [The network] has a lot of people who know how to make money, but Grant Tinker and Brandon aren't two of them. Brandon is a figment of Grant Tinker's irresponsibility."

What goes unstated in Klein's criticism is that despite NBC's ability to offer advertisers an upscale viewer profile, television remains a mass medium. A network's affiliated stations are its retailers—like shoe stores, they distribute their wares in all kinds of locations to all kinds of people. The owners of some of these affiliates see NBC as a purveyor of custom work in a ready-to-wear world, and they are not pleased.

"If the January replacement shows don't work, there'll be unrest, there'll be statements made," says Alvin Flanagan, president of WXIA-TV in Atlanta and formerly chairman of the Gannett Broadcasting group (owner of three NBC stations). "There won't be an eruption until May [when the affiliates meet]. It'll be rocky going then, and Tartikoff will take the brunt of it. Prime time programming has been a disaster. That's Brandon's doing. If he gets three or four hits in January, he'll get a new lease on life. But if not, he's in trouble. Of course, only Tinker really knows, but I don't think my opinion goes unshared."

In programming chess, rule number one is: Protect the living. That maxim dictated Brandon Tartikoff's initial moves in preparing for winter 1984. Even before the late-night session at NBC back in November, he was taking steps to shore up his existing programs. "My job is like the doctor in the cancer ward," he said one evening during this period. "The most you can do is get the patients comfortable for six or seven years. All of them are terminal. Some are going to die immediately. Some, through your help, will live longer and better. At times I feel like I'm telling a patient he should redirect his eating habits and his life protocol. When he doesn't, he ends up dying."

Tartikoff began his ministrations by focusing attention on *For Love and Honor*. There was still an outside chance that the show could be resurrected, and so one Sunday afternoon, Tartikoff, Sagansky, and another NBC vice

president drove to Bel-Air and spent several hours huddling with the producer, David Gerber, in the living room of his house.

Because the program was about the peacetime army, Tartikoff felt
Gerber's writers could not rely on the kind of militaristic scenarios that give
police shows and war movies a sense of jeopardy. He wanted more romance,
greater character development. In short, he hoped to push Gerber—who
made his name by creating action shows such as *Police Story*—to transform
the program into something along the lines of a prime time soap opera.

"I told him I was compromising," Gerber recalls. "But I told him I could
accept it. In this business, so many people feel like chattel or just pieces in a
puzzle, but when Tartikoff comes to you with that wonderful young, woeful
look of his, you really want to work for him. Couple that with his commercial
instincts, and he's hard to beat."

Tartikoff's prescriptions haven't always been greeted with such equanimity. He canceled *Fame* in May 1983 (the show is still in production and
flourishing in syndication), but during its death throes, he attempted to ad-
minister a number of plot transfusions. "NBC wanted more *Room 222* and
Mr. Novak," recalls Bill Blinn, the program's producer. "They wanted shows
with finite endings or more promotable shows about teenage prostitution,
child pornography." Blinn describes Tartikoff's suggestions as overly assertive and pat.

But as Tartikoff made his rounds this fall, he was rarely shy about offering his opinions. "I don't mention this out of arrogance," he says, "but the
fact of the matter is, I've worked on more series than any producer I've
worked with. If you do 35 pilots a year and you multiply it times the four or
five years I've been head of NBC programming, I've done a lot of work.
Now I'm not going to sit across from Norman Lear and tell him how to do a
pilot, but in the other 99 percent of the meetings I attend, I get my point
across."

For example, Tartikoff had long been urging the producers of *Diff'rent
Strokes* to marry off mighty mite Gary Coleman's stepfather, played by Con-
rad Bain; the show needed a new female character. Tartikoff's matchmaking
efforts prevailed. The knot will be tied this winter. That was an easy one.

But there was another, thornier problem—*Hill Street Blues*. Every
week, the class act of television was falling further and further behind CBS's
prime time soap opera, *Knots Landing*. After puzzling over the trend,
Tartikoff wrote producer Steven Bochco a letter.

The programming chief began by explaining the obvious. Ratings were dropping. Something had to be done to attract more viewers, especially more women; NBC's research figures showed that women were starting to turn to *Knots Landing* in droves. Then Tartikoff outlined a series of remedies.

First, he asked if Bochco would consider introducing a character—male or female—to entwine romantically with someone in the existing cast.

Second, he proposed that the producer and his writers think about creating a neighborhood association of housewives with whom the *Hill Street* precinct officers could occasionally interact.

Finally, and most dramatically, Tartikoff urged Bochco to thread a new and sensationalistic storyline through a number of the episodes. He wanted something hot, along the lines of the Alfred Bloomingdale-Vicki Morgan scandal.

When Bochco read the letter, his immediate reaction was anger. He believed that his show was, week in and week out, a finely cut jewel. It's not broken, and it doesn't need fixing, he thought. And he believed *Hill Street's* ratings ailments were traceable in part to Tartikoff himself. Bochco felt NBC had consistently violated one of the central tenets of effective programming by failing to give the show a strong lead-in.

Programmers believe that television viewers can be held entranced by one network throughout the night. It's the domino theory applied to the cathode-ray tube: Schedule a hit show early in the evening, and the rest of the night falls neatly into place. And what had Tartikoff given Bochco? Early in the night there were stragglers such as *We've Got It Made*. At 9:30 there was *Cheers*, a show that had taken a year to find its audience; now that it finally had one, Tartikoff was planning—or so Bochco had heard—to reschedule it.

Bochco waited five days after receiving the letter before calling Tartikoff. "I needed some time to let it settle," he says. The two talked on the telephone and agreed to meet later.

While a solution to the *Hill Street* dilemma was deferred, Tartikoff turned his attention to the problem of his 8 P.M. Monday show, *Boone*. Declared dead at the meeting in Burbank, the show had been carted down to the morgue where, upon examination, it had opened its eyes and breathed. Ratings were picking up. Tartikoff was involved in conceiving *Boone*, and he wanted the show to make it. Produced by Earl Hamner (creator of *The Waltons*), it was a folksy, sweet slice of American pie—the last "family" show on television.

As his deadline for constructing a second-season schedule loomed nearer, Tartikoff chose to spare *Boone*, at least for the moment. But he gave himself an out: Twice during the late weeks of the fall, he preempted *Boone* in order to test a Dick Clark special, *TV's Censored Bloopers*, and a *Johnny Carson's Practical Jokes* special in the time slot. Even though Tartikoff was irritated that Carson had vetoed a laugh track for his show, both the practical jokes hour and the bloopers program attracted strong 27 shares of the audience. Tartikoff charted the figures for use later.

Meantime, he telephoned David Gerber and gave him good news about *For Love and Honor*. "Keep your powder dry," Tartikoff said. He had made a hard choice: The ambitious *Bay City Blues* would be canceled to give the formulaic *For Love and Honor* one last shot in a new time period.

When not tending the wounded, Tartikoff was working to create new shows to fill the numerous empty spots left in his schedule by the dead. Some of these programs were springing to life in his head. One was *Not in Front of the Kids*, a comedy about children who are deposited on their grandparents' doorstep by a career-minded mother. The kids, feisty little pistols, think they'll be able to control the old folks. But they're wrong, as they keep learning.

As is de rigueur for budding moguls, Tartikoff had once done time in the mailroom of a New York ad agency, and he had some funny tales to tell. Thus, *I Gave at the Office* was another show he was plotting.

Comedy writing fascinates Tartikoff. NBC started the fall of 1983 with ten comedies in its lineup—more than in any season in recent memory. On some of the shows, most notably the innovative *Cheers* and *Buffalo Bill* (a dark half hour starring Dabney Coleman as a misanthropic radio talk show host), Tartikoff was encouraging producers to develop long, even surreal sketches—in essence, to labor against the grain of what he perceives to be a depressing trend. "The golden age of comedy has come and gone," Tartikoff says. "Imagine people in your life, if when you had dinner with them, every fifteen seconds they tried in a desperate manner to make you laugh. That's TV comedy today, and couple that with the fact that a lot of people doing it aren't funny, you've got problems. This trend has been caused by the zap box [remote-control channel changer]. Lucille Ball told me that, and she's right. Back in the old days, a viewer would be too lazy to get up and turn the channel, and that'd give you five minutes to set up a joke for a hilarious three-minute payoff. Not anymore."

By late November, Tartikoff had decided that his grandparents show might have a chance at a Friday night spot. But he would rely for his other new programs on breeders far more fertile than himself. One of the most prolific is Stephen J. Cannell, producer of *The Rockford Files* and *The A-Team*.

In Cannell's office on Hollywood Boulevard, writers were putting together a program upon which Tartikoff had pinned high hopes. The premise was this: Two ex-Vietnam MPs and a young computer nerd run a salvage business that doubles as a detective agency in Redondo Beach. The office, it turns out, is on a boat anchored across a gangway from a craft carrying the most beautiful women you'd ever want to lay eyes on. But that's all these guys can do—lay their eyes on them. The women are hands off, verboten. "It's like those girls in the Robert Altman remake of *The Long Goodbye*, who were always tempting Elliott Gould," Tartikoff said. "Guys will watch it because they want to be in great shape and living in Redondo Beach. Women will watch it for the same reason." The only problem: What should the show be called?

Cannell's nomination: *Pier 56*.

"Sounds like a fish restaurant," Tartikoff replied. "How about *The Naturals?*"

"That sounds like a bunch of hairdressers," Cannell said.

The final choice: *Riptide*—the name of the detectives' boat.

Elsewhere in Hollywood, other studios and suppliers were cranking out new ideas and re-circulating old ones to fill NBC's needs. At MTM, writers were working on *Duck Factory*, a sitcom about an animation studio. At Warner Bros., producers were creating *Night Court*, a comedy about a New York judge. At Universal, *The Legman*, a show about college kids who run errands for a shady shamus, was coming together. In New York, Lorne Michaels was casting a new variety show, episodes of which would not be taped until the day before they aired. Tartikoff had pretty firm ideas about where and when he would schedule these fledgling programs, and he now knew which old shows he would try to save and which he would let expire.

He was poised to make his moves.

No one could have been better prepared for the battles to come than Brandon Tartikoff. Ever since he was a kid on suburban Long Island watching *The Amos and Andy Show* and *The Honeymooners*, he has regarded the world—the whole catalogue of human experience—as raw material for a network programmer's magnetic board. Perhaps that is the best way to look at his own life as well—as a series of shows, some of them considerably more compelling than the material he was struggling over for his winter 1984 lineup. This is how Tartikoff's real-life schedule might appear in *TV Guide*:

IVY

The adventures of an irreverent Ivy League undergraduate who wants it all—athletic glory, literary dreams, and the prettiest girls on campus. An hour-long comedy drama.

Tartikoff is seen at Yale, a gangling, dark-haired English major who holds down the keystone on the school's baseball team. He wants to be a novelist, and his maiden effort is a novella about the efforts of one Saliva Schwartz to investigate a quartet of Siamese twins who are spreading a sexual disease across America. Tartikoff is not in the least offended when his senior adviser, Robert Penn Warren, urges him to enter another field: television. The Pulitzer Prize winner makes the suggestion after Tartikoff remarks in class one day that a short story by Tolstoy might have been more successful if one of the characters had been an automobile.

NIGHT WRITER

By day, he promotes television shows. By night, he writes poison pen notes about his industry. A searing hour-long drama.

In the season premiere, we see Tartikoff spending his days on routine station business at ABC affiliate WLS in Chicago, where he is promotions director, then hurrying home each night to sit before his old Royal typewriter. He writes a number of articles for *New Times* magazine—some under his own byline, others that are critical of television under the pseudonym Jordan Enid. In a 1975 piece about the demise of the game show *Jeopardy*, Tartikoff crafts an eloquent, funny paean to the program and its host, excoriating the NBC executive responsible for the show's cancellation. "Daytime TV is getting ready to play its own version of *Final Jeopardy*," he concludes. In other pieces, Tartikoff ranges farther afield. In one, irony of ironies for a television executive, he lovingly champions that most un-mass form of communication—the letter.

BRANDON'S SONG

That is how Tartikoff himself refers to this period in his life. It is the story of a young man's efforts to deal with cancer.

One morning when Tartikoff is 24 and working at WLS, a jogging companion—the host of a Chicago TV talk show—collapses unexpectedly. The man has cancer of the bone marrow, and within months he is dead. Shaken, Tartikoff decides to visit his own doctor for a checkup. It is a fateful trip. He learns that he has Hodgkin's disease. The illness is detected at an early stage, and soon Tartikoff begins the debilitating process of exorcising the demon through chemotherapy. He loses weight. His hair falls out. He suffers chronic nausea. His cheeks become swollen. His complexion turns mottled and gray. "He never complained," recalls his friend Larry Lyttle, now a vice president of comedy development for Warner Bros. Television. "He'd get sick all night at dinner then get up the next morning and play basketball. That's how he decided to beat it—by just not acknowledging it. He's very tough."

Of course, it isn't that simple. "I had to confront the reality that I might not get better," Tartikoff remembers. "I had to admit that I might die. The treatment was very humbling."

WLS IN CHICAGO

The zany efforts of a big-city television promotion whiz to win a larger audience for his station. A half-hour sitcom.

At a time when WLS's daily 3:30 P.M. movie is drawing lukewarm ratings, Tartikoff notices that the station owns about 60 gorilla movies. The young promotions director goes to station manager Lou Erlicht (now president of ABC Entertainment) and asks to run ape movies every afternoon for a week. Erlicht says yes. Tartikoff then takes a few hundred dollars, films a promotion, and voila, "Gorilla My Dreams" week is on the air. Ratings for the afternoon movie shoot through the roof. After that comes "Thrilla Gorilla" week.

Then Tartikoff begins applying a bit of method to the madness, using the station's computer to cross-reference movies by subject matter. He feeds in the subject "evil," and the computer coughs out a slew of titles such as *Secrets of Evil*, the *Evil Garden*, and *Evel Knievel*. "In its own warped way, the computer did the discriminating for me," Tartikoff recalls. A week of evil films is soon on the air. And so forth. Ratings are climbing even higher when he receives an audience with Fred Silverman, then the president of ABC Entertainment. Would Tartikoff be interested in coming to Los Angeles?

THE COAST

A promising young executive gets his big break and moves west, only to discover that Hollywood dreams are laced with disillusionment. A prime time soap.

Three years after fighting cancer to a draw, Tartikoff lands in Los Angeles as a programming executive at ABC. Like many would-be impresarios, he feels he has a gift for reading the public's needs and desires. He regularly visits a Westwood shop called Postermat and places bets with friends that he can pick out the three top-selling T-shirts at that particular moment. He rarely loses.

Tartikoff is driven, and he makes all the right moves. Yet he doesn't really share the perceptions of the people who dominate the industry. He tools around in a beat-up Toyota whose salt-eaten floorboards show pavement below and he refuses to own either a color television or a credit card. Shortly after he arrives in Hollywood, he drives to the MGM lot one night to see an industry screening of Paddy Chayefsky's film *Network*, a jeremiad attacking the shameless striving of television executives. Tartikoff believes that the movie rings true on a dozen important levels. But after it's over he's shocked to find that he may be alone in his reaction. Beneath a big tent on the studio lot, TV executives are attacking the cheese dip, jostling for positions at the bar, and generally enjoying an uproarious good time. Whenever Tartikoff stops someone to ask, "What did you think of the movie?" he receives an answer like, "I think it'll make money in New York and L.A. but die in the sticks." Tartikoff concludes: Nobody got it. On the way to his car, he stumbles upon a tableau that crystallizes the whole night for him. A woman television executive who holds a job similar to that of Faye Dunaway's character in the film is ranting to her date, "That's me up there. I'm going to sue those motherfuckers."

The woman's companion hears her out then jokes, "Oh, you don't come that quick"—a barbed reference to the fact that Dunaway's character suffers from hair-trigger orgasms.

As Tartikoff drives away, he thinks: To them, this is just another night out in Hollywood.

After a year at ABC, he switches to NBC to work for his college classmate Dick Ebersol, then vice president of comedy and now producer of *Saturday Night Live*. Although Silverman hired Tartikoff at ABC, the student beats the master to the new network by several months. Shortly after Silverman arrives at Burbank, he makes Tartikoff vice president of West Coast programming. In another year and a half, he gives his protégé his present job.

But under the Silverman aegis, there are considerable limits to Tartikoff's power. At a Hollywood Radio and Television Society luncheon, he is asked, "Is it true that no one at NBC makes a decision without checking with Silverman?"

"Could I get back to you on that?" Tartikoff jokes.

FLIPPER

A comedy of manners about a network executive and his wife who sit at home in front of the RCA console TV, eating Popsicles and hurling barbs at actors who unnerve them.

Tartikoff is a notorious homebody, happiest when he's curled up on the sofa of his ranch-style house near the Beverly Hills Hotel. Armed with a remote-control channel changer, he savagely flips from show to show. *The A-Team* flashes on, and Mr. T is seen spying on an office while the song "Roxanne" plays in the background. "That's Cannell's trademark, getting contemporary music into a show." Flip, and ABC's *Three's Company* appears. "She's totally unfunny," he says of the series' star, Joyce DeWitt. "I can't take too much of this." But he stays with ABC, and *Oh Madeline* appears. Even worse: "This is a terrible show." Flip, and up comes a skinny gospel singer on an Orange County cable station. "What is this, an anorexia telethon?" Flip, and it's back again to ABC, where *Hart to Hart* offers up a death scene. "Do you get the feeling more people die in episodic TV than on the news?" It's now 10:33 P.M., and Tartikoff turns down the volume. "Let's have some fun," he says. He picks up the phone and calls New York, where it's 1:33 A.M. Dick Ebersol answers. Tartikoff has called to suggest that *Saturday Night Live* do a parody of *Yentl*. "I've got an idea, Dick. Let's get Mary Gross to do a sketch called *Dentl*." After Tartikoff hangs up, he returns to his rapid-fire channel changing. "Boy, this is Brandon," Lilly says.

BURBANK CITY BLUES

A feisty group of young television executives determines the fate of a network that, like some ghetto police precinct, is besieged with problems. A one-hour drama of intertwining relationships and corporate danger.

The very night that Fred Silverman is shown the door at NBC, his successor, Grant Tinker, telephones Tartikoff and asks him to stay. Tartikoff now calls the shots, rarely having to clear decisions with those on high. To protect his autonomy, he develops a seductive style, often consulting his superiors, seeking their advice in a disarmingly ingenuous manner that endears him to most of them.

Yet by the fall of 1983, there are rumblings. It is, after all, Tartikoff's fourth consecutive losing season. Even his strongest boosters believe he needs to pull some rabbits out of the hat. Still, Tartikoff and his assistants evince a cocky esprit. They make fun of the programs aired by ABC and CBS. They joke about their dilemma. And Tartikoff is often the biggest joker of them all. In October he appears as guest host of *Saturday Night Live*. In one sketch, he wanders through the streets of New York desperately pressing handbills for failing NBC shows on uninterested passersby. Finally, a doorman bellows, "Move along," and Tartikoff skulks away into the uncaring throng.

It was now early December. In New York, the plaza at Rockefeller Center had undergone its seasonal conversion from café to skating rink. But upstairs at 30 Rockefeller Center, headquarters of NBC, the men who control the network's purse strings weren't in the holiday spirit. They were worrying about just what kind of schedule their young programming president on the West Coast was going to produce. In Los Angeles, though, Brandon Tartikoff was confident, even buoyant. He felt that his second-season lineup was beginning to fall into place, and he also believed he was making progress in correcting some of the network's long-term deficiencies.

On a balmy Friday night shortly before he would fly to New York to unveil his plans, Tartikoff sat in a red Leatherette booth at the rear of the Hamburger Hamlet on Sunset Strip.

"I just came from a great meeting with Michael Nesmith," he said as he sipped white wine. "He's agreed to do a show for us called *Video Ranch*. He directed the first 56 MTV videos, and I called him up after seeing a cassette he did called 'Elephant Parts' to see if he'd be interested in doing for comedy what he'd done for rock music." The idea Tartikoff was suggesting was as easy to see as it was revolutionary: Comedy videos could do for jokesters what rock videos had done for pop stars. It would be a new form. Nesmith, formerly of the singing group The Monkees, had already begun shooting and had signed up Martin Mull, David Steinberg, David Letterman, and several others. He planned to give Tartikoff a one-hour pilot in February.

"If the pilot is good, I'll give him an order for twelve or thirteen more," Tartikoff said. "I'll get them on in September. I think it could be the new *Laugh-In*. It could be an explosion. Every teenager in America will watch it. Nesmith is so good. It's great to be in the presence of people to whom you say, 'How do you do that?' as opposed to most people, to whom you say, 'Here's how you should have done it.'"

Tartikoff was in high spirits. He'd had lunch with Fred Silverman at La Serre in the Valley, where he had informed his mentor that he was going to renew *We've Got It Made*, a mindless piece of fluff Silverman was producing and about which Tartikoff had taken a lot of ribbing from old friends. Since Silverman's ouster from NBC three years ago, he and Tartikoff have remained close, although there was a tensely funny moment the first time they got together professionally following the change in their roles. Silverman traveled to NBC to attend a meeting, strolled into the boardroom, and sat in the seat that had become Tartikoff's at the head of the table. Tartikoff ribbed him about how some things never change. Everyone laughed, including Silverman, but he kept the seat.

Following lunch, Tartikoff had returned to his office to meet with Steven Bochco of *Hill Street Blues*. Bochco had cooled down, and he announced that he planned to implement two of the three suggestions Tartikoff had made in his letter—the new love interest for one of his regulars and the sex-scandal plot line. In return, Tartikoff promised to air more promotional spots for *Hill Street Blues*.

Then Robert Blake, Mr. Baretta, dropped by to pitch Tartikoff a show that only Robert Blake could have dreamed up: a drama about a dead-end kid who finds Christ in prison. It was called *Father on Hell Street*.

"I know a buncha writers and I'll get 'em and I'll deliver four of the best scripts you ever seen," Blake promised. He seemed determined, and who could tell—maybe something was there. Tartikoff gave him an order for four episodes.

And throughout the afternoon, Tartikoff basked in the glow of a phone call that he'd received the day before from Michael Eisner, president of Paramount Studios. Eisner wanted to thank Tartikoff for helping Paramount to land a movie that was fast becoming a Christmas hit—*Terms of Endearment*. The financing for the moving story of a cancer victim had been cinched after Tartikoff committed $3.5 million for television rights.

Tartikoff was further cheered by the fact that the occupants of the booth next to his were engaged in a spirited discussion of the previous evening's episode of *Hill Street Blues*, in which Lieutenant Howard Hunter had put a gun to his head and pulled the trigger in what viewers would not know was a foiled suicide attempt until the next week.

"I didn't pay them to be here," Tartikoff said of his neighbors. Then he smiled blackly and added, "There's a yin and a yang to this." He pointed up at a television set crouched behind the bar. It was turned to CBS.

After a while, Lilly—an ex-dancer with the New York City ballet— came in to get a sandwich and take her husband home. Tartikoff was facing another night before the tube, this time screening cassettes of *Buffalo Bill*. He had to decide whether to open the second season with an episode full of racial undertones or go with a tamer one.

When the Tartikoffs left the restaurant an hour later, they had to pass within several feet of the bar TV. The channel had been changed, but now it was on ABC. Tartikoff clenched his fists and said, "That really burns me up." He wasn't kidding.

On Thursday, December 8, Brandon Tartikoff took the elevator up to the sixth-floor boardroom of NBC's Rockefeller Center offices in New York City. As the doors opened, he might have smelled gunpowder burning in the air. Reuven Frank, his counterpart as president of NBC News, had just resigned, partly because of the news division's low ratings.

Awaiting Tartikoff was a group of twelve men in suits (back in LA., all the deliberations had been conducted in shirtsleeves and sweaters), sitting around a large table. Among them were representatives of the sales and research departments and Tartikoff's three bosses—Ray Timothy, group executive vice president of NBC, Bob Mulholland, president of NBC, and Grant Tinker, the chairman. In every way, this room was a long distance from the chamber in Burbank where a month earlier Tartikoff and his team had begun picking up Humpty Dumpty's pieces and trying to put them together again. But walking in Tartikoff felt upbeat and calm. He believed he had come up with some winners.

Of course, he had done it with a few artfully placed mirrors. On Tuesday, for instance, he had been faced with the problem of how to capitalize on the network's only monster hit, *The A-Team*. The evening had been falling apart at 10, first with *Bay City Blues* and then with *For Love and Honor*

(David Gerber's show had climbed to a 16 share in its new slot—not good enough).

Tartikoff presented the assembled executives with a gambit that he felt would not only help the network win the 10 P.M. hour but also turn the evening into a juggernaut. NBC's 9 P.M. show was *Remington Steele*, a clever, campy hour-long drama about a female sleuth and her bumptious but witty and sexy male partner. By mid-December, the program had climbed into the ranks of the country's twenty top-rated shows. Furthermore, the program's TVQ score (a measure of fan loyalty) suggested that its following was committed enough to stay tuned, no matter what time the show aired. So Tartikoff informed the NBC brass that he was shifting *Remington Steele* to the 10 P.M. spot and in its place inserting *Riptide*. The first two hours of Tuesday night would belong to Stephen Cannell, and if Tartikoff's instincts were correct, *Riptide* would not only be a hit in its own right but would serve as a seamless conduit through which millions of viewers would pass from *The A-Team* to *Remington Steele*.

Everyone at the table agreed with Tartikoff—Tuesday looked good. If they liked that, Tartikoff said, they should see one of the shows he was considering for Wednesday. The lights went down, and Tartikoff turned his colleagues' attention to a screen recessed into a far wall. Up came two episodes of the new comedy *Night Court*.

As the shows played, the room filled with laughter. *Night Court*, in fact, elicited so many yuks that Tartikoff made a snap decision to put it on his schedule instead of *Duck Factory*, the other show he had been contemplating for the 9:30 slot.

On Thursday and Saturday nights, Tartikoff explained, he was essentially shifting around various comedies and dramas, hoping that new configurations might unlock some magic. His only adventurous move on either of these nights was to position *Buffalo Bill* in the coveted 9:30 Thursday slot before *Hill Street Blues*. (He refused to bite the bullet, however, and chose to begin with a milder episode than the one he had originally considered.) The Dabney Coleman series was bold, and Tartikoff's decision to give it such a prominent perch sent a strong signal.

On Sunday, Tartikoff made no changes whatsoever. This left Monday and Friday, the two evenings that had stumped him from the start.

On Monday night, Tartikoff confessed, *Boone's* revival had been too little, too late, so the program was going to be killed. Then the question became: Will two half-hour comedies or a one-hour show of recombinant video garbage provide a better lead-in for the evening's movie? The answer was easy. The November test runs of *Bloopers* and *Practical Jokes* had caused the Nielsen ratings to jump as if they had received a jolt from the adrenal gland. Thus Ed McMahon and Dick Clark would be hosting a new show molded from these two hours of slicked-up bits of business in a spot where only a month earlier a fledgling drama had been airing.

But it was Friday night that was the black hole, and as the group discussed the network's plans for that evening, it became obvious that Tartikoff was flying on a wing and a prayer.

At 8 P.M., he was scheduling *The Legman*—because he believed in the group at Universal producing the show. He had nothing to screen at Rockefeller Center. "Well, I wish we had a pilot," one executive said.

Tartikoff was not, however, completely empty-handed. He had a 35-minute demo for his 9 P.M. Friday show, *The Master*. The lights went down, and he focused the group's attention on the screen, where actor Lee Van Cleef kicked, jumped, and strutted his way through a Bruce Lee repertoire.

As for the 10 P.M. program, which would be called *The New Show*, Tartikoff had only his abiding faith in Lorne Michaels to share with the men seated around the table. Tartikoff knew that Michaels had done it before. Surely he'd do it again.

A cynic responded, "Maybe we should just call it *The Old Show*."

Yet there was little dissension in the ranks. While a couple of the programs Tartikoff was scheduling were called "shit" by some in the room, most of his efforts met with approval. Like football quarterback Fran Tarkenton eluding massive tacklers while scrambling for daylight, Tartikoff had managed to keep the ball in play—maybe even keep alive the hope that a receiver was going to break open downfield and catch a touchdown pass.

There was irony in the moves Tartikoff had made. Last season, he had taken the low road with some shows in an effort to attract large audiences. Such programs had betrayed his professed desire for quality, of course, but even worse, they had failed spectacularly in the ratings. Now, in spite of the death of *Bay City Blues* and the birth of a half-baked video smorgasbord like *TV's Bloopers & Practical Jokes*, Tartikoff was scheduling several dramas and comedies of style and wit. By default, NBC would again assert itself as a network with high standards. But would anyone tune in?

Watching his young protégé present the schedule, Grant Tinker, NBC's white-haired chairman, wasn't worried. A veteran of the production side of the business, he himself had sold a dozen shows simply on an idea, a hope. History had taught him that this was a dangerous way to proceed, but he knew in his gut that it could be done. In fact, Tinker had a sneaking suspicion that Tartikoff just might have come up with some new hits.

Five days after the New York meeting, Brandon Tartikoff was back in Burbank, sitting in the booth at Chadney's, the restaurant across the street whose neon sign had lit his nights for the past month. The Rockefeller Center session was still on his mind—especially the fact that so much of his new schedule was built on blind faith.

"I remember when we put on *The A-Team* [last winter], we had only a few days of dailies and some scripts," he said. "And it became our hit of the season. And we'd seen four hours of *Bare Essence*, thought it was great, and ended up yanking it after six episodes. So how can you really tell?"

He took a bite of his cheeseburger. "I just can't believe we're not going to move ahead. We can't do as bad as we did before. It's almost a given we'll improve."

There was a long pause. "Well, most TV just doesn't work," Tartikoff said finally. "But there's failure, and then there's dismal failure. If I get another string of shows with 13 and 14 shares, well...I've always said that if I'd had my shot, they won't have to come to me and ask me to step aside. I'll do it myself. If certain of these shows are abject failures then maybe they should get somebody else. I could produce shows. Of course, people wouldn't laugh at my jokes so readily."

As the winter wore on and the premiere dates for the new lineup approached, Grant Tinker would remain firmly in Tartikoff's corner. "I can tell you that he's not going to get fired," Tinker said. "His job is in no jeopardy. If he were to come to me and say, 'I've bombed again, and I'm packing it up,' I'd talk him out of it. I'd say, 'You just can't pack it in as a loser.'"

Tartikoff is not, however, naïve in these matters. After all, he remembered the supportive utterances that network types always made in the weeks preceding an executive's demise. So it was no surprise that he would tell one joke quite often as he waited for Nielsen's 1,700 families to bless or blast his new season.

"Do you know the difference between a dead dog by the side of a road and a dead network executive by the side of the road?" Tartikoff would ask.

Then, smilingly knowingly, he would supply the punch line. "With the network executive, there aren't any skid marks."

Brandon Tartikoff ultimately succeeded in taking NBC to the top of the Nielsen ratings. Along the way he was instrumental in creating such defining programs as Family Ties, Miami Vice, *and* Seinfeld. *In 1991 he left the network to become chairman of Paramount Pictures. He died in 1997 following a recurrence of Hodgkin's disease.*

The Big Mocker

The most influential and intimidating gossip in Hollywood lives and works in a two-bedroom unit of a nondescript apartment complex in Los Feliz. Most of the celebrities about whom he writes wouldn't be caught dead in his neighborhood, nor would they recognize him if they ran into him. He's a goateed 31-year-old named Mark Lisanti, who dresses in jeans and T-shirts (a favorite features a picture of Sean Penn snapped after a nightclub scrap and the legend *Spicoli Forever*). He doesn't hang out at hot spots like Mood or the Cabana Club or lunch at power restaurants like Orso or the Grill. Rather, he holes up in his home office, a small space outfitted with a Sony computer and battered Ikea furniture and decorated with a Sigmund Freud action figure, a few snow globes, and a framed still of Ralph Macchio from the 1986 film *Crossroads*. In his 18 months as editor and sole writer of Defamer.com, Listanti has revolutionized Hollywood gossip. Wickedly funny (CBS president Les Moonves is a "generously betoothed future galactic despot") and reflexively impious ("Katie Holmes's Virgin Birth," roared the headline announcing the pregnancy of Tom Cruise's fiancée), Defamer has won a vast following. According to comScore Media Metrix, a firm that measures Internet audiences, the site—which is part of the New York-based Gawker empire—attracted nearly 1 million visitors in the first quarter of 2005, placing it just behind such blogosphere behemoths as the Drudge Report. For people in the Industry, Defamer has become the preferred but never publicly acknowledged source of both news and attitude. "I read Defamer every day, sometimes twice a day," says the head of a division at a major talent agency. "It's hilarious, but it's not the kind of thing I advertise." Few comments could better attest to Lisanti's impact. Not only are Hollywood potentates loath to speak ill of him, they're loath to speak well of him, for fear of offending any of the actors, directors, or moguls he's skewered and on whom their livelihoods depend.

On this fall day, Lisanti has cranked out 12 items. One celebrates the season premiere of Fox's *The OC*. "The show is my guilty pleasure," Lisanti says. "It sums up Defamer's worldview—repulsion and attraction at the same time." Another pairs an announcement that Bruce Willis had been selected to judge the Miss Italy contest with an account of Sean Penn's efforts to assist victims of Hurricane Katrina in New Orleans. "It just seemed logical to me," says Lisanti. "Willis is looking for Miss Italy. Penn, accompanied by a photographer, of course, is looking for survivors. In each case there's a ridiculous Hollywood angle."

But the breaking news involves Tara Reid, the star of *American Pie* and *American Pie 2* and long a mainstay of Defamer. "They're Fake and They're Unspectacular," boomed the headline atop an early-summer item reporting the actress's admission that her breasts—one of which previously popped up on the site after it slipped out of her dress in the presence of paparazzi—had been surgically enhanced. Reid's pronouncements shortly thereafter on the London subway bombings ("I wish all the mean people, if you want to be mean to each other, just buy a country and blow each other up") generated even more copy. Which is why the rumor that came in the previous day to tips@defamer.com ("anonymity assured") demanded attention: *Taradise*, the E! channel travel series chronicling Reid's margarita-fueled jaunts to exotic locales, was facing cancellation.

"I happen to watch *Taradise* because it's an incredible train wreck," says Lisanti as he leans back in the chair at his computer. The show's demise is exactly the sort of revealingly inconsequential story he loves. As he likes to say, it's "extra useless." Though the intelligence regarding *Taradise*'s fate had struck Lisanti as "detailed and solid," he took pains to verify it, confirming the basics via an e-mail to another source and further satisfying himself by scanning *Variety* and *The Hollywood Reporter*, which in relating that the E! channel had renewed its *Gastineau Girls* series failed to mention *Taradise*. "Usually," he says, "networks announce pickups in bunches." By mid-afternoon, Lisanti believed he had the piece nailed and beneath the headline "Taradise Lost" posted his item:

> It is with a heavy heart that we inform you that our beloved *Taradise* is no more. Our spies have told us that E! has cast out Tara Reid and her globetrotting, club-hopping crew from its movable Eden, calling them back stateside and plunging our televisions into a postlapsarian wasteland devoid of the party-positive innocence that only a half-in-the-bag Reid could deliver.

"I don't want to say it's reporting, but it's closer to reporting than what I usually do," says Lisanti as he rereads the *Taradise* story. Then, a bit wistfully, he wonders whether Reid's banishment from the E! channel lineup will make for fewer appearances in Defamer. Just that quickly, however, his spirits brighten. It will take more than the cancellation of a cable series to keep Tara down. "As long as there's not prohibition," he says, "she'll always be in the news."

Occasionally, Mark Lisanti scores scoops bigger than the cancellation of *Taradise*. Rumblings concerning layoffs at Miramax were first reported on Defamer; so, too, Tom Cruise's engagement to Katie Holmes. Sometimes the site itself makes news. Defamer's photomontage of Cruise's sofa-hopping gyrations on *The Oprah Winfrey Show* early this summer, which Lisanti's girlfriend, Kristen Stancik, captured by shooting TiVoed images with a cell-phone camera, went a long way toward alerting America to just how out there the actor is. More important than the site's contents, however, is the absurdist prospective it brings to the Industry. "Defamer supplies our daily minimum requirement of irony," says Allan Mayer, managing director of the crisis management firm Sitrick and Company, which deals extensively with the entertainment press. "We live in a total-immersion celebrity culture, but it's all so packaged. The *New York Post* will write about whether Lindsay Lohan has breast implants as if it's an issue as significant as what's going on in Gaza, but Lisanti writes about it in a way that makes it clear he knows the matter is absolutely trivial and a national obsession."

Defamer is both creating and embodies a fundamental shift in the culture's view of celebrity. Over the years the assumption implicit in most entertainment reporting was that the stars and the executives behind them were deities. Even stories exposing their foibles and faux pas, far from tarnishing them, actually reinforced their stature as objects of fascination: Only higher forms of being could command such attention. Defamer will have none of it. Neither traditional journalism nor old-fashioned social criticism, the site is a new form of hybrid that uses satire and technology to strip the veneer off Industry grandees. In Defamer, Hollywood, which is feudal and hierarchic, has at last met the Internet, which is radical and anarchic. If the site did no more than challenge the established order, that would be enough, but what elevates it is that it's also artfully written. Like much of what's on the Web, Lisanti's voice is offhand and pithy, yet there's something more. Populated by well-known recurring characters, fixated on status, laced with interlocking narratives, and located in a fabulously familiar playground, Defamer is an ongoing nonfiction novel. The place is Hollywood, the time is now, and the ambition—to turn Truman Capote's maxim on its head—is to make all gossip literature.

To click onto Defamer.com is to enter a world that suggests there's not much difference between the supermarket scandal sheet depths and the *Vanity Fair* Oscar party summits. The bad girls—Tara Reid, Lindsay Lohan, and Britney Spears—and one very naughty boy, Jude Law, appear on a sometimes daily basis. Frequently they're captured in the act ("We did it every way we could," the site reported Spears's first husband enthusing) or with their pants down ("Jude Law's Smoking Gun Revealed," blared the headline when the inevitable nude picture emerged). Capitalizing on the Internet's ability to link to anything and everything, Defamer ensures that its subjects' previous indiscretions live on into mortifying eternity. Thus an item on the September birth of Spears's son ("Spears Baby Equipped with Penis") leads directly to an item (with photos) detailing the entertainer's breast-baring romp two years earlier on a high-rise balcony. Likewise, a feature on the possible pregnancy of Law's fiancée ("Sienna Miller Wombwatch") not only reopens Defamer's "celeb schlong locker" but dredges up multiple items on the actor's admission of an affair with the family nanny. Not that Defamer is passing judgment. "Awww. We can't stay mad at Jude," it declared soon after the "nanny-diddling" scandal broke in July. "What a lovable scamp."

Like Charles Dickens's serialized tales, Defamer relishes its protagonists' peccadilloes and delights in their vanities. The site's coverage of Hollywood royalty almost always strikes a note of appalled bemusement. Earlier this year, it congratulated "Malibu feudal lord" David Geffen for allowing "access to the public beach blocked by his enormous Gay Mafia Xanadu" a "mere 22 years" after promising to do so. Beneath a photo of carb-deprived producer Brian Grazer that originally appeared in *Variety*, the site observed:

> Wanting to ensure that his boss would look his best for Monday night's *Flightplan* premiere, producer Brian Grazer's Special Skin-Tightening Assistant cranked the winch on the back of Grazer's neck one too many times, rendering him unable to blink or close his mouth. Luckily, Grazer's Director of Emergency Facial Lubrication also attended the event and periodically misted [his] face to prevent his gums or eyeballs from succumbing to any uncomfortable dryness.

The power player who consistently merits the most attention (29 appearances in the first nine months of 2005) is scene-making director Brett Ratner. Best known for the *Rush Hour* pictures and currently finishing *X-Men 3*, Ratner is invariably referred to on the site as "America's favorite fauxteur." Here he is "grinding his private parts against an attractive woman" at the new Wynn Las Vegas. There he is paying homage to that desiccated icon of showbiz virility, producer Robert Evans. Defamer has also written up Ratner on multiple occasions for parking his Bentley in the handicapped-only spaces at such fancy dives as Fred Segal's Café Mauro. Once again, though, the site refuses to sit in judgment, asserting that the director's "lack of natural born ability with a camera" constitutes a legitimate disability.

Whether it's in its weekly Privacy Watch feature, which publishes reader e-mails ("I witnessed…Tori Spelling, joined by a male companion who was not her now ex-husband, in a full-on, tongue-down-the-throat make-out session at Buddha's Belly"), inventive monikers ("Butterscotch Stallion" for Owen Wilson) or updates on job changes (typically accompanied by a mug shot of the Endeavor Agency's president, the "secretly pleased" Ari Emanuel), Defamer creates a tableau of contemporary Hollywood life. Like an anthropologist, Lisanti has captured the rites of a strange and insular society. At the moment, that society's tribal lodge is the Tropicana Bar at the Hollywood Roosevelt Hotel, where another of Defamer's favorites, singer-actress Courtney Love, overdosed this summer. In its Tales from the Trop, the site portrays an after-hours torrid zone that is simultaneously out of control ("Doing it Outdoors at the Tropicana," boomed one headline) and off limits ("Keeping the Plebes Away from the Pool," boomed another). Always at the velvet rope is the Tropicana's proprietress, Amanda Scheer Demme, whom Lisanti has dubbed the "hotness calibration technician." Her job is to turn away the unwashed. Lisanti's job is to make certain they get in.

The Web, of course, has spawned millions of sites, thousands of which focus on Hollywood. But they all pale in comparison with Defamer. Go Fug Yourself publishes countless unflattering celebrity photographs yet is less culturally aware. Awful Plastic Surgery, as its name suggest, focuses on a limited aspect of celebrity culture. Ted Casablanca's popular The Awful Truth captures the manners and mores of red-carpet Hollywood but is unremittingly campy. Although the Superficial also traffics in celebrity misadventures, it lacks wit ("Tara Reid Is Unemployed" was its bland headline announcing the demise of *Taradise*). None of these sites is as plugged in as Lisanti's. The executives and agents whose machinations generate the Industry's big stories rarely appear in their pages.

As with other sites under the Gawker Media umbrella, Defamer combines the irreverence for which the blogosphere is celebrated with some of the more conventional virtues of journalism. Early on Nick Denton, the founder and CEO of Gawker, understood that the Internet was the perfect medium for gossip. It's fast, accessible, and cheap. A 39-year-old British expatriate, Denton worked as a reporter for the *Financial Times of London* and later as an entrepreneur in Silicon Valley. His sites—the best known are Gawker, which covers New York media, and Wonkette, which covers Washington politics—are all about compiling information and presenting it with maximum amounts of spin. The formula is ingenious and successful, and of the company's 14 sites, Defamer just might possess the most potential. Already it has attracted such major advertisers as Sony, Warner Bros., and Fox and is turning a profit. Where the bulk of Denton's blogs are of interest to narrow segments of the population, this one is of interest to those in the know and everyone else. For a culture in which even outsiders now fancy themselves as Industry insiders, Defamer exudes a nearly irresistible combination of attitude and authority.

Every weekday at 7:30 A.M. Lisanti powers up his office computer and, much like old-fashioned police reporters who started their shifts by paging through station-house docket books, goes online to ferret out what the night has left him and what the coming hours might bring. "The first thing I do is check the trades and the *New York* and *Los Angeles Times*," he says. "They're the only places that do original Hollywood reporting." Lisanti then consults his RSS reader, software that constantly updates a customized list of 193 sites that have proved to be productive sources of gossip. As his links attest, the British papers (especially the *Sun* and the *Mirror*) provide frequent items, as do the *New York Post*'s Page Six and the *Daily News*'s Rush and Molloy. Fellow bloggers, among them Totally Unauthorized, BoingBoing, Egostatic!, TVgasm, and Flickr, also offer a bounty of material.

Lisanti generally posts items taken from the news by midmorning and then, as the studios and agencies begin to buzz, starts fielding tips. "I get 60 to 100 e-mails during the day," he says early one evening as he sits at his desk draining the dregs of a day-old cup of coffee. Soft-spoken and self-effacing, Lisanti initially comes across as a good citizen, yet as he talks, sharp glints of subversiveness reveal themselves. "I have a lot of eyes and ears out there. It's great." Some of those eyes and ears, cell-phone cameras at the ready, attended parties the night before. "Technology has turned everyone into potential spies," he says. "The pictures don't have to be good. They work on two levels. They show a celebrity caught off guard, and they show that you're so pathetic you went into a dark club and took a shot of a celebrity." Other tips come from people in the trenches. "During every transaction in Hollywood," Lisanti points out, "five people are silently on the line. That's how the junior people learn the business, and they wind up knowing things." Although not all of the information he receives from these sources is usable or even right, it keeps him up-to-date. For instance, Lisanti's sources regularly apprise him of new deals appearing on what's known as the tracking boards, confidential databases to which the studios, agencies, and production companies subscribe.

Unlike most Hollywood journalists, Lisanti avoids publicists. "They are all about trades," he says, "and I don't do them. They give you dirt if you scratch the back of a favored client. That's antithetical to how Defamer works." Not only this, he does no on-scene reporting. He never speaks to any of the people about whom he writes. Of the bad girl who reigns supreme on the site (65 appearances in the first nine months of 2005), Lisanti shrugs and allows, "I wouldn't know what to say to Lindsay Lohan." Nor does he patronize the Industry's most notorious "celebrity glory hole," as he calls it. "I've never been to the Tropicana," he says. "I guess I want to see what it's like, but the not going is as good as the going. No place could live up to such hype, and besides, three months from now it'll all be over." He views material less for its news value than for its comic potential. "People shouldn't care about Lindsay Lohan or Tara Reid," he says, "but this is what the cultural tennis ball machine is firing at us. This is what I have to swing at. I'm basically a guy writing jokes about famous people."

Although journalism school professors might scoff, Lisanti's distance and approach are the very things that give Defamer its impertinent omniscience. If Lisanti were part of the game, he couldn't be so sardonic. He couldn't channel Hollywood's id. That's what makes him different from the Industry's two most legendary gossip columnists—Hedda Hopper and Louella Parsons. Hopper, whose syndicated column was featured in the *Los Angeles Times*, was a stylish former actress of marginal abilities who enjoyed a reputation for bitchery and a fondness for conservative politics. Her bête noire was the left-leaning actor Charlie Chaplin, and she hounded him almost until the day she died. Parsons, who wrote for the *Los Angeles Herald Examiner* and the Hearst syndicate, was a dowdy print veteran of questionable writing skill who loved the movies and all the people in them except for Orson Welles, whom she never again mentioned following his portrayal of her boss in *Citizen Kane*. Hedda and Louella were at heart similar. Both were provincial, small-town girls who were wittingly and unwittingly used by Hollywood. (Indeed, each studio employed publicists for the sole purpose of planting items in their respective columns.) In cahoots with the Industry, they dined with moguls, drank with actors, and except when the powers dictated otherwise, cleaned up personal scandals. Unlike Lisanti, they functioned as Hollywood's superego, attempting to control both the stars' behavior and the business's image. At the height of their influence, their columns reached a combined readership of 75 million.

In the aftermath of Parsons's retirement in 1964 and Hopper's death in 1966, Los Angeles's outlets for Hollywood gossip began to dry up. For several years Parsons's former assistant Dorothy Manners carried on at the *Herald Examiner*. Later, Page Two kept the Hearst paper's hand in the game. At the *Times*, meanwhile, Joyce Haber and Mary Louise Oates covered the beat, although both were more concerned with high society than with the Industry. In 1989, with Oates's departure from the *Times* and the folding of the *Herald Examiner*, Los Angeles was left without a full-time local gossip columnist. At the same moment, national outlets for celebrity news were proliferating. Not just *People* and the tabloids covered Hollywood, but so did *Us* and the television newsmagazines *ET* and *Insider*. Soon enough they were joined by *In Style* and, more recently, *In Touch*. The paradox, however, was the more that was written or broadcast about the Industry, the less insightful any of it was. Because magazines needed celebrities to push newsstand sales far more than celebrities needed magazines to promote their careers, stars instructed their publicists to broker reportorial access, making celebrity journalism an oxymoron.

"People in Los Angeles believe they can control what's written about them," says Gabriel Snyder, a *Variety* reporter who once covered the media for *The New York Observer*. "They only talk to the press when it's time to publicize their movies, and the reporters go along with it because they don't have to worry about getting beat. That's why gossip columns are important—they feed the dailies, the national weeklies, TV. Media is a pyramid. Someone on the bottom needs to get things started."

This is the process that Lisanti has begun, and what it portends is not just the end of the Industry's decades-old stranglehold on scuttlebutt but a devaluation of celebrity as an unquestioned cultural currency. If Defamer publishes the unvarnished truth about Paris Hilton, an orchestrated and expurgated *Vanity Fair* cover story is of less worth in the marketplace. The upshot is that leverage will shift out of the hands of stars and into the hands of bloggers and—should magazine editors realize that what stars have to sell no longer sells—journalists.

No wonder that for every Hollywood executive who finds Defamer amusing, there are many who despise it. "I read Defamer four or five times a week," says the vice president of media relations for one of the major studios, "but I don't like it. I think it is mean-spirited and furthers its own agenda. It's a very specific example of what's wrong with the internet. Things are posted very quickly and not always with enough care. The only recourse I have is to point out an inaccuracy and ask them to take it off the site. I've done this a couple of times. But I can't be quoted by name criticizing them. If I take a shot at Defamer, he'll just post it on his site and make me look like a fool. He has a forum I don't really have."

The one figure who will go on the record with complaints about Defamer is the entertainment lawyer Bert Fields. "My problem with Defamer is that it has no standards," says Fields. "It feels that it can say anything about anyone. Humor is one thing—nobody minds a spoof—but these people go substantially beyond humor. He can do enormous personal damage to people."

Fields, whose clients include Warren Beatty, Dustin Hoffman, and Tom Cruise, has been jousting with Defamer since shortly after it posted its photomontage of Cruise's bizarre performance on *The Oprah Winfrey Show*. The lawyer took his first run at the site in early August when it published a synopsis of a *Radar* magazine article on Cruise's affiliation with Scientology that quoted a former church member who alleged the actor had doubts about the religion. "Your story about Mr. Cruise is false and defamatory," Fields wrote Defamer. "Please correct this misrepresentation as quickly as possible." The lawyer took aim again several weeks later after the site ran two photographs purporting to show a nine-year-old Cruise dressed up as Dorothy for a grade-school production of *The Wizard of Oz*. "The picture of the child dressed as a dancer is not Mr. Cruise," declared Fields in an e-mail. "It's his sister, Cass. At nine he once put on a costume in the picture for a Halloween party. He did not go around dressed as a girl as your report suggests. I must ask that you cease any publication of those photographs and retract the suggestion that he dressed regularly as a girl."

It didn't take long for Fields to hear back from Defamer. The site responded to the lawyer's initial letter by reprinting it in whole then proclaiming, "There you have it, straight from Team Cruise: The actor's faith in L. Ron Hubbard was, is, and forever after shall be unshakable." The second complaint prompted an even more arch retort. Beneath the headline "Defamer Clarification: Tom Cruise Dressed as Dorothy Once," the site asserted, "Even though we never suggested an ongoing predilection for women's clothing on the part of Mr. Cruise, we retract, we retract, we retract."

For Fields, Defamer's mocking replies were beside the point. "I always contest," says the lawyer. "If bloggers are entitled to the protection of the newspaper statute—and I don't think they are—I'm required to ask for a retraction. The law demands that." Fields was laying the foundation for a libel action, should that be the course Cruise wants to pursue.

As Lisanti sees it, Fields decision to mix it up with Defamer proves that the site is succeeding in its mission. "Isn't it the height of absurdity that Tom Cruise's lawyer writes and says he only wore the dress one time?" he asks. "These people take themselves so seriously. Our job is not to take them seriously. Truth be told, we don't get enough hate mail. We should be getting more."

Nick Denton encourages Lisanti's stance. "People in the press live in fear of the Hollywood lawyers," he says. "Maybe we'll learn to live in fear of them, too, but right now, we don't. One of the main reasons we started Defamer is L.A. seemed so woefully under-gossiped. My sense is that on the phone and over lunch, people in L.A. gossip all the time. But very little of that gossip makes it into the *L.A. Times*, which looks down on it, or into the trades, which are so beholden to the Industry. We're not owned by a big media company, and we don't owe anything to anyone. It may sound trite, but we're only loyal to the audience. We have the luxury of writing what we feel like. It'd be idiotic for us to tone down our content or attitude. That's what sets us apart."

Despite such bravado, Defamer has taken down material that might prompt legal trouble, particularly nude photographs, including ones of Cameron Diaz and, most notably, Jude Law. Even so, the site usually gets the last word. In removing its shot of "lil' Jude," Defamer expressed regret for depriving its readers of the chance to ogle: "God, it looked like he could fit two nannies onto that thing!"

In the new Hollywood gossip, nothing is off-limits. To look at the Industry otherwise, Lisanti believes, would be selling out. Still, as he gets up from his computer, he acknowledges that a part of him is chagrined by Defamer's contents. "My mother says she reads Defamer, and I said, 'Please, don't tell me that. I write filthy, disgusting things all day.' I don't want to picture her reading them."

To a soul, Lisanti's friends are surprised that he became a gossip columnist but not at all surprised that he became one who specializes in pillorying his subjects. "Mark was not the sort of guy who had celebrity magazines lying around," says Greg Kampanis, who has known Lisanti since the two were freshmen living in the same dormitory at Georgetown University. "He was very much a regular guy, a sports guy, a big Yankees fan." Nonetheless, Kampanis, now director of business development for the E! channel, sees a straight line from past to present. "Mark was always a funny, sarcastic guy, just bitingly sarcastic in conversation. So Hollywood is really the perfect target for his point of view." Duncan Birmingham, a screenwriter who met Lisanti when both were pursuing graduate degrees in creative writing at Boston's Emerson College, concurs. "I thought Mark would end up becoming a novelist. But from the first day of our program you could see he was a real wiseass. I read Defamer every day, and it's the same guy I knew at Emerson, the same voice."

The son of an architect father and a school administrator mother, Lisanti was raised in the New York City suburb of Yonkers. He grew up addicted to popular culture. "People from my generation were more immersed in TV than those from earlier generations," he says. "We had cable, MTV, and all those crappy shows like *The A-Team* and *Knight Rider*. My generation has an ironic appreciation of Mr. T." Like so many other children of the 1980s, Lisanti developed more than just a soft spot for the era's cult entertainment figures. Overexposure to celebrity culture bred a general skepticism about the mainstream media. These kids didn't buy into the Hollywood myth, and thanks to the development of the Internet, they had access to a medium that encouraged them to vent. By the time they came of age, they were striking back online at traditional news and entertainment outlets.

After earning his MFA at Emerson, Lisanti was at a loss. He did want to write a novel, but he also wanted to earn a living, so he moved to Hollywood. "There are jobs writing on TV and in the movies," he says. "Otherwise, you're just alone writing fiction, and it's so speculative." As it turned out Lisanti couldn't land the sort of position he sought. After interning on *Malcolm in the Middle*, he fell into low-level jobs on various other sitcoms, among them *Raising Dad* and *Bram and Alice*. "I came out here to be a writer," he says, "but the only thing I proved was that I was competent to put brads in scripts and take lunch orders."

In 2002, frustrated by his inability to break into Hollywood, Lisanti launched a blog called Bunsen.TV, named for an obscure character in *The Great Gatsby*. From the outset its only subjects were stars and show business. "Celebrities," states the legend beneath the site's masthead, "are just like any other people with multibillion-dollar industries dependent on propping up their fragile egos." Lisanti posted daily on Bunsen, addressing such issues as "How to Talk to Your Kids about the Paris Hilton Sex Video" and raising the question "Were Starsky and Hutch Gay?" By 2004, as plans for Defamer were being formulated, the site had hit its stride, and Denton had noticed. "I hired Mark because he had a good blog," he says. "It's a different skill than that for print journalism. It's more conversational, and the standards are simultaneously lower and higher. Bunsen showed me that Mark would never descend to doing things in a straightforward way."

During his 18 months as the Defamer, Lisanti has written nearly 4,000 items—a staggering amount of work. "I feel like I'm on a treadmill," he says as he sits at a Coffee Bean & Tea Leaf late one afternoon. "If I were still doing this in 20 years, I'd kill myself." The likelihood of Lisanti being in the job for even another year is slim, however. The site has made him what he's always wanted to be—a sought-after writer.

"Media people are now approaching me," he says. "Hollywood people, too. I've got two or three meetings next week." Editors of other Denton sites have parlayed their highly visible but low-paying positions into something bigger (Gawker has gone through four writers in just three years), and Lisanti feels he needs to as well. He drives a 1994 Honda Civic, and though he won't discuss his salary he reportedly earns around $50,000 a year. Yet much as he hopes to capitalize on what he's accomplished with Defamer, he faces difficult choices.

Lisanti has been in preliminary talks with the *Los Angeles Times* about writing a gossip column for the daily's online edition that would also appear in the Calendar section. "If Mark cleaned up his language and tightened up his fact checking," says a *Times* editor, "everything he does could appear in the paper."

The other undoubtedly more lucrative path would take Lisanti into television, and he has recently engaged the United Talent Agency to explore just such a possibility. Lisanti would like to produce and write a series that covers Industry news much as Jon Stewart's *The Daily Show* covers political news. Although Comedy Central's new *The Showbiz Show* with David

Spade beat him to the punch, it has received uniformly negative reviews, making Lisanti look good by comparison. "On an average day," wrote *Variety*, "Defamer.com delivers more chuckles than Spade and company could muster in a half hour."

Each of Lisanti's options, though, is problematic. While the *Times* needs a gossip columnist, it's not an ideal outlet for someone who derides the very entertainers its writers usually treat with equanimity. Moreover, its editors typically have the final say. At Defamer, Lisanti isn't edited at all. "It's just me and spell check," he says. "Luckily I'm a stickler." While some judicious editing wouldn't hurt Lisanti, he would almost surely find the *Times*—or any other newspaper—resistant to his caustic fancy.

As for television, it, too, is fraught. Most channels would be as scared of his approach as a daily newspaper. "Someplace like the E! channel would never hire someone like me," says Lisanti. "They'd lose their access to celebrities if they put me in charge of a show. They're going for a mass market. They want their celebrity news with no attitude. They don't want irony."

Both newspapers and television, in sum, are traditional media. Defamer is anything but traditional. Still, there's no question that Lisanti presents an appealing commodity. Editors and entertainment executives are shrewd enough to look at Defamer's numbers and see that the site drives traffic. Furthermore, Lisanti's vision of celebrity is not only addictive, it's plainly in the vanguard.

Lisanti could, of course, stay at Defamer, using it much as his colleague Ana Marie Cox, who recently took a leave of absence from her job as Wonkette to write a novel, has used her position. "The site could really set me up to do a Hollywood novel," he says.

Besides, Lisanti possesses a tremendous pride of authorship in Defamer and doesn't relish the prospect of watching Denton anoint a replacement, which he would do in the blink of an eye.

Ultimately, however, Defamer's chief attraction for Lisanti is that as long as celebrity subjects keep providing free material, the site remains fun to produce. "He has a very good time mocking an industry that's so easily mockable," says his girlfriend, Kristen. After Lindsay Lohan's publicist tried to blame the paparazzi for the actress's October car crash with a delivery van on Robertson Boulevard, Lisanti noted, "We should never believe the 1st, 2nd, or 3rd through 17th thing that issues forth from a publicist's mouth." The same week, he observed that Nicolas Cage's decision to give his newborn son Superman's birth name, Kal-el, proved that "the actor has finally made a clean break with reality." Then there was his reaction to Jake Gyllenhaal's remarks that his liberal Los Angeles upbringing allowed him to plunge into his gay love scenes with Heath Ledger in the forthcoming *Brokeback Mountain* without any homophobic panic:

> Credit Gyllenhaal's tolerant and forward-thinking parents for rearing such an open-minded son. Sure, the less advanced kids at school laughed at eight-year-old Jake when he insisted on playing "Gay Cowboys and Transgendered Indians" at every recess, but that uncomfortable period is definitely paying dividends now.

Restless though Lisanti is, he can appreciate that Defamer gives him one of the most liberating platforms in all of journalism or entertainment. Defamer wrests power from the stars and their handlers. Defamer offers an antidote to a mindless and obsequious celebrity culture. Defamer slaps the kings and queens of Hollywood and their minions. "I like my job," Lisanti says as he leaves the Coffee Bean for a quiet night at home. "On good days, I laugh while I'm working."

ACTORS

Part of the act of self-invention involves putting on a public face. That's what actors do, sometimes in very different ways. When I profiled Nick Nolte for *Premiere*, I was astonished by the painstaking lengths he goes to fashion that face. Harrison Ford, whom I profiled for the same magazine, is the opposite. What you see is what you get, and if he doesn't want you to see it, you won't.

An Ordinary Man

Premiere, March 1988

Harrison Ford is walking purposefully along a wooden plank sidewalk in a town somewhere in the Rockies. He moves with a sturdy grace, well-muscled shoulders shifting against the yoke of his denim shirt, hips working like ball bearings inside dirty Levi's. Save for his sunglasses, which he wears as armor against chance recognition, he could be just another cowboy.

By Ford's calculations, he only makes it into the big city—a one-stoplight affair on the edge of a National Park—about "0.3 times a week." Although the place retains a smidgen of western integrity, it has largely gone the way of all mountain resorts. The streets are lined with white-water-rafting outfitters, real estate offices, and ski shops. The main square is anchored by a Ralph Lauren boutique. Ford feels fenced in here.

No wonder. On his 800-acre spread seven miles out in the country, elk and deer roam freely, bald eagles wheel overhead, and cutthroat trout shoot through the creeks. The ranch is dominated by a two-story house of Ford's own design that a friend, relishing the obvious contradiction between the dwelling's massive size and plain style, terms a "Shaker mansion." Ford calls the compound a "refuge for animal animals and human animals."

But even a man more at home on the range than in civilization has to take care of business from time to time. The sooner the actor gets his chores done, the sooner he can get back to the Ponderosa.

At a sporting-goods store, Ford buys a pair of size-twelve boots with leather uppers and rubber bottoms. "These are basically industrial-strength slippers that I can pull on to step out into the 8-degree cold while the dog is encouraged to do her business," he says.

At a bicycle-repair stand that doubles as a wood-stove retailer, Ford picks up a couple of fireplace grates. "I don't want nice—just something that works," he says, setting two unadorned pieces on the counter. The proprietor, an unreconstructed hippie, is friendly with Ford, and as he rings up the purchase, he nods at a fellow who's shadowing his famous customer. "Is this guy getting local color?"

"Yeah," Ford answers and in parting adds, "Thanks, local."

Back outside, Ford pauses to savor the joke. Laughter softens his rugged features—the imposing eyebrows, stern nose, and that trademark little scar just below the lip. For an instant, he seems like a playful golden retriever: boyish, open, mischievous.

But the moment quickly passes. One more task and Ford can retreat to the hills. He has a lunch date at the White Buffalo Club, a restaurant duded up in faux Victoriana that he says provides "a place for us to bring out-of-towners and show them we're as capable of excess as they are." In response to the suggestion that there must be a homier spot for a conversation—a location that speaks to his heart and reveals something about the life he has fashioned for himself in this high, pristine setting—Ford stops and faces the man trailing him. "I'm going to give you no options," he says evenly, his eyes narrowing, his aspect suddenly hardening. "You cannot see the backstage part of my life. You cannot come to my ranch."

With that, Ford's mood again lightens. "My wife and I came up here because we wanted a private place with four seasons—three of them winter. But enough about me."

Harrison Ford will be taken on his own terms or no terms at all. And what's more, he won't even go that far unless he has a good reason. On this late fall afternoon, that reason is his new movie, Roman Polanski's *Frantic*, a project about which Ford is excited. "I'm more than happy to talk about *it*," he says. The picture, which was shot in Paris last year, should complete the process that *Witness* and *The Mosquito Coast* started: the elevation of the actor's place in the Hollywood pantheon from pulp genre hero to legitimate leading man.

Because of Ford's winning performances as interplanetary knight-errant Han Solo in the *Star Wars* series and swashbuckling Indiana Jones in *Raiders of the Lost Ark* and its sequel, *Indiana Jones and the Temple of Doom*, he had become stereotyped as a comic-book figure. Yes, he had dangerous good looks. Yes, he had presence. Yes, he made more money than just about anyone in Hollywood. But when it came time to cast the role of a serious male protagonist, he was always far down the list. "The way it used to work," says Thom Mount, producer of *Frantic*, "is that scripts would go to Jack Nicholson or Warren Beatty, and if they turned them down then they'd go to Harrison. But they're all growing too old for such parts. Now Harrison gets them first."

As a star vehicle, *Frantic* provides Ford with the kind of part that comes along very rarely indeed. In the role of Dr. Richard Walker, an

American cardiologist whose wife is kidnapped by Middle Eastern terrorists after she mistakenly picks up the wrong suitcase at Paris's Orly Airport, the actor is in nearly every scene. The movie's success depends almost entirely upon him giving a convincing portrayal of a man willing to go to any lengths to save what is dearest to him.

But as far as Ford's career goes, the most rewarding thing about *Frantic* may well be the opportunity the film gave him to work with Polanski. "I think Roman is one of the best directors I've ever worked with," Ford says. Adds Mount: "The difference between Ford as Indiana Jones and the Ford of *Frantic* is that Polanski, unlike Steven Spielberg [director of both Indiana Jones pictures], recognized Harrison's complexities and brought them to life. He saw that Ford is much more than a cartoon character."

Ensconced in a secluded booth at the White Buffalo, Harrison Ford is making short work of a pasta entrée. Now that he has set the ground rules—not only is the ranch off-limits but the town is to remain unnamed and the state to go unmentioned—he seems less edgy. He's willing to come along real peaceable-like as long as one agrees to look down the barrel of his preconditions.

"This is just too small a pond," he says, hoping to explain his wariness. "I have people show up in my driveway with Wisconsin plates and long lenses on their cameras, and I don't like it. They might not even be freaks, but they're just not operating on the same wavelength I am."

Ford feels that such intruders "deny me a real life, and I don't want to be denied a real life." His sense is that he can hold the wolves at bay by keeping a low public profile. Anyway, he says, the kind of celebrity bestowed upon actors by the press is distasteful at best and always transitory. Take, for instance, *People* magazine, which Ford has disdainfully renamed *Peephole*. "It just absorbs, digests, and shits out personalities like yesterday's prunes."

But on an even deeper level, Ford believes that by the nature of his job, he's already revealed everything that anyone should reasonably want to know about him. "I just can't imagine how much more you can expose yourself than what I've done onscreen," he says. "You can't know a person better. Who the hell do you think that is up there? Some total stranger? That's me."

By this logic, Ford's work in *Frantic* can be taken as that of a veritable exhibitionist. For starters, both the way he got the part and the motivation that drives his character attest to one of his central obsessions: a fear of being unable to protect the people he loves.

"A year ago, near Christmas, my wife [screenwriter Melissa Mathison, author of *E.T.*] was working on a script for Roman about Tin-Tin, the Belgian children's book hero," he says. "She had to go see him in Paris, and it was at the height of that terrorism business. She was pregnant, and I didn't want her to go alone. So I tagged along. That was the first time I met Roman."

During his stay in France, Ford sat down with Polanski at the director's apartment, "and he told me the story of *Frantic* in two hours. It was terrific—a compelling story about a man who loved his wife." Because of the actor's worries about his own wife, the tale hit especially close to home. "I was very receptive, because I'm always worried about her. That pretty much defines my reality."

While watching Polanski act out the movie, Ford realized that the horrors he could only contemplate were, for the director, hideously real. Because Polanski had endured the murder of his wife, actress Sharon Tate, by Charles Manson and his disciples, he "lent elements to it that I could never begin to imagine. It was clear that this was deeply emotional for Roman. To think how I'd feel if the circumstances had happened to me was… Well…When it was over, I said, 'If that's what it's going to be like when it's written down, I'll do it.'"

Frantic also reveals other aspects of Ford's personality. "Harrison is simultaneously very loose and very tight," says a longtime friend. "Polanski saw that and used it."

In a casual encounter with Ford, these contrasting traits crop up immediately. Over lunch, as he watches the waiter expertly uncork a bottle of wine, pour without spilling a drop then drape a towel with a matador's precision, he blurts out, "This guy is no actor." Almost simultaneously, however, as he tries to describe a heart surgeon he met while preparing for the new film, he haltingly belabors the point. "Aspects of his personality…were…expressed by the way he used his hands…a certain authoritarian aspect…Uhh…authoritative is perhaps a better word? In fact, it is a better word. This was a particular kind of guy."

It wasn't until after he got to know Ford that Polanski suggested that the character of Richard Walker should be a cardiologist—a profession that demands meticulousness. The director's goal was to capitalize on his star's conflicting impulses. Set him up as a figure accustomed to operating in an environment of scrupulous detail then plunge him into a netherworld where he will not survive unless he trusts his instincts. "In just a few moments at the start of the movie," Ford says, "we have to show that this guy is used to wielding authority." The actor hopes he accomplished the task by focusing on those aforementioned hands ("Surgeons have an incredible vanity about their hands") to create an impression of assuredness. But as Walker grows more and more frenzied about his wife's abduction, that sense of resolve vanishes, and Ford relied on "shadings of anxiety and degrees of frustration" to show a man who must fall back on his wits.

Ford believes the task of capturing his character's metamorphosis was made easier by the latitude Polanski gave him to improvise with the script, which the director co-wrote with long-time collaborator Gerard Brach (*Tess, The Name of the Rose*). "Roman is actually pretty free in the shooting process," the actor says. "If he can see it working before him, he doesn't care as much as other writing directors whether he gets a word-by-word interpretation."

Up to a point, Polanski approved of Ford's tendency to tinker with his dialogue. "Often when Harrison read a line, it was a different reading than I anticipated, but it worked," the director says. "Somehow it was more original, but it's a bit dangerous. Later on during the rushes I said, 'Oh, golly, I should have shot it the way I originally conceived it.'"

Since Ford invites speculation about the self-revelatory nature of his acting, another clue to his personality that *Frantic* provides can be found in his dedication to the movie as a whole and "not the character I play." Ford's style is Hemingway-esque. His mantra: proportion, discipline, appropriateness. His aim in a scene: "To make sure that we've got every drop that we can, that we've realized the thematic elements to the greatest, that we've made everything clear as a bell." He believes he will have succeeded in the film if viewers remember Richard Walker's problem and forget that Harrison Ford even exists.

Over coffee, while Ford is willing to continue talking earnestly about *Frantic*, he is, upon reconsideration, less eager to go any deeper into what the picture reveals about him. If he's not going to give a tour of his back forty, he's surely not going to open up the inner landscape. Everyone's welcome to draw his own conclusions, but, Ford says, the iciness back, "I don't have to explain how the damn thing works." Then, shrugging like a lowly employee asked to justify management policy, he adds, "I just work here."

A little embarrassed by how he knows he must sound, Ford relaxes his hostile expression, and something almost like pleading enters his voice. "I'd just rather be on down the road, back at work, attending to the myriad details that need to be attended to. Right now I've got to call a contractor about some storm-window adjustments. I want to look at a color going down on the floors at the house. I want to check with my wife about a rash on the baby's back. I'm gonna call my kid and tell him that a plane ticket for his great-aunt's funeral is coming. That's all important shit."

Holding his hands up as if to say "enough" Ford rises from the table and heads for the door. "I've got work at the *secret place*," he says, his tone acknowledging the ludicrousness of it all. But come quitting time—"beer 30," he calls it—he promises another audience.

Those who have actually been given leave to pass a day with Harrison Ford on his own ground describe it as a place that makes the actor "blissful." It is so isolated that Ford had to cut a new road, bring in electricity, and bury septic tanks just to begin construction on the buildings—aside from the house, there is an office, a workshop, a hay barn, and a tack shed. It is so untamed that 65 species of mammals live there. In hopes that the property will remain undeveloped into perpetuity, the actor has granted an easement on it to a nature conservancy. "I really have more of a sense of stewardship about it than ownership," he says. "I really want to preserve it for my kids—to let them know that this is what's dear to me rather than a big pile of money in the middle of the floor."

On a good day—"a day without reporters," he deadpans—Ford is up early, mending fences, checking on damage caused by beavers, and making lists of things to do, occasionally inking them right onto the palms of his hands. He also tries to spend as much time as possible in reverie. "I look at a creek with fish in it, and it just sets off a chain of thoughts. The fish are there because the water's clean. The water's clean because somebody took care to see that irrigation ditches don't flow into the creek. Or maybe the fish are there because somebody cleaned out a deep hole under a tree for them to live in."

Ford's love of the life he is building in the hinterlands leads him to believe he'll never leave—and certainly not for Los Angeles, which he calls "one of the most hostile environments known to mankind." With a new baby (ten-month-old Malcolm), a good marriage, "a business that lets me live anywhere I want," and a few close friends (singer Jimmy Buffett appeals to "the shit-kicker in me," the actor says, while L.A. gallery owner Earl McGrath satisfies a longing for intellectual debate), Ford, at 45, seems genuinely happy. It wasn't always so.

Ford flunked out of Wisconsin's Ripon College three days before graduation. His academic decline was brought on by "a tenuous hold on the minimum grade-point average and cosmic inattention." This following a "bumbly adolescence" in Chicago during which he was "never real popular or real athletic or real anything." The son of a Catholic father and a Jewish mother, he was neither fish nor fowl.

The one thing Ford was good at was getting jobs. "I'm real polite. I know how to sit straight and keep my head up. People think I'm not going to steal from them. Getting jobs is like acting." In Chicago, Ford talked himself into a position as a chef with a Great Lakes cruise outfit even though he'd never cooked a meal in his life. Arriving in Southern California in the mid-'60s, he hit the ground running on the same course, working by turns as a yacht broker in Laguna Beach, a management trainee for Bullock's department stores ("I must have said something that led them to believe retail sales would be my life"), and a pizza maker in Hollywood. When he decided to become a carpenter, he simply went to the public library and read every book on the subject.

Of all Ford's early jobs, carpentry was the one that actually spoke to his creative instincts. Stylistically his work was traditional. Technically it subscribed to the maxim "Form follows function." When it came to quality, he urged clients to spare no expense. "'Spend the bucks. Spend the bucks,' that's all he ever said," recalls one customer. The work led to his break in show business.

Ford had always been interested in acting. While living in Laguna Beach, he appeared in a few plays. In one he caught the eye of a talent scout from Columbia Pictures and was given a contract, but it led only to bit parts, mostly on television, as bank robbers or bellhops. At the age of 30—already married to his first wife, Mary, and father of sons Willard and Benjamin—he did not seem headed to the big screen. Then he scored some carpentry jobs in Hollywood. He built Sergio Mendes's recording studio and Sally Kellerman's sun porch. Most important, he built a bed for Fred Roos, a casting director.

"Harrison was not conventionally good-looking," Roos recalls. "He was also tight-lipped, standoffish, and most people thought he had an attitude. He's an incredibly cranky guy. But I thought he was going to be a star, and we got along famously."

Roos started auditioning Ford for "anything he was remotely right for." Finally, he prevailed upon George Lucas to cast the actor as Bob Falfa, the straw-hatted badass who shows up in the closing minutes of *American Graf-fiti* (1973) to engage in a classic bit of teenage ritual jousting: drag racing. Ford turned in a memorably sneering performance that attracted favorable attention.

Roos, who by this point had begun producing films, became Ford's angel. He gave him a part, for instance, in *The Conversation* as Robert Duvall's leaden-eyed hatchet man. But it was on a picture for which he served only as a consultant that Roos engineered Ford's big break. "I pretty much badgered George Lucas into casting him in *Star Wars*. He wasn't high on George's list. He didn't know him like I did."

Ford was on his way, but his ascent would not be seamless. "After *Star Wars* a funny thing happened to Harrison," says Roos. "As good as he was people in the industry thought the movie succeeded because of its special effects. He was dismissed. He went off to Europe and made a sequel to *The Guns of Navarone*, and people started saying, 'Oh, he isn't a star after all.' Even his work as Indiana Jones didn't help."

Then came *Witness*, and suddenly everyone was talking about Ford. "People started saying, 'He's really good,'" Roos remembers. "But he was always that good. He was always good with women. He was always funny. There's a gag in *Raiders of the Lost Ark* where Harrison, after defeating all these swordsmen in hand-to-hand combat, has to face this huge guy in a turban carrying a gigantic scimitar. Well, Harrison just pulls out a gun, shrugs, and shoots him. That was Harrison's idea, and it's the funniest thing in the film."

In the tone of a proud father, Roos adds, "He's really a star in the mold of Bogart—tough, cynical, capable of taking care of himself. And maybe there's a little Clark Gable, about whom there was absolutely nothing senti-mental. I hate to say I told you so, but..."

Success, however, did not soften Ford's "don't tread on me" demeanor. During the filming of *Blade Runner*, in which he starred as a replicant hunter, he nearly came to blows with director Ridley Scott. "It was a gruel-ing movie, and Ridley demanded so many takes that it finally wore Harrison out," says Bud Yorkin, the film's producer. "I know he was ready to kill Rid-ley. One night on the set, he would have taken him on if he hadn't been talked out of it."

Distant, recalcitrant, on occasion surly, Ford is in the end a man who goes to greater lengths than most to control what he will or will not do. Not only this, he makes life difficult for those who actually care about him. "In any encounter he's always the senior and you're always the freshman," says actress Carrie Fisher, who first got to know Ford when she played Princess Leia opposite him in *Star Wars*. "I think he always felt I was too loud and a little out of control, and he's the kind of guy who'd kick me under the table or fix me with a withering look to let me know it."

In spite of Ford's tendency to scold her, he and Fisher have remained close. She finds his prickliness well worth enduring. For one thing, she says, "I respect Harrison, which is an odd thing for me to say about anyone. He's well-read, thoughtful. When I was twenty, he told me I was one of the smartest girls he'd ever met—I can't tell you how that thrilled me." But more than admiring Ford, Fisher genuinely likes him. She believes that his stormy moods are little more than thunder squalls tracking across a basically mild climate. "Just don't wear the wrong clothes around him," she says, "because then he'll get you. He'll turn into your dad."

The Million Dollar Cowboy Bar is a fantasy out of Nudie's of Hollywood. The bar stools are fashioned from tooled leather saddles. The bar top is embedded with hundreds of silver dollars. The chandeliers are huge, light-bulb-studded wagon wheels. In glass cases located strategically around the cavernous, main room, gigantic stuffed bears and bobcats stare down on cowboys and cowgirls who dance the western swing as a country band twangs away on stage.

After taking a long pull on a Corona, Harrison Ford looks up from his table with a chagrined expression. "I don't come here very often, man." Although the place is authentic in a campy kind of way, it is, to Ford's thinking, a little bit of Vegas plopped down in paradise.

"I don't go out much," he says. "By the time dinner is over and the dishes are done, it's time to think about what to do the next day, try to read part of *The New York Times*, watch a little TV. Generally, I go to bed early because we get up early with the baby."

Tranquility is what Ford seeks here at home, not bright lights. He sees enough of those at work. He's already signed up to do his next film, Mike Nichols's *Working Girl*, a dry comedy he won't discuss other than to acknowledge that he's cast in a Cary Grant-like role. Then, in late 1988, shooting will begin on yet another installment in the Indiana Jones series. He won't talk about that, either—"No can do," he snaps when asked what the picture is about—but without prompting he offers his prediction of what the reviewers will say: "'Now that Ford has done these very creative roles,

189

why does he do another *Raiders* film?'" Clapping his powerful, work-begrimed hands in a gesture of delight, he provides the answer: "Well, I'll tell you, it's the same process whether it's a so-called serious movie or a not-serious movie. The job of acting is the same. What I really enjoy is the kind of problem-solving aspect of getting stuff off the page and on its feet, and for that there's no one better than Steven Spielberg. He's got one of the most facile minds you're ever going to meet in movie making. And besides, playing Indiana is fun. It's every boy's dream. Jesus."

During Ford's speech, a king of the wild frontier wearing a black, ten-gallon hat appears at the table. Identifying himself as "Davy Crockett—a distant cousin of the original," he extends his hand to the actor. "We're mighty proud of you, Harrison. Mighty proud to have you live here."

A pained smile flashes across Ford's face as he returns the handshake. "Thank you, Davy," he says in the same tone he often used in the *Star Wars* films when encountering some odd, extraterrestrial life-form.

In hopes of avoiding a group of Davy's friends, Ford quickly settles his tab and hustles out the door. Already, a chill is in the air. In front of his truck—a serious, winch-equipped Chevy Scottsdale pickup—he pauses for a second to give the little metropolis a last once-over. Then he opens the driver's door, bends over, and produces his new dog, Betty, who's been asleep on the floor. A chocolate Labrador puppy not much bigger than a football, she's cute as can be. "Come on Betty, this is no place for you," Ford says as he climbs behind the wheel. While warming up the engine, he rolls down the window and with a leveling gaze tells his inquisitor, "I know I haven't satisfied you, but I'm leaving you the same way I found you." With that, he drives away into the night's all-encompassing solitude.

Moon over Hollywood

Playboy, July 1995

A couple of hours before the sight of his naked, middle-aged fanny began filling television screens across America, Dennis Franz sat in his trailer on the Twentieth Century Fox lot in Los Angeles replaying a cassette of the soon-to-air footage. The actor had filmed the scene without makeup after convincing himself that a tiny scar from a spider bite was dramatically plausible. (His character, Detective Andy Sipowicz, had been shot in the wallet in *NYPD Blue's* pilot episode.) But now that the moon, so to speak, would soon be rising, Franz was less sure, and he kept scrutinizing the image of his nether region, searching for that pinprick of red until the absurdity of it all dawned on him and he asked: "What kind of guy am I? I've got a beautiful woman in the shower with me, and I'm rewinding the tape to look at *my* ass?"

The woman was Sharon Lawrence, who in the role of Sylvia Costas shares this moment with Sipowicz, baring not just her own derriere but an area of her lover's psyche that has long been off-limits. At first, Sipowicz tries to push Costas away, protesting: "I usually shower alone." Then, when she not only persists but also begins sudsing what can only be his most private parts, he flat-out balks: "Whoa, whoa. I usually wash myself down there." Finally, however, he submits, allowing tentatively: "Boy, that'll sure be clean."

As Sipowicz's lines suggest, his character's nudity is almost secondary to something else, a story that has been unfolding on *NYPD Blue* since it premiered in September 1993, the story of an angry cop recovering elements of his humanity. "Sipowicz hadn't been devoid of sex in the past," noted Franz, "but those were financial transactions. When he wanted it, he paid for it. Last year, he admitted he hadn't had sex sober in 20 years. Now, he's having to learn how to play, to be naughty—like an adolescent. That's part of the charm of his character. It's rare to see a man his age, with his outward gruffness, act in that sort of manner."

Yet for all that, it was Franz's behind that would tonight be exposed before a nationwide television audience. He was understandably thinking less about Andy Sipowicz's demons than about the fact that he was joining an exclusive club, the handful of TV actors—most of them courtesy of *NYPD Blue*—who've revealed on camera as much of their anatomy as network strictures allow. Call it full dorsal nudity. On the one hand, he was flattered that someone might want to see his less-than-svelte self in the altogether. "Back when we were conceiving the show," he remarked, "I was asked if I had any qualms, and I said, 'If they want to see it, they're welcome.'" By the same token, however, he was aware that he was opening himself up to ridicule, confiding: "I know that my friends, my family, my loved ones—people I don't ordinarily show my rear end to—are going to see it. I imagine tomorrow I'm going to be the rear end of a lot of jokes."

With that, Franz emerged from his trailer, which is moored next to the soundstage that houses *NYPD Blue's* sets, and stepped across the lot to the space where his Jaguar was parked. All he could do now was await the outcome at home.

Predictably, the calls started coming the next morning, yet the day was nearly over before the rump roast commenced in earnest. As it happened, it was Thanksgiving eve, and Franz and his longtime inamorata, Joanie Zeck, were up baking, the TV tuned to *The Tonight Show*, when Jay Leno plunged into his opening monologue.

"So, Dennis Franz bared his butt on *NYPD Blue*," Leno began.

Pause. Then: "Did they think we needed to see that before Thanksgiving? I guess a lot of people won't be eating white meat."

Laughter. Encore: "Franz intended this as a public service ad: This is your butt. This is your butt on Twinkies."

Like Leno's studio audience, Franz and Zeck found this to be genuinely amusing. For an actor, Franz is surprisingly devoid of vanity, and he appreciated the broad comedic target his posterior offered. Which was lucky. The episode scored one of the best ratings in *NYPD Blue* history, making it the week's fifth-highest-rated show and meaning that 16.7 million households, more than a fourth of the viewing audience, saw Franz's buns of molten steel au naturel.

That it would be the unveiling of Dennis Franz's bottom—and not that of his decidedly more buff former sidekick, David Caruso, or present partner Jimmy Smits—that sent *NYPD Blue's* Nielsens through the roof seems, at first blush, astonishing. As Franz will willingly confess, he's not exactly matinee idol material.

Fifty years old, weighing 210 pounds, and standing just over 5'11", Franz is the very picture of a Rust Belt man. Though he doesn't carry much fat, his physique can best be described as lumpy, and he admits that when it comes to dieting, the most he ever does is "occasionally pass up a doughnut." (Indeed, in contrast to the preparation of other actors, Franz didn't try to get in shape before his *NYPD Blue* nude scene.) Then there's the mug—balding, of course, and jowly, with a beak of a nose, mustache, and cartoon eyebrows. To learn that Franz was born Dennis Schlachta in an ethnically balkanized Chicago suburb (his stage name, which rhymes with prawns, was his father's first name) comes as no surprise.

But whether he looks the part or not, Dennis Franz is a star, a sex symbol even, who receives indecent proposals in his fan mail, is accorded "heart-throb" status by the *National Enquirer*, and pops up on the cover of *People* magazine's Valentine's Day issue. And not only that, there has been exceptional critical acclaim. For his work on *NYPD Blue*, Franz took home both the 1994 Emmy and the 1995 Golden Globe for best actor in a dramatic television series.

The reasons for Franz's success are many. For starters, he's a legitimately skilled performer. Steven Bochco, who along with David Milch created and produces *NYPD Blue*, has been using Franz ever since he cast him as the fiendish Sal Benedetto in *Hill Street Blues* 13 years ago. Bochco speaks of Franz's "big, big engine" and his "meticulous" work habits. Then there's the fact that *NYPD Blue* was basically written for Franz. "When David and I conceived the show," recalls Bochco, "the first thing I did was hire Dennis. We didn't even have a script." Yet finally, there's something else, something specific to Franz as a man.

Spend time around those who know Franz and they will invariably volunteer that he's that rarest of items, a virtuous soul. Bochco, who's not the sort to sing false praises, vows: "He has a genuinely good heart. He's fiercely ethical. That's what I respond to. My dad was that way." David Milch echoes this sentiment: "Dennis is a gentleman—civil and sweet-spirited." Actor Joe Mantegna, whose friendship with Franz dates back to when they started out together in Chicago theater in the early '70s, goes even further: "If I had to choose three human beings to watch my backside if such an occasion arose, Dennis would be one of them. It's that Midwestern mentality—no pretense, no hidden agendas. You always know where you stand with Dennis. If he's your friend, he's your friend."

Considering that acting is a profession dependent on artifice, the link between Franz's decency and his power on-screen may seem unclear—but not to Bochco. "To use Milch's word," he says, "there's an interesting 'doubleness' about Dennis. You're always attracted to his blue-collar toughness. But inevitably, as his characters progress, his goodness begins to emerge through that blue-collar toughness."

It's this inner aura, Bochco believes, that draws viewers to the outwardly repugnant Andy Sipowicz. "In Sipowicz, we've created a very edgy character, in many ways a bigot, loaded with biases. But endlessly leaking through the cracks of that façade is Dennis's goodness. The trap for us as writers, in fact, is not to give in to it. It's important to take Sipowicz back to that darker side."

The dark side, of course, is from whence Sipowicz sprang in all his glory in *NYPD Blue's* pilot. Alcoholic, misogynistic, and armed, Sipowicz announced himself to the world—and to Costas, the assistant D.A. who later becomes his lover—by grabbing his crotch and snarling: "Ipso this, you pissy little bitch."

And it is the dark side that has informed countless subsequent Sipowicz outbursts. Not since Archie Bunker has anyone voiced as many insulting or off-color sentiments in prime time. But where Bunker delivered them in the form of armchair rants, Sipowicz serves them in your face.

During the course of *NYPD Blue's* two seasons Sipowicz has unleashed a number of memorable verbal sallies. Some are shots across the bow of polite sensibility. For instance, his crack to an aging, gay screenwriter who wanted him to estimate the value of an Academy Award statue stolen by some rough grade: "Mr. Rickman, I'd love to sit here with you figuring out what someone would pay to whip his skippy while he looks at your Oscar, but we're working a multiple homicide right now." Likewise, his crack to a wife-killing chiropractor who asked about Sipowicz's bad back: "Maybe I can get over it thinking of you in Ossining getting acupuncture up your dirt chute." Others, however, are blows at political correctness, particularly a tirade he unleashed at an obdurate black man named Futrel who believed he was being interrogated in a murder investigation solely because of his skin color:

SIPOWICZ: Hey, pal, I'm trying to find some assholes before they murder another innocent family. It so happens that these particular assholes are black. Now, how do you want me to go about this? You want me to put the questions, "I'm sorry for the injustices the white man has inflicted on your race, but can you provide any information? I'm sorry your people have been downtrodden for 300 years, but did you discuss the layout of the Sloan house with any of your friends?"

FUTREL: Yeah, do it that way.

SIPOWICZ: O.K. I know that great African American George Washington Carver discovered the peanut, but can you provide the names and addresses of these friends?

Like Bochco says, there's not a lot on the surface to love. Yet the audience loves Sipowicz, and that it does is testimony to Franz. Admittedly, *NYPD Blue*'s writers have endowed Sipowicz with enough saving grace to give the actor a starting place. How could a hardened cop who collects tropical fish not tug at heartstrings? And the romance between Sipowicz and Costas has softened a few edges. But finally, it's Franz who furnishes the transformative magic. "The dimension and subtlety and depth Dennis brings to that character are something to see," says David Milch, who scripts the bulk of Sipowicz's dialogue.

To illustrate his point, Milch described a moment he witnessed when *NYPD Blue* was recently filming in New York. In the episode, Sipowicz probes the sexual violation and murder of an immigrant boy as he comes to grips with the distance between himself and his estranged son. During the course of his investigation, he visits the dead boy's parents, who in their grief embrace the belief that their son's soul has taken residence in a bird perched on their windowsill. They want to know what Sipowicz thinks. It was a difficult scene for Franz—because of the conflicting perspectives Sipowicz brought to it as father and cop, because central to Sipowicz's persona is a disdain for self-delusion, and because Milch was still rewriting, handing Franz his lines on the back of an envelope.

"Dennis was able to convey Sipowicz's impatience with the parents' mendacity," Milch recalls, "yet express his empathy by looking at the bird and telling them he thinks he can see a light coming out of it. It was amazing. There were a lot of ways to do the scene badly, but Dennis found a way to do it well."

In short, the light radiated from Franz. What made the light so strong was not just its beneficence but its authority, too, an authority forged during a traumatic time the actor rarely discusses.

On a rainy morning several days after he received his Golden Globe, and several weeks after the nation got its look at his backside, Dennis Franz was padding around his spacious home in Bel Air. The house where television's fiercest lawman lives looks more like an antique shop than a precinct station. Over the years, at swap meets and estate sales, Franz and Joanie have amassed a sizable trove. Much of it goes under the heading of Country Cute—old railroad signs, cow tchotchkes, bottle racks, American flag pillows, vintage radios, an enameled turn-of-the-century stove. All of it means something to its owners, most particularly an upright piano they bought for $35 at an auction in Lake of the Ozarks, Missouri, loaded into a U-Haul trailer, and drove home through a blizzard only to discover it would cost $1600 to refurbish. Suffice to say, six years later, the piano sits on the porch, untouched.

As Franz was recalling all this, the doorbell rang and he answered. Congratulations for the Golden Globe were still pouring in—this one in the form of a bottle of Cristal champagne from Ted Harbert, president of ABC. Considering everything *NYPD Blue* has done for the network, the champagne seemed a rather paltry gesture.

After scanning Harbert's note, Franz puffed out his chest, cocked an eye, and let loose a barrage worthy of Sipowicz: "This is all I'm worth to you Ted? This is it? Where are the car keys?

"This is nice but what happened to the days when they gave you a car? I could use a new four-wheel-drive vehicle."

For an instant, Franz seemed genuinely perturbed. But then he smiled, for he knew that ABC would begin expressing its gratitude two mornings later. A limousine would whisk him to the waiting Learjet in which he, Bochco, Jimmy Smits, and Bill Clark—the former New York cop who works as *NYPD Blue's* technical advisor—would fly to Miami for a Super Bowl weekend that would include dinner with Diane Sawyer and other network notables, a round of golf with Harbert, nonstop soirees, and, almost as an afterthought, a football game. The Cristal was merely a prelude.

After pouring coffee, Franz walked into the den where his dogs, Bigelow and Gallagher—mammoth husky mixes, one of whom had recently lost a leg to cancer—were lolling around. Outside, visible through a sliding door, rain danced across the dark surface of a swimming pool.

Unlike so many actors, Franz does not revel in self-revelation. Although not exactly guarded, he is neither insecure enough to seek validation through confession nor egotistical enough to presume others are really that interested. Yes, he has tales to tell, but he doesn't force them on you, especially if they involve Vietnam.

In much the same way that Franz's friends are in accord that he is a prince among men, they are also in accord that to a one they didn't learn about his service in Vietnam until years after they met him. With Milch, who's worked with the actor on *NYPD Blue, Hill Street Blues,* and the short-lived *Beverly Hills Buntz,* it took a decade. Even then, he says, Franz was cryptic about it all. With Joe Mantegna it took three years, and the conversation was likewise brief. Mantegna, who'd opposed the war, realized he had no frame of reference from which to respond. "What could I say?" he asks. "Bummer?"

When apprised of his friends' unanimity on the subject, Franz seemed somewhat taken aback. But then he admitted: "It's not something I preface a relationship with. I don't say, 'Hi, I'm Dennis Franz and I went to Vietnam.' But if I'm asked, I don't hold back. It was a terrifying, life-altering experience, yet I wouldn't trade it for anything in the world."

It was 1968, and Franz had recently graduated from Southern Illinois University with a degree in drama and speech. His student deferment up, the draft board calling, he enlisted. After basic training at Fort Dix he entered officer candidate school. Franz takes pains not to paint himself as a would-be hero but as a confused and terrified young man whose actions were predicated on a desire to avoid combat. "It was strictly out of fear," he said. "I did not want to get shot. The plan was to get into special services and somehow entertain the troops."

Franz's illusions, however, were soon dashed. There was no hope of hoofing his way through the war—the Army wanted its second lieutenants at the front. And Franz realized he wasn't cut out to be a leader of men. So three weeks into officer candidate school, he requested reassignment to infantry duty. The next day, he was ordered to Vietnam—orders, he confides, he almost disobeyed. "I was due to ship out of Oakland, but I had a friend living in San Francisco, and there couldn't have been a worse choice in 1969 than between Haight-Ashbury and Saigon. I was three days late reporting. I toyed with the idea of going AWOL. But it's not in my makeup. I couldn't disgrace my family. I couldn't live a life always looking over my shoulder."

In country, Franz was assigned to a recon unit of the 82nd Airborne and was soon immersed in the fighting. "Our primary function was to set up ambushes along enemy trials," he recalled evenly. "At night, we went out in 15-man teams and stood in rice paddies with the water up to our waists. We received fire and dispersed fire, sometimes into darkness, sometimes at targets."

After five months in the Mekong delta, the 82nd pulled out. Franz was detached to a unit of the 101st Airborne, which was patrolling wooded terrain. There, he saw his worst action.

"One time, we were walking down a road. That was wrong. We usually went down the sides. But we'd been climbing up through trees, and it was a luxury to walk down a road. I was next to the last man in line. We'd all passed this point. I was carrying my rifle at the ready, and the guy behind me yelled, 'Denny, why you carrying your rifle like that? Sling it over your shoulder and enjoy the walk.' Fifteen second later, there was a huge explosion, and I saw the guy who had just spoken to me ten feet in the air, his leg going in the other direction. He'd stepped on a land mine. He lost a leg, an arm, and his eyesight. The most frightening thing about it was that we'd all just walked over the same point. We had all walked over the mine. He was just behind me.

"There was another occasion," Franz went on, "where we were in a village conducting a cordon search for VC. It was daytime, and we were going hut to hut looking for any info indicating they were there—guns, bullets, military clothing. We were quite unsuccessful, but they were there. That night, our position came under attack. I was in the dirt, trying to crawl right into the dirt, holding my rifle over my head and firing. Next to me I heard people getting hit, screaming. Bullets were going right over my head. I was shaking involuntarily, but I kept firing, not necessarily to kill anyone but because that was the only way to make it stop. I had to make it stop. The next day, we returned to the village, and it was like the day before. No sign of them. That was the frustration of the war."

Upon completion of his tour of duty, Franz was honorably discharged. Back in Chicago, he experienced some of the difficulties that afflicted other Vietnam vets. "Having subjected yourself to all that to save others—or so we naively thought—and come back and try to adjust to the hostility directed at us was hard," he said. "I had to try and understand that behavior and in some cases forgive it. I spent a year not doing very much."

But Franz's re-entry problems notwithstanding, he returned from Vietnam unscathed. While he may not have relished the war, he relished having served. "I did it. Stood up to it. Came back," he said. "I left my youth behind. I was no longer a boy. I had earned a certain sense of manhood."

With that, Franz rose from the sofa and walked into the kitchen for another cup of coffee, a man who will talk about Vietnam after all but doesn't need to. Which, not to profane the sacred, breeds the kind of confidence that most actors would kill for.

Whatever confusion Franz felt those first months back from Vietnam, he was on his feet by 1972, making a concerted effort at launching his acting career. Initially, he worked the Chicago dinner-theater circuit, appearing in such period pieces as *Luv*. Then, in his life's pivotal creative turn, he landed a part in the Organic Theater's production of Ray Bradbury's *The Wonderful Ice Cream Suit*.

Headquartered in Chicago's tough Uptown section, the Organic was at the time the city's premiere art-theater company, a precursor to Steppenwolf. Here, director Stuart Gordon—who would later become known for writing *Honey, I Shrunk the Kids*—assembled a cadre of talented actors and staged numerous original works. The most notable production was *Bleacher Bums*, the story of a group of long-suffering Chicago Cubs fans that went on to a profitable second life as a touring show (it ran for 11 years in Los Angeles) and was made into a PBS movie.

The Organic attracted the usual pot-smoking, war-protesting artistes. Except Franz. "He was very solid, Mr. Status Quo," recalls Joe Mantegna, who was one of the ensemble's mainstays. To begin with, Franz owned a car—not just any car but a new Chevy on which he made monthly payments. If that wasn't far out enough, he had a day job as a security guard at the Pick-Congress, a downtown convention hotel. In other words, the latest recruit to this band of countercultural gypsies was a house dick.

Yet no matter how out of place Franz might have seemed initially at the Organic, he soon established himself as one of its stars, winning numerous excellent notices, particularly for his work in *Bleacher Bums* (for which he also received a writing credit). Moreover, he began developing the acting style that would sustain him, a style that plainly lent itself to portraying policemen.

"There was just something about him," remembers Mantegna. "One of the plays we did together was called *Cops*. As research, we would drive around the neighborhood in an old Buick to get a sense of what it was like to be on patrol. We'd pull up to a group of hookers on the corner, and all Dennis had to do was roll down the window and stare at them, and they'd squeal, 'We ain't doing nothing.' Dennis would say, 'Just watch yourselves.' And it sounded authentic."

After five years at the Organic, Franz was ready to take his shot at Hollywood. So, too, was Mantegna, and they drove west together. Mantegna and his wife towed Franz's car behind their own, while Franz drove the U-Haul truck that carried the two households' belongings.

On the coast, Franz found that his gritty stage presence was a double-edged sword—it got him work, but it also got him typecast. The cop in Brian De Palma's *The Fury* (1978)—that was Franz. The detective in De Palma's *Dressed to Kill* (1980)—that, too, was Franz. The airport security chief in *Die Hard 2* (1990)—Franz again. In all, Franz has played 28 different lawmen. Still, as confining as the roles may often have been, it was while playing a cop that he entered Steven Bochco's orbit.

Although Sal Benedetto skulked through only a few episodes of *Hill Street Blues*, he was one of the most idiosyncratic characters ever to be written into a show famous for idiosyncratic characters. Bad to the bone, a disgrace to his shield, he came to a grimly memorable end. Caught in the process of trying to rob a bank, he went *mano a mano* with a bomb-squad robot. Then, as Officer J.D. LaRue (Kiel Martin) urged him on, he committed suicide.

Bochco and company immediately regretted dispatching Benedetto—not so much because they missed him as a character but because they missed working with Franz. And from that day forth, they cast the actor whenever they could. In the short-lived baseball drama *Bay City Blues*, Franz appeared as pitching coach Angelo Carbone. Then, when MTM productions fired Bochco at the end of *Hill Street*'s fifth year, his replacements—Milch and Jeffrey Lewis—brought back Franz as Norman Buntz, an oleaginous, polyester-clad detective whom Milch characterizes as "Benedetto benignly mutated 20 percent." Buntz, who was accompanied almost everywhere by a trusty snitch named Sid (Peter Jurasik), proved to be such a hit that when *Hill Street* finally came to an end in 1987, Milch and Lewis gave Franz his own series, *Beverly Hills Buntz*. The spinoff, though, did not win a wide audience and was canceled after 13 episodes. Yet Franz emerged untarnished, and when Bochco and Milch reunited to do *NYPD Blue*, he was, of course, at the top of their list.

Franz obviously relishes the success of *NYPD Blue* and relishes playing Andy Sipowicz. "I'm riding this thing until the end," he maintains. "I think so much of the writers, the producers, and the show. There's so much still to explore with Sipowicz." Yet he adds that if he never portrays another cop, it won't be too soon. And he may not have to. With the recognition and the ratings come, of course, opportunities. In February, Franz played attorney Richard "Racehorse" Haynes in the miniseries *Texas Justice*. In May he hosted *Saturday Night Live*. Meanwhile, he's been cast as one of the three leads in Tristar's forthcoming feature production of David Mamet's *American Buffalo*.

Quite simply, it's been a sweet year for Franz. "There comes a time when metabolism, numerical age, and enthusiasm all mesh," he reflects. "For me, it didn't happen when I was 20. It's happening now." And the best part of it had nothing to do with Hollywood.

To characterize Franz's romantic life as unsettled wouldn't be exactly right. He and Joanie Zeck have been together for 13 years. To say he's had a problem with commitment would also be in error, as he has not only lived under the same roof with her for most of that period, but he has also acted as a father to her two daughters. Franz, however, had never given any sign of being the marrying kind. Indeed, throughout the relationship's first decade, he kept his own apartment in Los Angeles's Fairfax district. True, he never spent a night at the place, using it chiefly as a retreat where he could read scripts and listen to music. Yet he held onto it defiantly, much as a man might hold onto an unrealized fantasy. It was a last bastion of independence.

Late in 1993, however, Franz gave up his bachelor pad, prompting friends to nod knowingly. No one, however, was prepared for what he would do at his 50th birthday party a few months later. Least of all Franz.

Joanie, a tough, redheaded fireball who's in the corporate promotions business, had rented a room for 200 at a San Fernando Valley restaurant, transforming it into an homage to Franz. The walls were covered with blown-up photographs from his childhood. The tables were topped by chocolate centerpieces shaped to resemble TVs, the screens filled by a likeness of the birthday boy. As a final touch, a Hirschfeld caricature of Franz had been etched into the champagne glasses at the head table.

All of Franz's family and friends were in attendance, as were most of the gangs from *Hill Street Blues* and *NYPD Blue*: Steven Bochco and David Milch, Jimmy Smits, Sharon Lawrence, Nick Turturro, Peter Jurasik, Charlie Haid, Bruce Weitz, and Joe Spano.

Not surprisingly, there was much drinking, much dancing and, at the end, much toasting—most eloquently from Joe Mantegna.

"Shlachta is 50," Mantegna exclaimed as an opener.

Then, more solemnly, he saluted Franz as a friend, actor, and "the man who 30 years ago, when we were smoking pot and saying what a horrible country this is, was running around in rice paddies on the other side of the world so that today, we could all sit here together in this beautiful room."

"Dennis, if you were my brother, I couldn't love you more."

With emotions running high, a sharply attired but nervous Franz took the stage.

"Joanie, come up here," he began, and she did.

Then, with Joanie by his side, he said: "This is gonna knock me out. I'm totally unprepared for this. I don't have anything in my pocket, but—in front of all of you—will you marry me?"

There was, of course, bedlam. Not until the pandemonium died down was Franz able to be heard: "She said yes." Six months later the two exchanged vows.

So in the same year, Dennis Franz—a man not given to exhibitionism, a man for whom restraint is still a virtue—had twice bared all. To the television audience, he'd shown that part of himself upon which the sun does not shine. To his wife-to-be, he'd exposed his heart. In each instance, the response had been profoundly affirming. At 50, Franz had chosen the exact right moment to reveal both the man within and the man without.

The Nolte Nobody Knows

Premiere, March 1989

Standing on the fringe of the Calabasas Golf & Country Club's fifth green, Lee Majors is a $6 million vision in a pink argyle knit vest adorned with the logo of Arizona's exclusive La Paloma links. Then there's Powers Boothe, so natty in a blue-and-buff ensemble that's it's easy to forget his numerous turns as a Hollywood heavy. Bill Cross—maroon sweater bearing the insignia of Hawaii's majestic Kapalua Bay eighteen—would be at home on any course from Augusta to Pebble Beach. Yes, it's a sporty group, a trio of successful, middle-aged Americans indulging in a little male bonding. But wait: still out on the fairway, the fourth member of the party is preparing to hit over the water hazard that guards this hole. A moment of silence, the familiar thwunk of club striking ball, and, oh my God...

Nick Nolte's drive—a careening slap shot that was headed into the drink before it skipped through a flock of unsuspecting ducks and bounced onto dry land—is ugly enough, but Nolte...well, club members pay exorbitant dues to avoid such apparitions. This late-November morning, the actor's hair is tequila-sunrise orange, and it hangs limply over his tinted rimless glasses like a mop of radioactive noodles. Then there's Nolte's bulk. At six feet one, 210 pounds, he's certainly a big old boy. Yet above and beyond the actor's distinctive physical characteristics, there's the matter of his taste in leisure wear. Mismatched surgical scrubs—inside-out lime green top, surf gray bottoms—girdled by a grimy elastic back brace might be correct attire in an insane asylum, but in this WASPy setting, they're just a tad inappropriate.

As Nolte lumbers toward his buddies, a couple of Palm Springs types, mouths agape, tool by in their golf cart. "Where'd you get these guys?" one of them asks Majors, meaning, of course, where did he get the lunatic?

Without missing a beat, the erstwhile bionic man gestures toward Nolte and replies, "Well, I got this one in the green out of the institution. I gotta get him back by lunch. What time is it?"

The leather faces simply nod and speed away, their incredulous expressions sending Majors, Boothe, and Cross into paroxysms of laughter. Nolte is pleased to be a source of amusement to his friends. After all, his weekly round with these fellows is a favorite diversion. But he's not going to let them off without paying a price. Extracting his putter from a bag choking with clubs pilfered from at least half a dozen different sets, the actor takes a bead on the pin and then—snorting and growling as if he just might hack the tiny, dimpled spheroid at his feet into a thousand pieces—calmly taps home. Once the ball drops into the cup, Nolte looks up at his companions, and in a gravelly voice that is simultaneously triumphant, threatening, and goofy, he sputters, "Fuck you, you fucking dickheads."

On the golf course as on the screen, Nick Nolte is adept at presenting himself as a pretty deranged sort. Indeed, if his behavior in a country-club environment seems a trifle unbalanced, consider the parts he's played on film. In *Who'll Stop the Rain* (1978), his terrifying evocation of a Vietnam veteran caught up in a heroin-smuggling ring captured the insidious ways in which the war haunted its participants even after they returned to America. In *North Dallas Forty* (1979), his blackly humorous portrayal of an alienated, drug-addled professional football player forever destroyed any romanticized illusions about the NFL. And as a bedraggled street person in *Down and Out in Beverly Hills* (1986), he managed to bring a crazed gusto to the task of eating dog food from the can.

This spring, Nolte will appear in three major new pictures that to greater and lesser degrees also trade on his ability to portray disturbed—or at least off-center—individuals. In John Milius's *Farewell to the King*, he plays a World War II Army deserter named Learoyd who organizes a group of tribal headhunters to fight behind the lines against Japanese troops. As an embittered ex-con in *Three Fugitives*—yet another Touchstone role-reversal vehicle—he is forced to endure being taken hostage by an inexperienced bank robber (Martin Short). And in Martin Scorsese's segment of Touchstone's *New York Stories*, he plays an expressionist painter obsessed by his beautiful apprentice (Rosanna Arquette).

Meanwhile, in late January, Nolte is scheduled to begin shooting what could well be his most challenging film to date—Arthur Miller's *Everybody Wins*, costarring Debra Winger. As Thomas O'Toole, a disillusioned private investigator, the actor must not only untangle a complicated murder cover-up loosely based on an actual 1970s cause célèbre (the Peter Reilly case, in which Miller was deeply involved), but he must also confront his character's cynicism regarding the very concept of justice.

Several of Nolte's forthcoming roles—especially those in the Scorsese short and *Everybody Wins*, which is being directed by Karel Reisz (*The French Lieutenant's Woman*)—are the kind that any movie star would covet. Smart career moves, they establish Nolte, in the words of Disney Studios chairman Jeffrey Katzenberg, "as a really major star, one of the two or three most sought-after leading men in the industry." They are the kind of parts that advance the actor into the select group of bankable male leads who can command exorbitant fees—the producers of *Farewell to the King* reportedly paid him $3 million. Yet Nolte insists that such calculations did not influence his decisions to take any of these jobs. "I've just decided to put the blinders on as far as business and making money go," he says. "I don't deal with it anymore. I refuse to. The actor's problem is to find stories he wants to be part of. Then, if the studios make money and the public goes, that's fine. But that's not my intent out front."

The stories Nick Nolte wants to be a part of are those that somehow mirror his own psychological obsessions. A self-diagnosed manic-depressive ("That's why I wear the medical clothes everywhere. It's sort of a joke, but it's serious"), Nolte was initially attracted to acting because it "would let me put the pieces of my life together if I could do it," and through the years the basic idea has remained essentially unchanged. The actor's desire to probe his psyche on celluloid has led him to make some commercially ill-advised decisions—when offered the title role in *Superman*, Nolte responded, "I'll do it if I can play him as a schizophrenic." It has also involved him in more than a few box-office and creative disasters. Perhaps the most dismal was *Weeds* (1987), a clumsily earnest account of a San Quentin inmate named Lee Umstetter, who rehabilitates himself by writing and producing a play behind prison walls. But to Nolte, such misfires are preferable to premeditated successes. At 48, he still believes that by exploring his madness in his work, he just might find himself.

The process always begins the same way. Facing each other across a beat-up wooden table, Nick Nolte and Bill Cross are tearing apart several nicely bound copies of *Everybody Wins*. It's only a little after nine in the morning, but the actor's Malibu office—a junk-strewn warren lined with cinder-block bookshelves containing titles ranging from *Nautical Archaeology* to the complete works of Stanislavsky—is already hazy with cigarette smoke. For an hour now, the two men—one a stocky bantam in a pearl-buttoned Wrangler shirt, the other an unshaven slab clad, of course, in his operating room best—have been grappling with an important creative question: Would private investigator Thomas O'Toole carry a gun?

"Karel doesn't think he should," Nolte says, "but this guy used to be a cop, and if you've grown up as a policeman your gun is always your friend."

"The trouble is," responds Cross, "if you introduce a gun, the audience says, 'What's he going to do with it?' If it'll make you feel better, maybe we should just take a prop and strap it on your leg, but you can't show it, because then this becomes cops and robbers."

On every movie he's made during the past ten years, Nolte has relied on Cross (who, when not serving as the actor's sounding board, is often seen on television and film in supporting roles) for this kind of advice. The two men met in the early 1970s at a theater on Los Angeles's Melrose Avenue, where Nolte was appearing in a production of *Picnic*. Cross—who had just returned to the States from a tour of duty as an Army captain in Vietnam—was a constant presence, leaning against walls, tense, bowed up as if he were still in combat. The actor instantly identified with the obviously troubled vet (others at the playhouse thought they were brothers), and when Nolte was cast in *Who'll Stop the Rain*, he sought out Cross to help authenticate his performance.

Nearly a dozen pictures later, the boys have it down to a science. Starting a couple of months before a film goes into production, they meet daily for several hours. On three-by-five note cards, Nolte jots headings for each segment of the movie in which he'll be appearing. Some examples from *Everybody Wins*: "Drive Angela Home," "Laid & Leave," "Go Back to Cemetery." Then the actor and his friend speculate on his character's probable motivations during these scenes. Cross records the musings on a yellow legal pad and feeds the information into a computer, producing a running analysis of their thoughts. The goal: to come to a consensus on how Nolte should interpret every aspect of his part.

At least that's how it functions in theory. But as a Xeroxed photograph of a Texas Ranger named Joaquin Jackson tacked prominently on the wall in Nolte's workroom testifies field research is also often required. In 1986, the actor sought out Jackson, a righteous western lawman, when he was preparing to make Walter Hill's *Extreme Prejudice*—a film whose ludicrous violence mars Nolte's fine performance as an incorruptible white hat.

Tales of Nolte's struggles to get ready for parts are legion around Hollywood. Before filming *Down and Out in Beverly Hills*, he disappeared for several days into Los Angeles's skid row, where he drank cheap wine and slept in vacant lots. "When he first showed up for rehearsal he really upset Bette [Midler] and Richard [Dreyfuss]," recalls director Paul Mazursky, "because he quite literally stank." Prior to playing a policeman in his comeback blockbuster *48 Hours* (1982), he accompanied San Francisco cops on the obligatory rounds. And during the shooting of *Farewell to the King*, he and Cross transformed their hotel suite on location in Borneo into a situation room that, apart from its mess, was worthy of General Douglas MacArthur: battle charts, arcane historical accounts of Allied objectives in the Pacific theater, a dog-eared copy of the script into which the relevant pages of the novel that it was based on were inserted for background. The actor's war research was so exhaustive that director John Milius took one look at the stuff and barked, "What the hell does any of this have to do with acting?"

To Nolte, the answer was *everything*. "You have to think it out," he says, "otherwise you get on camera with just generalized bullshit."

Most directors eventually get used to Nolte's method. Milius did. "I don't know why more actors don't work like Nick," says the director. "There's no ego involved. He just wants to understand his character." So did Mazursky, who asserts, "Nick would never be so pretentious as to call himself a Method actor. He just does it." And so did Scorsese. "His preparation on *New York Stories* was exhaustive," he says. "He spent a tremendous amount of time with the artist we based his character on [Chuck Connelly]. It really pleases me when people do their homework."

Nolte admits that he's compulsive about his preproduction ritual, although he insists he knows when it's time to quit. "Preparing for a role is when I get to indulge," he says, "but when we start, it's a collaborative effort, and I feel strongly about that. It comes from theater, where you very seldom see an actor who tries to take over a stage production, and from athletics, the ethics of sports. I'm a team player."

But on this early-winter's day, Nolte is a long way from being ready to regard *Everybody Wins* as a communal enterprise. In fact, he and Cross have just begun to transform Thomas O'Toole from a vague image in the actor's mind into something real and concrete. Once they decide that the character won't use a pistol, they move on to the next issue. In the screenplay, Miller describes his protagonist as an opera lover. To Nolte, this is the kind of entry point he likes to exploit, which is why his work surface is cluttered not just with pencils and paper but also with dozens of brand-new audiocassettes. Shortly, *La Traviata* begins booming from the office's custom sound system: a cheap plastic ghetto blaster.

It's a safe bet that in the past, neither the actor nor his sidekick has spent a lot of time cozying up to Pavarotti, but as the Italian tenor's voice fills the room, they listen like devoted cognoscenti. Nolte, especially, seems transported. "Yes," he says at one point when, for at least a moment, he sees himself as a weary PI driving through the playwright's cold New England countryside, florid melodies wafting from his car stereo, a mystery on his mind. Later, he will tentatively reflect, "I think all an actor's technique is, is learning that he'll survive, finding the knowledge that he'll survive this thing he's going to have to go through. Only then can he deal with his insecurity and his fear."

The face staring up from beautician Lori Davis's chair does not look insecure. Wild? Yes. A hell-raiser? Hell, yes. But scared? Not Nick Nolte. For one thing, the wide forehead, ain't nothin'-bashful-about-me nose, and massive jaw look as if they were carved out of a clean hung of Iowa limestone, weathered just long enough to gain some complexity, then happily fixed at a point between boyishness and maturity. The only flaw: jug ears. For another, there's not a doubt-plagued male alive who would go out in public on a pre-Christmas Saturday looking like the actor does at this very minute. It's not just the hospital getup—by now, that's routine. No, it's the fact that Davis has wrapped Nolte's locks with so many small pieces of aluminum foil that he looks like a cross between a glitter-bonneted Sioux chief and a human TV antenna.

Davis, a plump blonde all dolled up in scarlet, describes herself as "hair doctor to the stars." Her patients have included Sean Penn, Barbara Hershey, and Laurence Olivier. She is treating Nolte this afternoon on an emergency basis. Something has to be done about that carcinogenic-orange mane—the by-product of several recent dye jobs—because the actor has just learned that he'll be journeying up the coast on Tuesday to shoot a new ending for *Three Fugitives*. During the next four hours, Davis will bleach and then re-bleach Nolte's hair in an attempt to reveal its natural light brown tones. Painstakingly, she must strip away multiple layers of color in a process analogous to how one must uncover the turmoil Nolte hides behind his rugged façade, for the actor—like all actors—camouflages himself in ways that submit only to a gradual unmasking.

With Nick Nolte, one needs to begin with a time—the late '70s and early '80s—he doesn't like to talk about and with a woman he'd really rather forget, his second wife, whose name is Sharyn but who was universally

208

known by a moniker that speaks volumes: Legs. About all the actor cares to volunteer on either the era or the marriage is that it was "a very chaotic period, and I was very messed up. I think, generally, there were a lot of troubles in the whole industry, and the relationship with Legs was tied up in this. It personified a whole self-destructive way of existing. We carried it on too far."

What Nick and Legs carried on too far was more than just an emotional folie a deux. Cocaine was an equal partner in their pathology. "Nick went right up to the edge of the danger zone," says Cross. Adds John Milius, whose relationship with Nolte far predates *Farewell to the King*, "The way Nick put it to me was that during that time he looked into the pit of hell."

Considering that Nolte's vantage point during those days was often little higher than ground level, it's no wonder things appeared so threatening. Following a separation from Legs that took place while he was filming *Cannery Row* (1982), the actor beached his bloated bulk on the floor of costar Debra Winger's trailer. About this time, Cross recalls seeing his friend sprawled in the middle of the driveway trying to keep Legs—who was in the process of backing the car into the street—from leaving home. And Nolte himself will admit to awakening hung over one day in a gigantic, empty mansion on Zuma Beach, hearing a creaking buoy, and vaguely realizing that during the bender that had dropped him in this unfamiliar setting, he had agreed to rent the place.

That the actor sank to such a disoriented state was due, he now believes, to "what started out in the '60s as being very pure becoming very corrupted." Perhaps so. But Nolte's dilemma was also distinctly of his own making.

Ever since he was a boy, Nolte has had a self-destructive streak. The son of Iowa State football player Frank Nolte, young Nick was a superb high school athlete, lettering in baseball, basketball, wrestling, track, and—most notably—football. Avidly recruited by legendary Arizona State coach Frank Kush, Nolte left his native Midwest following graduation to join the team. But after a semester in Tempe, the would-be Sun Devil quarterback simply stopped studying. Forced by poor grades to leave the university, Nolte dutifully agreed to rehabilitate himself. But instead of enrolling as planned at Eastern Arizona Junior College, he pocketed the money his mother had given him and moved into a Mexican whorehouse.

"I took off in a little MGA," the actor recalls, "and it was a little Kerouacian. Boy, I found Canal Street in Nogales, and being from the Midwest and finding a place like that, I just stayed there. You wake up in the morning and you're miles from Iowa, and life is pretty complete."

Thus began Nolte's life on the road. Over the next several years, he played ball at five different schools, dropping out whenever it became apparent he was going to have to attend classes. He probably could have continued the pattern for a while longer, but after his 1961 season at Pasadena City College, he came to a wrenching conclusion: he lacked the physical skills to make it to the next level. "You take a young man and build up this athletic myth as the great pursuit of life," he says, "but then it ends, and it's so abrupt. Really, all that's left is a shell."

Washed up as a jock, Nolte stayed in Hollywood—not because of the movies but because he found a job as an iron-worker, installing storm drains in the hills by day, rolling around in the gutters outside Barney's Beanery by night. The cinema held no attraction for him, yet when a friend associated with the Pasadena Playhouse took him to see a production there, Nolte felt a glimmer. "I realized there was something I could feel intensely about again," he says. "Theater was a rebirthing process for me."

Many struggling actors spend years trying to get to Los Angeles, but Nolte's instincts told him to leave almost as soon as he decided he had found a new calling. "The problem for young actors in New York or Los Angeles or any of the big centers," he says, "is that their only experience is classes or minor roles. Inside, they're churning. I didn't have time for that. If you really want to act, you have to play Biff in *Death of a Salesman* while you're still in your twenties. And you certainly want to play John Osborne's *Luther* when you're a young man, and there's only one place you can do that—regional theater."

For the next fourteen years, Nolte gypsied across America performing at the Actors Inner Circle Theater in Phoenix, the Old Log in Minnesota, and the Little Theater of the Rockies in Colorado. He regards his long period of self-imposed exile with surprising equanimity. "It was really great," he recalls. "Some of the best plays I've ever seen were done in these theaters. Everyone had so much intensity and integrity."

During his travels, Nolte married his first wife, Sheila, and he picked up a pretty good education by auditing classes at various universities—he attributes his early rebellion against academia to the fact that on his mother's side of the family everyone was either a professor or an administrator, and he grew up feeling they were all a bit smug. The actor was also convicted of a felony. The charge: counterfeiting draft cards. The sentence: five years' probation.

"The crux of it," Nolte recalls, "is they thought I was in some way attached to the war resistance. Truly, I wasn't—although philosophically, I was. But I sold thousands of cards at just about every school in the Midwest. It's all in *Down and Out in Beverly Hills*. I have this little speech about my background, about how I got to be a bum. In the script, Mazursky just had a line that went, 'I was politically active in the '60s.' But I said, 'Paul, why don't we just insert this little thing I wrote instead.' And he did."

Nolte didn't return to California until 1973, when playwright William Inge, enamored of a Phoenix production of *The Last Pad*, in which the actor was starring, insisted that the players be given a chance to reprise their work in Los Angeles. The show opened at the Westwood Playhouse on the night Inge committed suicide, and it ran for many months, making Nolte locally famous. In 1976, national adulation followed when the actor played a leading role in the Irwin Shaw TV miniseries *Rich Man, Poor Man*.

Soon, Nolte was a star (his first major role was "opposite Jackie Bisset's wet T-shirt" in *The Deep*). And soon, in his own hardheaded way, he began behaving like one. He ran with a motorcycle gang whose members played pinball in joints up and down the Pacific Coast Highway for ludicrous stakes—losers had to disrobe and ride naked on their bikes from Santa Monica to Malibu. He hung out with the Allman Brothers Band's Dickey Betts. He frequented clubs on Sunset Boulevard, drinking with abandon, while also indulging other vices. And, inevitably, he met Legs.

A dancer of Lebanese descent, Legs was the most exotic and impassioned female Nolte had ever encountered. According to the actor's close friend, ex-Dallas Cowboy Peter Gent, she also seemed intent on destroying Nolte. "It was the most psychotic relationship I've ever seen," says Gent, who met both Legs and Nick while the actor was filming *North Dallas Forty*, which was based on the football player's novel of the same title. "I remember seeing her rip the phone out of the wall of Nick's apartment, throw all his clothes in the swimming pool, then knock Nick over the head with the phone and push him in. After that, he came and hid out with me in my room at the Westwood Marquis for the rest of the production."

"Ultimately," Nolte confesses, "I had to climb away from it. At a certain point, the only sanity left for me was in my work."

The actor's salvation was his third wife, Rebecca, whom he married in 1984. "Becky saved Nick's life," says Bill Cross. The daughter of a West

Virginia surgeon (in fact, she comes from a whole clan of doctors, which, if nothing else, assures her husband of a steady supply of medical garb), Rebecca quickly asserted herself as the sustaining force in Nolte's recovery. The couple set up housekeeping both at a comfortable ranch in a Malibu canyon and in "an unpretentious little house in Charleston" (another beach place is under construction in North Carolina) and had a child—Brawley King, now two. Moreover, the new Mrs. Nolte began managing Nick's career. The old rebel, it seemed, had been domesticated.

Indeed, Nolte now enjoys nothing more than expounding on such subjects as family values and middle-American verities. He wants to build a life in a town where he doesn't have to worry if the kids aren't home at a certain hour, can trust his neighbors to watch his yard, and won't have to discuss the industry but can instead listen to common folks talk about common concerns. He sheepishly admits to becoming a homebody, and in a sense it seems a natural development. In spite of his many escapades, Nolte is at heart a gentle soul. His innate goodness shows through even in his most idiosyncratic film characters, from *North Dallas Forty*'s Phil Elliott—who was ultimately the one honorable individual in Gent's book—to *Down and Out in Beverly Hills*'s Jerry Baskin, who brought a sense of decency to the life of hanger maven Dave Whiteman (Richard Dreyfuss).

However, something about the actor's contention that he's ready to become a responsible citizen doesn't ring completely true. Many things still seem unsettled in him; in fact, they may never be resolved except during those few moments of artificial reality onscreen—and even then not satisfactorily.

It's dark outside, and the rain is pouring down in a cold, steady shower, but in the clubhouse of the Calabasas Country Club, things are warm and cozy, and Nick Nolte, Lee Majors, Powers Boothe, and Bill Cross are settling in for a fine drunk. At first, Nolte tries to be good, ordering only light beer, but Majors—who insists on buying double screwdrivers for the table—is an evil influence. The Six Million Dollar Man has just returned from New Zealand, where he married the 1985 *Playboy* Playmate of the Year while earning $500,000 for appearing in a Toyota Commercial, and he's in no mood to be denied. Soon, neither is anyone else.

"I don't like movies that have plots in 'em," the bionic hero is contending.

"Lee, you gotta have plots," Nolte counters.

"Hell, your films don't have plots. What was the plot of *Down and Out?*"

"It was that I was gonna screw everybody in the house."

And on it goes. Talk about the racehorse Nolte and Cross have recently purchased and named Walter Hill. Talk about point spreads for the weekend's football games. A lot of lying about youthful athletic accomplishments.

As spirits rise all around, Nolte turns to Cross and mutters, "I've been too serious lately, haven't I?"

"Yeah."

"I should relax?"

"Yeah."

With that, Nolte orders another double. Rebecca will have to call the club twice tonight before he drags himself home.

A Character Actor Reaches Cult Status

The New York Times Magazine, November 16, 1987

On a warm afternoon earlier this fall, Harry Dean Stanton, wearing an old denim work shirt, Levis, and deck shoes, sat on the sofa of his Mullholland Drive home high above Los Angeles dispensing shopping instructions to a female assistant regarding the purchase of a present for his maid. "Get Maria something nice," Stanton said. "Spend $200, $300. She works so hard." Then, in a nearly incredulous tone, the 60-year-old actor added, "I'm not rich, but for the first time in my life I have money."

Grizzled and lean, with a face dominated by hollowed cheeks and deep-socketed brown eyes, Stanton possesses the hungry look of a man who knows about living on the run. No surprise that he has usually played tough guys, psychopaths, and criminals. Somewhere along the way, he even began to live like a marginal character. His house, a small wooden structure that clings to a hillside overlooking the San Fernando Valley, is the epitome of a disheveled bachelor pad.

The bedroom contains a mattress on the floor and not much else. Save for a beer or two, the kitchen refrigerator is usually empty. In these Spartan quarters Stanton—despite all evidence to the contrary—long nurtured the hope that film directors would see him as more than just an onscreen slasher.

After giving his assistant her marching orders, Stanton slipped on a pair of half frame reading glasses and in a pile of bills and magazines located the script for Beth Henley's *Crimes of the Heart*, a movie he had turned down.

"They wanted me to play a corrupt Southern senator," Stanton said. "I could have really scored with it, but I would have been a heavy. There's a scene where the character they wanted me to do kicks the hell out of a black kid, and that's why I didn't take it. The role is superbly written, but it's gotten debilitating over the years to have people say to me, 'You're the bad one. You're the one who gets shot.' Give me a break for a change. I know I've got the ability to bring a sense of menace to the screen. I have that specific competence, and it's kept me working. But I don't want to do anything else that's life negative."

Standing up, Harry Dean walked to the fireplace. Outside, it was 85 degrees, but a blaze was roaring on the hearth. "It's for company," he said. For several minutes, he stared into the flames.

It is all now finally beginning to change for Harry Dean Stanton. After an apprenticeship of nearly three decades, he is no longer numbered among Hollywood's character actors, those hard-working cogs whose faces and roles are more memorable than their names. With anonymity only a bad memory, he has just completed work on *Slam Dance*, in which he plays opposite Tom Hulce, and John Sayles is talking to him about starring in his next film. Earlier this year, a trio of movies featuring him opened almost simultaneously.

In Robert Altman's *Fool for Love*, Stanton is the deranged, ornery, but ultimately benevolent "Old Man," father to both Sam Shepard and Kim Basinger. In *Pretty in Pink*, he plays Molly Ringwald's dad. In an episode of Showtime's *Faerie Tale Theater* directed by Francis Ford Coppola, he is that most innocent of American folk heroes—Rip Van Winkle. These were quickly followed by Disney's *One Magic Christmas*, in which the actor portrays an angel named Gideon.

Recently, celebrity has also come to Stanton in other ways—his friendships with such members of the well-publicized "brat pack" as Madonna and Sean Penn, several appearances on *Late Night with David Letterman*, and even a gig as guest host of *Saturday Night Live*, where instead of delivering the traditional opening monologue, he belted out a blues number with the house band.

Stanton's rise is unusual for his breed of actor. Supporting performers do not ordinarily attract powerful agents or managers, nor can they afford to throw high-visibility parties. They must audition several times a week, thus living with constant rejection. Their pay may range up to $25,000 per picture, but when they do get a break, they are usually cast in the same sort of generic roles—mothers, the hero's best friend, or small-time villains. Most character actors are stuck in such niches for life.

Prior to 1983, the year things started to turn around for Stanton, his 50 or so film credits read more like a rap sheet than a resume. After breaking into the movies in a 1957 western, he was picked the following year to play a bad guy opposite Alan Ladd in *The Proud Rebel*, and the type was cast. What followed was a cinematic crime spree—films like *Hostage, Day of the Evil Gun*, and so on. During the 1960s there was no respite in his television work—in each guest spot he reprised a version of the violent persona that provided his bread and butter.

Occasionally, Stanton rose up out of his rut to deliver gemlike performances that revealed greater depths. In *The Missouri Breaks*, he was winning and dignified as the co-leader of a gang of horse thieves on the lam from Marlon Brando. In *Cool Hand Luke*, he was the sweet and melancholy convict who serenades Paul Newman with gospel music. In *The Godfather, Part II*, he played the taciturn F.B.I agent assigned to guard Frankie Pentangeli.

The turning point for Stanton was Wim Wenders's film *Paris, Texas*, winner of the 1984 Grand Prize at the Cannes Film Festival and the first movie in which the actor, after 27 years in the business, was cast as the leading man. When Stanton talks about the picture his voice takes on hushed tones. "That opening scene parallels my own personal quest for the grail, as it were," he observed recently.

Paris, Texas begins out on the parched Southwestern badlands. To the eerie strains of Ry Cooder's guitar soundtrack, a solitary figure marches resolutely toward some unknown destination. The face is that of a man who has been deeply wounded, and it belongs, of course, to Harry Dean in the role of Travis.

The film ends with Travis's rejuvenation. After a reunion with his brother and son, he musters the courage to visit his estranged wife (Nastassja Kinski). Their encounters are heartbreaking, and Stanton gives a wrenching performance as a character working through the debris of his life to arrive at the strength and resolution to quit running and begin again.

Stanton got this breakthrough part because Sam Shepard, author of *Paris, Texas*, looked across a barroom in Santa Fe, New Mexico, one evening in 1983. The place was thronged with people attending a film festival, and Shepard's eyes fell upon Harry Dean. Over shot glasses of tequila, the playwright-actor and the character actor fell into conversation.

"I was telling him I was sick of the roles I was playing," Stanton recalled. "I told him I wanted to play something of some beauty or sensitivity. I had no inkling he was considering me for the lead in his movie."

Not long after Stanton returned to Los Angeles, he picked up the telephone to hear Shepard offering him the part. "My first question was, 'Why aren't you doing it?'" Stanton said. "Sam replied that it was too indulgent, and besides, he was also doing *Country* at the time. So I said yes."

When Harry Dean Stanton arrived in Hollywood during the 1950s, he was convinced that within a couple of years he'd become a star. His optimism, however, was undercut by the insecurities and frustrations he'd carried with him since childhood.

Stanton was born in the little town of West Irvine, Kentucky, into a troubled family. His mother and father were constantly separating. During the worst years of the Depression, the brood moved frequently. Often, Harry Dean felt as if there were no place he belonged. Whatever solace he drew from his parents' strict, Southern Baptist faith evaporated as he began to sense that fundamentalism was anathema to his rebellious spirit.

When he was upset during boyhood, Harry Dean sang about his woes. If the house was empty, he'd climb atop a stool in the kitchen and practice the songs. He was about 8 when he started such performances.

"One day I just got up and started singing 'T for Texas, T for Tennessee, T for that girl who made a wreck out of me,'" he offered not long ago. "I guess you could say that was the birth of my blues, but it's also when I went into show biz."

Stanton, however, never seriously considered acting until he was in college. Following a tour of duty in the Navy during World War II, where he served on an LST in the Pacific and received a commendation for coolness under fire, he entered the University of Kentucky. During his junior year, he settled on a major in drama after a successful campus production. But he quit school without graduating.

"I made it a point not to graduate," Stanton said. "I thought that was a positive, independent kind of statement. I never liked being ordered around—which, of course, was an overreaction. I eventually found out that I didn't mind being ordered around at all when it was by someone who knew what he was doing."

After an interval as a student at the Pasadena Playhouse in California, Stanton joined the American Male Chorus on a national tour (he also drove the bus). Then he moved to New York and signed on to the road company of the Strawbridge children's theater. Soon he was back on the highways. By 1957, when he'd had his fill of touring, he settled on the West Coast for good and began his long run as a movie bad guy.

Harry Dean Stanton's friend Fred Roos, a producer and casting agent, remembers that throughout the 1960s, "Harry always had so much hostility and resentment. There was a long period when he couldn't get anything but bit parts, and the frustration level was extremely high. You read interviews with other character actors, and they're proud of their work, proud of being able to bring a touch of authenticity to a small part. But not Harry. He kept saying, 'I have to get out of this.'"

From the perspective provided by his newfound good fortune, Stanton said recently, "I don't blame anyone but myself for the kind of parts I got. To blame external circumstances is absolute folly. I hated being typecast in those roles. It was personally limiting, only playing stereotyped heavies. But I got those roles because I was angry, because that's what I projected. I was angry at my mother and father because they didn't get along, angry at the church. On top of that, I had an extreme lack of self-confidence."

During his early years in Hollywood, Stanton had numerous brief entanglements with women, none lasting much longer than a year. "I was troubled by all the life problems—finding a mate, having a family, settling down. I just couldn't get those things right." Stanton's longest-lasting relationship was with a young actress, Rebecca de Mornay. However, it ended badly, too. Ultimately, Stanton began to develop the Beat-era persona of a man living on the edge of reality. He was mercurial, nocturnal, and often unconscious. He had a knack for making improbable statements and winding up in the wrong place at the wrong time.

Jack Nicholson, who roomed with Stanton in a house in the Hollywood Hills during the early 1960s when both men were scrounging for small character parts, came to regard Harry Dean as "one of the truly unpredictable entities on the planet."

At his worst, Nicholson said, Stanton "could drive people crazy." For example, during the filming of *Pat Garrett and Billy the Kid*, Stanton, who was only a bit player in the picture, ruined an expensive shot by accidentally jogging across a set while cameras were rolling. Kris Kristofferson, the film's star and one of Stanton's old friends, recalled that the movie's director, Sam Peckinpah, "had waited all day just to get this one shot right in which James Coburn rides off into the early-morning light after killing me. Peckinpah was furious. He yelled at Harry, 'You just cost me $25,000.' Then he picked up a bowie knife and threw it at him. It was a pretty close call."

At his best, however, Stanton was not awed by Hollywood's biggest stars. "On the set of *The Missouri Breaks*," Nicholson was saying not long ago, "I saw Harry Dean make one of the bravest and most inspired moves I've ever had the chance to witness. You remember that Brando wore a dress in that picture. It was all in keeping with his character, a deranged lawman chasing me and Harry. On the day he was finally supposed to kill Harry—it was awful; he was supposed to impale him on this stake—Marlon briefly turned his back, and Harry snuck up on him, jumped on top of him, and ripped off the dress. Now, I have a singular admiration for that event. Marlon knew what an honest thing Harry was doing. The whole time Harry was wrestling him down, he was smiling."

The only thing Stanton cared to say about the episode with Brando was, "I just couldn't stand the idea of getting killed by a man in a dress."

Although Stanton is proud of his distaste for artifice and his refusal to be bound by convention, he's a little sheepish about his reputation. "I sure wish I'd matured earlier. There was such a long period in my life in which I was struggling to bloom, and as a result I did a lot of stupid things. I'd say that I'm now a lot more stable. I was just a very late bloomer. It was Eastern mysticism that began to help me. Alan Watts's books on Zen Buddhism were a very strong influence. Taoism and Lao-tse, I read much of, along with the works of Krishnamurti. And I studied tai chi, the martial art, which is all about centering oneself."

But it was *The I Ching* (The Book of Changes) in which Stanton found most of his strength. By his bedside he keeps a bundle of sticks wrapped in blue ribbon. Several times every week, he throws them (or a handful of coins) and then turns to the book to search out the meaning of the pattern they made. "I throw them whenever I need input," he said. "It's an addendum to my subconscious." He now does this before almost everything he undertakes—interviews, films, meetings. "It has sustained and nourished me," he said. "But I'm not qualified to expound on it."

Stanton contends that his quest for self-awareness has given him the courage "to begin the next phase of my career." In fact, he suggests, "I've only started getting good parts because I've changed, because I'm no longer so angry. I'm much more confident now, and it comes through."

Still, Harry Dean Stanton has retained just enough of his rambunctious, childlike self to have grown into a peculiarly complex man—part tyro, part tough, and part teacher. "Harry Dean has got a rebelliousness in him, a freedom, a youthfulness, that even most young people don't have," commented Madonna. "At the same time he has the wisdom of the ages, an Eastern philosophical point of view." In other words, Stanton is 60 going on 22, a seeker who also likes to drive fast cars, dance all night, and chain-smoke cigarettes with the defiant air of a hood hanging out in the high school boy's room.

Although Stanton abhors the term brat pack—"It's just a handle for the media, and it confines everyone to the kiddy table when a couple of these people are way beyond that"—he regards several of the young stars grouped under the heading as his best friends.

The attraction, which is mutual, grew out of his work in the title role of the cult-classic *Repo Man* in 1983. A hard, nihilistic film set in a sterile California suburb—a place where all the products are packaged in plain wrap, burned-out hippie parents sit comatose in front of TV preachers, and most folks can't keep up with their car payments—the movie limns the desperation experienced by teenagers who see no place for themselves in the modern world. When one such teenager (played by Emilio Estevez) goes to work for a car repossession agency, Stanton instructs him in the art of legally stealing automobiles. More important, Stanton imbues the boy with what he calls "the Repo code," a set of commandments for an unglued society: "Repo man don't go running to the law; Repo man goes it alone; Repo man would rather die on his feet than live on his knees." When Stanton is shot down by the police at the film's conclusion, he is seen as a martyr.

Stanton's role in *Repo Man* elevated him to the position of punk icon, and thereafter he became one of the few Hollywood old-timers easily embraced by young actors, particularly Sean Penn.

Penn, perhaps the most accomplished and surely the most outrageous of the movie's new stalwarts, sat down beside Stanton one night at On the Rox, a private West Hollywood club, where the two quickly struck up a friendship. "It was just one of those things where I met someone I really liked," said Penn. "He's a good companion, and he could keep up drinking with me all night. After we met, we went to France together for the Cannes Film Festival where *Paris, Texas* won the prize. Then we spent a week in New York hanging out. The amazing thing about him is that unlike most older guys he treats you like an equal. I think this is because he's so adaptable himself. Behind that rugged old cowboy face, he's simultaneously a man, a child, a woman—he just has this full range of emotions I really like. He's a very impressive soul more than he is a mind, and I find that attractive."

Penn was so taken with Stanton that he and his soon-to-be wife Madonna began going out with the older actor almost weekly. Now, the three of them—often accompanied by Sean's parents—spend many evenings together eating dinner, attending the movies, or dancing. Stanton is so fond of

Penn and his connections that he's come to see them as his surrogate family. He calls Sean and Madonna "the kids."

Similarly, Penn and Madonna feel a strong family tie to Harry Dean. "I know he's lonely sometimes," said Madonna, "but I think he's reconciled himself to being a lone figure in the universe."

Nowadays, Harry Dean Stanton shows signs of channeling his self-exploration toward becoming the kind of actor remembered for his artistry. His conversations are peppered with words like "good taste," "quality," and "significance." He seeks roles that are "righteous," using the word in its street connotation to mean "serious and profound." What he wants is that one magic part, the one they'll mention in film dictionaries, that will finally make up for all the awful parts from early in his career.

"The role for Harry Dean really is still out there," said his old friend Fred Roos. "I've been in his corner so long that I'd like to be the one to give it to him, so I'm looking, waiting."

The danger in the tack Stanton has taken is that he may become so selective that producers and directors will regard him as a prima donna. "I think Harry Dean's a victim," said Robert Altman. "He's 60, and he's been doing this all his life, and now he wants adulation and respect. He's so thirsty for it. Not only does he want the acclaim, but he wants the things that our industry uses to confer worth—more money, a bigger makeup trailer. As much as I wanted him in *Fool for Love*, he almost didn't get the part because his agent was gouging us for these things, making outrageous demands. I hope Harry Dean gets beyond this."

Stanton, however, is willing to take the chance of alienating Hollywood's powers because for so many years he feels that he did exactly what he was told and it got him nowhere. "Life is very short, and I have to take advantage of the chance I now have," he said one evening at dinner at City Restaurant, a hot, new Hollywood dining spot.

Stanton was seated at a good table, and from time to time other patrons glanced over, recognizing that a star was in their midst. It was a new sensation for Harry Dean—something that rarely happens to a character actor—and he liked it. Buoyed by the attention, he said, "I don't really want a career right now. What I want to do is what is artistically right, to make an impact."

Stanton, for so many years the touch of evil in film after film, looked across the table and added, "Well, there is one part I really want to play, but it hasn't been written yet, although some people are talking about it. I want to play Henry Clay, the man who held the Union together for so long before the Civil War. I want to play him because he's credited with the line, 'I'd rather be right than be president.'"

It all seemed so improbable yet so apt. Clay, like Stanton, was a Kentuckian. He also had a weathered face, but he is remembered for his noble aspirations. After playing so many men with weathered faces and ignoble desires, it was hard to blame Harry Dean for dreaming of finishing his acting career not as a sinner but as a saint.

G'Days

GQ, April 1990

The picture had finally wrapped, and now, after the short flight from Sydney and the long drive through the emerald countryside, Bryan Brown was home.

Up the dirt lane, across the plank bridge, under the overarching limbs of a dozen bunya-bunya trees he came, until at last he pulled to a halt before a yellow clapboard cottage. Built in 1914, the house is typical of its era—galvanized-iron roof for coolness, cistern for drinking water, veranda for tea. The current owners have done little to alter this simple, pretty place.

When Brown emerged from the car, his wife greeted him with mock severity. "You've got to shoe the horses, do the branding, and put up the weather vane," she ordered.

"But I just got here."

At that, Rachel Ward smiled and took her husband's hand. Yes, as master of a 300-acre cattle farm, Brown does have certain responsibilities, but for the moment, they could wait.

The first order of business was getting reacquainted. After corralling his 5-year-old daughter, Rosie (3-year-old Matilda would have to stay behind with the nanny), a shovel, and a couple of weeping-willow seedlings he'd purchased on the road that morning, Brown held open the paddock gate while his wife bridled a standard-bred trotter, jumped on bareback, and pulled Rosie up beside her.

It was late afternoon, and as mother and child rode ahead, the country squire strolled behind, enjoying the soft play of light on his rolling expanse of pasture and copse, hillock and dale. At the edge of a tiny grove he caught up with Rachel, who had stopped to observe the handiwork of a quite particular bird that was building its nest exclusively with blue artifacts—clothespins, threads, Bic ballpoint tops, disposable razors, milk-jug caps—pinched from the backyard garbage. Moving on, the family reached a gentle promontory overlooking a far valley and stood in silence while five kangaroos swept across the horizon.

Eventually, everyone arrived at the lily-pad-laden pond where Rachel had decided the trees were to go. "I really want them in there," she said, indicating a boggy bottom.

"That's all water," her husband objected, but realizing the location was actually quite splendid, he quickly set to work. The job didn't take long, and once finished, Brown leaned against his shovel, Rosie at his knees, while his wife rode briskly toward the west.

Silhouetted on horseback against the Australian sunset, Rachel Ward was a majestic sight. An exotic in a rude land, she is a woman who left a noble English house to live here in what was once, after all, Her Majesty's penal colony. But as Brown began to walk up a grade to join his wife, he certainly evinced no surprise at the fact that he—not just an Aussie but a boy from grim, working-class Panania, a Foster's-quaffing, football-loving commoner who at 25 was still toiling at a life-insurance agency—could have captured a foreign princess and brought her back to his native soil. Indeed, his marriage to the exquisite actress, like his burgeoning movie stardom and the trappings that go with it—this bucolic spread, a seaside retreat just outside of Sydney, a pied-a-terre high in the Malibu hills—strike him as, well, inevitabilities.

"I remember a conversation I had with another actor back in 1974, when I was struggling to make a name for myself in England," he said. "We were in a very depressing shopping mall on a cold day in a northern city, and he asked me, 'Why are you doing this?' And I said, 'Because someday I want to have a farm with horses and go off and do a couple of films a year.'"

For a second or two, Brown let this recollection hang in the air. Then, with a conspiratorial grin that revealed a sliver of gold front tooth, he confided, "I guess you could say that I'm a pretty confident sort of person."

Buried up to his neck in a desolate sand dune overlooking Sydney's Cronulla Beach, a bulldozer piloted by costar Karen Allen bearing down on him at twelve o'clock, Bryan Brown had better be self-assured.

On this gusty late-autumn morning, the actor was filming the trailer for his forthcoming feature. Tentatively titled *Sweet Talker*, the picture tells the story of a slick grifter named Harry Reynolds who descends on a struggling ocean-resort town, fills its citizens with visions of grandeur while stuffing his valise with their hard-earned cash, and winds up in an awful predicament.

Today's first shot—a slightly rejiggered restaging of one of the movie's climactic scenes—concluded, of course, with the piece of heavy equipment grinding to a halt at the last possible instant.

Brown's ordeal, though, was only beginning. For the next three hours, he would sit patiently in what amounted to a grave—underground, the dirt was held back by jacks and construction forms; up top, a plywood lid into which an opening for the actor's head had been cut sealed the hole—while director Michael Jenkins ordered take after take.

The whole procedure was delayed by a rain squall blowing in off the Pacific and by Allen, who pouted that her position at the earthmover's controls wasn't visible enough to the camera. Through it all, Brown kept up a cheery façade, singing to himself and bantering with the crew. This despite the fact that with his hands trapped beneath the surface, the makeup girl periodically had to wipe wind-whipped grit and brine from his mouth and nose.

In part, Brown was simply staying in character, keeping himself primed to deliver a series of lines that required a sangfroid belying these uncomfortable surroundings. In part, he was just being a "good bloke," remaining true to the unwritten Australian law forbidding whimpering and whining. But the actor's grace under pressure was also inspired by the fact that this film is crucial to his career.

In the decade since Bryan Brown first attracted international attention with his portrayal of a cocksure Australian Army lieutenant in Bruce Beresford's *Breaker Morant*, he has generally made two kinds of pictures. His domestic films—thoughtful, emotionally honest pieces such as *The Good Wife*, co-starring his own spouse—have won critical praise but done little to increase his worldwide stature. Meanwhile, his Hollywood features—among them mindless blockbusters such as 1988's *Cocktail* opposite Tom Cruise—have made exorbitant amounts of money but incurred reviewers' wrath.

What he now wants is to combine quality and commerce, and as one of three Australian actors—along with Paul Hogan and Mel Gibson—whom producers can actually build a project around, he suddenly finds himself with the power to fulfill his wishes.

Unlike his famous fellow countrymen, however, Brown has achieved this position without relying solely on the de rigueur "G'day, mates" and macho postures that audiences have come to expect from the land of "Crocodile" Dundee and Mad Max. Yes, the actor projects all the vaunted national characteristics—straight-forwardness, a lack of pretense, and a strong predisposition to devilry. In fact, his screen presence is imbued with the same rowdy spirit that in life gets him into more than his share of mischief. Take, for instance, his audacious attempt one night not long ago at New York's Elaine's to reenact the crazed liquor-bottle-juggling stunt from *Cocktail*—a performance that left the restaurant's floor carpeted with broken glass. Or consider his behavior at a recent Malibu dinner party, where he initiated the postprandial entertainment by stuffing a couple of coins between the cheeks of his rump, squatting indecorously, and releasing the change into a brandy snifter, an act that prompted such otherwise well-behaved companions as actor Sam Neill, producer Jerome Hellman, and pedagogical songster Sting to follow suit.

Yet there is something more to Brown. "Bryan is one of those rare actors who combines a hard assed quality with a poetic sensibility, a tenderness," contends director Michael Apted, who cast the Australian as a wildlife photographer opposite Sigourney Weaver in *Gorillas in the Mist*, a picture that not only tested Brown's patience ("Sigourney is a bit schoolteacher-ish, always saying, 'Do this; don't do that'") but his mettle ("I was absolutely petrified of the gorillas"). Adds director John Duigan, who used the actor in *Winter of Our Dreams*, a well-received art-house film, "In the mold of such people as Mitchum and Bogart, he can express a tremendous amount economically, but he can open up in ways that those two couldn't—someplace there's a great comedic part out there for him."

Twice during recent years, Brown appeared to have been on the verge of the long-expected breakthrough. In 1985's *F/X*, the story of a New York special-effects whiz who finds himself enmeshed in a Mafia sting, the actor gave a complex and exciting performance, but the film failed to put him over the top, winning, at best, an enthusiastic video following. Meanwhile, *Tai-Pan* (1986), a $25 million epic in which Brown played the title role, was an out-and-out disaster. Briefly touted as a sure bet, the James Clavell-inspired saga ultimately collapsed under the weight of an unwieldy script and inept direction and contributed significantly to the eventual bankruptcy of its backer, the De Laurentiis Entertainment Group.

Many believe that Brown has been less than discriminating in some of his film choices. "There's no doubt," he admits, "that *Tai-Pan* failed. It was a badly conceived, badly made movie. But I don't think I made a bad choice. I'm simply playing the game. It'd be bloody nice to win every time, but it's also necessary to lose. It's just part of the cycle of life."

With *Sweet Talker*, due out this fall, the 42-year-old actor may have finally positioned himself in exactly the right spot, for from the start the project has been designed to retain its homegrown integrity while attracting a global audience. Conceived by Brown, blessed at the treatment stage by director Peter Weir (*Witness*), written by Tony Morphett (*The Last Wave*), produced by Ben Gannon (*Gallipoli*), and shot on location in a tiny beach community several hundred miles south of Sydney, the movie is Australian to the core, drawing on what its star calls "the strengths and weaknesses of my own society" and striking a blow against what he terms the "homogenized product" that so often emanates from stateside studios. At the same time, the film is being bankrolled by an American company, New Visions Pictures. Though the firm has been beset with financial difficulties, its president, director Taylor Hackford, promises *Sweet Talker* will open in the U.S. with the kind of backing rarely accorded a foreign effort.

Little wonder, then, that on this storm-threatened fall day, Brown happily submitted to the final indignities attendant to what had been a long and arduous project. But once the promotional footage was in the can and he emerged from his earthen tomb, the actor's buoyant spirits collapsed. In fact, something suddenly hit him hard, a loss from which this job and the obsessive work it demanded had briefly insulated him.

"My mother died two weeks ago," Brown said as he sat in a director's chair, the surf pounding in the background. "She was 76, and she was sick during most of the two months we were shooting—first she broke her hip, then a heart attack, then her kidneys went.

"Strange how I didn't acknowledge it while we were filming," he added. "Now, I'm going to have to admit that she's really gone."

For a second, Brown gazed up at the leaden sky. Then: "She raised me from the age of 3 with no husband, no money, no nothing. You can really have no idea of the kind of devotion my mom gave me, how everything she did when I was a boy said I was important, how she gave me the only true gift a parent can give a child—a great security."

Shortly after dusk on his first night back at the farm, Bryan Brown found himself sitting at the plastic-place-mat-bedecked kitchen table of his nearest neighbor. In Brown's estimation, Paul Schadel is "a terrific bloke," but the man's many fine qualities were not what inspired this visit. Rather, Schadel's wife, Gail, brews a mean homemade beer that earns Bryan's highest accolade: "You can get pissed on two bottles."

After exchanging pleasantries, Gail produced a Styrofoam cooler stocked with beaded brown bottles of varying sizes, and soon enough, mugs were clinking and conversation was flowing. Like Brown, Schadel is a working-class city boy. Until computer technology came along, he was employed by one of Rupert Murdoch's Sydney newspapers as a Linotype repairman. Now he labors at a saw mill, cutting railroad ties. As he and Bryan—both in white T-shirts, both with foam-flecked upper lips—discussed the intricacies of lumbering, it became quite apparent that not only was the actor catching up with an old friend, but he was truly in his element. In fact, had it not been for his mother, Brown might himself be simply another of Australia's terrific blokes.

In the Sydney suburb where Bryan grew up in a government-subsidized apartment, the odds were slim that a child would reach adulthood open to life's larger possibilities. For Westies, as the denizens of these benighted, Irish-Catholic precincts were known, economic survival was triumph enough.

To keep her little brood afloat, Molly Brown worked days doing cleaning and laundry and three nights a week played piano for ballet classes. "The hardest thing for Mum," Brown remembers, "was having to meet the rent. When she'd get home, she'd put her money in these glass bottles on the kitchen counter—one bottle for light money, one for gas, one for rent. There was never much left over."

The Browns' plight, Bryan believes, was directly attributable to his father, who abandoned his wife shortly after the birth of Bryan's younger sister. "Between the time I was 3 and 17," the actor recalls in a voice devoid of emotion, "I saw him eight times."

In the 1950s, in a Catholic neighborhood, parents simply did not divorce, and the lie Bryan told to explain his father's absence suggests that the separation hurt more than he will admit. "I always told people my father was killed in the war. That got me through school. I'd fantasize him as a hero."

Bryan was not, however, a delicate child. If anything his difficult upbringing made him a determined extrovert, one of those pint-size entrepreneurs who run deliveries for the local chemist, recycle their comic books, and comb trash cans for old newspapers to sell for a penny a pound. By the age of 15, he was laboring in a chair factory, holding metal frames in place while grown men welded them.

After graduating from a parochial high school, Brown—still living with his mother, still packing the brown-bag lunches she prepared for him each morning—went to work for one of Australia's largest insurance firms. Although he aimed to become an actuary, he quickly saw that "the blokes who had a good time were salesmen."

Brown thrived as a policy peddler—"It's a lot like acting"—and odds are his business career would still be in full flower had he not signed up to appear in an employee theatrical revue in 1968. "It was a bit of a giggle," he says now, but, in truth, the experience marked a profound turning point. "It was one of those rare moments," observes a longtime friend, "when your whole life comes into focus."

While nothing in Brown's background suggested dramatic inclinations—"We never had any books," he remembers, "and there was certainly no theater"—his mother's love of music had stimulated his imagination. The way she revved up for every piece, no matter what style, with a vaudevillian "da-da-da-da-da-da!" inspired in Bryan both a sense of wonder and a natural hamminess.

Moreover, despite her bleak circumstances, Molly Brown came from impressive stock. In fact, Robert Hughes, author of *Fatal Shore* and *Time* magazine's art critic, is Bryan's maternal cousin. While the actor grew up in an environment so far removed from his talented relative's that he didn't even meet the writer until the mid-1980s, he obviously inherited a few of the family's distinctive characteristics. Asserts Hughes: "Bryan is not quite the son of the horny-handed proletariat that he says he is—he's well read; he knows how to handle himself. Don't let him romanticize, as so many Australians do, his humble heritage."

Yet even if Brown does tend to mythologize his low beginnings, there can be little doubt that when he arrived in England in 1972, his insurance career recently concluded and only a few amateur parts behind him, he was one of the unlikeliest aspiring performers ever to knock on the door of a London casting agent.

Following the time-honored path, Brown took any stage work he could find. His first job was as a scenery pusher for Max Bygraves, an Ed Sullivanesque promoter whose revue featured dancing girls and magicians. Next, he signed on with a provincial company in the industrial town of Billingham. Finally, after sending out scores of resumes, he finagled an audition with Peter Hall, director of the National Theatre.

Brown began his reading for the renowned impresario with the expected recitation from Shakespeare. But when Hall wanted to hear the would-be actor sing, Bryan fell back on his roots, belting out a game but tinny rendition of "When the Red, Red Robin Comes Bob, Bob Bobbin Along."

Meanwhile, the previous hopeful—an overly emotive Master Thespian—had raised the rafters with a thunderous operatic aria. It's all over, Brown thought as he walked out the door.

But that night, of course, it was Brown's telephone that rang, and for the next year, it was Brown who trod the same boards as Olivier, Richardson, and Gielgud. Seeing these legends, working with them—albeit in the rather limiting roles of Fairy and Tree—Bryan experienced an epiphany: "What I saw of them offstage was what I saw of them onstage. When they acted, they didn't suddenly become something they weren't. They were reflecting their own intelligence, humor, sensitivity, lack of it—whatever it was, that's what they were projecting through their characters. So it clarified to me very quickly what acting was: You bring yourself to a character."

For Brown, few revelations could have been more liberating. No longer did he feel he had to copy the styles of more-refined, better-educated actors. No longer did he "feel uncomfortable" with his lack of formal training. Instead, he realized that he could trust his own instincts.

By the time Brown returned to Australia in 1974, he had utterly embraced his new calling. In fact, he exuded such certainty that others couldn't help but stand back in amazement. "I'll never forget the first time I met him," recalls Stuart Green, Bryan's best friend and a longtime gaffer at the Australian Film, Television and Radio School. "We were both auditioning for a movie, sitting in this little room waiting, so I said, 'What do you do?' And he answered, 'I'm an actor.' And I said, 'No, really, what do you do?' because no one then would have had the balls to say he was an actor. For instance, I was driving a taxi, and I told him I was a cabbie. But he just stared at me and repeated, 'I'm an actor.'"

And so he was. Initially, Brown appeared in "rude, crude" revues staged at pubs in and around Sydney. The shows' titles—among them *TV or Not TV* and *Smiles and Piles*—speak for themselves. Eventually, however, he began working in more respectable venues, although he continued to win parts that drew on his rough-edged, ragtag sensibilities. "I was a bit of a basher in me early days," he says, somewhat embarrassed as he recalls his work in such projects as *Love Letters from Teralba Road*, a black-and-white short in which he portrayed a wife beater.

Such performances, however, got Brown noticed, both at home, where he soon starred in the hit television miniseries *A Town Like Alice*, and abroad, where Hollywood handicappers—agents, studio vice-presidents, and their ilk—promised instant stardom if the actor would just make one tiny alteration: They wanted him to lose his distinctive accent.

But Brown refused. "A person who actually gave me a lot of confidence during this period was Michael Caine," he says. "Not that I'd ever met him, but I'd always thought if a man who's that bloody cockney can be an international star, then there's no reason I can't be."

Brown's perseverance paid off, and by 1982 he was big enough to command a leading role in the American miniseries *The Thorn Birds*. As an abusive Australian sheep farmer whose Mrs. lusts after a celibate clergyman (Richard Chamberlain), the actor "made more money for one bloody show than I'd made in the ten previous years." He also fell in love with his on-screen wife—Rachel Ward.

Bryan and Rachel were married at her parents' Oxfordshire manor house just nine months after they met. The ceremony was conducted in a chapel on the grounds, an Anglican vicar and a Catholic priest officiating. To Stuart Green, Brown's best man, the setting embodied "the very things Bryan had always ridiculed—power, privilege, and inherited wealth." To the bride's family, the groom epitomized the upstart from the outback, a point her brother exploited to great comedic effect by presenting Bryan with a joke wedding present: a classic Australian Akubra hat, the fly-swatting cork replaced by a dangling tampon.

Indeed, it would have been difficult to imagine a more improbable pairing. Rachel's uncle is the Earl of Dudley, her mother's beau a former Tory member of Parliament, her past inamoratos both rich and tragic (the late David Kennedy) and rich and spoiled (playboy Phillippe Junot), and her career a seemingly effortless ascent from *Vogue* cover model to star of such glossy vehicles as *Sharky's Machine* and *Against All Odds*.

Yet from the moment the two were introduced, each was drawn irresistibly to the other. At first, the fascination was sexual, a passion, as one journalist on *The Thorn Birds*' set later put it, "so hot people had to step back not to get scorched."

The class differences between the lovers only intensified the allure. Although Brown contends that he initially didn't comprehend just how rarefied Rachel's background was, she immediately delighted in the fact that Bryan bore no resemblance whatsoever to anyone listed in *Burke's Peerage*. "She loved the fact that she was with this brash, uncouth guy," recalls an old friend. "Rachel's always been a rebel," Brown agrees. "She went away at 16 to live in France then she went to America to model. She searches for ways to go through life on her terms—not society's. She's a very game sort of woman."

Ultimately, however, it was Brown's self-certitude that spoke most deeply to Rachel. "I suppose I'd just never met anyone who was so confident," she says. "I'd been living in the States for seven years, so his lack of insecurity was all the more striking. American men are much more open about their fears than the Australians, who are innately cocky. He knew exactly what he was doing; there was nothing two-minded about him. He didn't dither about."

Not that Brown's almost constitutional inability to equivocate is an altogether positive trait. "The fact that he's so clear about everything has its disadvantages," Rachel observes. "Indeed, he can be bloody stubborn and annoying."

From the start, Brown's hardheadedness—which, like almost everything else about him, is attributable to his mother, a woman his wife remembers as "a little ball of determination who had a point of view about everything and would side with her boy about anything"—sparked tremendous rows with Rachel's aristocratic parents.

"There have been heated dinners," admits the actor, "and I don't mean microwave."

Most of the arguments between Bryan and his royalist relatives involve politics. No wonder. Aside from being a child of poverty, Brown is a combative Labour Party supporter, a man who cites Studs Terkel and the George Orwell who wrote *Down and Out in Paris and London* as his favorite authors. Moreover, he scorns not only conservative ideologies but the outward trappings of wealth. Just the sight of a Rolex-adorned Yuppie causes him to sputter "All clock, no cock." At the Wards' ancestral estate, the signs of affluence—limousines, gilt-framed portraits of lords and ladies, a formal garden—are considerably more extravagant and imperial than any gold wristwatch.

Such battles also erupt closer to home, where Brown has on more than one occasion sparred with his wife regarding manners and class. Typical of the couple's confrontations was a recent set-to that began when Rachel told daughter Rosie she was pretty. "There's too much importance placed in this world on looks," snapped Bryan, who proceeded to denigrate beauty as an arbitrary ideal invented by the privileged few to keep the masses in their place. Rachel—who has been called one of the world's loveliest women—immediately fired back, contending that art and culture were proof enough against her husband's argument. Then, with an eye toward ending this encounter with a smile, she asked, "Bryan, didn't your mother ever tell you you were pretty?"

What has generally kept these debates from getting out of hand is that despite his strong opinions and tendency to reduce any issue to black-and-white simplicities, Brown is neither arrogant nor rancorous. Although he baits his wife and her connections mercilessly, he rarely loses his good humor. "I'm exceedingly lucky," Rachel says, "for from his confidence grows a quality I hadn't counted on—kindness. He's the most moral man I've ever known."

Seven years, two daughters, and several continents after exchanging vows, Rachel and Bryan seem to have bridged any difficulties that might ordinarily arise in a marriage whose partners come from such disparate circumstances. Indeed, the one issue that plagues them most is the thorny, practical problem faced by so many working couples: how to manage dual careers while maintaining a stable home for the children. Here, Brown believes that the financially trying conditions of his youth actually give him an advantage.

"Let's face it," he says. "To me a woman is a breadwinner, because that's what my mom was. In fact, I've always lived in a matriarchy. I grew up with two women. Now I live with three. When it comes right down to it, I appreciate women's position in the world better than men's. Consequently, I think I'm aware of how important Rachel's work is to her.

"The simple fact of the matter," Brown adds, "is that my wife works, so there are times I'll say, 'Well, it's useless for me to read a script now because I'm not going to be working for the next six months. It's Rachel's turn.' While we don't do this in any formal way, one of us always tries to be at home with the kids. I'm not interested in having a family that's apart. It just doesn't make any sense. As much as I want to be a successful actor, I want more to be a successful husband and father."

Still, keeping all parties happy is a difficult task. Although Rachel certainly receives her fair share of roles—she recently finished filming *After Dark, My Sweet* with Bruce Dern in California after eliciting glowing notices for her work in *How to Get Ahead in Advertising*—there can be no doubt that it's Bryan who's presently positioned to the greater professional advantage. "Here I am, sitting on the farm," she says wistfully, "while there are so many good actresses in London and Hollywood ready and focused. On top of that, the things I want to express as an actress arise from my own culture. Everything that gives me color as a person is British. Now that Bryan is exploiting the very fact that he's Australian, I'm having to suppress who I am.

"But I have no regrets," she adds after a minute's reflection. "I don't want to give up this to pursue that, because it's really not that important. In fact, when I'm here on the farm, I don't even want to waste an afternoon reading. If I was to sit down with a book, I'd feel rotten. I could be out with the children or riding a horse. I guess I feel that the kids will grow up, the pets will die, and then there will be nothing but time."

At sunset a couple of nights after repairing to the country, Bryan Brown sat on the deck of the Pub with No Beer, a legendary Australian watering hole that most decidedly does not live up to its name. Since completing *Sweet Talker*, the actor had been concentrating on his cattle business. Already today, he had attended an auction, instructed his foreman to discontinue a worrisomely high-tech embryo-transplant program he'd been using to fertilize their Black Angus heifers, conferred with a vet regarding the death of a little bull named Ferdinand who'd eaten some poisonous bracken, and spent the better half of the afternoon traipsing along an overgrown creek bed to round up a lost calf. Now, the tired stockman wanted to hoist a few schooners of Tooheys before supper, which his wife was preparing back at the farm.

Soon enough, Brown would be off to Los Angeles to discuss the sequel to *F/X*, which begins filming in Toronto this month. Then he would be back in Sydney, starting preproduction work on another feature, *Blood Oath*, a true story of the Japanese-war-crime trials conducted by the Australian government during the late 1940s.

But as the actor lingered at the bar—an iron-roofed roadhouse, its walls covered with rusting broadaxes and pit saws commemorating the region's timber-harvesting past—his movie career was far from his mind. He was attempting to reconcile himself to the loss of his mother, something he knew would take time.

Inevitably, there were regrets. "My mom didn't come to our wedding," he said softly. "I was in the middle of a movie [*Give My Regards to Broad Street*] at the time, and I only had one day off. She'd never been to England in her life, and she was getting on. I just thought I wouldn't be able to look after her properly and that it might be emotionally difficult for her. But I did the wrong thing. She should have been there on that day."

For a second, there was silence. Then: "I did take her to China when I did *Tai-Pan*. That was great. She'd never been out of the country her whole life. To say hello there, you say, 'knee-how.' I'd say to Mom, 'When you go downstairs for dinner, tell the girl, "Knee-how."' And she just couldn't get it together. She kept saying, 'Lego.'"

Laughing at the memory, Brown mused, "I believe that things go on. I don't believe this is the be-all and end-all. I believe in energy, that within this body and within this mind there's something that floats, and when all this falls away, that spirit moves off."

After another round, Bryan regained his ebullience, and soon he was serenading a companion with the well-known Australian folk song inspired by the old tavern:

So it's lonesome away from your kindred and all,
By the campfire at night
Where the wild dingoes call,
But there's nothing so lonesome, morbid or drear,
Than to stand in the bar
Of a pub with no beer.

This was the quintessential Bryan Brown, the irrepressible carouser, the larrikin, as Australians call their wild and impulsive revelers. As darkness fell this evening, he was still going strong, holding forth on any and all subjects, ready for everything the night might bring. But the actor restrained himself from serious misbehaving. Supper would be ready shortly, and with Rachel and the children waiting at home, he didn't want to be late.

DESPERADOES

A man's life may not require him to seek trouble, but it demands that he be open to it if it comes. Harry Crews called this "getting naked." His theory, as he articulated it to me, was that "you can only find out about a thing when you're vulnerable to the experiences of the world." Crews believed that the payoff was personal renewal. Not that this process always ends well.

Fallen Angel

Los Angeles, June 2005

On a Friday morning in November 2001, several hundred mourners filed into the spacious sanctuary of Trinity Life Center, a Pentecostal church just east of the Las Vegas Strip, to pay final respects to one of the congregation's most unlikely members. Robert "Bo" Belinsky had died of a heart attack a week earlier at the age of 64.

Gathered on Trinity Life's pews were people who had known Belinsky in many of his incarnations. Up front were the former ballplayers who, on May 5, 1962, had watched the left-handed pitcher for the Los Angeles Angels take the mound at Chavez Ravine and throw California's first major league no-hitter. In one row were Dean Chance, the Angels' 1964 Cy Young Award winner and Bo's closest friend on the team, and Albie Pearson, the Angels' center fielder at the time. Nearby were Dick Williams, most famous for managing the Oakland Athletics to consecutive world championships during the 1970s but on the night of Belinsky's masterpiece left fielder for the opposing Baltimore Orioles (in three at bats Williams struck out twice and fouled out), and Steve Barber, the Orioles' starting—and losing— pitcher that evening. These men had been best acquainted with the old Bo, the one who in the wake of his singular triumph used his good looks, charm, and knack for getting his name in the newspapers to woo Hollywood starlets. Among them were Ann-Margret, Tina Louise, Juliet Prowse, Connie Stevens, Mamie Van Doren, and *Playboy* playmate Jo Collins. Their Belinsky was the rebellious, sporting-world Casanova who pointed the way for the athletes as sex symbols who followed. Before Joe Namath, there was Bo.

Elsewhere at Trinity Life were those who'd seen a different Belinsky, whose largely unpublicized post-baseball descent into alcoholism and cocaine addiction took him to such depths of degradation that for nearly a decade he seemed past redemption. Some, like Mark Greenberg, former vice president of business development at the Betty Ford Center in Rancho Mirage and current executive director of Michael's House, a treatment facility for men in Palm Springs, were involved in Belinsky's rehabilitation. Others, in the manner of Alcoholics Anonymous members, were known to Bo merely by first names and last initials. These mourners possessed a keen aware-ness of his travails. As Belinsky once said at an AA meeting, "It's a terrible feeling when you're in pain and you know you're going to remain in pain. You tell yourself, it's gotta get better, but no, the game is just starting. There's no limit to going down the tubes."

Belinsky's services attracted a few Las Vegas notables—chief among them boxing promoter Bob Arum—but most of the others in attendance were either members of Trinity Life or friends Bo had made during his 12 years of residency in the city. People like Rich Abajian, general manager of Findlay Toyota, Irving Marcus, director of guest relations at Arizona Char-lie's Casino, Lou Rodophele, a retired plumbing supplies distributor from Boston, and Don Richardson, sales manager of Saturn of West Sahara. These people knew Belinsky as a genial soul who, despite perilous finances, always over-tipped waiters and frequently quoted from the Bible. To them, Bo's religious conversion was both brave and undeniable. "I had a spiritual awakening," he liked to say. "It was a beautiful thing. There's a power great-er than any other power on this earth, and it came into my life and left me with a feeling that no matter what happens, everything is going to be all right."

It was an impressive funeral, but as the Reverend Randy Greer stepped to the pulpit, it became obvious that the body of the man who was being remembered was not on the premises. The reasons, like so much with Belin-sky, were complicated. Divorced three times and estranged from his only sibling and three children, Bo had left no instructions regarding the disposi-tion of his remains. Until the legalities could be sorted through, his body would stay at the undertaker's. Later Don Richardson would comment, "Nothing was ever easy with Bo." Yet the absence of Belinsky's corpse also spoke to a deeper enigma, one rooted in Bo's sense of alienation. "Nobody could ever figure me out," he once remarked. "I wouldn't show what was really inside me, inside Bo Belinsky. I was just a façade I'd carried along all my life." On another occasion he said, "I was born apart. My mother was Jewish, my father Polish Catholic. To Jews I was a Polack. To Poles I was a kike. I was removed—removed from people in my family, people in my school. Even in my youth, I didn't know where to park myself."

Two days before his death, Bo Belinsky was at work in the showroom of Findlay Toyota on Auto Show Drive in the Las Vegas Suburb of Hender-son. The former pitcher suffered from an array of illnesses, most seriously bladder cancer and diabetes. These diseases, along with a recent hip replacement operation, the years of substance abuse, and one unconquered vice— he chain-smoked unfiltered English Oval cigarettes—had taken a toll on Bo's appearance. Skin pallid, eyes dark circled, and hair sickly gray, he was not well. Yet as he gazed out the dealership's windows onto the lot, where the sun burst off Camrys and 4Runners, he seemed happy. "Bo was proud of what the last 10 or 11 years had been like," says Rich Abajian, his boss, who spent time with him that November morning. "He was proud that he could conform to a business structure. He and I had the longest employer-employee relationship in his life."

Findlay Toyota was perfect for Belinsky. The dealership's owner, former University of Nevada Las Vegas basketball standout Cliff Findlay, believes in hiring retired athletes (among others who have worked for him are onetime National League batting champion Bill Madlock). Abajian, a boyish 51-year-old charismatic Christian, enjoys helping people in trouble. "I work with people who've had problems," he says as he indicates the spot where Belinsky's desk sat. "I give people second chances, third chances, and usually I don't get much back. But once in a while with people like Bo, things work out. This place became his world. And that's rewarding."

Belinsky's job at Findlay was that of a public relations emissary. He represented the dealership at celebrity golf tournaments and gave Toyota-touting talks to civic groups, but according to Abajian, although Belinsky's position provided him with a high profile, he never behaved like a big shot. "By the time Bo got to us, he'd learned humility. He'd go wash a car. He'd walk new salesmen around the lot. He'd keep our morale up. In the car business, if by two in the afternoon nothing is happening, it can get depressing. But Bo would walk around the dealership saying, 'It's gonna be okay,' which meant a lot to me."

Once a week Belinsky ate breakfast with Irving Marcus at Arizona Charlie's, a rambling casino on the north side of Las Vegas that attracts mainly locals. He liked talking to the 85-year-old guest relations director about boxing and gambling. Occasionally, Bo ducked into a sports bar called Instant Replay for lunch. Every Sunday, there were services at Trinity Life. But otherwise, Bo stayed to himself in the tiny apartment he rented at the Duck Creek Condominiums not far from his work. There, night after night, he ate supper, watched old movies on television, read the Bible, and took obsessive care of a tabby cat named Choo-Choo.

At the end, Belinsky's existence was subdued. In fact, it may have been the life he was best suited for all along, not that those who knew him at the height of his glory or the nadir of his madness would have predicted that it would turn out like this. Indeed, when he was in the midst of it all, Bo—who over the years had put his thoughts regarding these matters on tape—could never have imagined such a finale. Speaking of his seasons with the Angels, he said, "In those days it was all sex and champagne, champagne and sex. The two were a lot like each other. When it was good, it was good, and when it was bad, it was still pretty good." As for the dark times, he was appalled: "I was an alcoholic of the worst kind, not only dangerous to myself but to my loved ones and friends—and they fled from me."

Even before Bo Belinsky arrived at the Angels' 1962 spring training camp in Palm Springs, he was already famous. He had done what in those days was unthinkable for a rookie—held out for more money. He was insulted by the Angels' $6,000 offer. Anything under $8,500, he said, and he would stay home hustling pool in Trenton, New Jersey. After the club agreed to renegotiate his deal at midseason, he accepted the $6,000, but his labor action had made big news. When he reached the team's Desert Inn headquarters, he was whisked to the swimming pool, where reporters had gathered for a press conference. Turned out in dark sunglasses, cashmere sports jacket, yellow sports shirt, tight pants, and suede shoes, Bo dazzled this hardened bunch. Boasting of the "compromise" he'd exacted from the Angels, the self-professed "crazy left-hander" scoffed at the "yes sir, no sir...zis-boombah" attitude of conventional athletes. "He gave them what they wanted," team publicist Irv Kaze subsequently reflected.

Unlike most big leaguers, the 25-year-old Belinsky had never played an inning of high school baseball. He instead was spending his after-class hours on the streets of Trenton, where his family had moved when he was a baby and where his father eventually opened a TV repair shop. By age 10 Bo had smoked his first cigarette, by 12 he had lost his virginity, and by 14—thanks to evenings spent at Joe Russo's Pool Hall—he was an accomplished pool shark. Under the tutelage of an old hand known as "the Goose," Belinsky learned not only how to sink complicated combinations but also how to seek out marks. At age 16, he made his first big score in a neighboring small town, taking $1,200 off a seasoned hustler named "the Masked Marvel." For the remainder of his teens, Bo apprenticed himself to the likes of "Cincinnati Phil" and "the Farmer" and worked the eastern seaboard, preying on the gullibility of grown men. Along the way, he acquired the cunning skills that would carry him through the first years of adult life. As he would later proclaim, "You gotta remember the laws of hustling. You never hustle anybody. They hustle themselves. You never try to snow a snowman."

From an early age, Belinsky possessed a live left arm, and summer days often found him on Trenton sandlots blowing fastballs by hitters. On May 15, 1956, after a scout saw him strike out 15 opponents, Belinsky signed a contract with the Pittsburgh Pirates' Brunswick, Georgia, farm club for $185 a month. When he arrived at the team hotel, he didn't even own a baseball glove. Instead, he carried a pool cue. From the start—he went AWOL from Brunswick to hustle pool—his minor league career was dodgy. In Pensacola, where his 13-6 record marked him as a comer, he had to be smuggled out of town under a blanket to avoid a statutory rape charge. In Miami, he and a roommate were accused of drilling holes in their hotel bedroom wall to spy on the Miss Universe contestant staying next door. Finally, after six years of spectral lights and long bus rides while playing for Knoxville, Aberdeen, Stockton, and Little Rock, he was drafted by the newly minted Los Angeles Angels. During winter ball in Venezuela in 1961 he had developed a screwball. The difficult-to-control pitch can be a devastating asset, as it allows left-handers to throw a ball that breaks away from right-handed batters, making it hard to hit. In Belinsky's case, as sportswriters duly noted at the time, the screwball was also something of a metaphor.

The Los Angeles Angels and Bo Belinsky were made for each other. The club was entering only its second year of existence. So much did owners Gene Autry, the singing cowboy, and Bob Reynolds, a former Stanford all-American football player, resent being overshadowed by the better-established Dodgers that although they played their home games at Dodger Stadium, they refused to refer to the park by its given name. Their home field, they maintained, was Chavez Ravine. Autry and Reynolds were looking for someone who could make them both a contender and a rival for the city's affections. They were not only willing to tolerate the eccentricities of a pool shark turned pitcher, they were prepared to celebrate them.

Belinsky won his first three decisions of the 1962 season. Still, only 15,886 were in attendance at Chavez Ravine on May 5 to see him face the Baltimore Orioles. The game that these fans took in, declared Bud Furillo of the *Los Angeles Herald Examiner,* "made history." Over nine innings Belinsky dominated the opposition. Wrote Braven Dyer of the *Los Angeles Times*: "I can report that the Birds didn't even come close to getting a hit." Though

Belinsky walked four men, he struck out nine and faced only one serious threat—a bases-loaded jam in the fourth. When the Orioles' last batter popped out in the ninth, giving the Angels a 2-0 victory, the city had witnessed its first big-league no-hitter. Bo Belinsky, not Dodger great Sandy Koufax, would forever hold the record. After the game, as his teammates celebrated, Belinsky posed for pictures, including one with former vice president Richard Nixon, California's Republican gubernatorial candidate that year.

Among the handful who saw Belinsky pitch that night was 65-year-old gossip columnist Walter Winchell. For three decades Winchell—with his punchy items, access to places high and low, and, on his radio and television broadcasts, trademark salutation ("Good evening, Mr. and Mrs. North and South America and all the ships at sea")—had been an unavoidable presence in American journalism. Of late, however, he had been slipping. Frequently descending into red-baiting and Kennedy bashing, his work seemed increasingly dated. Still, because his column appeared in the *New York Daily Mirror*, the nation's second-largest-circulation daily, and the *Los Angeles Herald Examiner*, he possessed a huge readership. Moreover, he narrated the popular television drama *The Untouchables*.

Winchell recognized Belinsky as a great source of copy who could restore relevancy to his work. (The pitcher reminded the columnist of his younger self—a city kid, a Jew, and a handsome rogue with an eye for a well-turned ankle.) A few days after the no-hitter, Winchell published his initial item on Bo: "New York-born no-hitter rookie Bo Belinsky of the Angels should be in *The Untouchables*. His fastball is that unbelievable." Several days later, there was this: "Bo Belinsky, pitching curves and catching headlines. The most exciting player to hit the major leagues since Mantle's debut." A few days later still, Winchell convinced Belinsky to join him onstage at the Ambassador Hotel's Cocoanut Grove in a comedy sketch with headliner Eddie Fisher. By early June, Winchell and Belinsky were inseparable. Cruising Los Angeles in the pitcher's new candy apple red Cadillac convertible, which a local dealer had provided in return for promotional considerations, the two took in premieres, attended parties, and made after-hours clubs. Each was hustling the other, and both were getting what they wanted.

Thanks to Winchell, Belinsky suddenly seemed bigger than baseball. When he started a game at Chavez Ravine the night of June 1 against the powerhouse New York Yankees, a then-record crowd of 51,584 (among them Marilyn Monroe, Bob Hope, and Ann-Margret, who the *Herald Ex-*

aminer reported "came to plead for Bo") filled the stadium. While the Yankees beat Belinsky that night, it nonetheless seemed that he could do no wrong. Even at the time, however, Bo knew it wouldn't last. "I needed that no-hitter like GM needs more engines," he said years later. "I wasn't ready to handle it. All the pretty blonds, the actresses, the notoriety." The task of keeping up appearances—a task that had consumed Bo since he worked his first pool room—had become infinitely more demanding.

At 5 A.M. on June 13, as Belinsky, accompanied by Dean Chance and two young women, steered his Cadillac through Beverly Hills, he made his first misstep. While stopped at the intersection of Wilshire Boulevard and Roxbury Drive, the foursome, on their way home from the Cocoanut Grove, got into an altercation. Ultimately, 33-year-old Gloria Eves jumped from the car, blood pouring from a jagged wound over her left eye. "He's beating me up," she screamed. It was at this point that Officer B. E. Gruenzel arrived on the scene. While the policeman concluded that Eves, who refused to press charges, had sustained her injury accidentally, the incident took some of the shine off of Belinsky's image. Blared the headline in the next day's *Times*: "Belinsky, Chance Fined After 5 A.M. Ruckus."

The fallout continued for several weeks, and it hit Belinsky—who went out of his way to absolve the married Chance of wrongdoing—the hardest. "Someone should talk to Bo and give him some advice," Eddie Fisher told the *Times'* Hedda Hopper, who also reported that Gene Autry had admonished the pitcher, informing him, "Hollywood will wine you and dine you as long as you win, but you...start losing a few games and they'll forget you're alive."

In the wake of this highly visible lapse—which cemented the improbable friendship between the streetwise Belinsky and Chance, a slow-talking farm boy from Wooster, Ohio—Bo did go on a losing streak. After Belinsky started the season 7-2, his record fell to 10-11, and he narrowly averted being traded by the Angels' old-school general manager, Fred Haney, who disapproved of the pitcher's antics. Nonetheless, 1962 had been an astonishing year for the Angels, who finished in third place, and for Bo.

By season's end, Belinsky had moved into a bachelor's pad atop La Presa Drive in the Hollywood Hills' Outpost Estates. The one-room apartment, which featured a lavender Formica bar, a black sunken tub, and a king-size bed, looked out on the Los Angeles skyline through enormous windows. This would be the heart of Bo's romantic universe, the lair to which he'd invite not only starlets but such exotic diversions as Queen Saroya of Iran, the ex-wife of the shah. "Bo's idea was that every day should be thrilling," says a sportswriter who knew him. "By that he meant the most gorgeous women, the biggest tits, and the best sex—then he could talk about it to 15 people the next day. Bo lived by the line: 'Live fast, die young, and leave a beautiful corpse.' I didn't think he'd make it to 40."

Belinsky even had dates with such elegant older women as actress Paulette Goddard and tobacco heiress Doris Duke, but he took none seriously. All that changed one night in late 1962 when Winchell, who was sitting with Bo at Hollywood's Peppermint West disco, picked up the phone and invited Mamie Van Doren, the star of *Sex Kittens Go to College*, to join their party. Though the actress for whom Universal Studios created the "bullet bra" rejected this first invitation, she accepted when it was tendered again the next evening and spent several hours on the club's dance floor with Belinsky. "He could do the mashed potato better than James Brown," she says. "He was a sexy dancer." Bo and Mamie went their own ways that evening, but by the time the Angels' 1963 spring training camp was under way, they were together. On April 1, the two were engaged.

For Belinsky, the 1963 season was a wash. He pitched poorly, but he and Mamie were happy. "Bo was just full of sex," she says. "We'd be up all night making love, and the next day he'd wonder why he didn't have a fastball. We spent a lot of time in his apartment. He'd walk around naked. He was always splashing on Aqua Velva cologne. I'd done that commercial, 'There's something about an Aqua Velva man.'"

On May 26, with his record a dismal 1-7, Belinsky was sent down to the Angels' AAA farm team in Hawaii. Though Fred Haney hoped Bo would feel chastened, the pitcher was overjoyed. He loved the islands, where he learned to surf and, with Van Doren far away, resumed chasing women. Minor league baseball seemed a purer form of the sport: no front-office politics, no contract fights, just bats and balls and fans. Part of him wanted to stay there forever. But after recording some impressive victories, he was recalled to the big leagues; on his better days he knew he belonged there. Bo adored his teammates, particularly Chance. The two spent time gambling, playing practical jokes, and making scenes—the wildest of which, courtesy of Winchell, saw them hanging out with FBI director J. Edgar Hoover. "J. Edgar! Man, he's a swinger," Bo told the press afterward. "He let me shoot tommy guns at FBI headquarters. He said, 'Bo, there'll always be a place for you on the force.'"

Belinsky had fashioned a persona as both bon vivant and rapscallion. He possessed the brio of a Dean Martin, yet he also bore the anti-establishmentarian markings of a Jack Kerouac. In him, the lounge lizard and the free spirit commingled. Little wonder that he was soon guest starring on that most emblematic of early '60s television series: *77 Sunset Strip.*

If Belinsky was ever going to fulfill the promise of his 1962 no-hitter as an Angel, he would do so in 1964. To begin with, his engagement to Mamie Van Doren was over. "He didn't trust me at all," Van Doren says. "He thought because he was doing it, I was doing it." With Mamie out of the matrimonial picture but not out of his life ("We were very sexually compatible," she says. "We couldn't stay away from each other"), Bo worked hard during spring training, and he began the season pitching well. But the Angels failed to give him much offensive support, and by midsummer his record stood at 9-8. "Bo was brilliant that season," says Bob Case, the team's then visiting clubhouse boy and a close friend. "If he'd had any help, he'd have been 15-2." No matter: Belinsky's year—and his Angels career—came to an abrupt conclusion at 3 A.M. on August 14 in Washington, D.C.'s Shoreham Hotel. Several days earlier Bo had lost a tough game at Chavez Ravine to the Cleveland Indians. In the locker room afterward, he told the Associated Press that he was going to quit baseball. By the time the Angels arrived in the East for a three-game series with the Senators, the wire-service story was all anyone was talking about. This was evidently why Braven Dyer of the *Times* came to Belinsky's door. According to Bo, Dyer barged into his room demanding to know why he wasn't given the scoop. According to Dyer, it was Belinsky who initiated the conversation. The pitcher, he maintained, had reconsidered his retirement decision and wanted to get the word out. What happened next, however, is not in dispute. Following several nasty comments by both men, Belinsky flattened the 64-year-old Dyer with a left to the head, causing blood to spurt from one ear. The 27-year-old southpaw had knocked out a sportswriter more than twice his age. Fred Haney suspended Belinsky. For years the pitcher would argue that Dyer had been at fault, but in time he would accept responsibility for what happened, admitting, "I screwed myself out of a job with the Angels." After just two and a half years, Bo's Los Angeles playing days were done.

Although Bo Belinsky was finished with the Angels, he was hardly out of baseball. After spending the off-season in Hawaii, he reported with considerable fanfare to the Philadelphia Phillies. On March 1, 1965, *Sports Illus-*

trated featured Bo and Phillies ace Jim Bunning on a cover captioned "The Phillies—old and new—try again." In Belinsky the team believed it had found an answer to its pitching problems. "I went to a great deal of trouble to get Bo," says Gene Mauch, the Phillies' manager at the time. "People said, 'You're crazy' But I was pretty cocky and thought I could take on anybody." Convinced that Belinsky's fastball was his most effective pitch, the manager did his best to persuade him to abandon the showier but less consistent screwball. "Early on, I told him I was going to show him what he could do without the screwball." At first Mauch appeared to make headway. "Bo went to Houston and pitched a three-hitter relying on the fastball," he recalls. Then in an aggrieved tone suggesting that even after 40 years what happened next still galls him, he says, "Four days later, we get to Los Angeles, Bo gets two strikes on a hitter in the first inning, and here comes the goddamned screwball. I go to the mound and say, 'One more of those and you go to the bench.'" At that moment Mauch realized that Belinsky was a lost cause. "The fastball wasn't flashy enough for Bo. Flash meant a lot to him, more than baseball did, which he saw as sort of a hors d'oeuvre to get things started—girls, parties."

Mauch, who would conclude his career as the manager of the Angels, liked Bo. "How could you not like him? He had such a great personality." But in the wake of the pitcher's insubordination, he sent him to the bullpen. There Belinsky, who had spent most of his career as a starter, stewed. Worse, he began a habit whose terrible consequences he would only see in retrospect. "I'd occasionally used greenies, amphetamines, as a starter, but in Philadelphia they had red juice [liquid amphetamines]," he later said, "and when I got into the bullpen, I started getting loaded every day, because as a reliever, you never know when you might have to play. This chemical started coming into my life. I thought I could handle it, because I was strong and still had that phony smile. But something was happening to my system."

The remainder of Belinsky's major league career was an exercise in futility. He began 1966 still in Philadelphia, but having compiled a 4-9 record the previous year, he was soon sent to the club's AAA farm team. In 1967, Belinsky popped back up in the big leagues with the Houston Astros, where he pitched indifferently but made headlines by adopting a dog and getting the club to agree to give it a locker in the Astrodome. When the season ended, he repaired to the place that increasingly enthralled him—Hawaii. There he met his first wife.

Looking across crowded Michael's Restaurant in Honolulu in January 1968, Bo spotted Jo Collins, the 1965 *Playboy* Playmate of the Year. Wearing a white backless mini-dress, she sat amid a gaggle of advertising men and Ford executives who'd gathered in Hawaii to kick off a promotional campaign for Lincoln-Mercury. "Bo came over and introduced himself, and everyone made a fuss over him," Collins says, "but I wasn't a baseball fan and didn't know who he was. I'd been dating Donny Anderson, a running back on the Green Bay Packers."

The next morning Collins received a bouquet of roses from Belinsky in her room at the Royal Hawaiian Hotel. Several nights later she accepted his invitation to dinner. "We went out that first night," she says, "and were inseparable afterward. I never went back to the mainland. Everybody was wondering where I was. I was with Bo."

Though Belinsky reported to the Astros' spring training camp in February, he failed to make the team and spent the bulk of the 1968 season on the Hawaii AAA club, which delighted him. "Hawaii was just his playground," Collins recalls. "He was the star of Hawaii." In June, Belinsky and Collins married. For the next two years—save for a brief return to the big leagues with the Pittsburgh Pirates late in the fall of 1968 and an abortive flirtation with the St. Louis Cardinals the next spring—Belinsky remained with the Hawaii club. On June 19, 1969, Jo gave birth to a daughter they named Stevhanie Lehua to honor their attachment to the islands.

Belinsky got his last shot at the major leagues in 1970 when he reported to spring training with the Cincinnati Reds. He made the team but only got into a few games, and in late May manager Sparky Anderson cut him. That night, when Bo returned home to the suburban town house he and Jo had rented for the season, he began to drink. By 4 A.M. the two were fighting, at which point Bo pulled out a .38 pistol. "He threatened me with the gun," Jo says. "I called the police, but when they came and saw it was Bo Belinsky, they let him go. So I took Stevhanie and spent the night with Pete and Karolyn Rose." Later Bo and Jo patched things up, but the career that had begun so promisingly with the no-hitter at Chavez Ravine was over. In five and a half years in the big leagues, Belinsky had won only 28 games. To reporters he boasted, "I got more out of 28 victories than any major leaguer in history. Anybody can be a star if he wins 300 games. Let him try being a star winning only 28 games." In truth, Belinsky was crushed. Since 1956, baseball had been all he'd known. "I never liked baseball that much, at first anyway," he later said. But by the end he'd experienced a change of heart.

"That's funny, isn't it, babe?" he asked writer Pat Jordan. "Me, the guy everybody said didn't love the game enough. Ha! Man, I loved the game. I just didn't take it seriously I don't take myself seriously, so how could I take a game seriously?"

On a November evening in 1970, Bo and Jo, now living in Malibu, were speeding down the Pacific Coast Highway in yet another Cadillac. They had just finished a dinner where they both drank too much, and they were quarreling. As the two argued, Bo lost control of the car, smashing it head-on into a steel utility pole. Jo's right arm was so badly crushed that emergency room doctors initially considered amputating it. "That was the beginning of the end of our relationship," she says. It was also the start of Bo's headlong descent into the bottle.

"When I got out of baseball," Belinsky would say, "I sat down and had a drink, and that drink never stopped." The causes of Belinsky's binge were many. "He didn't know what he was going to do, and panic set in," Jo says. Ultimately, however, the explanation went deeper. Bo's terrors had been with him in one way or another since childhood. "I didn't have a chemical problem as a kid," he said, "but I had the personality and the fear of an alcoholic, and I was ready to have the chemical catch up with the personality." Even as a 16-year-old pool shark, Bo had often been consumed by dread. He had developed his hustle as a tactic to, in his words, "down those people" who might hurt him. The same approach had worked, albeit to a lesser extent, in the big leagues, where the screwball replaced the pool cue and Walter Winchell stood in for the Goose and Cincinnati Phil. Once the games were done, Bo could no longer count on such props or hide behind such glib maxims as "never snow a snowman." Suddenly naked, he surrendered to the addictive disposition that had emerged when he began using speed in Philadelphia. "The disease ran over me," he said. "It caught up that quick. That's how it is. It knocks you over. Boom! A year and a half later nobody knew what to do with me."

After recovering from the injuries sustained in the car wreck, Jo accepted a job as Bunny Mother at a new *Playboy* Club in Denver, taking Stevhanie with her. Soon *Playboy* promoted her to a public relations position in Chicago. Periodically, Bo visited in an attempt to reconcile, but it was not to be. "We needed to pull our lives together," Jo says. "I was capable of that. Bo wasn't." Living with a prostitute in Malibu, Belinsky became, as he put it, "a flat-under-the-table drunk. There wasn't a sober day for quite a while. I stayed drunk for two years, blew out my pancreas, almost died. It was total insanity."

In 1972, through the intercession of his old Angels teammate Dean Chance, Belinsky was admitted to St. Thomas Hospital in Akron, Ohio, near Chance's home. "It wasn't too nice," Bo recalled. "It was a lockup type of an institution. There was a guarded gate. They'd throw you down and get you to sign." Every weekend during Belinsky's stay, a group from Alcoholics Anonymous visited. The smiles, slogans, and omnipresent Styrofoam coffee cups offended Bo's sense of cool. "I couldn't figure them out. They'd treat each other like they hadn't seen each other in years, shaking hands and spilling coffee on their shoes." Following 28 days of treatment, Belinsky was released. "I had two or three dollars, and the first thing I did was bought a bottle of wine and stuck it in a brown bag, and I went crazy. I didn't even know where I was. I wound up under this bridge in Akron. It was about 18 degrees and slushy, and I said, 'One and a half years ago, I'm in the major leagues in Cincinnati, and now I'm under a bridge in Akron,' and I thought, 'Boy, it can't get any worse.' *Wrong!*"

Back in Malibu, Belinsky began traveling with a criminal crowd. "The pimps and gangsters in Los Angeles were the only ones who'd accept me," he recalled. "As a matter of fact, they gave me a couple of draws and were going to put me in the business, but I was too drunk. They introduced me to cocaine. I had to stop drinking, because it was bad for me, so I did cocaine."

Hair now flowing over his collar in greasy strands, boyish smile masked by a dirty mustache, Belinsky spent much of the early '70s roaring up and down the PCH on a Harley-Davidson, stoned out of his mind. "It was unreal," he said. "I never killed anybody, and I'm fortunate. The things that happened to me, the physical damage that happened to me—I just didn't care. I wanted to die. I didn't want to die. I had no idea. All I knew is that I was in pain."

Not that there weren't ways out. In 1973, Dial Press published *Bo: Pitching and Wooing*, by veteran *New York Post* sportswriter Maury Allen. The author, as the jacket copy boasted, received "the uncensored cooperation of Bo Belinsky." Allen and Belinsky were equal partners, and as the release date approached, their editor became convinced that they had a best-seller. It was the age of the athlete as antihero, and the work's subject was the prototype. When the *Today* show booked Belinsky to plug *Pitching and Wooing*, the hype began. All Bo had to do was catch a red-eye flight to JFK, where a limousine would whisk him to NBC's Rockefeller Center studio. "Much as I liked Bo," says Allen, "I was wary, for I knew there was a chance he'd miss the *Today* show date. Not only did I talk to him two hours before the flight, but I insisted that the Dial publicists walk him to the gate in Los Angeles, and they did. The problem was they left before the flight boarded. There was a beautiful girl on line. She and Bo started talking, and they went off and spent the night. The next morning on the *Today* show there was no Bo. That was a killer for us. That was to have been the big break. I was so angry. I told myself I'd never talk to that cocksucker again." Allen pauses for a second before adding, "But I couldn't stay mad at Bo. He called and apologized, and I said, 'All right.'"

In 1974, Belinsky made another effort to overcome his addictions, relocating to the state that had always been charmed for him—Hawaii. There he embarked on a program that prescribed Valium and other drugs to dispel his desire for alcohol. He stayed sober several months. While walking on the beach, he met Jane Weyerhaeuser, heiress to the timber and paper fortune of the same name. Like so many others, she was at first smitten, and in 1975 they married. "She's a lovely gal," Belinsky would recall, but that was only part of the attraction. "Now I was back in the ball game. Now I could buy all the cocaine I wanted."

For a year Bo and Jane Belinsky used cocaine—he heavily, she less so. In 1976, when Jane was seven-and-a-half months pregnant, she gave birth prematurely. "The day I brought her in for a checkup," recalled Bo, "the doctor said, 'Your wife is giving birth today.' On top of that he says, 'You're gonna have twins.' I couldn't handle the pressure. She went into the hospital, and I got loaded. I brought all my friends over, and with all the dope and everything, I couldn't even make it to the hospital. I think I was drinking. I may have had a nip. I don't know. All I know is that I was coming apart at the seams. I was dying inside. I was so dead that when I finally came to the hospital and saw those two little girls, I had no feeling for them whatsoever, and I had no feeling for Jane. All I could think about was me."

Because the twins were born prematurely, they stayed in the hospital when Jane returned home, where Bo immediately got high. It was then that he snapped, retrieving his .38. "I started shooting all over the place. Next thing I knew, I was gonna play 20 Questions with my lover. I go back to the bedroom and am waving the gun around at her. I'm ready to pass out. I don't know what I'm doing. I thought I would fire it in the closet. But somewhere along the line I knew I was going to shoot her. And I did. The bullet went through her hip. Maybe a quarter of an inch up and she's dead.

Simple as that. After I gave her the whack with the .38, I had seen what had happened. I walked off. I was going to put the gun right to my head and fire it. Cocked it, too. Then I heard her say, 'Bo.' I was going to pull the trigger real fast. And she said, 'What are you doing? What are you doing?' And I didn't do it."

Jane's wound was not serious. "I was very lucky," she says. "The bullet didn't hit any bone. I should have called the police, but I didn't. I loved him." After a physician stitched her up, Belinsky fled to Los Angeles, where he went on a bender. "All I wanted to do was get into the bottle, back into alcohol, so I could totally blot out this incident." But Bo could not blot it out, and following several trips back and forth between the mainland and Hawaii, he checked into another rehab clinic.

During Belinsky's first two weeks at Saint John's Hospital in Santa Monica, he made little progress. "I wasn't responding to the treatment. The counselors kept saying, 'Let's get him down the street. He ain't doing it.' But the program director, Dave Thomas, kept saying, 'Let's give this guy one more day.' There's always someone in a program who won't give up on you, and that's what happened to me."

While Belinsky always had a religious bent—in times of trouble he would recite the 23rd Psalm—he'd rejected faith as being unhip. But shortly after Thomas interceded, this Jewish boy from Trenton opened himself to Jesus. 'After all those years of not God losing me but me losing Him," Bo said, "I found Him. I had to beat myself down so low and get it down so deep and so far to be receptive. But there it was. I stopped shaking and started to swell up inside."

Belinsky then did something that a couple of years earlier would have been inconceivable—he agreed to attend an Alcoholics Anonymous meeting. "It's AA or amen for you, Bo," Thomas informed him. Bo's first meeting was in Manhattan Beach. The room was plastered with posters bearing all the familiar slogans. As Bo looked around, he told himself, "It's so corny." Yet as he heard one alcoholic after another relate their stories, he couldn't help being moved. "I thought I was a sensitive, giving person, but I started taking a cold, hard look at how egotistical and self-centered I was and how much fear and resentment ruled my life, and I started to open my eyes. I knew I would always be insane, but I saw I didn't have to drink behind it. I didn't have to be dangerous. I was given a gift. Something was happening. This was where I belonged."

Once Belinsky emerged from Saint John's Hospital, he performed the suggested follow-up work of attending 90 AA meetings in 90 consecutive days. He soon began to venture out into the world, always traveling with a list of names to call should the temptation to drink arise. Astonishingly, Jane Weyerhaeuser and Bo remained together, moving to Doheny Estates, where Bo drove a Maserati and played golf at the Riviera Country Club. "He was the father of my daughters," she says. The relationship, however, did not last. According to legal filings, Belinsky beat his wife. "He grabbed me by the throat and pushed me in front of our children," she alleged. In 1981, the couple divorced, with Bo relinquishing custody of the twins. Through the years he visited them infrequently, then once they turned ten, not at all. "They always thought he'd ride out of the hills on a white horse and rescue them," says Jane. "But he never did."

As often happens with recovering alcoholics, Belinsky preached the gospel of sobriety. For much of the early '80s, he teamed with Dr. Joseph Pursch, a Laguna Beach-based psychiatrist who specializes in treating patients suffering from substance abuse. "It was the Bo and Joe show," says Pursch. "We were contracted by business organizations, the Betty Ford Center, and several major league baseball teams to discuss the problem of alcoholism. Bo would tell his story as one who'd been to hell and back, then he'd introduce me, and I'd give the scientific facts to hang on the bones of Bo's firsthand account." At such sessions, Belinsky held little back. "It hurts me when I tell you of shooting my wife," he would typically say. "But I tell you because I love you, and if you ever forget where you were, I'll tell you again." The point was clear: If Bo could rise from the depths, so could his audiences. There was, of course, another point as well. In providing hope for the hopeless, Bo was gaining a sense of accomplishment and making the sort of personal connections of which he'd previously believed himself incapable. "You're my family," he'd tell AA groups. "You saved my life."

Not all of Belinsky's work was public. In 1980, when he heard that his former Angels teammate Eli Grba was in an alcoholic tailspin, he drove to the Yorba Linda home where Grba had crashed. "Bo and I had never been that close," says Grba. "He was too Hollywood. But he came and got me and took me to an AA meeting. I was nervous, but Bo said, 'Don't worry, Eli, they're all drunks just like you and me.'" Grba has been sober for 24 years.

By the mid-1980s, Belinsky was back in Hawaii and remarried, this time to a waitress named Bobbi. Living on the North Shore of Oahu, he spent his days windsurfing. In 1989, the two split. Subsequently, Bo would attempt to make light of the breakup. During an appearance at the Betty Ford Center with Pursch, he remarked, "You know, I'm not too successful with wives. So I asked Joe, 'Every time I go to Hawaii, I get married. What can you advise me about my relationships?' He said, 'Simple, stay away from Hawaii.'" Despite such stabs at humor, the divorce from Bobbi was another indication that Bo, his decade of sobriety notwithstanding, still didn't know what to do with his life.

That Belinsky would find his ultimate path on a golf course was, considering all that was to come, fitting. "I met Bo at a scrambles tournament in 1989," recalls Don Richardson, sales manager at Saturn of West Sahara in Las Vegas. "He was living on a small pension from baseball, but he loved cars, so we put him to work in sales at Saturn. We soon found out he didn't have what it took to do sales, but Rich Abajian, who was then my boss, said, 'Bo, relax. I'm gonna pay you $1,500 a month to do PR.' For the rest of his life, he essentially played golf and schmoozed."

Judging by appearances, Belinsky adjusted easily to life in Las Vegas. "Bo had a magnet that drew everybody to him," says Richardson. "He had an ability to be in a group, and everybody liked him." Building goodwill for a business came naturally to Belinsky. When Abajian moved to Findlay Toyota, he took Bo with him.

For the first time in decades, Belinsky's fortunes seemed on the uptick. In 1994, thanks to Alana Case, a successful European model and the wife of his old friend Bob Case, Bo was featured in a major fashion layout in Italy's *L'uomo Vogue*. No longer young but not yet old, he photographed well, projecting a hard-earned wisdom. In 1997, he was invited to play in an Angels old-timers' game. This honor not only recognized his place in the team's history, but amounted to a homecoming after the extended exile that followed the ugly 1964 incident with the *Times'* Braven Dyer. On the field that evening in Anaheim, Bo exchanged warm greetings with Gene Autry and cavorted with his former love, Mamie Van Doren. At a news conference, he received more attention than did 300-game winner Nolan Ryan, thus confirming his view that he'd gone a long way on his 28 wins.

Still in all, Belinsky's Las Vegas friends often sensed that beneath his upbeat public persona lurked a profound sadness. "He kept a lot hidden from us," says Lou Rodophele. "Don, Irving Marcus, and I knew Bo very well, but none of us knew where he lived." Belinsky not only kept his address a secret but resisted the efforts of his newfound pals to make him an intimate. "On holidays I always included Bo in my family," says Rodophele, "but he'd only stay an hour or so. He couldn't stay longer because he couldn't tolerate it emotionally to see a happy family life, which he didn't have."

Out of touch with his children, Belinsky was alone. Even dalliances with beautiful women—whom he'd once hustled as avidly as he'd hustled pool—were no longer satisfying. "The fucking you get isn't worth the *fucking* you get," he'd crack to Abajian. Bo would then laugh, but he was putting up a brave front.

The gap between the face Belinsky presented to the world and his tortured private self opened on New Year's Eve, 1997. After falling off the wagon, Bo attempted suicide at the high-rise apartment where he'd long been living. First he drank half a bottle of vodka. Then he slashed his wrists. Next he plunged a dull hunting knife into his stomach just below the rib cage and slashed downward. Bleeding heavily, he dragged himself to his unit's balcony. "He later told me he was going to throw himself off," says Rodophele, "but he was hurt so bad he didn't have the strength." Eventually, Bo crawled to a phone, and soon help was summoned.

For several days Belinsky was in intensive care at the University Medical Center Hospital. "The emergency medical technicians told me they were surprised he lived," recalls a friend. Once Bo was strong enough, Rodophele bundled him into the backseat of his Lincoln Town Car and drove him to Palm Springs, where he would again battle alcoholism. "When Bo had his relapse," says Mark Greenberg, who had gotten to know the former Angel during the years when he spoke publicly on substance abuse, "I assisted him in getting help." The help began with a stay at Michael's House, Greenberg's new employer. There Greenberg perceived that for all the progress Belinsky had made, he had yet to deal with some of the underlying reasons for his despair. "I told him to clear things up with his daughters and clean house," he said. "But that's one step I don't think he really took. He didn't make amends."

Still, Belinsky fought his way once more to sobriety. On February 28, 1998, at a clinic called Life's Journey, he signed a "No Suicide Contract" in which he agreed not to take his life and to phone Greenberg should he ever find himself entertaining suicidal thoughts. Then he returned home.

Back in Las Vegas, the members of Belinsky's circle now possessed a sharper awareness of how fragile Bo was. Rodophele, who was charged with cleaning up Bo's apartment, was shocked by what he found. "I broke down crying," he says. "It was squalid. Not only was there blood from where he'd knifed himself, but trash was piled up everywhere. You couldn't even see the kitchen table. It was covered with empty cans, unopened bills, dirty clothes. This is what depression looks like."

For the first few months Belinsky lived with a succession of friends, among them Rich Abajian and his wife, Jo Ann. As he'd done during his initial recovery, Bo kept himself clean by helping others do the same. Jo Ann had a drug problem. "Bo helped her stay sober, and she helped him," says Abajian. Adds Jo Ann, "We'd sit on the balcony and talk about our lives. It wasn't all 'Woe is me.' There was a lot of laughter. He was an inspiring gentleman." At the Abajians' urging, Bo joined their church—Trinity Life.

"I met Bo right after the suicide attempt," says the Reverend Randy Greer. "He told me that he'd had a vision of Christ that night he tried to take his life." According to Greer, Bo realized that "his life was empty. He wanted to fill that void that Billy Graham calls 'a God-shaped vacuum.'"

Trinity Life became the pivot around which Belinsky's existence revolved. Not that he acted pious. "Bo was always going to be rough around the edges," says Greer, citing as example his habit of sitting in the back of the sanctuary during services so that he could duck out for cigarettes. Equally telling, Bo continued to indulge in language better suited to a dugout than a house of worship. "He'd come up to me after church and say, 'That was a helluva sermon, Pastor Randy.'" Belinsky also resisted what for a Pentecostal is the acid test—speaking in tongues. Nevertheless, Greer believes that his new congregant found true salvation. "Bo would tell me, 'I need Jesus. Without Him, I'm lost.' He gave his life to Jesus. He wanted to be part of everything here."

On the morning of December 7, 2001, Bo Belinsky was finally laid to rest in the Garden of Peace at Paradise Memorial Gardens, a perpetual-care facility just across a busy four-lane road from McCarran International Airport. After the initial confusion as to the legalities, Lou Rodophele was appointed administrator of Bo's estate. The spot that he, Don Richardson, and Dean Chance chose for their friend is five plots away from where the remains of another tortured 1960s sports icon—former heavyweight boxing champion Sonny Liston—are interred.

As the Reverend Greer pronounced words over Belinsky's body, questions regarding Bo's troubled 64 years still eluded easy answers. On one level, he was a man who had it all—looks, athletic talent, stardom, and charisma. Yet he couldn't face life's realities. "God knows, Bo was of this world," his friend Dr. Joseph Pursch would later say, "but he was not for this world.

He was like a child. All his life, by acting out socially and sexually, he tried to defend himself. Then he lost baseball, and he had nothing left. That's when alcohol and drugs got him." But whatever the sources of Belinsky's pain, by the end he had achieved some degree of self-knowledge. "Bo was becoming more normal, thinking about the continuity of life," says Pursch. Adds Chance, "For the first time, Bo got around quality people, and that made him feel much better about himself."

For Belinsky's brass grave marker, two of those people—Lou Rodophele and Don Richardson—selected a motif that honors his greatest achievements. Beneath an image of a baseball appear the words NO HITTER and the date 5/5/62. Next to the legend is another image—a cross. At long last, Bo had found a home.

A Sinner's Second Chance

Esquire, November 1984

As the black bus barrels southward, the sun begins to drop below the horizon, and up ahead, far away, the spires of New York City glimmer in the dusk. Gregg Allman, his lead guitarist, Danny Toler, and his pianist, Tim Heding, are sitting around a small table in the front of the coach, with the rest of the band members asleep in bunks at the back. Toler taps Allman on the knee and asks, "Brother, you remember that dream you had when you were nine?"

Allman winces. "If I saw some guy on TV explaining that dream, I'd think he was crazy."

"What was it?" Heding asks.

Allman lights his tenth cigarette of the day. "Well, about the time I was in third grade, I had this recurring dream where I was being led up a high set of steps. At first I thought it was to the gallows. People were behind me, and there were all these bright lights. When I got four steps from the top, I saw a solid block of finished wood—something fine, like walnut. And then I heard this roar. It was a happy sound, like everybody had gotten together for a big barbecue. I jumped up and down, but I couldn't see over the top of that piece of wood."

Allman takes another drag from his cigarette. "I had that dream thirty or forty times then it stopped. I didn't think about it again until years later, when one night at Madison Square Garden I was walking up the steps to the stage and there was my Hammond organ, all shiny and beautiful, and light was coming over it, and the crowd was roaring, and my brother was in front of me. I froze. It was the dream."

But that was long ago. When New York draws so tantalizing close that Allman can almost reach out and touch it, the bus veers west onto another highway. Gregg Allman doesn't play the Garden these days. Instead, he's headed to a cold little club with concrete slab floors and graffitied plywood walls in Hackettstown, New Jersey, where the band will earn $5,000 then pack up the equipment and head on. In a sense, the job isn't all that different from the kind Gregg and his late brother, Duane, used to take when they were just starting out in the '60s, playing dates in Mobile, Alabama, and Jackson, Mississippi, on what Allman calls "the chitlin circuit...clubs where we played 'Try a Little Tenderness' to rednecks who wanted to get drunk, listen to music, and get laid—in that order."

At thirty-six, Gregg Allman has returned to the road, hoping that it will lead him back from obscurity. This current trip is a swing through the Northeast. The shows, for the most part, go unnoticed, but Allman is here with friends who have stuck by him through very hard times, and he is determined to make the most of it.

In Boston, he is playing the Channel, a cavernous club in a warehouse district near the water. The Channel's regular patrons are more accustomed to the cacophonous grating of Black Flag than to Allman's stock-in-trade— Southern blues—but this evening the crowd is different. Wandering among scores of kids who can't have been much older than ten in 1973, when the Allman Brothers Band headlined the Watkins Glen music festival in upstate New York, are women with long, center-parted hair and cosmic gazes and bearded, balding sorts reminiscent of the Zig Zag rolling paper man. When Allman walks onto the stage and takes a seat behind his organ, applause erupts. The singer smiles, waves, and then, counting off the beat begins playing a blues progression. At the last possible instant he pulls the microphone to his lips, and in a jagged but mournfully sweet voice that both cuts and caresses, growls, "Just one more morning...I had to wake up with the blues," the opening lines from "Dreams," a song that appeared on the Allman Brothers' first album. No matter what toll the past years have taken, Allman is still the blackest white boy ever to sing about being done wrong.

It promises to be a powerful performance. Things move right along, the band "in a groove," as Allman likes to say, until someone in the crowd accidentally knocks a drink over into the snake—an electrical junction box at the front of the stage that connects nearly every important wire in the band's sound system. Suddenly, half the speakers go dead. Then, as technicians struggle to correct the problem, another disaster strikes. Guitarist Danny Toler sets his instrument down and rushes out the club's back exit, where he falls to the ground, violently sick.

Allman apologizes to the audience and, after tucking his sweat-drenched hair down the back of a black leather jacket, makes his way out to the tour bus, where he finds Toler, his face ashen, curled on the sofa in his compartment at the back. Toler, who has played with Allman since the late '70s, is the singer's closest friend.

Immediately the driver puts the bus in gear and speeds away through the empty, late-night streets toward the nearest hospital.

"Tell him to hurry, Gregg," Toler moans.

"I will, my man." Allman stares off an instant then muses, "You know my granddaddy used to say, 'If you have one friend in life, well, you've been a successful man.' I've been successful all right." Whereupon in an exaggerated Dixie drawl meant to conjure a grizzled old man he adds, "Alfred. That was my granddaddy. He ran a saw mill in Tennessee, but it was a front for a still."

Before Allman can go on with the story, the bus arrives at the emergency room, and Toler is taken off in a wheelchair. As his band mate disappears through the hospital doors, Allman urges the driver to get him back to the hotel, where he's going to see about scraping together a hundred dollars to pay for his friend's treatment. When the coach brakes to a halt in front of the forlorn Bradford Hotel, Allman bounds out and heads up to the eighth floor, where he finds a small mob of ready-to-party roadies and hangers-on gathered in the hall.

Tonight Allman's in no mood to celebrate. Then someone tells him that the group's insurance will pay for Toler, and someone else mentions that the hospital has called to say that nothing is seriously wrong with the guitarist. It takes a second for this to sink in. When it does, Allman locates in the throng a tall, raven-haired woman who bears a striking resemblance to his ex-wife, Cher, takes her by the arm, and smiling, steers her down a long hall to his room. Things, as he well knows, could be worse.

It is now difficult to remember that just ten years ago, with five platinum and three gold albums to their credit, the Allman Brothers were the highest paid rock act in America, often earning $250,000 a night. The group's sound was powerful, original, and perfect for the times—bluesy yet psychedelic. While fans seemed to be transported first and foremost by Duane Allman and Dickey Betts's guitar duets, it was Gregg Allman who gave the Allman Brothers their soul. He wrote nearly all of the Allmans' trademark songs and sang all but two or three. "People don't give Gregg enough credit," says Phil Walden, who was president of the Allmans' label, the now-defunct Capricorn Records of Macon, Georgia. "He was really the heart of the band. He knew the blues."

Not only did Gregg understand black music, but he taught it to his brother. It was in the early '60s that the two boys formed their first band, the

House Rockers, and started playing back-up for a group of black singers, the Untils, on the boardwalk at Daytona Beach, Florida. Then after a short stint with another hometown band—this one named the Allman Joys—the brothers found their way to Los Angeles and started a psych-pop band called Hourglass. By late summer 1969 the two were in Georgia, where Duane, who had established himself as a leading recording session guitarist, organized what would become the Allman Brothers. Soon the group recorded an album and started playing free concerts in public parks across the country. Then the band took off. But that, too, was a long time back.

A couple of nights after the disaster in Boston, the band is headed to its next gig, this one in Baltimore. As the tour bus barrels down Interstate 95, Allman has retreated to his private quarters, where he is cradling his Gibson Dove in his lap. He is in an unusually talkative and reflective mood, and between sips of lukewarm ice tea he bought fifty miles ago, his mind roams backward. "Man, I remember Watkins Glen like it was yesterday," he says. "I'd never been so scared in my life. We helicoptered into the place, and when we got near all you could see were people. It was a sight."

A radio recessed into the compartment's back wall is playing faintly, and it picks up the strains of a song by Prince.

"That boy ain't got no chops," Allman snorts. "He sure ain't no Little Richard." Then Allman smiles.

"When I met Little Richard the first time, it was around when our *Fillmore East* album was set to come out. I'd been to New York and bought myself some beautiful clothes in the Village—floral-patterned shirts, boots, bell-bottoms. And I'd bought this incredible belt buckle—a shiny, outrageous thing. Anyway, I went to see Little Richard in Atlanta. I idolized him. I got backstage and walked up to shake his hand, and he grabbed that buckle and just smiled at me.

"I said, 'Mr. Penniman, I'm honored to meet you. I'm an admirer of yours. But if you do that again, there's gonna be a dead nigger here.' We've been great friends ever since."

Allman chortles. Then, his voice straining into a high register, he begins singing, "Tutti frutti, aw-rootie, tutti frutti…"

Coughing, he grins and adds, "I'll tell you who can outdo Prince and Little Richard. That's Little Milton. I finally met him, too. Only one I didn't meet was Otis Redding."

Allman takes another sip of tea. Although he never knew Redding, Gregg inherited both musical and corporate sustenance from the late soul singer. Redding was the first star managed by Phil Walden and booking agent Alex Hodges out of Macon. Walden and Hodges used what they learned handling Redding to build a music empire in an otherwise backwater middle-Georgia city. By the mid-70s Capricorn Records was a force to be reckoned with, and it was no accident that Georgia governor and presidential aspirant Jimmy Carter eventually sought Gregg out.

As the bus rolls on, Allman is still reminiscing. "Back in the fall of '74, Jimmy Carter threw a party for Bob Dylan one night at the governor's mansion. I got there late, right as the last guests were going home. I had my limo driver stop at the gate, and the guard told us to come on. Carter wanted to see me.

"We drove on up to the front porch, and Carter was standing there on the steps, wearing old Levi's, a T-shirt, and no shoes.

"We went inside and sat down on the floor. We talked for a long time. I genuinely liked the man. Still do. He told me he was going to be president, and I started laughing. But he was serious, and he asked me to help him raise some money."

By the time Allman agreed to promote Carter, he had released his first solo album, *Laid Back*—a work that to date is his creative high water mark. Not only did the record include a hit ("Midnight Rider"), more important it contained Allman's most ambitious and successful effort as a songwriter, a demanding, disturbingly sad blues ballad called "Queen of Hearts."

Reaching into his wallet, Allman extracts a dog-eared Bicycle playing card—the queen of hearts. "That song saved my life. It gave me a sense of…for the first time I realized I wasn't the no-talent, procrastinating, don't-take-care-of-business flunky sheep I thought I was after my brother died." After things began to fall apart.

Allman sighs. Then he glances up sullenly and mumbles, "I can tell you some crap to make your hair curl. Once, I got myself off in the dark." He makes a muscle with his left arm then mimes giving himself an injection just above the elbow. For a second, deep furrows become visible around his eyes. Soon, he falls asleep.

In the fall of 1971, when Duane Allman was only twenty-four, he was killed in a motorcycle wreck in Macon. Accompanying himself on acoustic guitar,

Gregg sang "Melissa" to the hundreds of mourners at the funeral, and then everyone joined in on "Will the Circle Be Unbroken."

A year and thirteen days after Duane's death, Allman Brothers bass player Berry Oakley died from injuries sustained in a motorcycle crash only a few blocks from the intersection where Duane perished.

Never averse to taking whatever drug was put in front of him, Gregg began indulging a heavy cocaine habit. In 1976, after John "Scooter" Herring—the road manager who supplied Gregg's needs—was arrested, Gregg turned state's evidence, testifying against his friend in federal court. "They had me. I had to do it, and Scooter understands," Allman said. But other members of the Allman Brothers weren't so forgiving. Drummer Jaimoe Johanson wrote an open letter to Georgia newspapers contending that Gregg's actions had destroyed the band. Lamar Williams, the group's new bass player, said, "He really hurt everybody...I could never work with him again." On a wall near the offices of Capricorn Records, an anonymous protestor scrawled: GREGG ALLMAN HAS MURDERED THE BROTHERS AND ROCK 'N' ROLL.

Things went from bad to worse. Shortly before the Herring trial, Allman exiled himself to Los Angeles, where he'd met Cher one night after she'd seen him perform at the Troubadour. Following a passionate courtship, Cher became his third wife in a ceremony conducted at Caesars Palace in Las Vegas. Nine days later she filed for divorce. The couple reconciled long enough to produce a son, Elijah Blue, and one of the worst albums ever recorded: *Allman and Woman—Two the Hard Way*. In 1978 the marriage broke up for good. Cher recently said she doesn't care if she ever sees Allman again and that he never calls to check on their son. When asked about Cher, Allman said plaintively, "I still love her. I always will."

Allman had used heroin before, but by the winter of 1977 his addiction had become so bad that he sequestered himself back east in the house of a Buffalo physician who, in exchange for $29,000, promised to step him down. For several weeks Allman used methadone. Then he went cold turkey. For days he managed only a few hours' sleep, brief interludes disturbed by dreams of gore and dismemberment. But mostly, Allman was wide awake. It was the winter of one of Buffalo's worst blizzards, and he spent almost all of his time walking up and down four flights of stairs in the old house, watching the snow pile higher and higher and feeling his habit freeze over.

After fifty days of treatment Allman was clean, but his life had become a melodrama, and soon he sank into alcoholism. The first thing he'd do most days was upend a quart of vodka. ("Some mornings I had to use a straw, I was shaking so bad.") Always shy and laconic, he grew downright prickly. "He was nice one minute and mean the next," recalled Danny Toler. "He was distant and unreliable," said Phil Walden. Allman put it more succinctly: "I was an asshole."

During the next five years Allman was in and out of alcohol abuse centers all over the country, and he joined Alcoholics Anonymous. Yet somehow, in the midst of everything, he managed to reunite the disbanded Allman Brothers and record a final Capricorn album. The band then moved to Clive Davis and Arista for two uninspired albums. Davis and Allman feuded over creative control, and the records failed miserably. To top it off, deep wounds still festered in several band members because of the Herring trial. After an appearance on *Saturday Night Live* in 1982, the group disbanded for good and Allman repaired to his new home near Bradenton, Florida.

Save for a few fanatics—freaks with their flags still flying, blues musicians with whom Allman occasionally jammed in Atlanta, and those fans who remembered how superb Gregg was in his prime—many people forgot Allman ever existed.

In Baltimore the band plays an imitation Gilley's then it's on to a suburban shopping plaza hot spot in Columbus, Ohio. For Gregg Allman, the discouragement he is experiencing now is at least better than the despair he was feeling sitting idle at home. "I just got sick and tired of being sick and tired," he says. "I discovered I didn't have to hurt myself to live. I'm ready to be a top entertainer again. I want to have hit songs on the radio."

Wishing, however, isn't necessarily going to make things so for Allman, although from all accounts he has dried himself out. Allman's renunciation of liquor is regarded by several key members of the supporting cast from the Allman Brothers' glory years as an important sign. Veteran manager Willie Perkins, someone who loves Gregg but had given up on him, has returned to the fold. Alex Hodges never really lost faith in the singer, but lately he's intensified his efforts on Gregg's behalf.

From Hodges's offices at ICM in West Hollywood (and from the Atlanta suburb of Marietta, where Hodges headed up the Empire Agency before moving to the West Coast last spring), calls have been going out for months now to record companies in Los Angeles and New York. A balding, meticulous Southerner with an affinity for bird hunting, Hodges says, "What I've found is that there are a lot of roadblocks out there. They know Gregg's got a great voice and know he's got a following, but we've got to show them some great new songs, and then there are the perennial questions: How's his attitude? That means, Is he straight? And is he the classic artist of the '70s who's just not going to be able to make it in the music world of the '80s? The answer to the first question is yes and the second is no."

Still, as Lenny Waronker, president of Warner Bros. Records, puts it, "Gregg may have a chance to make a comeback, but it's a real judgment call. When he's clean, he's great. When he's not straight, he's just not focused or motivated."

Yet Hodges labors on. There's a possibility that CBS Records might sign Allman, but Hodges wants to guard against the chance that the label will regard the singer as an old war-horse. Then there are several so-called P&D deals in the air with relatively unknown labels that would require Allman to pay for his own production work in exchange for distribution. Finally, Hodges has even considered a television direct-marketing deal with a company along the lines of K-Tel. Hodges says that the TV group "wants to break the mold," but if that's the road he takes, it's hard not to envision Allman becoming a rock 'n' roll Slim Whitman, his records advertised late at night on Atlanta Superstation WTBS.

What Hodges has to offer record companies is an eight-song demo tape Allman and his band recorded in a small studio in Sarasota, Florida. Allman's new songs are good, and his voice is better than ever, but as one record insider puts it, "I just can't hear them on the radio." Phil Walden, who rarely speaks with Hodges (the two old associates have been embroiled in acrimonious disputes concerning the breakup of Capricorn), says, "Gregg's getting bad advice. He's such a great singer, but they've got to push him toward a more modern sound." Indeed, on careful listening, Allman's tape reveals that he's relying on the same arrangements that worked for him in the old days: two percussionists, two lead guitars, and a lot of the blues. If his sound has progressed at all, it's in the direction of the soulful fusion of such mystic redneck bands as the Dixie Dregs.

Of course, whether Allman signs a lucrative new deal or not, he will remain one of America's great blues musicians, and if he wanted, he could build a career as a white B.B. King. In fact, Allman appeared with King last summer at the Medgar Evers festival in Mississippi for a memorable jam session, but as Allman looked around that day he must have realized that he was the only young man on the stage.

Allman says he doesn't want to go out as yesterday's news. But he's got a lot of ground to cover just to catch up with the present, much less plan for the future. It's no surprise that Allman, a product of the era of Jim Morrison and Janis Joplin, the little brother of a rock 'n' roll martyr, would have his own romance with Thanatos. Now, after winning a hard-fought battle with drugs and liquor, he's embracing the idea that life is good. The clubs he's playing may be small, and the hotel rooms may be steerage class, but Allman—who's redefined the cliché about paying your dues to sing the blues—doesn't mind. No one ever promised him that it was going to be easy.

On a sunny late winter afternoon, Gregg Allman sits on the set of *Thicke of the Night* at Metromedia Studios in Hollywood. He's making a guest appearance in the hope of letting fans and record magnates alike know of his reemergence. But *Thicke of the Night*, one of the only shows in recent memory to flirt with zero in the Nielsen ratings, isn't exactly the perfect showcase. Appearing with the singer are the busty female publisher of *High Society*, who's pushing her new phone sex business; the film critic of *The Hollywood Reporter*, who's gushing about a couple current releases; and a white-haired psychic named Kenny Kingston, who's trying to communicate with Marilyn Monroe via a tiny artifact that he claims is one of her fingernails. As Alan Thicke prattles with his guests, Allman—perched at the far end of the banquette behind the host—plays nervously with his hands and stares at the floor. Finally, just before Allman and Danny Toler, who's waiting in the wings, are scheduled to play a couple of songs, Thicke turns toward the singer.

"I've read you don't like to do interviews, Gregg. What do you like to do?"

"Oh, I like to fish," Allman manages.

"Well, Gregg, that's why they ask you about Cher. They're afraid you'll want to talk about trout."

Following a couple of other equally inane exchanges, Thicke allows Allman to perform his songs. He's impressive.

Afterward, Allman and Toler retire to their room at the Hollywood Holiday Inn, another unimposing hotel in yet another unsavory part of a big city. Before ordering room service, Danny changes into his pajamas and Gregg unbuttons his jeans, unleashing the beginnings of an unruly gut.

Eventually, steaks, potatoes, fruit salad, and a huge container of ice tea arrive. The two silently wolf down the meal as a TV buzzes on the wall. Finished, they push the room service cart aside, and Danny tosses a couple of Frisbee-like plastic plate warmers onto a corner chair. Only seven years before, Gregg was retiring in splendor at Cher's Holmby Hills mansion about ten miles to the west. Now it's barely eleven o'clock, but he pulls a faded bedspread up to his chest. "I'm beat," Allman says emphatically, and Danny gets up and flicks off the TV.

Citizen Breitbart

Time, April 5, 2010

Andrew Breitbart sits in an Aeron chair at an iMac computer gazing out the sliding glass door of his Los Angeles home office. On the patio, a hula hoop and a portable basketball rim await his children's return from school. Breitbart, 41, dressed on this late-winter day in his standard work uniform of a dirty Oxford-cloth shirt and grungy khaki shorts, looks more like a surf bum than one of the most divisive figures in America's political and culture wars. Then his BlackBerry rings.

The woman at the other end of the line, conservative fulminator Ann Coulter, is among Breitbart's staunchest allies, and soon they are engaged in a spirited attack on liberals. "Their entire structure is writhing in diseased agony on the side of the road, and they don't even realize it," Breitbart says. But the left isn't the only object of disdain. "I'm sick of this effete GOP nothing sandwich," he adds, growing more animated. "As long as everyone is so pristine and socially registered, we're going to lose." Shortly before signing off, Breitbart says, "The second I realized I liked being hated more than I liked being liked—that's when the game began."

It's a game Breitbart plays extraordinarily well. He has become the Web's most combative conservative impresario—part new-media mogul, part Barnumesque scamp. Last fall, he launched Big Government, the flagship of his wickedly right-of-center sites, which also include Big Hollywood, Big Journalism—which described the House's March passage of President Barack Obama's health care reform bill as a "socialist putsch"—and the news aggregators Breitbart.com and Breitbart.tv. On its first day of business, Big Government produced a scoop: undercover filmmakers James O'Keefe and Hannah Giles—the would-be Borats of the right—had shot videos that appeared to show workers at ACORN, a liberal organization that lobbies for affordable housing, offering tips on how to open a brothel. For Breitbart, the videos proved to be a gold mine, putting the left on the defensive and Big Government on the map. That the filmmakers were accused of entrapping their subjects and editing in footage of O'Keefe dressed as a pimp seemed almost beside the point.

The stunt gave Breitbart—who like many online scribes had spent much of his professional life toiling in anonymity—a public persona. In January, O'Keefe was arrested in New Orleans on charges of entering the offices of U.S. Senator Mary Landrieu under false pretenses while preparing another undercover video. This only boosted Breitbart's profile. At the National Tea Party Convention in Nashville in February, Breitbart introduced the star speaker, Sarah Palin, and delivered a rousing jeremiad of his own. Assailing national reporters for portraying the movement as "racist and homophobic," he used the dais at the Gaylord Opryland Hotel to speak his version of truth to mainstream media power: "It's not your business model that sucks. It's you that sucks."

Breitbart perceives himself as a new-media David out to slay old-media Goliaths. As he sees it, the left exercises its power not via mastery of the issues but through control of the entertainment industry, print and television journalism, and government agencies that set social policy. "Politics," he often says, "is downstream from culture. I want to change the cultural narrative." Thus the Big sites devote their energy less to trying to influence the legislative process in Washington than to attacking the institutions and people Breitbart believes dictate the American conversation. Recently, Big Hollywood has gone after *Sesame Street* for a musical number titled "We All Sing with the Same Voice" that, it alleges, contains "controversial political messages designed to promote multiculturalism." Big Government has targeted the Obama Administration's safe-schools czar, Kevin Jennings, for a reading list, compiled when he headed the Gay, Lesbian, Straight Education Network, that includes books depicting adolescent homosexual encounters.

Such cultural crusades might seem to appeal mostly to the far-right fringe, but Breitbart is tapping a deep reservoir of conservative dismay. Former Bush Administration official David Frum says, "What matters to [this constituency] is not why the government is spending $15 million on something. What matters is a perception that hostile forces are invading your home, school, and family. Those forces come in on TV and in newspapers. An enormous amount of what conservatism now does is media criticism."

Andrew Breitbart was raised in Brentwood, on Los Angeles's privileged west side. The area is home to studio executives and producers, and the politics are Democratic. Breitbart was never fully comfortable in L.A.'s '80s social milieu. His parents are Midwestern Jews. (His father ran a Santa Monica steak house.) They saw life differently than the other kids' sophisticated dads and moms did. "My folks are from an older and very silent generation," Breitbart says. "My dad is as conservative as William F. Buckley was, but without the same presentation. He expressed his conservatism by working 16-hour days at the restaurant and never complaining."

By the time Breitbart entered the Brentwood School, an elite private academy, he was out of step with his classmates. "Andrew didn't fit the mold," says Larry Solov, a friend since childhood and now Breitbart's partner in the Big sites. "At Brentwood, you got A's and bought into a system set up to get you into an Ivy League college. Andrew got C's." Soon enough, Breitbart adopted the guise of skeptic and prankster, staging acts of subversion designed to win laughs and undermine the school's prevailing assumptions about wealth and meritocracy. It wouldn't be Harvard for this wiseacre. He was going to Tulane.

The South was a revelation for Breitbart. Southerners, whom he'd assumed from their depiction on TV to be Neanderthals, were warm and smart and less neurotic than Californians. The social life at Tulane was splendid. "I was a drunk," says Breitbart, who estimates he spent five nights a week at New Orleans bars with fellow Delta Tau Delta fraternity members. The classroom experience was less satisfying "I didn't read Mark Twain," he says. "I read critical theorists. I graduated with a degree in nihilism and nothingness."

After returning to Los Angeles, Breitbart met Matt Drudge, founder of the conservative Drudge Report. It was the mid-1990s, and the Web was in its infancy. Breitbart went to work for Drudge and served as his legman for 15 years, learning how to excavate news items from databases and wire-service feeds. More than that, he adopted Drudge's contrarian worldview. "Matt rejects entrenched thinking," says Breitbart. If Drudge taught Breitbart a new way of seeing, it was another former employer, Arianna Huffington, who whipped him into intellectual shape. Drudge introduced Breitbart to Huffington in the late 1990s when she was a right-wing provocateur. He worked for her as a researcher. "I was a slacker," he says. "Writing, rhetoric, argument—she demanded that I take a disciplined approach."

Breitbart helped launch the Huffington Post in 2005, but the marriage was destined to fail. Huffington had become a progressive. "It became impossible for me to work with Arianna's staff. They're liberals." But as he walked out the door, Breitbart experienced an epiphany.

The Big sites were born of Breitbart's realization that if Huffington could create a virtual salon for the left, he could create one for the right.

"Most conservatives are individualists," he says. "For years, they've been pummeled by the collectivists who run the American media, Hollywood, and Washington. The underground conservative movement that is now awakening is the ecosystem I've designed my sites to tap into."

Like some elements of the Tea Party movement, the Big sites can be crude. Also, Breitbart has shown an increasing propensity for bombast. While accepting an award at the Conservative Political Action Conference (CPAC) in Washington in late February for his role in breaking the ACORN story, he called *New York Times* reporter Kate Zernike "despicable" for saying in the *Times*'s Caucus blog that a young speaker used racially-offensive language. Two days later, Breitbart got into a verbal altercation with freelance writer Max Blumenthal. "You are the lowest life-form I have ever seen," Breitbart said. Blumenthal's putative offense had been to accuse O'Keefe in an article for Salon.com of attending a gathering that featured "white nationalists." All these outbursts were captured on cell-phone cameras wielded by members of competing camps. The videos went viral. The attack dog had become a mad dog.

While Breitbart is a polestar to many Tea Partyers, his excesses have the potential to cause the movement embarrassment. "The smarter conservatives who know Breitbart regard him affectionately," says Republican strategist Mike Murphy, "but they think he's a little out of it. In another age, the Big sites would have been produced on a mimeograph machine. I'd call him the first neo-crank."

Critics on the left are, of course, harsher. "The CPAC stuff was ugly," says Eric Boehlert, who writes for the liberal website Media Matters for America. "He's become known as the guy who yells at people in the halls. And his sites have little impact. The last time I looked, no one in the mainstream media had picked up the campaign Big Government has going against Obama's education guy."

Breitbart's online competitors are both impressed and wary. "Andrew has an eye for stories that never make *The New York Times*," says a journalist with experience in old and new media. "When I see him, he'll say, 'Why aren't you covering this?' And he's right. But some of what he publishes is irresponsible. He represents something fascinating about today's culture but also something deplorable." John Harris, editor of Politico.com, says, "I regard Andrew as a skilled media and ideological entrepreneur, but as he becomes a combatant, he is going to get scrutinized like one."

To Breitbart, the dismissive reviews are a form of flattery. To speak ill of people in the new media is to do them a favor, generating hits on their sites, which drives revenue. Furthermore, Breitbart is a true believer. "I'm Upton Sinclair 2.0," he says, "except instead of attacking rotten meatpacking houses, I'm attacking the rotten political establishment and the mainstream media that discourage dissent in this country." As for the charge that his sites pay too much attention to the prurient side of issues, he responds, "I like decadent. I like rambunctious. I like mirth."

However polarizing, Breitbart's efforts appear to be flourishing. Technorati, a website focusing on new media, ranks two of the Big sites—Big Government and Breitbart.tv—on its influential top-100 list. (At number 24 in March, Big Government—while trailing the number-one site, the Huffington Post—was ahead of such liberal sites as Daily Kos and Talking Points Memo.) According to Solov, he and Breitbart have not sought outside investors, funding the sites with their own money along with ad revenue. But this may change. In the months ahead, they plan to launch Big Peace, which will cover national security, followed by Big Tolerance (aimed at conservative gays, blacks, and Jews), Big Education, and Big Soros (which will address the world of institutional giving).

It is a brilliant weekday afternoon, and Andrew Breitbart is at the wheel of his Range Rover, driving to the Los Angeles bureau of Fox News to make a live appearance on Fox's politics and business show, *America's Nightly Scoreboard*. He'll then tape a segment for the late-night talkfest *Red Eye*, whose host, Greg Gutfeld, is a contributor to Big Journalism. On *Scoreboard*, Breitbart takes another jab at Blumenthal. On *Red Eye*, he shoots for bigger game. "I want it to be in the history books," he proclaims, "that I took down the institutional left, and I think that's gonna happen."

Breitbart observers are divided about what his future will bring. Political blogger Mickey Kaus, an acquaintance and longtime Breitbart watcher, thinks the Big sites will become exactly that—big. "I've always thought of him as an empire builder," he says. "He has the temperament of a tycoon, a conservative Ted Turner. He has what they all have—that slightly crazed look in the eyes." Boehlert sees a different ending: "What's ahead for Breitbart is some sort of spectacular flameout."

Maybe this is why Breitbart is in such a hurry. After dashing out of the Fox bureau, he races home via the sort of shortcuts only native Angelenos know. His wife, Susie (daughter of Orson Bean, a mainstay of the old TV game show *To Tell the Truth*), is preparing dinner for him and their four children. But the real reason for the rush is that James O'Keefe is visiting their house tonight to screen his latest effort, an undercover video revealing purported shenanigans at the offices of the Department of Housing and Urban Development. Breitbart hopes to debut the footage on Big Government. He believes it will be another scoop—and another blow to the liberal establishment.

"I feel very alive," Breitbart says as he whips along backstreets adjacent to the 405 freeway, where traffic is at a standstill. "We're in a battle, and in hindsight I can see that the moves I'm making are correct. I'm putting together something that's going to be extraordinary."

Less than two years after this story appeared, Andrew Breitbart was dead of a heart attack, but the raucous media world he created survives him. Indeed, Stephen Bannon, who became the site's executive chairman after Breitbart's death, served as chief executive officer of Donald Trump's 2016 presidential campaign. Following the election, Trump appointed Bannon assistant to the president and chief strategist.

The Talented Mr. Raywood

Los Angeles, November–December 2008

Part 1: Getting In

Almost daily throughout late summer and early fall 2007, someone else looking for Craig Raywood pulled into the porte cochere of the Granville Towers on Crescent Heights Boulevard just south of Sunset. Shopkeepers and craftsmen, limo drivers and process servers, one by one they marched across the lobby with its dated art and grand piano. Built in 1930, the Granville, an eight-story French revival apartment building, is the sort of place where Old Hollywood lived when it was young. Ricardo Mayorga, the 24-year-old doorman, never failed to call upstairs to announce the visitors, although he knew the tenant in number 61 would not answer. He also knew the reaction this would spark in those seeking Raywood: exasperated mutterings, the slamming down of writs or summonses, and increasingly, outbursts that culminated in threats of bodily harm. Everyone left disappointed or furious, whereupon the phone at the front desk would inevitably ring.

"Were they looking for me?" Raywood would ask Mayorga from his quarters six floors above.

"Yeah, they were here. You owe them money."

"They're wrong. It's a mistake. I'm not what they say I am."

Soon enough Raywood would emerge from an elevator, oblivious to what had just transpired. Tall and preternaturally tanned, dark hair brushed back from a high forehead, teeth glistening, he did not so much enter a room as make an entrance. If he was headed for a daytime charity event at Virginia Robinson Gardens in Beverly Hills, he would wear a violet seersucker suit from Kiton. If he was attending an evening benefit for AIDS Project L.A. on the Fox backlot, he affected something more bohemian: a sequined tunic-length black linen jacket unbuttoned to the sternum to show off a $15,000 strand of Tahitian pearls dangling from his neck. For business it was always Armani accented by a pocket-handkerchief and a tiny Hermès crocodile bag. Even casual outings were occasions for the stylish gesture. In a pink polo shirt, khakis, and John Lobb loafers, and with his whippet,

Giselle, in tow, he would depart by taxi for Barneys, where, once inside, he would let the dog wander off leash, or to Tiffany, where the sales staff would adorn her in jewels.

As Raywood liked to tell new acquaintances, he was a native New Yorker and "one of the preeminent international interior designers." Indeed his work had been celebrated in *House & Garden* and *The New York Times*. That the bulk of this attention had come in the 1980s and early '90s did not, in Raywood's mind, diminish his stature. Rather, it solidified his place in the firmament. "I live in a certain way, and that's a standard of my life," he often boasted. "Whether that's acceptable to you or anyone else, that's the way it is." For most of Raywood's 57 years the world of fashion and wealth had been his natural habitat, and the names he dropped—Italian countesses, Andy Warhol's Factory crowd, Manhattan hedge fund barons, Parisian aesthetes—suggested the guest list for a dazzling dinner party. Not that these luminaries weren't flawed. While Raywood praised them to his lessers, thereby elevating himself, he disparaged them to his betters—especially potential clients—thereby elevating *them*.

"Craig's an almost rascally figure whose charm lies in the old-fashioned comical disdain he has for people," says a Beverly Hills physician. "He has this way of projecting that nothing is good enough." Snobbishness, however, is just one of the faces Raywood presents. "His biggest talent is his disarming-ness," says Gil Garfield, a West Hollywood painter who has known Raywood for more than fifteen years. "He has an ability to make you feel immediately comfortable, that he's intensely interested in whatever you have to say. He makes you feel totally at ease. In twenty minutes you find yourself telling him things you'd only tell someone after knowing them a long time." The intimacies go the other way, too. The designer is adept at that most beguiling of gambits: the admission of vulnerability. Heartbreaks, a bad knee, reliance on pain pills—he speaks of them with pleading sincerity, sometimes hinting at more ominous difficulties in the not-too-distant past. "He seems sensitive, fey, almost beaten down," says a Westside businessman. "He seems like a victim, so you trust him."

The Granville Towers, which turned condo in the 1980s, were ideal for Raywood: a raffishly elegant apartment house. The designer had filled his unit—owned by the stylist Estee Stanley, who conceived the look of the Olsen twins and co-founded the women's clothing line Miss Davenporte—with exquisite things. The living room was dominated by a sofa and chairs created by the turn-of-the-century Viennese modernist Josef Hoffmann.

The master suite was papered in parchment, with a big pile of pillows where Giselle slept and a bed topped by a duvet cover from Pratesi. Meals were served on a shagreen dining room table. When guests were present, they pulled their leopard-print chairs up to place settings of Christofle silver in the "Cluny" pattern typically paired with yellow "Pompeii" china by Puiforcat, a line discontinued so long ago that a single plate, much less a set, is a rarity. In nearly every room specimen orchids vied with glass bowls of peonies. The most coveted spots, however, were reserved for framed photographs of the household's twin muses. The model and actress Marisa Berenson—grandniece of art historian Bernard Berenson and granddaughter of fashion innovator Elsa Schiaparelli—was, the designer told everyone, his best friend. As for Raywood's late mother, Ethel—herself an interior designer—she was the most elegant woman her son had ever known. She taught him everything.

By late September Raywood had been living at the Granville for two months, all the while dodging merchants and service providers and failing to exhibit much concern regarding the central fact of his tenancy: He had yet to pay Estee Stanley a security deposit or the $5,000 monthly rent, putting him $15,000 in arrears. It was sticky, but so was so much else about his life—and anyway, getting in had been a cinch. On a Friday in late July he and his realtor had met Stanley and her agent at number 61. Raywood was a bit coy, providing a credit report that did not contain a Social Security number, making a vetting of his financial history difficult. Even so, the match between the designer and the stylist seemed inspired, and they shook hands on a deal. A couple hours later Raywood returned and asked Ricardo Mayorga for the apartment's key, saying he wanted to admit a cleaning crew. Since the doorman had just seen the stylish figure standing before him exchanging pleasantries with the owner, he said sure. On Saturday Raywood moved in. The next week, after his deposit and rent checks bounced, Stanley called the sheriff, but since the new occupant of number 61 was in possession of a lease that he claimed both parties had signed, there was little the authorities could immediately do. What made it so galling was that by every outward appearance Raywood seemed beyond reproach. When Stanley's realtor dropped by the Granville to ask the designer to do the right thing, he still couldn't believe what was happening. "He can't be a scammer," the agent thought. "He's done up the apartment so beautifully."

Raywood made it all appear effortless. People invited him into their lives. It was as if by dint of his grandiosity and society references, he lifted them to the same fabulous plane he inhabited. In the process he distracted them from his true purpose. "Craig doesn't need burglar's tools," says a lawyer who has tracked him for years. "He breaks into your mind. He breaks into your heart. The rest is easy." Despite Raywood's cunning, as autumn 2007 approached his behavior became uncharacteristically erratic. He had been maintaining an illusion for nearly two decades, first in New York and now in Los Angeles, and he was growing exhausted. By material standards, his life had been phenomenal, overflowing with the best and the most expensive of everything. So much of it, however, had been obtained at the cost of others. He had multiple stories to keep straight and countless debts to elude. Just answering the phone or walking to the mailbox was work. The risk of slipping up was always there, especially if, as was presently the case, circumstances were desperate. Still, what occurred the evening of September 28 was unworthy of the designer's talents.

Later Raywood would say that he'd been in a daze, his faculties impaired by one of the prescriptions he was on. He would claim that he couldn't remember what happened. The police report, however, was detailed. Around 6 P.M. the designer walked into the West Hollywood Whole Foods Market. At the meat counter he picked out $43 worth of Spencer steaks and $31 worth of veal chops, yet rather than set the items directly in his cart, he placed them first in a chic leather bag to which he proceeded to add a half-dozen candles, three diffusers, two fragrance atomizers (one called "Heart Spirit," the other "Pure Passion"), and $31.66 of Crossings chocolates. Scattering a few less expensive items atop his haul, the designer headed to the wine department. From a high shelf where the better French vintages are displayed he grabbed a couple Latour-Giraud Meursaults ($44.99 a bottle) and Haut-Surget Bordeaux ($25.99 each), which he put into a cardboard six-pack, shoving it onto the cart's bottom rack, where it was hidden from view. As it happened, security had been watching and alerted the manager before Raywood got in line. During checkout the designer talked up the cashier but never opened his bag or gestured to the wine, paying only for those goods that served as camouflage. When he stepped into the parking lot, a guard handcuffed him. He was escorted back inside to the customer service booth, where he lay down and began to whimper. Once transported to the sheriff's substation, Raywood was booked on felony burglary and thrown into a four-man cell.

The episode created a host of new problems. To begin with, Raywood had to phone Steven Kay, someone he'd been avoiding. Otherwise Giselle, who'd been waiting in the car, would have ended up in the county animal shelter. A few months earlier the designer had borrowed $15,500 from Kay, a 50-year-old realtor who'd once posed nude for *Playgirl*. The loan, which Raywood had secured with two pieces of contemporary art and a Franck Muller wristwatch, was coming due. It was uncomfortable, but he couldn't think of anyone else to call. Then there was the $20,000 bail and the several-hundred-dollar fine for driving with a suspended license, not to mention retrieving his vehicle from impound. It was one thing after another, none of which the designer needed, especially now.

On the morning of October 1, two days after Raywood was released from jail, Judge Richard A. Stone called the case of *Stanley v. Raywood* in the Beverly Hills division of Los Angeles Superior Court. On August 10 Estee Stanley had served the designer with a notice to quit the Granville Towers. A couple of weeks later Raywood filed a handwritten response alleging in downloaded legalese that "landlord's reasons for eviction are not among those set forth in section 17.52..." Nonetheless, the judge ordered Raywood to make a $10,000 payment on October 12 and one of $2,500 on October 22. If he hit both deadlines, he'd be allowed to remain in the Granville until noon on November 30. If he missed either payment, he'd have to fork over a lump sum of $15,000. Raywood was in a bind. Which is not to say that the obstacles were insurmountable.

For someone with Raywood's gifts, Los Angeles was the land of opportunity. He could take advantage of the city's insecurity about fashion and decor. Despite all the wealth in L.A., much of it is temporal—a hit TV series, an executive position at a studio—and at least in matters of interior design, there's more concern with comfort and first impressions than with provenance. That's not true back east, especially in New York, where clients are willing to pay handsomely for important pieces—pieces that are not just beautiful but also have history. Because Raywood billed himself as an arbiter of style favored by Manhattan's old money, because he carried himself with such authority, he was accorded an added respect here. The setup was perfect—he might never run out of new prospects to seduce.

Part 2: Beware of the Biggest Scam Artist

Chen Loft in Hollywood is a vast open space packed with so much furniture and so many *objets* from such a wide range of places and periods that it is less an antiques shop than an emporium of wonders. "Joel Chen wants to own everything, and he's pretty much succeeded," says an admiring competitor. Sleek Robsjohn-Gibbings chairs stand next to giant plaster clamshells. Midcentury brass-and-glass chandeliers mingle with minimalist stainless steel benches, baroque lamps by Tony Duquette, and ivory dragons. In the thirty-five years he has been in business, Chen has done much to define Los Angeles's aesthetic—serious yet playful and unwilling to limit itself to a single look or era. On October 9, three days before his initial payment was due to Estee Stanley, Craig Raywood walked inside.

Over a two-week period Raywood returned to the Loft several times and also visited Chen Vault, a massive new showroom the dealer had opened in Culver City. His client, he told Chen's staff, was a Russian heiress who lived in a gated community off Benedict Canyon. He was, he said, transforming her Italianate mansion into something less gaudy, and Chen's holdings included exactly the right pieces. A Josef Hoffmann *demilune* seating arrangement similar to the one the designer had at the Granville—he wanted it. A Hoffmann "Sitzmachine" armchair—he had to have it, too, along with a circa-1940 patinated leather sofa by Kaare Klint. Because Raywood needed to let the client see the furniture in her home, he asked for and received the courtesy extended to top-of-the-line designers—he could take the pieces out on approval. He secured them by leaving an American Express card number: 3715 377353 52025. Since the antiques business still largely functions on trust and a handshake, Chen's sales associate didn't run the number, putting it instead on file for the date when, if all went well, the purchase would be completed. By October 18 Raywood had taken out 13 items valued at $102,800, and a trucking service had hauled them away.

In a world where a single antique can go for more than $250,000, Raywood's activities did not set off alarms. The more outrageous a designer's demands and the more imperious his demeanor, the more legitimate he seems to be. This is a profession whose major players think nothing of swanning into a place like Chen Loft, a cell phone at their ear and an assistant at their side. Between snatches of conversation with the person on the other end of the line, the tastemaker eyes the merchandise, indicating with a nod and a snap of the fingers the commode or armoire suitable for his multimillion-dollar project. The shopkeeper, aware he is in the presence of money's emissary, puts the pieces on hold. By these criteria Raywood seemed aboveboard.

On October 31 he reappeared at the Vault, where for the first time he met Joel Chen himself. The dealer was put off by the designer's get-up—on this occasion, something from the disco past—but he was impressed by the contents of the portfolio he'd brought along. Multiple magazine and newspaper layouts gave every indication that Raywood was who he claimed to be. The good feeling, however, lasted only a few hours. That evening Chen had a dinner date at Musso & Frank with Stephen Tomar and Stuart Lampert, old-line Los Angeles interior decorators. Conversation consisted largely of shoptalk until Chen mentioned that he was doing business with Craig Raywood. On hearing the name, Tomar and Lampert blurted in unison, "Watch out." Raywood, they said, had ripped off a dozen or so Angelenos, some of them rich clients, the rest in the design business. "Joel," says Tomar, "turned blue."

The next morning Chen's staff ran the American Express card number—it was invalid. By now they also had reviewed a surveillance tape shot during Raywood's visit to the Vault the previous day. It showed the designer reaching into a jewelry display case. Following his departure, an African ring acquired from the estate of the late actor Paul Winfield was missing. In a panic, one of Chen's associates phoned Raywood, who, the dealer says, acknowledged taking the ring and promised to return it and the furniture. That afternoon, however, when Chen and three workers arrived at the Granville Towers to collect the goods, Raywood refused to let them up to number 61. "At that point," says Chen, "I knew my pieces were in jeopardy. I knew it was going to be a long haul. This guy is there to hurt you. He's a professional."

From the black A Bathing Ape knit shirts, black Dior slacks, and unlaced black Converse All Stars that make up his standard uniform to his spiky, graying black hair, Joel Chen comes across as at once suave and defiant, the picture of contemporary L.A. cool. "He can be warm, but he can also beat you up," says a rival. The stance stems in part from the Shanghai-born Chen's experiences in the early '70s when he was getting started. He called on a Melrose Avenue antiques shop only to have the owner refuse him entry. Incensed by what he perceived as an ethnic slight, he borrowed money and launched his own firm. Three decades later he's just as combative.

Chen immediately filed a report with the Culver City Police Department accusing Raywood of stealing his pieces and secured a writ of possession from Los Angeles Superior Court ordering their return. He then hired process server Greig Donaldson, who staked out the Granville Towers from a window seat in the second-floor dining room of a McDonald's across Crescent Heights. Donaldson's intent was to swoop down on Raywood, but after two days of watching, he never saw the designer. Not that this was a surprise. "Craig wouldn't come out," says doorman Ricardo Mayorga. "When he had to walk the dog, he took the rear exit." While Chen slipped Mayorga and his coworkers $20 here and $100 there to report on Raywood's comings and goings, it was to no avail. His flamboyance notwithstanding, the designer knew how to disappear.

As Thanksgiving approached, Chen had talked to enough people to grasp that Raywood's activities were much more extensive than Tomar and Lampert had imagined. After downloading a picture of the designer from a Web site and compiling a list of twenty Angelenos who said they'd been defrauded, Chen drove to the Granville, where for the next hour he nailed homemade "Wanted" posters to telephone poles and tucked them under the wiper blades of parked cars. He then drove to the Pacific Design Center, home to most of the city's design showrooms, where he distributed more posters. By the time he was done, they were nearly everywhere. CRAIG RAYWOOD: BEWARE OF THE BIGGEST SCAM ARTIST & CRIMINAL! roared the opening line. HE IS WORKING IN THE WEST HOLLYWOOD & BEVERLY HILLS AREA.

Several days after the posters went up, Chen received a call from a lawyer representing Raywood, who arranged for the recovery of four of the dealer's pieces; another lawyer negotiated the return of the ring from the Winfield estate. That was the last Chen would hear from the designer. On November 30 Raywood, having made his payments to Estee Stanley, moved out of the Granville Towers. Two more weeks would pass before Chen learned the fate of his most expensive items. Not only had the designer never delivered them to his putative client, but he had hocked them. The best ones, including the Hoffmann seating arrangement, went for $11,500 to South Beverly Wilshire Jewelry & Loan, a deluxe pawnshop where over the years stars in duress have liquidated their possessions. The others went to Uniquities, a Brentwood consignment house that also had acquired a couple of French Empire pieces Raywood had taken out on approval during the same period from Connoisseur Antiques on Melrose Place. Bijan Sotudeh, owner of Uniquities, estimates that he fronted the designer $30,000. Just that easily Raywood had generated more than $40,000, enough money to pay a few creditors, put his furniture in storage, and begin doing what he needed to do next. The designer gave no indication that anything was amiss, and from his perspective nothing was. He had not only survived—he had profited. Before Christmas he and Giselle were gone.

Part 3: Who Is This Guy?

For at least a few hours on a spring evening in 2005, two years earlier, Craig Raywood had been what he said he was—a sought-after interior designer around whom socialites and Hollywood players clustered. Raywood had moved from New York to Los Angeles several months before, and it's not much exaggeration to say he had devoted almost all of his time preparing for this occasion. He had spent, by his account, tens of thousands of dollars transforming his rented West Hollywood bungalow into "a charming romantic cottage, a little Italian, a little English, a little French." Just east of Doheny on Rosewood Avenue, the home sent exactly the right signal, and exactly the right people were now receiving it.

In the living room, HBO Films president Colin Callender was admiring a stunning floral centerpiece. In the master bedroom a clutch of society-page princesses—Wendy Stark (daughter of the late mogul Ray), Amy Lumet (daughter of director Sidney), Angela Janklow (daughter of agent Mort), and Cornelia Guest (daughter of the late style icon C. Z.)—peered into an open closet displaying rack after rack of suits arranged by color and fabric. Standing beneath an Austrian chandelier in the dining room, *West Wing* producer Lawrence O'Donnell rubbed elbows with Paris Hilton's publicist Elliot Mintz. Out back the painter Kenny Scharf and the novelist Bret Easton Ellis stood drinking amid freshly planted rosebushes and angel's trumpet trees as waiters passed trays of sliders. Floating everywhere was Nikki Haskell, the self-styled diet guru and perpetual debutante. Ostensibly the party was for Raywood's houseguest, the New York celebrity photographer Patrick McMullan. In truth it was all about the host. "Craig was very on," says Ryan Tasz, at the time McMullan's West Coast representative. "All these people were Patrick's friends, and Craig wanted to impress them and have them as clients. He was working it. He wanted to show off the house so people would ask, 'Who is this guy?'"

Raywood had left New York, he told most who asked that evening, because he was having difficulties with his boyfriend of sixteen years, Michael Cancellare, a Long Island divorce lawyer. The split was not final—Cancellare paid the first six months' rent at the Rosewood house with a $22,200 cashier's check—but Raywood wasn't looking back. Although he was loath to be specific, the designer occasionally alluded to professional misadventures that had also played a part in his decision to move west. "He had a dark cloud hanging over his head," says Leah Sydney, a freelance journalist who ran into Raywood at parties. Yet the shady aura, far from diminishing Raywood's appeal, further enhanced it, lending an air of mystery to the ambition plainly at work. The Rosewood house was nothing less than a showcase, and the event for McMullan marked the public unveiling of Raywood's campaign to establish himself in his new hometown. As the designer saw it, Los Angeles was a backwater. "Craig thought L.A. was very naive about style," says someone who worked with him early on. Making a splash, however, was only part of what it would take. To get in the game in a big way he needed entrée to the city's Westside bastions of affluence.

Raywood almost immediately met with success. Sanford Spielman, an architect who developed much of the property around Lake Hollywood and considerable chunks of the San Fernando Valley, and his wife, Lois, had been close to Ethel Raywood and had known her son forever. Over the years they'd introduced him to such friends as the painter Gil Garfield. When they heard Raywood was moving to Los Angeles, they put him in touch with some of the city's most status-conscious figures, among them Joe Babajian, who would become the designer's first L.A. client. A realtor with Prudential California, Babajian shared the listing on the $22 million property bought by David and Victoria Beckham. Most years he topped $100 million in sales. In late 2004, the realtor was putting the finishing touches on a mansion of his own in the upper reaches of Beverly Hills. Construction was nearly done, but the interiors had a long way to go, and Raywood went right to work, executing plans and ordering custom-made thermal-glass screens to front the living room fireplace, fabric for upholstering chairs and sofas, and shades for the sconces in the bedrooms and baths. "Craig has wonderful taste," says Babajian. "He knows about different stores and designers and is fun to be with." For a designer new to the city, this was a splendid start. He had landed a client whose job it was to sell palatial homes, many of them in need of decorating.

Raywood's second Los Angeles client was also referred by powerful patrons—Nathan Serota, who made his fortune building shopping malls on Long Island, and his wife, Vivian. During the 1980s, the couple had introduced Raywood to their friend Kenny Solms, the co-creator of *The Carol Burnett Show* and a producer of *The Smothers Brothers Comedy Hour*. Now that the designer was in town, he decided to renew the acquaintance. "Craig called me, and I invited him to lunch," Solms says. A graying 66-year-old, the producer favors dowdy checked sports shirts and nylon track pants and gives the impression of being perpetually distracted. "Craig told me he wanted to break into the design business here," says Solms, "so I took him to my home." A cluttered ranchburger also in the upper reaches of Beverly Hills, the house, like its owner, simply needed a new wardrobe.

"I bet you could jazz this place up," Solms told Raywood, and the two were off, parading through antiques shops on La Cienega and jewelry stores in Beverly Hills. "I found him delightful," says Solms. "He has a great eye." Within weeks the designer had purchased his new client a pair of leather club chairs, Convivio china, Fabergé wine glasses, and a set of Alain Saint-Joanis flatware that went for $8,292.

As he was moving forward on the Babajian and Solms jobs, Raywood met someone who could connect him to a higher and more glamorous stratum of Los Angeles. At a party for Planet Hope, a charity run by Sharon Stone's sister, the designer introduced himself to Vivian Turner, for years the actress's stylist. "He was incredibly charming, acted like he was loaded, and was flawlessly dressed," says Turner. Soon the two were inseparable. "I was his straight wife, and he'd call himself my gay husband," she says. "We talked constantly on the phone. He'd have me over to his house, and we'd get in bed under a Hermès blanket and watch romantic movies. He'd fix me chamomile tea. And he'd always want to buy me presents." One day at lunch with Turner and some of her girlfriends at the Polo Lounge at the Beverly Hills Hotel, Raywood had a salesman and a security guard from the lobby jewelry store—the California outpost of Asprey, gold- and silversmiths to the Prince of Wales—bring over a necklace for Turner to try on. "He wasn't really going to buy it for me," she says. "It was just for show. But a woman always dreams of having something like that happen. He was sealing the deal." The deal was that Turner would introduce the designer to Sharon Stone. He believed the actress was destined to be his new muse.

Part 4: We Got Screwed

So what if Craig Raywood's striving was obvious? Los Angeles rewards the obvious. If he was overly opportunistic, that was also not a problem. Members of his profession may create beauty, but most depend on the largesse of their clients, and the wealthier and more famous the clients, the greater the possibilities. Yet even as Raywood was making inroads, stories were beginning to circulate. Because interior designers are among the few members of the help who enter through the front door, they come to know a homeowner's most private details. They know whether the man of the house obsesses about his stereo components and whether the woman uses a bidet. They have access to information about diets, television viewing habits, sexual proclivities, and most intimate of all, budgets and bank accounts. Implicit in the relationship is an almost priestly level of trust. When that trust is broken, it's not just business—it's personal.

"The gist of it is I paid for stuff that was never delivered," says Joe Babajian. "I kept calling about the damn screens, and he'd say, 'They're in Brooklyn being refinished.' Worse, I ended up paying him for a lot of stuff twice. He charged my American Express card, and he billed me with invoices, and it happened more than once." Several months into the project, Babajian had spent nearly $134,000—by his lawyer's reckoning, some $25,000 of it on double billings—and was angry that the Spielmans had ever introduced him to the designer. Babajian says he would have been more on top of things if his partner hadn't been ill and died two weeks after he moved into his new home. "Craig," he says, "caught me with my guard down."

For Solms, the first inkling that Raywood might be trouble came when he opened a bill from Blackman Cruz, a renowned antiques dealer, to find that he'd paid for a $1,200 bronze studded lamp he never ordered. Raywood admitted that this was his own purchase and the charge was expunged, but Solms was discomfited. Then a more vexing incident occurred. Upon returning from a trip to Europe, Solms discovered that Raywood, without consulting him, had removed most of the contents of his living room, replacing them with extravagant new items. "He said, 'I have a surprise for you,'" says Solms. "I wasn't heavy about it, but I was pissed. I said, 'Craig, you may have meant well, but I want the furniture to go'—and you know what he did? He charged me for its removal." Three weeks later Solms opened his MasterCard bill to find an unexpected $3,000 charge from Neiman Marcus. When he confronted Raywood, the designer pleaded ignorance, but the store informed Solms that Raywood had made the purchase. The $3,000 was for a silk suit he had bought his ex-boyfriend in New York. "He'd overheard me give my credit card number to Blackman Cruz," says Solms, "and went to Neiman Marcus and used it. Neiman's credited my account and Craig returned the suit, but now I knew he was a thief." That Solms never received something he actually had ordered from Raywood, a $5,300 rug for the house's main hallway, seemed almost beside the point.

Vivian Turner also soon found out that she didn't want Raywood in her life. In February 2005, he hosted a birthday party for her—"an intimate party for a few people," she says. Raywood was determined that Sharon Stone come. He invited all the other guests by phone, but for Stone he went to a

boutique paper store, Soolip, and ordered a custom-made invitation executed by a calligrapher. He hand-delivered it to the actress's house. Stone didn't
attend. Several days later he asked Turner to take him to a baby shower for
Stone, telling her he'd already bought her child a present. That's when
Turner started to worry. She told Raywood the occasion was private and that
everyone had to sign a confidentiality agreement. "He was very offended,"
she says. "He said I had 'bad energy.' I was hurt, but it was my fault. I fell for
the attention he showered on me, when all he really wanted to do was get
next to Sharon. He called a few days later and said, 'Can't we start over?'"
Turner said no.

Had the clash with Turner and the problems with the Babajian and
Solms projects been anomalous, they could have been discounted. Design
jobs implode every day, and operators, if not always as ostentatious, are
commonplace in Hollywood. Yet as Solms was the first to realize, Raywood's actions were part of a larger pattern in which moneyed Angelenos
and the businesses that serve them were the targets.

Solms's best source was Raywood's housekeeper. On arriving in the
city, the designer had sought referrals for good help, and Solms had suggested his man. Luis Vargas quickly learned that the Rosewood bungalow was
practically under siege. Not long after Raywood moved in, he installed a
$1,729 video surveillance system. To some, this strengthened the impression
that he was concerned about threats from back east. But to the housekeeper,
the designer's problems appeared to be local. Raywood would use his monitoring system to avoid the parade of shopkeepers and professionals who
stormed up the walk. If he were not at home, Vargas would open the door
and catch an earful. "Luis told me all of the gossip," says Solms. "He said,
'He owes the dry cleaner. He owes the drugstore. He owes the wine merchant. He owes the dentist.'"

Solms spent several weeks corroborating what Vargas told him. The
manager of Du Vin, a small, elegant West Hollywood shop that specializes
in French wine, told him that Raywood had ripped off $800 worth of mer-
chandise, including a case of Château Lafite's Duhart-Milon. "He came in
and said he was throwing a party for Sharon Stone—like we'd be impressed,"
says Robert MacMillan. "He wrote us a check and then returned a few days
later, before we'd received notification that the first check was bad, and
wrote us another one. It was bad, too." The owner of Mickey Fine Pharmacy
in Beverly Hills said Raywood had scammed him as well. "He came in and
told us he had just moved to town, and it was great to find such a good

pharmacy," says Jeff Gross. "He had a smooth story. He dropped the names of regular clients. He told us his credit card had been misplaced, and he was waiting to get insurance, so we opened a house account for him. He may have made one payment, but he never paid us another cent." The drugstore was out $2,172. Helene Cohen Hale, a sales associate at Gearys Beverly Hills who'd known Raywood in New York, offered a similar tale. "He got Buccellati silver and William Yeoward wine glasses," she says. "He had a house account he didn't pay and an AmEx that was no good. Afterward he had the nerve to come in with Giselle like nothing had happened. I said, 'Craig, you have embarrassed me in my place of work.' He had no shame." The loss was just over $10,000.

Solms also uncovered an incident in which Raywood had turned violent. It involved an encounter with Chung Sun Sohn of Artistic Hand Laundry, where the designer took his high-thread-count linens. According to the sheriff's report:

> Raywood entered the cleaner and wanted to pick up his cleaning. Sohn said that over the course of several months every check that Raywood has given them…has bounced… Sohn said he went into a drawer behind the counter and produced several bounced checks… Sohn said Raywood became upset at the sight of the bounced checks and attempted to grab the checks from his hand. Sohn said when he tried to pull away from Raywood's grip Raywood punched him in the face.

The litany went on. Raywood had taken Doheny Cleaners, which pressed his suits, for $2,741; Connect Television, which installed his flat-screen sets, for $1,759; and Dr. Phillip Gorin, a Brentwood dentist, for $2,700 of oral surgery. When the six months of prepaid rent on the Rosewood house came to an end, the designer stiffed his landlord, Joel Ring. For Solms, however, the most astonishing bit of news concerned the party Raywood threw to introduce himself to the city's glitterati. "When the night ended, Craig went into his bedroom and closed the door even though he hadn't paid the chef and waiters, who were still cleaning up," says Patrick McMullan, the guest of honor. "They had worked for him before, so they figured they'd get their money the next day. A month later a friend called and said, 'You're not going to believe what happened. Craig never did pay them.' I'd always liked Craig. I thought he was funny. But I felt defrauded, too."

The scope of Raywood's activities mesmerized and appalled Solms. Here was a designer of talent. Affected? Yes. Exploitative? Undoubtedly.

Still, you wanted to believe in him. He could be so convincing. He was great company. He seemed to care so much. But quickly a duplicitous person emerged. It was a puzzle. More than that, it was an affront. "I'd like to have sympathy for Craig," Solms says, "but I can't. He's too social. There's too much name-dropping. He uses people. And when I think of his expensive things—if he'd just gone to Bed Bath & Beyond for his sheets, I might have dropped the matter, but the linens from Pratesi rankled me." In the initial flush of his resolve, Solms sat down and wrote Raywood:

> It must be so tedious and exhausting being you. What's it like to know inside that every day and minute of your life you cheat and swindle? ...Are you just immune to all the daily reminders of your lying ways? Do you somehow switch it in your mind and blame everybody else for your deceits and dishonesties? ...Do you think we're all naive and are yours for the taking?

Solms ultimately decided against mailing the letter. It felt like a futile gesture. Instead, in concert with Joe Babajian, he put together an event that became known as the "We Got Screwed by Craig Raywood Party."

The gathering, which was a cross between a support group meeting and a strategy session, convened late in the afternoon of July 28, 2005, in the conference room of Babajian's Prudential California office in Beverly Hills. Among the victims attending were Mason Citarello, chef at Mason Jar Cafe (a West Hollywood restaurant that had catered several Raywood events); Citarello's lawyer; a couple of antiques dealers; Jeff Gross of Mickey Fine; the proprietors of Du Vin and Doheny Cleaners; Dr. Phillip Gorin; and the designer's landlord, Joel Ring.

The session started off with people competing to top one another with tales of outrage and woe, but as the talk turned to what they might do, the enthusiasm dissipated. To a person, the group's members agreed that if they went public, it would be mortifying. They would be forced to reveal themselves as dupes who'd been taken in by no more than some fancy talk and a confident demeanor. Those in the design business were especially fearful of exposure: They wanted to avoid anything that reflected badly on their stock-in-trade—their images. The lawyer said they could band together in a class action suit, but the results would be uncertain. "I got the sinking feeling," says Babajian, "that there wasn't anything we could do." Adds Solms, "Raywood relies on attrition. He knows that you'll get worked up, but he counts on the fact that you'll fade away." Still, no one was ready to surrender. They had all been victimized in a peculiarly unsettling way. Unlike a mugger, Raywood had taken more than their money—he had violated their faith.

As for Raywood, he seemed vaguely cognizant that he'd made some mistakes, yet he was unwilling to assume responsibility for them. "He'd call me," says Solms, "and say, 'I know there have been things we've disagreed about and that you might find my behavior not what you think it should be, but I really love you, not just as a client but a friend.'" His problems, Raywood felt, stemmed not from his actions. Rather, they resulted from the inability of most people in Los Angeles to appreciate his refined sensibilities. "I think there are some jealousy issues," he would say. As a consequence, Angelenos persecuted and conspired against him. They didn't understand him. Worse, some of them were saying things that undermined the designer's most cherished possession—his own image. But he knew how to deal with that.

"When we'd talk," says Solms, "he'd make these slightly threatening jokes. He'd say, 'I'd be careful what you say about me because your house might burn down with you and that housekeeper in it.'" Raywood made the same type of comment to Vivian Turner. After the stylist told a friend that the designer was a "scam artist," thereby nixing an invitation to the GLAAD awards banquet, she says he left a message with her answering service. "He said I better keep my mouth shut, because he had way more money than me and a lot meaner dogs—like he had the power to ruin me. I took it as a death threat."

Part 5: The Swan

Several weeks after the "We Got Screwed" meeting, Craig Raywood walked into the Haworth Institute in Beverly Hills for a consultation with the founder, Dr. Randal Digby Haworth. A plastic surgeon who starred in *The Swan*, Fox's extreme body makeover series, Haworth approved of Raywood's buttery cashmere sweater and his Tod's driving shoes worn without socks. Raywood, in turn, was impressed by the doctor's swept-back locks, English manners, and Pirelli sneakers. "Oh, I've got a pair of those," the designer said. That Raywood liked to carry a portfolio of magazine clippings and that Haworth had a portfolio of his own—with articles from *Vogue* and *People*—open on the waiting room table made what followed all but inevitable.

Raywood didn't like the way he looked anymore. His face was too puffy, his chin too droopy, and his belly straining too noticeably against the fabric of his fitted shirts. He wanted Haworth to do something—now. Because a mutual friend had introduced the designer to Haworth, and because the doctor's experience told him that when a man wants plastic surgery, it's best to act before the impulse passes, he promised to get him right in. "We generally have set rules," says Haworth, "but our rules were bent. We accepted payment that was rendered without confirming the source of the funds. We usually have a two-week window, but we took a check from him five or six days before surgery." That was September 12, 2005.

Five days later Raywood underwent a seven-hour procedure that included facial sculpting, multiple-site liposuction, and a tummy tuck—the works. That evening he returned to Rosewood and the care of two female nurses from Majestic Recovery Retreat, a firm that typically treats postop plastic surgery patients at the Hotel Angelino in Brentwood but also offers in-home services. From the outset nothing went right. Although Raywood was undoubtedly in pain ("He looked like the Mummy," says one of the nurses), he behaved, by all accounts, abominably. "He was a nightmare," says a friend who dropped by to check on his progress. "He cursed at the nurses. He threw pill bottles at them." At eleven o'clock on the second night of his convalescence, Raywood called Haworth to complain that the nurses were destroying his valuable stemware and to demand he locate a male nurse to replace them. "He's screaming, a total prima donna, like out of a Sidney Sheldon novel," says Haworth. "How can you find a male nurse at that hour?" Scrambling, the doctor located Jim Wade, a big, blond, former law enforcement officer. "He's delicious," the designer later cooed over the phone to Haworth.

Wade looked after Raywood for three days, seeing him through a complication—a neck hematoma—that he believes could have been caused only by the designer's decision to remove his bandages prematurely. "You want to keep pressure on the area," says the nurse. "The first thing I did was re-wrap his head." Raywood healed, and both Haworth and Wade say the operation was a success. "I delivered beyond expectation," says the plastic surgeon. "Everything was beautiful." Adds the nurse, "I compared pictures I saw of Craig before to pictures I saw later—he really changed his looks, like an old gangster who'd changed his appearance."

A week or so after the procedure, Haworth learned that the check Raywood had given him bounced. "Craig said, 'Redeposit it,'" says the doctor. "I never like that. So I went to the bank and discovered the thief in him. The check had been drawn on an account that had been closed six months." When Haworth pressed Raywood, he was unrepentant, maintaining that the hematoma provided sufficient basis to withhold payment. What was occurring began to sink in. "You slowly realize you've been conned," says Haworth. "It's like Elisabeth Kübler-Ross's five stages." His loss was $18,272. Majestic Recovery was having a similar experience with Raywood. "He said our nurses were incompetent," says the firm's manager, Ruzica Leskovar. "He's very clever. He'd planned it all along." She was out $1,181.

Altogether the designer had conned more than $19,000 in medical treatment. According to Jim Wade, Raywood was pleased with the results. In fact, he praised Haworth's skills. "He said, 'I don't like the asshole,' but then said, 'He does very good work.'"

Part 6: To Court

The worst thing about getting scammed is that on the deepest level the victims believe it was their fault. Why didn't they see it coming? How could they have trusted the guy? Shame, blame, embarrassment, depression—the innocent experience the emotions associated with the guilty. Hold them inside and they'll fester. Let them out and you risk a scene. By late 2005, Craig Raywood's victims were starting to accost him on the streets. The owner of Du Vin spotted Raywood in his car and pounded on the window. Joe Babajian's new boyfriend got into a shouting match with the designer outside a West Hollywood nightclub. Then there was Haworth.

Several months after operating on Raywood, Haworth strolled into the Little Door, a 3rd Street restaurant where the designer enjoyed hanging out. "It's like you're in Morocco, a place I happen to be partial to," Raywood liked to say. As the doctor was waiting for his date, he spotted Raywood at the bar and walked over. "Craig looked me up and down and said, 'Oh, how are you?' I said, 'Not so good since I see you. You owe me money.' He said, 'What about my scars?'" At this Haworth exploded: "I don't give a fuck about your scars. Go screw yourself, you cocksucker." The doctor then stormed off, but any satisfaction he felt was short-lived. The encounter left him shaken. "I've never said that to a patient before," he says. "I'm sorry I didn't come up with an Oscar Wilde retort." Exactly so. Even when the designer's victims confronted him, they often felt like fools.

Raywood, on the other hand, was unflappable. "The guy has zero remorse," says Haworth. "He did what he did to me with the cool calculation of a serial killer. He's a sociopath." Robert Burnside, a realtor who worked with the designer during this period, uses a different analogy. "Craig's a vampire," he says, "and L.A.'s culture is tailor-made for him. He preys on people who think they have style. He sneers at them behind their backs. Getting their money is like getting their blood. It's thrilling for him."

The only possible source of relief was civil litigation, and on December 14, 2005, when Haworth sued Raywood for $25,000 in Los Angeles Superior Court, the lawsuits began. Since most of the designer's victims had been taken for relatively minor sums, they were forced to file in small claims court. Over time everyone from Kenny Solms and Joe Babajian (who ultimately assessed his losses at $7,500) to the proprietors of Mickey Fine Pharmacy, Doheny Cleaners, Connect Television, Majestic Recovery, and a number of other businesses, among them International Flooring, Quatrain antiques, Jean De Merry antiques, Blackman Cruz, and LA Caractere Jewelry, filled out the appropriate forms and submitted them to the court clerk.

It was the start of a long and tedious process. In small claims court plaintiffs and defendants, all operating without counsel, can repeatedly delay hearings, a tactic at which Raywood proved excellent. Hiding behind his home security system, the designer made it almost impossible for process servers to deliver the necessary papers. On those occasions when he was served, he sought continuances, asserting that a nagging knee injury had incapacitated him. "I will be recovering from surgery then out of state," he wrote on February 2, 2006, to avoid appearing in the matter of *Solms v. Raywood*. The designer couldn't duck every date, but even when he appeared, he seemed immune. Sauntering into the Beverly Hills Courthouse, Los Angeles's main forum for celebrity justice, Raywood was so tailored and coiffed that he turned the heads of county employees otherwise inured to A-list litigants. Female clerks begged him for fashion and grooming advice, jotting down his tips and posting them on their computers. "Cologne— wonderful," wrote one, specifying the name of Raywood's scent and the store where it was sold: "Barneys, A La Nuit, Serge Lutens." When the designer actually faced a judge and lost—as he did in the matter of *Majestic Recovery v. Raywood*—he countersued. The nurses from Majestic, he claimed, were incompetent, and he'd been forced to fire them and hire someone else.

The sole encounter with the legal system that Raywood couldn't finesse involved his landlord. On January 6, 2006, Joel Ring had served him with a three-day notice to pay back rent on the Rosewood house. When the designer failed to meet the deadline, Ring's counsel filed an unlawful detainer motion, and on February 21 the two parties met in the Beverly Hills division of Los Angeles Superior Court. Raywood told Judge Richard A. Stone, who was getting his first look at the designer, that the dispute had little to do with money. It was about sex. "I've been harassed for the past eight months in this home," he said. His lawyer elaborated: "Mr. Ring had a crush on Mr. Raywood. Mr. Raywood would not reciprocate." The implication was unmistakable—the landlord's actions were retaliatory. That the 40-year-old Ring, who suffers from a degenerative neurological disorder and is confined to an electric scooter, could have sexually tormented anyone seemed absurd, and the judge didn't buy it. Nor did he buy the other argument advanced by Raywood's counsel: Because his client had eventually attempted to make good on his back rent, he should be allowed to stay. "There's no gray," said the judge. "When he gives you a three-day notice, so long as the particulars are on the notice...you've got to tender. If you don't, you're out."

On the morning of March 16 a crowd of Raywood's victims stood outside the Rosewood Avenue house as two Los Angeles County sheriff's deputies pulled up to evict the designer. When Raywood, dressed in a blue bespoke shirt and carrying crutches, emerged with Giselle, the group broke into applause. "There were a dozen of us cheering," says Claudia Sanchez of Petrossian café, who says Raywood stiffed her for $1,200. "It felt awkward, but I finally felt a little justice." Raywood did not acknowledge the throng. He climbed into the driver's seat of a Lexus SUV and headed to the nearby L'Ermitage, where he checked into a $425 room. But the experience was horrible. To the designer the Rosewood property had come to represent so very much.

"There is a difference to me between a home and a house," Raywood would later say. "Being that I was leaving a life, my whole life in New York, I wanted to make it as comfortable, as beautiful, as to represent what I do, what the gift God gave me... I took care of that home. I made that house into a very special place with a lot of love and a lot of caring." Never mind that he had missed several months' rent—to him a technicality. His dream had been stolen from him, and he had no doubt whom to blame. His former landlord, the designer was soon informing friends, had tried to ruin him, and he would be sorry.

Part 7: The Art of Living

Whether it was chutzpah, delusion, or a combination of the two, Craig Raywood betrayed no outward signs of being chastened by all that had gone on during his first 18 months in Los Angeles. Within weeks of being evicted from his West Hollywood bungalow, he'd installed himself in the nearby Isola Bella Apartments, a luxurious faux-Mediterranean complex. The truth, however, was that as the summer of 2006 began, Raywood was struggling. He'd gotten into the Isola Bella only because a friendly merchant had co-signed the lease, and while a few small jobs were in the offing—redecorating an apartment in Hollywood, reupholstering a chair for a friend in Beverly Hills—for the most part the designer had been reduced to filing insurance claims and peddling. He had collected $29,200 from Chubb insurance for two wristwatches (a Bulgari and a Cartier) he'd reported missing. He was also selling timepieces online. "Here are 2 attached pics. 18 K Breguet," he wrote in an e-mail to two prospective buyers. It was all depressing, and Raywood, who was in therapy, on some level realized as much. He enrolled in an online dating service, declaring in his profile, "I am a very loyal person. Once you are my friend I will protect you always." He joined Debtors Anonymous but attended only a few sessions, saying, "I got out of it what I thought I needed to." His psychiatrist had him on 40 milligrams a day of the antidepressant Lexapro and doses of the antianxiety drug Klonopin.

It was at this moment that Raywood thought of how to get back on top: He would become a television personality, dispensing design and entertainment advice. This, after all, was Los Angeles. Not only were many home improvement shows in development in Hollywood, but the designer's public persona—so cultivated, so assertive—was made for TV. For all its glamour, interior design is a difficult business. Impossible clients. The knowledge that you'll never be as rich as the people you work for. To be paid to talk about the craft as opposed to practicing it is something even the best would leap at. For someone in Raywood's position, such a gig would have been a godsend. "He was looking to see if I could help him cross over and become on-air talent," says Tom Marquardt, an ICM agent who took a meeting with the designer. "He wanted to be a star. He was definitely charismatic."

Throughout the first weeks of July, publicists and advisers called on Raywood at the Isola Bella. "What Craig wanted to do was create a brand out of himself," says Boden Stephenson, a business consultant who agreed to be his manager. "My job was to get him press, work on a book deal, and ultimately get him on TV." The goal was to land Raywood a spot on either HGTV or Bravo's interior decorating competition series, *Top Design*. Stephenson came up with a plan for what amounted to a high-profile audition, booking Raywood into an auditorium at the Pacific Design Center to give a demonstration of floral arrangements and table settings. He engaged a film crew, set August 2 as the date, and billed the event, which was open to the public, "The Art of Living with Craig Raywood."

A week before the big day, Raywood and his whippet, Giselle, walked into Privé, a salon that occupies the old Spanish Kitchen restaurant space on Beverly Boulevard and counts Christina Ricci and Uma Thurman among its patrons. The designer occasionally had his hair cut there, but this time he also received an eyebrow waxing and eyelash tinting. As Giselle roamed, Daniel McFadden, who runs the in-house makeup concession, taught Raywood how to use a $350 apparatus for spraying on foundation. Many TV personalities swear by the device, and since Raywood was about to join their ranks he decided he had to have one. The tab for the visit came to $771, which the designer waved off, telling a receptionist as he made for the door that his manager would take care of it.

That same week producer Kenny Solms eased into a booth at Jan's Restaurant Coffee Shop, just east of the Beverly Center. Solms, the first Angeleno to raise doubts about Raywood, was there to confer with Greig Donaldson, the process server, who had been recommended by one of the many plaintiffs the producer had met outside small claims court in Beverly Hills. Merchants and clients, laborers and professionals, those suing the designer had begun to form friendships built around their frustration at the difficulty of bringing him to justice. "We can't get him served," Solms told Donaldson, "so we can't get him into court. But I know where he's going to be next week." Solms then pushed a list of names and phone numbers across the table. By August 2, Donaldson had 12 clients, among them realtor Joe Babajian, dentist Phillip Gorin, and Jeff Gross, owner of Mickey Fine Pharmacy.

"The Art of Living with Craig Raywood" attracted an audience of 75, mostly women from the Westside, who watched for an hour as the designer put together beautiful centerpieces and unveiled elaborate place settings, all the while keeping up an informed patter. The verdict on Raywood's performance was mixed. One person in attendance found him "extremely polished," but Peter Fitzgerald, who has directed documentaries on Alfred Hitchcock and Joan Crawford for Turner Classic Movies and who was supervising the crew shooting the event, found him "condescending." Afterward, a receiving line formed. When the last person reached Raywood, he asked Fitzgerald to turn the camera away.

"Oh no, this can't be good," said Raywood.

"You're served," said Greig Donaldson, handing the designer a thick envelope.

Fitzgerald at first felt bad for Raywood. The feeling didn't last. "He'd asked me to front my crew's expenses," says the director. "I never do that. But he touted himself as a bigwig, and because a friend of mine was the go-between, I said OK. I did a favor that ended up being a $1,300 kick in the pants." Fitzgerald sued Raywood in small claims court, and he wasn't the only new plaintiff. "Craig's manager never showed up at Privé to pay us," says Daniel McFadden. "I confronted Craig, and he told me, 'Oh, I had no idea.' He acted like he was stunned. He gave me a credit card number over the phone. I put it right through, and it was declined. I tried it again, and it was declined. But it finally went through. In a couple of days we got a call from the credit card company saying he was disputing the charges and wasn't going to pay. The guy is a little Mozart of deception."

Raywood didn't appear fazed by any of this. In September he recorded a test for a podcast, holding forth on the basics of pulling together a room. He also booked a session with Paul Gregory, a head-shot photographer. Most of Gregory's clients are actors for whom his $595 fee is a major investment. Raywood, however, seemed different. "He brought props—a chair he said was worth $100,000, flowers, and candles," says Gregory, who works out of a studio in his Laurel Canyon home. "He also brought a man bag filled three inches thick with $100 bills. I thought, 'Holy cow! This guy doesn't need money. Yeah, I could get used to this.'" The photographer shot Raywood alone and with Giselle, and the results were exceptional. The designer looked a decade younger than his 57 years. Afterward, the two sat around talking. "You need drapes," Raywood soon exclaimed. The remark struck Gregory as so full of concern for his unformed design sensibilities that when Raywood asked for his American Express card number, its expiration date, and the security code so he could buy the necessary fabric and supplies, he thought, Why not?

Raywood invited Gregory to dinner at Falcon, the Sunset Boulevard celebrity hangout. "He talked about Marisa Berenson after she did *Cabaret*, about so-and-so's yacht, and the Hamptons," says Gregory. "He was very East Coast and upper-crust. I'm successful, but I'd never met anyone like him. I thought he could be my mentor." Following several nights out, Raywood offered Gregory work as a consultant. To get him on the payroll, he needed his Social Security number. Soon after, Raywood added himself to Gregory's credit card account. On September 16, using Gregory's information, he opened a new American Express account under the name CR Designs. The number: 3715 377353 52025. The photographer says he was unaware of Raywood's actions until he received a call from American Express alerting him to unusual charges on the recently activated card. There were more than $50,000 in purchases, including clothes from Bergdorf Goodman and a stay at the Montage resort in Laguna Beach. Gregory told the company he knew nothing about the new card and asked to be notified on his home phone to verify any further transactions. At that moment Raywood was trying to use the card. Half an hour later, says Gregory, the designer, accompanied by Giselle, appeared at his house. "He said, 'Paul, don't do this.' I said, 'It's too late. I've done it.' While Craig was there, the dog pooped on my lawn. Craig was so mad he picked the poop up and threw it in my garage, then left."

Soon after, the photographer received an email from Boden Stephenson, Raywood's manager:

> Paul...if you're going to do business with the big boys, you need to grow some balls and not freak out over 5 digit Amex bills... You have done something beyond the pale by cutting off [the] cards... You have done something that has set in motion what will be a series of events that will leave you puking in the toilet from fear...

Eventually, says Gregory, Raywood returned the merchandise, which reduced the charges by half. Still, American Express stripped Gregory of his card.

Stephenson says the American Express incident led him to quit, derailing Raywood's Hollywood hopes. "Craig's ethics and sense of morality are off," he says. So too, he's convinced, is the designer's sense of reality. On some days, he says, Raywood sat in front of the makeup device he'd taken from Privé, applying foundation even though no filming was scheduled.

Part 8: To Court Again

By December 2006, Craig Raywood was at an impasse. He had alienated old friends and burned new acquaintances. He was the object of numerous lawsuits. His bad knee, long a source of unbearable pain, was deteriorating. Yet when he checked into Cedars-Sinai Medical Center for knee surgery, he was as imperious as ever. Right away he redecorated his private room, replacing the institutional sheets with high-thread-count linens, laying down an earthtone rug, and hanging a couple of minimalist paintings. He imported his own silverware, dishes, and crystal. Breakfasts were catered by Jerry's Famous Deli and lunches and dinners by Sweet Lady Jane. As for pastries, there was a box from Boule, a patisserie he was devoted to. Best of all, at the request of his psychiatrist, the hospital agreed to let Giselle stay with him. To walk and care for the dog, the designer hired the service Citizen Kanine.

After the operation Raywood developed an infection, and he required eight weeks of in-home care. As had occurred following his plastic surgery in 2005, Raywood didn't pay his caregivers. "We helped him get dressed, helped him take his medication, helped him learn to walk again, and he conned us out of $15,000," says Earl Sherman, vice president of finance at AAA T.L.C. Health Care of Encino. "He convinced our people he was affluent, but when the check came, it was no good." Raywood had his reasons. AAA, he said, had ruined some of his pricey sheets. "I am very unhappy about certain things," the designer told the firm's lawyer during the run-up to the inevitable lawsuit. "I am aware of other things that transpired which I do not know whether you are." There was also another new litigant: Citizen Kanine. "He kept telling me he'd pay," says Will Bratten, who walked Giselle every day for several weeks. "He was so sincere, I believed him." Citizen Kanine was out $1,800.

Once he recovered, Raywood focused his energies on the individual he'd come to hold responsible for everything that wasn't right in his life— Joel Ring, the landlord who had evicted him from the Rosewood bungalow. Several months earlier the designer had sued Ring in Santa Monica Superior Court for $2,875,000. The grounds were various and the allegations devastating. Raywood claimed "unjust enrichment," asserting that Ring had profited from the thousands of dollars in improvements the designer had made to the Rosewood house. He charged that Ring had extended, then retracted a right of first refusal to purchase the property. He contended that Ring had repeatedly ignored repair requests. As a consequence, leaks had destroyed one-of-a-kind drawings. He also revived the explosive claim of sexual harassment that he had raised in his 2006 eviction hearing. The trial was set for April 25, 2007.

At the same time Raywood was seeking satisfaction from Ring, the dozen merchants, antiques dealers, and former clients who'd filed suits in small claims court were losing patience. They had viewed Greig Donaldson's encounter with Raywood at the Pacific Design Center as a victory. But the designer, in the aftermath of his knee operation, now had a legitimate reason to seek a delay. "...Have developed a bacterial infection which will take 30 days of treatment," he wrote to the Beverly Hills court on December 5,

2006, "then another knee surgery—need a minimum of 60 days." On February 2, 2007, a group of plaintiffs petitioned the court:

> It is with utter outrage that we who are the plaintiffs, who have been owed the monies, can't ever get our day in court. And when we do...the [defendant] isn't there... In some cases this stalling tactic and rubber-stamped extensions have been going on for years. When will this charade end?

In response to the petition, which appeared over the names of old hands like Solms, Babajian, and Gorin and new complainants like Privé's McFadden, the court re-summoned Raywood. A hearing was set for April 25, 2007.

Faced with being on the docket in two courtrooms on the same day, Raywood chose Santa Monica. After all, if he prevailed against Ring, he might become a millionaire. As for the proceedings in Beverly Hills, the designer believed he could provide sufficient rationale for his absence. "Craig Raywood has been under my care for the past year for management of chronic pain with intermittent exacerbations," Dr. Howard Rosner wrote on the designer's behalf. "His current medical status is guarded; he is unable at the present time to engage in any jury, court dates, or depositions..." Another doctor, Andrew S. Wachtel, wrote that Raywood's use of painkillers prevented him from acting in his best interest: "It is...my opinion that...dilaudin...renders a person incompetent to testify on their own behalf."

When Judge Richard A. Stone, who had now presided over several cases involving the designer, noted that Raywood seemed to have genuine medical concerns, the plaintiffs who'd assembled in the Beverly Hills courthouse groaned. It was a frustrated and angry crowd. It was also a crowd wise to Raywood's ways. "Kenny Solms stood up and told Stone that Raywood was not only well enough to be in court," says Gorin, "but that he was in court in Santa Monica at that precise moment suing his landlord." At this, Stone issued a $10,000 warrant, phoned the court in Santa Monica, and said loudly enough for everyone to hear, "Pick him up." The judge presiding in Santa Monica, though, released the designer on his own recognizance.

Craig Raywood v. Joel Ring began with David Denis, the designer's lawyer, summoning witnesses to attest to the work his client had done at Rosewood. Denis then called Raywood. The designer was on the stand for nearly three days and told a story in which he cast himself as put-upon and misunderstood. Ring, he said, had rented him a house so unready for occupancy that he'd been forced to check into L'Ermitage. But once he moved in, he had created a masterpiece. "I purchased sinks, toilets, towel bars, toilet paper holders, I believe shelves...shower hose," he testified. He got his fixtures from such smart suppliers as Altmans and Davis & Warshaw and his limestone tile from Walker Zanger. Painters glazed the dining room walls and lacquered those in the bathroom. Despite all his efforts, things were never right. The toilet overflowed in the guest quarters. The roof leaked. The landlord didn't care. Worst were the unwanted attentions. They began with Ring trailing him "like a puppy." Then, Raywood said, the landlord became more aggressive:

> He would come by on his wheelchair to the French doors... I had to go to work. And I said... "I have to go take a shower." He said, "Can I come and watch you," and my response was, "You know what Joel, I don't even watch myself take a shower, so I don't think you're going to be allowed that."

The harassment persisted. "I would get up," Raywood testified, "have coffee...have a towel wrapped around my waist, and you know, he would be there... And then I started locking the gates." Over dinner one night at the Little Door on 3rd Street, Raywood said, Ring went too far. He kissed him. When the designer resisted further advances, the recriminations began: testy dealings, ignored repair requests, a rent increase, and finally eviction.

Tim Lane, Ring's lawyer, went at Raywood hard. He paid special attention to the dinner at the Little Door, eliciting the admission that the designer had sent Ring mixed signals, driving the landlord to the restaurant and picking up the tab for a bottle of splendid burgundy ("It was Gevrey-Chambertin, to be exact"). The two men, Raywood conceded, had enjoyed a lovely meal during which they'd sat next to each other and had exchanged intense feelings. "I wear my heart on my sleeve," the designer said.

With his client watching from the defense table, Lane then took Raywood in a different direction.

"How tall are you, sir?"

"Six feet tall."

"And how big is Mr. Ring?"

"I never measured him, but he's shorter than I."

"Like around five-five?"

"If you say so."

"You notice that Mr. Ring has a disability, right?"

"Yes, of course I do."

"You observed that Mr. Ring has trouble maneuvering with his muscles, right?"

"Yes."

"Is he very fast?"

"No."

"How did Mr. Ring get at you to kiss you at the Little Door?"

"He just leaned over."

"What did you say after Mr. Ring kissed you?"

"I kind of made light of it."

Lane's point was unavoidable. True, Ring was infatuated, but Raywood had not only done little to dissuade him, he'd led him on. The lawyer then secured the concession that in return for the initial improvements the designer had made to the Rosewood house, Ring had waived the rent for a month and a half. Moreover, the lease stipulated that any additional work had to be approved in writing. Raywood acknowledged that the landlord had never given such approval. Lane also established that Raywood had been accorded a ten-day period during which he could have purchased the home. The lawyer concluded by taking the designer through the circumstances of his eviction, winning the admission that he had not paid his rent and that the matter had already been adjudicated.

Although the trial took five days, the jury needed only two hours to return a verdict in favor of Ring. The judge ordered Raywood to pay his former landlord's $125,727 in legal costs. David Denis has no doubts why his client lost: "The court felt sorry for Ring because he's a handicapped guy." Tim Lane is just as certain why his client prevailed: "Craig Raywood was my best witness. He was so outrageous and pompous, the jurors could tell he was trying to take advantage of Joel."

Raywood's defeat in court was the first in a new series of indignities. For one, he lost a job he had been bragging about: a redesign of the art deco Temple of the Arts on Wilshire Boulevard. "I am renovating and restoring the theater," he told people, "and I'm also designing a sanctuary that I'm very excited about." Raywood's role, in fact, was minor, and even then he failed to deliver. The designer didn't pay subcontractors he had hired. "It was a bad experience," says Rabbi David Baron. Around the same time, the painter Gil Garfield, the designer's old friend, publicly denounced him. When someone had attacked Raywood in the past, Garfield had always defended him. "I'd think they're exaggerating," he says. "Craig is so gracious, it couldn't possibly be true. But then there was such a blanket of accusations from too many people to overlook." Specifically, Solms, Babajian, and the interior decorators Stephen Tomar and Stuart Lampert sat Garfield down and told him what had been going on. Not long after the conversation, Garfield spotted the designer at the 3rd Street restaurant Orso.

"He was wearing a shawl," says Garfield, "and when he saw me he tried to hide behind it. I stared right at him like in a silent film, looked at his guests, and said, 'Do any of you know the kind of man you're sitting with? If you knew, you wouldn't be sitting with him. Everybody in this city can tell you what he is really like.' I vilified him. I was so mad and disgusted. My voice was trembling. It all came from hurt over his fakery."

Anyone else would have crumbled, but in the wake of the encounter with Garfield, Raywood sent an upbeat e-mail to his new pal, Steven Kay. A Westside realtor, Kay had already loaned Raywood $15,500, and now the designer was asking for more: "I think that things are beginning to turn around for me... Things are beginning to happen. My head is clear. My focus is on ... I am trying to be out there. I will make it happen. Like the phoenix." This time Kay said no.

A couple of weeks later Raywood wrecked his car. It turned out he had been driving with a suspended license and had a number of outstanding tickets. On July 19, 2007, five months after the owner filed an unlawful detainer complaint against him, Raywood left the Isola Bella.

Part 9: The Prince

It is impossible to say exactly why Craig Raywood turned out as he did, but there are clues. He grew up in Manhattan, living briefly in Miami Beach. Summers were spent in the Catskills, where his maternal grandparents owned a resort. He and his younger sibling were close. "He was a very caring brother, and that's the truth," says Keith Raywood, longtime set designer for *Saturday Night Live* and now a production designer for *30 Rock*. Before Craig turned ten, his parents divorced, and his mother married Shelly Raywood, who was in the garment business. "There was nothing traumatic about it," says Keith, but others aren't so sure. "Shelly was psychologically impotent," says Robert Regni, personal assistant to the heiress Isabel Goldsmith and for years one of Raywood's closest friends. During his teens, Raywood looked to his godmother, Geraldine Lipshie, for guidance. The grande dame of an Upper East Side family, Lipshie adored Craig. "She treated him like a spoiled child," says someone who knew them both.

By every account, the person who loomed largest in Craig's life was Ethel Raywood, his interior designer mother. "She was very pretty, dressed beautifully. She was darling, just a good lady—fun, terrific, what all of us think we are," says an old friend. Yet as much as Craig idolized her, the relationship was fraught. "Ethel didn't approve that he was gay," says Regni. "Ethel was in total denial," says the old friend. "She kept trying to find him girls." Conversely, Craig had trouble seeing his mother for who she was. Although he told everyone that Ethel was a brilliant designer, she was a workaday practitioner who turned out corporate offices and a few homes. "She just wasn't all that talented," says Regni. "Her personality was cold and hard-edged, and so was her design." Betty Ann Grund, the longtime senior fashion editor for *Harper's Bazaar* and for years a friend of Craig's, recalls visiting Ethel's home. "Craig told me that his mom was fabulous, with fabulous jewels," she says. "But she was not fabulous, and the apartment was anything but glamorous." Misunderstood by his mother, yet intent on exalting her, Craig became adept at maintaining illusions. "He had to keep creating an aura of fabulousness," says Grund. "He'd do anything to keep that aura real."

Following graduation from the High School of Performing Arts in Manhattan, Raywood flirted with a singing career (he cut a demo tape of cabaret songs). Soon, though, he drifted into fashion. "During the mid-'70s, Craig used to hang around Seventh Avenue buying couture samples, which he'd sell at a fantastic profit to people looking for one-of-a-kind gowns," says Grund. "He kept an expensive beaded gown by Mollie Parnis under his bed." The leap from frocks to decor seemed natural.

Early on, Raywood's decorating business thrived. He claimed an impressive list of clients, among them fashion designer John Anthony, singer Paul Simon, socialite Denise Rich, and most critical, real estate developer Nathan Serota and his wife, Vivian. Raywood's work on the couple's Park Avenue duplex received an eight-page spread in *House & Garden* in 1982, a heady validation of his talent. Although a Picasso hung in the living room and a Renoir in the master suite, the den—a warren of mohair-upholstered walls, burgundy leather banquettes, and a revolving brushed steel column that served as both sculpture and TV cabinet—attracted the attention. Raywood called the look "minimal opulence," but there was nothing minimal about it. This was the 1980s in all its excess. The Serotas entertained regularly, and after the apartment was finished, they kept Raywood on as a consultant. "He made me feel safe when I was a hostess," says Vivian. "I used to give big parties, and famous people came—Joe Papp, Raul Julia, Mary Tyler Moore, Debbie Allen. I once needed something spectacular for my foyer. This party was for the cast of *Tango Argentino*. The guest of honor was Robert Duvall. I didn't want the usual red-and-black thing. So Craig went to the garment center, bought gold and silver cloth, and created a tent. You came in like you were coming into a tented palace, and photographers snapped your picture."

Raywood played the part of successful designer to the hilt. Friends referred to him as "the Prince." Whether attending the opera or dancing with Marisa Berenson at Studio 54, he expected to be catered to, and he usually was. "We'd go to La Grenouille without reservations," says Martha Kramer, former head of American operations for the fashion house Emanuel Ungaro and at the time a confidante of the designer's. "Craig would say, 'We're hungry. Can you feed us?' They'd end up sitting us at a table next to Oscar de la Renta. Craig was very amusing. People treated him like a pet." Raywood's five-and-a-half-room East Side apartment reflected his high self-regard. Anchored by a futuristic copper-tube coffee table and a French Directoire armchair and lit by an Italian gilt-wood chandelier, the apartment, reported the *New York Times*, was "meant to impress, and it does." As Raywood put it: "It's very rich-looking here. But it's neither old money nor new money. I guess it's my money."

By the 1990s, Raywood had become involved with Michael Cancellare, and his life increasingly revolved around the village of Muttontown in Oyster Bay, where the lawyer owns a home. "Michael played the WASP, Craig the Jew," says Robert Regni. The two began purchasing purebred whippets, one of which they entered in competition. They socialized with theatrical producer Marty Richards, who lived nearby, and Janet Brown, whose Port Washington boutique catered to clients who arrived by shuttle from Manhattan's Regency Hotel. "Craig had excellent taste," says Brown's former business partner, Simone Levitt, widow of Bill Levitt, founder of the giant planned Levittown communities. "He knew the best places to buy anything—always the fanciest and most expensive." The designer also exhibited a penchant for camp. At dinner parties he'd pull up his slacks, don high heels, and strut. "He had the best legs I've ever seen," says Levitt. "The women all envied his legs." Raywood and Cancellare eventually became such a part of Long Island society that they could spend a New Year's Eve with

former Bergdorf Goodman fashion director Robert Burke, costume jeweler Kenneth Jay Lane, the *New York Post*'s Suzy, and couture designer Carolina Herrera at the home of their neighbor, style doyenne C. Z. Guest.

Raywood, though, was living beyond his means. For all of his talent, he hadn't developed the skills necessary to run a business. "Famous designers land big clients," says Regni, but they need "draftsmen and billing processes. Craig didn't have the discipline or temperament." Surrounded by so much wealth, Raywood succumbed to an occupational hazard. "The big thing with designers when they work with wealthy clients is they want to live like their clients, but they can't," says a former friend. "It's an old story." By the late 1980s, the New York civil courts had assessed thousands of dollars in judgments against Raywood. The plaintiffs included Neiman Marcus and Eastern Air Lines, but many were friends. "He took $15,000 in cash from my parents, plus some furniture," says Betty Ann Grund. "They'd hired him to re-cover a few pieces. He told them he needed an advance. My father thought, 'Oh, he's a friend.' We never got any of it back." A couple of years later Grund ran into the designer at a New York bar. "He tried to act like nothing happened," she says. "He came over to where I was having drinks with some people. I said, 'Craig, you're a thief.' He threw a glass of champagne at us."

Raywood's fall was unfortunate, for as a designer he was the real thing. His taste, at first too flashy, had evolved. He'd become enamored of early European modernism, embracing its clean aesthetic. He particularly loved French deco furniture. His floral arrangements, always a strength, had become more subtle and poetic. Talent, however, had never been the issue. Throughout the 1990s, the judgments against him began to add up: Baccarat was awarded $10,859; Reymer Jourdan Antiques, $18,359; the Paul Stamati Gallery, $15,510. He also began to victimize an ever-increasing number of people close to him. "Craig took advantage of me," says Simone Levitt, who hired Raywood to work on her Fifth Avenue apartment. "He designed things for me that were never delivered and never made but that were paid for in advance. He did unpleasant things. He threatened me. I hate to even remember or talk about it."

Of all the intimates Raywood betrayed, Beth Rudin DeWoody took it the hardest. The philanthropist daughter of New York real estate magnate Lewis Rudin, DeWoody was among the designer's best friends. "Beth loved Craig," says Vivian Serota. The two traveled together to the Caribbean and spent weekends at DeWoody's vacation home in the Hamptons. Michael

Cancellare represented DeWoody when she and her husband, Jim, divorced. According to DeWoody, Raywood repaid the years of friendship by bilking her of $20,000 and then taking her cousin, Eric Rudin, for an even greater sum. With Raywood's assistance, Rudin bought two highly collectible Andre Arbus chairs from a dealer in Paris. When, after numerous delays, they finally arrived in New York, Rudin realized they were knockoffs. He contacted the dealer, who told him Raywood had never given her a cent. The designer had pocketed Rudin's payment and sold him fakes. Rudin's attempts to get the district attorney to prosecute Raywood failed. The event, however, changed the way New Yorkers viewed the designer. "When the Eric Rudin thing happened, we knew Craig was out of control," says Martha Kramer. "The Eric Rudin story is famous among people with Craig experiences."

If not for two events, Raywood might have continued to run amok in New York. On June 5, 2003, he walked into Lafayette Antiques at the Warehouse and took out $35,340 of furniture on approval. He secured the pieces, which included a French deco walnut table and chairs and a pair of 19th-century urns, by giving the Upper East Side business a check. Several days later, when the check bounced, Lafayette's owners engaged Marc Bengualid, a lawyer who had an office in their building. A slight 47-year-old who shares a no-frills work space with his father, Bengualid typically practices personal injury and medical malpractice law. Like many who have seen through Raywood, he is indifferent to fashion, inclined to wear off-the-rack suits and birthday-gift ties. He was so offended by the designer's brazenness that he took a step no one else had: He filed a theft report with the New York police and persuaded a detective to telephone Raywood.

"I was always taught that if you create stress, people crack," says Bengualid. "Come at people on 20 fronts, they may catch 18, but they'll miss 2." The call, which Bengualid says "freaked Raywood out," was just his first move. The lawyer also secured a copy of the designer's bank records. "That's what really got my blood boiling," says Bengualid. "The records show that Raywood put a stop payment on the check for the furniture from Lafayette before it was picked up from the warehouse. He had a clear intent not to pay. What more do you need?" On July 11 the lawyer sued Raywood on Lafayette's behalf in New York Supreme Court and served the designer with discovery demands. "He didn't respond to my discovery," Bengualid says. "He would have had to swear through his attorney to the truth. I don't think he could have done that."

307

On July 25, 2003, when the New York Supreme Court awarded a $190,632 judgment against Raywood in a civil suit filed by former clients Eric and Simona Brown, the designer's problems grew worse. The Browns, who had hired Raywood to decorate two residences, alleged that he had defrauded them. "It is my belief," declared Eric Brown, that Raywood "simply took our money without any intention of providing the goods and services...As far as I am concerned [his] actions constituted out-and-out theft, which has cost my wife and me a substantial sum of money...Apparently, this is Raywood's modus operandi..."

On October 24, 2003, Raywood filed for Chapter 7 bankruptcy in New York federal court. In his petition he said he had between 16 and 49 creditors, among them the Internal Revenue Service and the State of New York. He owed $500,000 in back taxes alone. All told, there were $1,100,000 in unsatisfied liens, warrants, and judgments against him and his various companies. Although the judgment in the Brown case played a part, Bengualid believes he forced the action. "I pushed him on criminal and civil fronts, and I wasn't going to give up," says the lawyer. "The only way he had to stop me was to file bankruptcy. My case against him was frozen."

In early 2004, Raywood was hospitalized for several days following a breakdown. A few months later he called Vivian Serota. "He was crying," she says. "He told me he'd broken up with Michael. He certainly didn't tell me anything about other problems. We were in the south of France, and he asked if he could stay in our apartment. I said yes." When the Serotas returned to New York, Raywood told them he wanted to change his life. They gave him $10,000 to help him get on his feet in his new home—Los Angeles. In Los Angeles, he said, he could be a different person. That, of course, is the myth, but the truth is that the city, far from transforming people, does the opposite—it brings out their deepest selves, revealing not who they wish to be but who they are. "Craig Raywood will always be a con artist," says Bengualid. "He finds the human flaws in individuals and attacks them."

Part 10: Justice

On a late December afternoon in 2007, Craig Raywood stood at the corner of Rodeo Drive and Santa Monica Boulevard in Beverly Hills, his face streaked with tears, his chest heaving. Just a few weeks earlier, the designer had fled the Granville Towers, the third Los Angeles residence he'd been forced out of in two years. Many of the homemade "Wanted" posters distributed by antiques dealer Joel Chen before Thanksgiving were still up. It was a rough time. Which is why Raywood had called Bijan Sotudeh, the proprietor of the consignment house Uniquities. The shopkeeper already knew that the ownership of the furniture he'd bought from Raywood the previous month was in dispute, yet he'd agreed to meet because the designer had told him he had nowhere else to turn. "He said he had no money," says Sotudeh, "and that his boyfriend was sick and dying. He said he had to get to New York. I knew he was bad. But I felt so horrible to see a grown man crying. I gave him money."

Raywood flew to New York and on Christmas Eve checked into the Soho Grand Hotel, where Sotudeh had booked him a $434 room. "At least I had the presence of mind to authorize payment for only three nights," says Sotudeh, who thought little more about the matter until mid-January, when he received a call from the hotel's manager. Raywood had remained at the Soho Grand for eight days, running up a $4,327 tab, which the hotel wanted the store owner to make good on. "I ended up paying around $1,500," says Sotudeh. The hotel got stuck for the balance. Says Lizette Nieves of the Soho Grand accounting office: "We now have a case pending against Mr. Raywood."

Raywood spent much of last winter and spring shuttling between Manhattan and Long Island. At a 3,000-mile remove, the designer received only the occasional reminder of the havoc he had wreaked in Los Angeles. One came in a phone call from his friend Steven Kay. December 28 had been the deadline for Raywood to repay his $15,500 loan, and he had missed it. Kay had discovered that the paintings the designer had left to secure the debt were worth little and that the Franck Muller wristwatch was counterfeit. On January 16 Raywood e-mailed Kay, telling him not to worry. He said he had a painting at auction and that he'd send him a check as soon as it sold. Two days later the designer e-mailed Kay again. This time there was no mention of settling up, just a signature kiss-off: "Steven, I am a good person. You know that. Otherwise you would not have done for me what you have, whatever conflict you had. I miss you. Think of you often. Craig, '08."

Raywood would have liked to close the door on everyone else in Los Angeles that easily, but he couldn't. Joel Chen was adamant that the designer be prosecuted for the theft of $102,800 of antiques from his two stores, and in Kirk Newman, the Culver City police detective assigned to the matter, he had found an ally. A Southern California native with graying blond hair, Newman saw the case as emblematic of L.A.'s obsession with image. "What caught my eye," he says, "is that in this world of interior design, of surface and facade, this guy was able to put up a bigger facade, walk among them, and pick their pockets. With these people it's not who they are—but how they are. Here's a con man adept in his trade. You may not like what he did, but you have to appreciate his methods."

Chen wanted fast results, but Newman counseled patience. Yes, a surveillance camera at the dealer's Culver City store, Chen Vault, had caught Raywood reaching into a display case. Yes, a ring that had once belonged to actor Paul Winfield had vanished. Yes, Raywood had hocked the furniture he had taken out on approval, forcing Chen to repurchase his own goods from Uniquities and the high-end pawn shop South Beverly Wilshire Jewelry & Loan. But Newman believed he could nail the designer on more than that. "We can throw a pebble and hit Raywood in the shin," Newman told Chen, "or a baseball and hit him in the forehead."

The baseball was the American Express card number Raywood had given Chen's staff as collateral: 3715 377353 52025. This was the account that Raywood had opened under the name CR Designs but that belonged to Paul Gregory. The head-shot photographer, Newman wrote in his report, "stated that he knew Craig Raywood, but that he did not give him permission to...have an American Express [card] issued in his name." Gregory agreed to testify against Raywood, and the detective took the case to the Los Angeles County District Attorney's Office. On February 29 Judge Robert P. O'Neill issued a $70,000 warrant for Raywood's arrest on three felony counts: for theft of the Winfield ring, for theft of the $102,800 of antiques, and for identity theft. Raywood was no longer running from judgments handed down in small claims court. He stood accused of violations punishable by prison time.

With Raywood in New York, there was little Newman could do. In late June, however, the designer returned to Los Angeles. He had filed another lawsuit against his nemesis, Joel Ring, this time alleging that the former landlord's negligence had caused him to fall several times at the Rosewood house and injure his knee; the designer was seeking $3 million in damages. Raywood was also thinking of resuming business in L.A. and was hoping to renew social ties. He attended a cocktail event at Spago for the Luxury Marketing Council, mingling as if nothing was wrong with at least one merchant he'd scammed. But something was wrong. Antiques dealers and showroom owners were wary, and friends shunned him. Even party girl Nikki Haskell declined the designer's dinner invitation, a sure sign that the city's beau monde had had enough.

On the morning of July 10 Raywood walked into the lobby of 333 South Grand Avenue downtown. He was there for a mediation hearing to resolve his suit against Joel Ring. Waiting for him were Newman and four plainclothes Culver City detectives. As soon as Raywood, dressed in khakis and a blue blazer and carrying an Hermès crocodile bag, approached the check-in desk, he was surrounded and handcuffed.

"You're under arrest," declared Newman.

"Oh, I've already taken care of that," Raywood replied.

For the next ten minutes, as Raywood sat on a metal bench in the courtyard of the pink granite high-rise, Newman talked intently into a cell phone. As it turned out, Raywood had gotten into a dispute the previous week with yet another landlord. Los Angeles police officers were summoned. During a background check, they discovered the outstanding Culver City warrants and arrested Raywood. Although the designer celebrated the Fourth of July weekend behind bars, his brother eventually bailed him out. Newman had no choice but to let him go.

After unlocking Raywood's cuffs, the detectives gave him back his bag.

"Is my passport in there?" the designer asked as he walked off.

"Yes, everything is there," the detectives answered.

Two and a half months later, on September 29, 2008, Raywood was arraigned. With his lawyer, West Hollywood city council member John Duran, at his side in the LAX division of Los Angeles Superior Court, Raywood pleaded not guilty to the three counts.

When Judge Keith L. Schwartz proposed October 31 as the date for a preliminary hearing, he looked down from the bench and asked, "Do you have any trouble with the hearing taking place on Halloween?"

"Should I be wearing a mask?" Raywood responded.

Part 11: Damage

As of late October, little more than four years after arriving in Los Angeles, Craig Raywood had been involved in some forty separate cases in the county courts. More than thirty suits had been filed against him. In turn, he had brought suit seven times, three times against Joel Ring. Several cases are still outstanding, but the results are inarguable. Nineteen judgments (including ones for plastic surgeon Randal Digby Haworth and realtor Joe Babajian) resulting in a cumulative $200,000 in damages have gone against Raywood.

The criminal charges Joel Chen is pursuing will undoubtedly come down to a matter of interpretation. Although Raywood's lawyer would not comment, the designer will likely maintain that he intended to return the pieces taken out on approval, contending that the antiques dealer overreacted. He will assert that Chen was so hostile and aggressive that he denied him the chance to honor their agreement. He will probably argue that the identity theft allegation also grew out of a misunderstanding—that he and Paul Gregory were legitimate business partners and the photographer had jumped the gun.

The lone penalty so far imposed on Raywood arose from his 2007 shoplifting arrest at Whole Foods Market in West Hollywood. The designer pleaded no contest to a reduced misdemeanor charge and was placed on thirty-six months' probation and ordered not to venture within 100 yards of the store.

As for Raywood's grievances, he has prevailed only once. On October 2, at a hearing in the Stanley Mosk Courthouse downtown, the designer settled his negligence suit against Ring. Though he was seeking millions, Raywood agreed to $45,000. "We had a great case," says David Denis, Raywood's lawyer. "But Craig wanted to get it over with. He's tired of all the drama." Edward Hess, Ring's lawyer in this matter, sees it differently. "The settlement was motivated purely from economics," he says. Ring's insurance company had calculated it would spend at least that amount to hire medical experts for a trial. Notes Hess, "Why you'd pursue a case you said was worth millions and settle for $45,000 answers itself."

New Yorkers who knew Raywood when he was young fall into two camps about all this. "I'm discreet about people I know," says Marisa Berenson. "I'd be happy to talk about a different subject." Keith Raywood will go only a bit further. "My brother and I aren't that close anymore," he says. "Nothing about Craig has ever struck me as being criminal. I never thought he'd try to swindle people." Then, with the slightest edge in his voice, he adds, "If he did, I wish he'd been better at it."

Others are more overt in their disappointment. "He could have made it big," says Beth Rudin DeWoody. "He had the eye and the talent. If he'd only been honest, he could have been successful." Vivian Serota is more blunt. "The Craig Raywood that I knew died," she says. "There were two Craig Raywoods. The Craig Raywood that I remember was a loving son and a caring person. Now he's done these terrible things. When I heard what he did to Kenny Solms, I cried. Kenny Solms is my good friend. Why would he rip him off?"

In Los Angeles there is less effort to understand. The owners of several antiques stores and a long list of physicians and merchants refuse to talk about their experiences with Raywood. Either so abashed by what they went through or so relieved to have Raywood out of their lives, they see no benefit in further discussion. As for those who have chosen to speak out, they're incensed not only at the designer but at the impotence of the justice system. Kenny Solms vented his emotions in an October 17, 2007, letter to Lisa Hart Cole, a judge who'd sat on several of the small claims cases against Raywood in Beverly Hills:

> It's soon going to be over three years since Mr. Raywood took a check of mine in the amount of $5,500.00 for a rug that he never ordered or delivered. I've been to small claims court to fight this countless times which I'm sure your files will reflect. (Incidentally, I'm only one of the dozens of people seeking claims against Raywood on other matters.)... Nothing seems to ever seal Raywood's fate... The bottom line is, WHAT DO I DO NOW? Is there no way the court can satisfy my grievances?

Cole's response, dated December 5, 2007, did something that Raywood could not. It left Solms speechless:

> [Your] letter clearly expresses the frustration you are experiencing in collecting on the judgment you received against Mr. Craig Raywood in the above referenced case. Unfortunately, you are correct: there is nothing the court can [do] to force Mr. Raywood to pay you the money he owes... I apologize that I cannot be of any further assistance to you. Best of luck and I wish you well in this holiday season.

Almost everyone who has brushed up against Raywood is struggling with the same questions. They debate whether he is aware of his wrongdoing or acts unconsciously. They wonder whether he needs psychiatric care or should do hard time. Most of all, they ask why. Why did it happen to them? What made them so vulnerable? "Craig Raywood enters your life to teach you a lesson," says the designer's former friend Robert Regni. "After him, you will look at the world differently. You'll never be naive." The bulk of his victims, though, are less philosophical. "Craig Raywood," says dentist Phillip Gorin, "is a sharp stick up your ass." Joel Chen is more measured but no less fierce. "Most of us in life never meet a true adversary," he says. "That's who this guy is." A month before Raywood was arraigned on the charges stemming from the antiques dealer's allegations, Chen received an e-mail that originated from a server in Oyster Bay:

> ...You are in the mist of allot of trouble. Mr. Raywood is very connected and there is people who will make your world change very dark. My advice is stay away from him moving forward...I receive 1 phone call and the tornado that will strike will be like no other...If you think this is a game then lets play the game. Only difference is you are the game, and will be hunted.

Part 12: Dubai

On a summer afternoon as his world closed in on him, Craig Raywood drove across Los Angeles. He was headed to the Chateau Marmont, where he and Giselle had checked in. Speaking by cell phone, he wanted to explain himself. "I know there are people who are upset with me," he said. "There's a lot of untruth. A lot of people have it in for me. I don't know for what reason. I'm a very good guy. People take advantage of me."

His accusers should be the accused, he claimed. Look at former client Joe Babajian, who'd charged him with double billing. The realtor had been recently indicted on mortgage fraud, and Raywood could not have been more gleeful. "He owes me $39,000, and he's saying terrible things about me. Is that right?"

Joel Chen is just as awful: "He put up posters in my neighborhood. It was disgraceful. He's a thief. His people were so happy they were doing business with me, and then they turned on me. I was sick, under medication. I suffered two concussions in a car wreck. I have to have two more surgeries on my leg. I live with pain. I'm in pain every day."

It was all too much. Raywood had moved to Los Angeles to practice his art, to spread grace and beauty, but the city hadn't appreciated him. Like so many who've failed elsewhere, he had been seeking a second chance. Now he would seek it abroad. "I'm through with L.A.," he said. "I'm not sure I'll ever come back. I've been offered to do a very big project, to move to Dubai for four or five months. I'm extremely excited about it. I'll be doing special events. I'll design the dishes, the flatware, the stemware. I've met with the sheikhs."

Raywood could not recall the sheikhs' names—the painkillers he was taking had dulled his memory—but he could see the future, and it looked bright. "I'm going pretty soon," he said. "They're sending a plane for me. The sheikhs have their own 747."

In 2009, Craig Raywood was arrested on the outstanding charges involving Joel Chen and incarcerated at the Los Angeles County Jail. He ultimately pleaded no contest and was sentenced to three years probation.

Getting Naked with Harry

The Atlanta Journal & Constitution Magazine, May 15, 1977

It was all of two o'clock on a sultry, Thursday afternoon, and Harry Crews was poured into a corner booth at an ersatz nautical bar in Gainesville, Florida, called the Winnjammer. Bits of sailing rigging were scattered about. The place was as dark as the hold of an Eastern European freighter. Light from a flickering wall lamp played upon Crews's face, and there was a shock in seeing him, discernably electric, as if he were stripped of psychic insulation like a wounded animal that has retreated to its lair. "The craziness is in me," he was growling. "I'm self-destructive, masochistic." He was slouched into the booth, and one of his legs, crippled from childhood polio, hung limply to the floor. His large, brutal torso, fitted into a decaying mauve sweatshirt, coiled lazily. His massive head, eyes set deep into the brow, turned on a thick neck around which he wore a silver and turquoise chain. "My private life is a shambles," he said. The voice was almost indiscernible, lost in a glass of Scotch and milk. "I get into trouble. I can't cope. I louse things up, wreck cars, lose money. But a fictional world—I can make it do what I can't do with my own life."

Here at the Winnjammer, Crews was fighting to gain control of himself. He had just endured a long, hot drive back to Gainesville from Ashburn, Georgia, where his mother was ill with appendicitis. He was trying to pull his mind together before going home to finish an article about jockeys for *Sport* magazine. Facing him at 7 P.M. was the initial meeting of a quarterly fiction-writing class he teaches at the University of Florida. In the back of his mind, hanging like a millstone, was the thought of the writing he still needed to do on his first work of nonfiction: *A Childhood—The Biography of a Place*. Scheduled for release in the fall, it is to be a dissection of past and present in Bacon County, Georgia, Crews's birthplace. It will be his ninth book, and it follows a string of novels that began appearing yearly in 1968 with the publication of *The Gospel Singer*. Whether the new work will come from what could be called Crews's world is difficult to say. Crews's world is hard to understand. He doesn't comprehend it completely. However, an observation that Flannery O'Connor made about her own fiction could just as well apply to his: *It is in the extremities of evil circumstance that the possibilities of grace are more nearly perceived.*

"Oh man, man. I feel like I'm gonna die," Crews was saying. "My mama just worries, worries, worries. I had to go up there to check on her because a son has got to do what he feels he's got to do." A second Scotch and milk was in his hands. "I may die, though. Damn drive."

Lighting a Marlboro, the writer backed up from the thought of his demise. "I ain't gonna die, but damn if I don't feel like it. Bring me another of the same and less milk," he called to the barmaid.

Harry Crews's novels abound with the extremities of evil circumstance, the products of evil circumstance. There is Joe Lon Mackey, protagonist of his most recent effort, *A Feast of Snakes*, which is set in Mystic, Georgia, at the time of the town's annual rattlesnake roundup. Joe Lon is a college-caliber football player left with nowhere to play because of poor high school grades. He re-channels the brutality his coaches encouraged in him by blowing away a number of acquaintances with shotgun blasts.

Then there is the Gospel Singer, in the novel of the same name, a golden sheep born from the fold of a depraved white-trash family in Enigma, Georgia. The Gospel Singer has a honeyed voice that has allowed him to escape the insularity of his hometown. He returns to sing at one last tent revival and ends up getting hanged from a tree. The people of Enigma perceive that he's a charlatan and exact their vengeance.

Appearing in almost all of Crews's novels are midgets, people without legs, the lame and the halt. There are also crowds in every book—milling, destroying, and running awry with the license granted to those in large groups where anonymity triumphs over responsibility.

A fresh drink in hand, Crews took a shot at explaining his literary landscape. "I'm not really a product of William Faulkner," he said, his voice at once filled with jazz and Georgia. "Graham Greene has influenced me more than any other writer. People are always talking to me about being a Southern novelist, about being out of the Southern tradition, and all of that crap. All I can say to them is I've lived in the South all my life. I was born and raised in Bacon County. But I don't think of myself as a Southern writer. I don't think any novelist of any consequence wants an adjective in front of the word novelist. You don't want to be ah, I don't know, a gothic novelist or a black-humor novelist. You just want to be a novelist. It's true that a writer is told by a lot of stupid people, like English teachers, to write about

317

what you know. But that's bull. You write about murder, and you never killed anybody. You write about a woman, and you haven't been a woman, and on and on. What English teachers mean, I hope, and they probably don't, but what they should mean is that to write and write well you have to be on incredibly intimate terms with the manners of a people, the culture of a part of the country."

That, however, was it for now. After tipping his glass up over his nose and draining it, Crews declared, "I'm splitting."

Writers like Harry Crews run the risk of not just being mythicized but stigmatized. Already, the cultural elite have consigned him to a place that one critic said was beneath the dark root of the Southern literary tradition. Because Crews writes about people who on the face of it are freaks and evil interlopers—Jean Stafford called his bailiwick "a Hieronymous Bosch landscape in Dixie"—he is regarded primarily as a purveyor of the abnormal and the gut-wrenching. Obsessive, violent, grotesque, gratuitous, bizarre, macabre, harrowing, and wild—these are the labels reviewers tack to Crews's fiction. "I don't even read that crap anymore," the writer will bellow. "It's too hard to write, and if you read enough of that, you flip and lose your confidence. It does happen."

Although Crews has received his share of plaudits, the general perception holds that he is nuts, that he writes about nuts, and that his work is rife with uncalled-for ugliness and perversity. The consensus is that he sits at his 1929 Underwood typewriter in his stultifying stucco rental house in Gainesville and busies himself with creating ever more bizarre scenarios to be marketed to the freak-reading public. Even his friends promote this view. *Playboy*, where Crews's articles appear frequently, labeled him its "resident weirdo." *Esquire*, for which Crews writes a monthly column called "Grits," created a standing logo that suggests the cracking skin of the Marvel comic book character the Thing. The paperback editions of Crews's books fall all over themselves to promote the transgressive nature of the writer's vision. The jackets are adorned with everything from paraplegics in tank tops rotating on their middle fingers to sexy karate fighters in bikinis.

Then there are the hard facts of Crews's own life. His behavior has been so outrageous that many accuse him of being drunk on machismo. Already this year, he has been forced into an out-of-court settlement with a man whom he says "leaned on me too hard, just wouldn't let me out of there without going back to the parking lot and then, what could I do? When it's gone that far, there's nothing to do but go on with it." Anyway, Crews ended up breaking the man's hip in the ensuing brawl outside a Miami lounge. There have been other incidents as well. He was thrown into jail in St. Augustine after a ruckus at an establishment called the Slipped Disc Disco. While in Tulsa, Oklahoma, reporting an *Esquire* story about allegations of sexual impropriety involving evangelist Garner Ted Armstrong, Crews took up for a Tex-Mex in a fight with an immigration agent and was again jailed. The writer's day-to-day existence seems as extreme as his work.

Jed Smock was gyrating like a drunken top on a worn spot of grass in a quadrangle near Harry Crews's office in the gothic fine arts building at the University of Florida. Smock, a well-known Gainesville street evangelist who dresses in white suits and embellishes the impending doom of the Old Testament with his own febrile imagination ("Do you think those people on the 747s that collided the other week in the Canary Island knew they were going to die? Did they know Jesus? Will you know Jesus if you are called tonight?"), considers the Gator student body to be his personal flock. His admonitions wafted up to Crews's window on this Friday morning as they do most every day.

It was just a little past eight, and Crews was well into his third large Styrofoam cup of Krispy Kreme coffee. The previous night had been taxing. It began with a two-hour lecture to his fiction-writing class and ended with a drop-in friend curling up with a stun-gun in the living room. A never defined threat—an angry husband, an unpaid drug dealer—was looming, and the writer felt the need for protection. Now, however, he was shaking all that off, slurping coffee, smoking cigarettes, and stoking his nerves. Outside, Smock was telling a group of Krishna consciousness devotees that they and their saffron robes were going to burn eternally.

"God, I don't know. I don't know," Crews mused. "One of the things that writers live with is the terror—fear—that they're not going to be able to write a book. And if you write one, you're scared that you're not going to be able to write another one or that if you do write it, it's going to be terrible. And writers who are truly writers, that's about all they got to live for. It's what keeps them together. It gives them something to hold onto. William Inge, the playwright out in Los Angeles who wrote *Picnic*, killed himself because he couldn't get any work anymore."

Crews finished his coffee and grunted. "I think precisely what people mistake in me as being macho, that thing in me that wants to get as far on the edge as I can of anything that I can, the thing I like to call getting naked, is my need to keep myself going as a writer. You can't find out about a thing—well, you can find out about a thing vicariously and you can find out about it by reading a book—but you can't find out about a thing as well as you can when you're naked and vulnerable to the experiences of the world.

"And that's the only reason that I can live more or less in a university community and still not write academic novels. I go out into the world and do whatever I do. Now people can just say what they want to say. I don't think anybody who's ever met me or known me for any length of time, intimately, would say that I go out and do these things, this machismo stuff. I'm just out there, and if you're out there long enough, things happen to you. And then you write about them.

"There is a cost. There is. My gig is to get naked, but guys make me out as a brawler and a drunk, and sure, I howl sometimes, just like anybody, I howl.

"What I wonder about, however, are things like when I went into this bar last week and a guy I don't know from Adam asks me about the time I was out at the Blue Pine and got into a fight with a cue stick with some guys. I say to this character, 'That never happened, man. How do you think I get any work done, hunh?' That's the thing they don't realize. People think I'm always lying in some gutter someplace, sleeping something off. There are times I am, but not that often. I try to take reasonably good care of my talent. I figure I'm just hitting my stride. A good writer ought to be able to get 22, 24, 25 books in a career. After all, no matter what anyone says, we're just trying to get through this thing, trying to have something to do until we die."

Harry Crews has paid a stiff price to get this far. Born into horrific poverty at the height of the Depression, he began writing fiction when he was five years old about the models in Sears, Roebuck catalogs. "Those models were always perfect, and my home life was pretty awful." In spite of his polio-damaged leg, Crews talked his way into the Marine Corps at age 17. He stayed three years, leaving to enroll at the University of Florida, where he studied fiction writing under Andrew Lytle. He was, Crews said, his great teacher. Lytle had been a member of the Vanderbilt University Fugitive group of writers, which included Robert Penn Warren and John Crowe Ransom, and he saw potential in the upstart from South Georgia.

When Crews left the university, he took an unlikely job as a seventh grade English teacher at a junior high school in Jacksonville. It was 1962. There, living with his young wife and a son who would later drown, the budding novelist made his most important investment into learning how to write.

"I wrote a novel that year. What I did was take Graham Greene's *The End of the Affair*, and I reduced the damn thing to numbers." Crews had gone out for still another cup of coffee, and he spilled it on his desk with a sweeping punch from his right fist as he warmed to the story. "Nerves," he observed, "Pure nerves." Then he picked right back up. "Anyway, I determined how many characters Greene had, how much time was in the book—present time and past time and the time of memory and of flashback, all of it. I found out how many cities were in the book and how many buildings and how many rooms in the buildings and how many transitions. And I pinpointed the climaxes, where action turned, found what pages they were on. I read that book until it was dog-eared and was coming apart in my hands.

"After that, I said, 'I'm gonna write a novel with the same number of scenes and on and on as are in *The End of the Affair*.' I knew I was going to waste a year—but it wasn't a waste—and I knew the end result was going to be a mechanical, unreadable novel. But I was trying to find out how you do it. I wrote it, and it ended up being the piece of crap I knew it would be.

"I mean, I ate that damn Graham Greene book, literally ate it. And after I wrote mine, I didn't let anybody read it but Mr. Lytle, and he gave it back to me and said, 'Well, son...' He was a hard taskmaster. But it didn't matter. Because of that year I knew how it was done, and I went on from there."

It was mid-morning, and Crews was in need of alcoholic sustenance. The Gainesville bars opened at eleven, so donning a black beret, he limped out from his office to make the drive to the house of his ex-wife, Sally, for a couple of vodka tonics. After hoisting himself into his silver van, Crews jammed a tape of Randy Newman's *Good Old Boys* into an eight-track player and pulled onto the blistering macadam of the highway. Driving loosened him, as if it worked the coffee out of his system.

"Yeah, it's very difficult for me to talk about. It's very difficult for me to intellectualize on all the work I've done," Crews said, "but it's easy to do about the work someone else has done." As he weaved in and out of traffic, Crews hummed along with "Kingfish," Newman's song about Huey Long.

"For instance, people have written that there is a midget in my first three novels. When I gave a copy of *This Thing Don't Lead to Heaven*, my third novel, to Sally, she said, 'You don't, do you, intend to make a career out of midgets?' And that was the first time it ever occurred to me that there were midgets in my first three books. There's Jefferson Davis Munroe in *This Thing Don't Lead to Heaven*, Foot in *The Gospel Singer*, and Jester in *Naked in Garden Hills*.

"This thing I'm writing for *Sport* about jockeys—I was down in the jockey room at the race track working on it, looking at all them little people, and they don't walk, they tick, like a watch. They're fine. I say in the piece that they are perfect of their kind. They are the absolute essence of what is needed to do what they do, which is ride thoroughbreds."

Harry Crews never relaxes long. The talk about midgets had rekindled his animosity toward critics. He was all wound up again, so much so that he nearly missed the turn from one of Gainesville's main drags onto the shady street that leads to his ex's home. "There are these guys," he was saying, almost spitting the words, "who say I write gratuitously about freaks. Some guy at the Atlanta papers said that in a negative review of *The Gospel Singer*. I wonder about that guy, if he's ever written anything himself. He said that I was a terrible writer and that you'd never hear from me again, that I'll never write another book.

"Anyway, there's a guy who has his head on wrong. Some people never get over that kind of criticism. I'm not saying this to be self-serving, but to be a writer and to sustain yourself for a long period of time, you need raw courage. You have to say to the world: 'OK. Say what you want about me. And I'm still gonna write and I'm gonna write the way I want to write, and I'm not gonna write books to satisfy you.'

"And if they're gonna say I gratuitously write about freaks and violence, let them go ahead and say it. I have a helluva lot of compassion and sympathy for those people who, as I said about Foot in *The Gospel Singer*, are special under God—or special people."

Crews had now stopped in the driveway of Sally's pretty ranch house, but he wasn't finished. "See, I can walk around and I'm not going to get any static. People will look at me and no one is struck by how ruined I am. I can think dreadful things, have dreadful notions in my mind and no one is going to know. But a guy who is three feet tall is going to have to deal with being three feet tall every day. And every time he turns a corner, he looks at a guy and he sees his own predicament in that guy's eyes.

"To write about one thing you have to talk about another thing, and that's the whole nature of fiction and poetry. You can say more about what the world out there calls normal by dealing with what the world calls abnormal. This is what I do.

"The reading public bothers me, though. They don't want to read about the blood and bones and guts of an issue. They want to read about something they're not going to have to think about, and if it does hurt them as, say, *Love Story* does, it won't last very long. What has happened in this country is a failure of the imagination."

Crews eased himself out of the van and began fumbling around in his pocket for a key. Finding it, he shoved his beret low on his forehead and shuffled to the side yard, where a brick doghouse provides a home for Brutus, his black mastiff. "I write out of this kind of outrage," he was saying. "And to write about the violence and stuff I write about, you've got to be angry. People wouldn't understand it if I said I was a moralist. They'd think I was some academic dude holed up with a bunch of facts and books who didn't live in the real world. But to write out of my kind of outrage, you've got to be a stomp-down, hard-core moralist."

Crews had begun to tease Brutus. When the dog growled at him he growled back. Soon enough, man was barking at dog and dog was barking at man. The encounter conjured a scene from *The Gospel Singer*, where a character named Didymus contemplates throwing himself to a massive beast.

Didymus said, "Go into strange lands where people have never heard of you and tell them things they do not want to hear and cannot understand. If you are lucky, they will kill you and eat you...or throw you to vicious dogs. That is the way to God, righteousness, and the moral life."

AFTERWORD

The first thing I see each morning when I sit down at my computer is a post-it note tacked to the bottom of the screen. On it I scrawled something Herschel Walker told me: "Every day I get up and fight. Every day I've got to fight." Although the former NFL star made the remark shortly after getting involved in the most brutal sport since the age of the Roman gladiators, he was not talking about mixed martial arts. He was instead articulating a basic tenet of manhood—you must fight to survive. His words now function as one of my mantras.

The lessons I've learned while writing the pieces that constitute *A Man's World* inform almost every part of my life.

Several weeks after my profile of Robert Penn Warren appeared in *The Atlanta Journal & Constitution Magazine*, a typed, single-spaced, four-page letter from the Pulitzer Prize winner arrived at my office. After warmly declaring that he and his wife, Eleanor Clark, considered me a new friend, Warren took me to the woodshed. First, he corrected errors of fact (Ford Madox Ford was not, as I had reported, a contemporary of Katherine Anne Porter—he was much older). Then, he attacked anachronisms (As a young man, Warren did not, as I had put it in '70s-speak, jog; he ran). Next, he addressed substance. While Warren believed that I'd largely succeeded in my task—sketching a portrait of his life—he was appalled at what he saw as an ethical breach. I'd kept my tape recorder running at dinner as he baited Clark about President Franklin D. Roosevelt. Warren felt I'd betrayed his trust although I think he was more worried that in my presentation of the exchange he came off as a boorish and unreconstructed Southerner who wanted to keep government out the lives of Americans.

Warren had given me a piece of his mind. Yet while initially stunned, within an hour I felt only gratitude. This writer whom I revered had done me the honor of subjecting my article to a version of the unrelenting but elevating critiques that he and his fellow Vanderbilt University Fugitives had applied to one another's poems and stories in the 1920s when they essentially invented modern Southern literature. He had treated me, if not as an equal, then as an adult. I took everything he said to heart (I've inserted his factual changes into the piece as it appears here), and in all the work I've written since I've been slavishly attentive to accuracy. However, I think it's telling that I never for a second regretted recording his set-to with his wife about FDR. Not only is the conversation smart and funny—it's a classic example of a type of ironic, high-brow japery at which Southerners are the undisputed masters—but it was my job to get it down and shape it into a revealing moment. Warren was the subject. I was the writer. I knew this. He knew it, too. Still, he could have crushed me. He chose instead to complete what he saw as a pedagogical exercise, and the point of the exercise was to make me better while putting me on notice. If I wanted to practice the art of writing at his level, I needed to respect the never-ending difficulties. To be the recipient of such grace was a supreme piece of luck. I was 25.

Not all the wisdom I picked up along the way came so dramatically. The bulk of it, in fact, came from hanging out, and some of the most compelling men I hung out with are actors. They are entertaining, and to a one they can do something I can't—project confidence as they're shaking on the inside. They can bluff their way through a tight spot, and of the many I profiled none does it as well as the Australian Bryan Brown. While I respect Nick Nolte's process and admire Harrison Ford's integrity, I am blown away by Brown's seeming certitude. Born a working class bloke, he learned how to convince his alleged betters in the film business that he was as good as if not better than they. After spending time with him on a movie set in Sydney and at his home in rural New South Wales, I came away believing that the ability to pretend is an attribute every man must develop. I still believe this and in a jam at least take a stab at brazening it out.

The flipside of confidence is fear, and that was the emotion I confronted in the piece in this volume that gave me the most trouble. I proposed a profile of Bo Belinsky after reading his obituary. It reported that the Jewish, former Los Angeles Angel and legendary playboy had died a born-again Christian car salesman in Las Vegas. In a bar on the strip, a friend of Bo's handed me some cassette tapes the ex-pitcher made shortly before his death. This was in itself eerie (I was going to get an interview with a dead man), but the topic Belinsky discussed on the recordings—his descent into alcoholism and cocaine abuse—unnerved me even more. I'd always suffered from stage fright, and here I was hearing a lost soul recount how he went down the tubes because he was scared of life: The drugs were a symptom. Listening to the tapes left me shaken, and I had trouble starting to work. Not until about 2:30 in the morning a couple days before deadline did I begin. Banging away on my IBM Selectric (I still use a typewriter for first drafts), I wrote, "Bo's terrors had been with him in one way or another since childhood. Even as a 16-year-old [he] had often been overcome by dread. Once his career ended, he could no longer hide. Suddenly naked, he surrendered to his addictive predisposition." Those sentences represented a break-through. I realized that for all the lessons my father failed to impart when I was 16, I'd discovered the vital thing—something Bo never did discover—on my own. The solution is to face whatever it is. You can't run. It's always out there. The correct move is to confront the darkness, even if you have to seek it. That's what Harry Crews advised in the earliest story in this collection, written in 1977 when I was a kid. Here I was in my 50s, coming back around to the same issue. It never ends.

Fighting, creating, acting, embracing danger—these are the things I had to teach myself. The profiles in *A Man's World* amount to a record of how I did it.

ACKNOWLEDGMENTS

In 1977 I had only a couple years' experience as a newspaper reporter, but Andrew Sparks, editor of *The Atlanta Journal & Constitution Magazine*, hired me anyway. He thought I showed promise, and I owe him my career as a magazine writer. At the *Journal & Constitution*, I also worked for Don O'Briant, David Osier, Nancy Smith, and Lee Walburn and with such gifted colleagues as Jim Auchmutey, Robert Coram, Jim Dodson, John Fleming, Phil Garner, William Hedgepeth, Paul Hemphill, Frazier Moore, Jr., Russ Rymer, Margaret Shannon, Mitchell J. Shields, and Ed C. Thompson. It was a charmed moment, and it happened because James G. Minter, editor-in-chief of Atlanta's then jointly owned but editorially separate newspapers, so wished it. At *California* magazine, I benefited from the guidance of the perspicacious Scott Kaufer and the legendary Harold Hayes, while at *Premiere* I was in the good hands of Susan Lyne and Deborah Pines. I wrote for a trio of fine *Esquire* editors—Betsy Carter, David Hirshey, and Adam Moss. At *GQ* the estimable Eliot Kaplan shepherded my stories. Stephen Randall edited my first article for *Playboy* in 1986, and he edited my last in 2012—a long, productive collaboration. In 2004 I took a job at *Los Angeles* magazine writing for the brilliant Kit Rachlis. Kit is the best thing that ever happened to me in journalism. He challenged me to undertake ambitious pieces then made them better, and he introduced me to a group of similarly tough but caring editors—chief among them Richard E. Meyer. Kit is a magnet for talent—Margot Dougherty, Jesse Katz, Patric Kuh, Mary Melton, J.R. Moehringer, Michael Mullen, Matthew Segal, R. J. Smith, and Amy Wallace to name a few—and during his editorship *Los Angeles* was the best magazine in the West. Last but not least, my agent, Beth Vesel, believed in the idea of collecting my stories into a book, and Marc Jolley at Mercer University Press made it happen—my thanks to both, and to Lisa Bayer at the University of Georgia Press, publisher of the work in paperback.

CPSIA information can be obtained
at www.ICGtesting.com
Printed in the USA
LVHW031915040619
620117LV00004B/332/P